The Property-Contract Interface

OXFORD PRIVATE LAW THEORY

Oxford Private Law Theory publishes leading work in private law theory. It commissions and solicits monographs and edited collections in general private law theory as well as specific fields, including the theoretical analysis of tort law, property law, contract law, fiduciary law, trust law, remedies and restitution, and the law of equity. The series is open to diverse theoretical approaches, including those informed by philosophy, economics, history, and political theory. Oxford Private Law Theory sets the standard for rigorous and original work in private law theory.

ALSO PUBLISHED IN THIS SERIES

Conflict between Equals
Tort Law beyond Wrong, Harm, and Costs
Avihay Dorfman

Responsibility for Negligence in Ethics and Law
Aspiration, Perspective, and Civic Maturity
Verónica Rodríguez-Blanco

Property Law in the Society of Equals
Christopher Essert

The Property-Contract Interface

Historical and Theoretical Perspectives

Edited by

JAMES PENNER

Kwa Geok Choo Professor of Property Law,
Faculty of Law, National University of Singapore

IRINA SAKHAROVA

Assistant Professor in Commercial Law, Durham University, UK

HENRY E. SMITH

Fessenden Professor of Law, Harvard Law School, USA

ZHONG XING TAN

Associate Professor of Law, National University of Singapore

OXFORD
UNIVERSITY PRESS

OXFORD
UNIVERSITY PRESS

Great Clarendon Street, Oxford, OX2 6DP,
United Kingdom

Oxford University Press is a department of the University of Oxford.
It furthers the University's objective of excellence in research, scholarship,
and education by publishing worldwide. Oxford is a registered trade mark of
Oxford University Press in the UK and in certain other countries.

Published in the United States of America by Oxford University Press
546 Fifth Avenue, New York, NY 10036, United States of America.

British Library Cataloguing in Publication Data
Data available

Library of Congress Control Number: 2026940458

ISBN 9780198951988

DOI: 10.1093/9780198951995.001.0001

Printed and bound by
CPI Group (UK) Ltd., Croydon, CR0 4YY

The manufacturer's authorized representative in the EU for product safety is
Oxford University Press España S.A. of Parque Empresarial San Fernando de Henares,
Avenida de Castilla, 2 – 28830 Madrid (www.oup.es/en or product.safety@oup.com).
OUP España S.A. also acts as importer into Spain of products made by the manufacturer.

FSC www.fsc.org
MIX
Paper | Supporting responsible forestry
FSC® C013604

Preface

This collection was conceived in 2023, both as a 25th anniversary celebration of Thomas Merrill's and Henry Smith's seminal paper, 'The Property-Contract Interface' ((2001) 101 Columbia Law Review 773), and as an opportunity to reconsider the paper's central themes and relate them to a broad swathe of issues in private law. It would be an understatement to say that the paper 'made a splash': it is widely recognized as a path-breaking modern work addressing the ways in which in personam contractual rights and duties interact with in rem property rights and duties. This collection examines, and re-examines, how its insights have borne fruit over the years and how they continue to do so.

The essays are arranged as follows:

Part 1, 'The Nature of Property and Contract', comprises three essays, by Rebecca Stone, Aditi Bagchi, and Irina Sakharova, which challenge 'property approaches' that see property as prior to contract and offer accounts of the basic role of contract in private law.

Part 2, 'Property, Contract, and the Structure of Private Law', comprises five essays, by Henry E. Smith, Nick Sage, Robert Chambers, Zhong Xing Tan, and Richard R. W. Brooks which, in ascending order of generality, discuss issues pertaining to the *numerus clausus* principle and broader issues of categorization in private law and its relation to extra-legal social and economic structures.

Part 3, 'Institutions Along the Property-Contract Interface', comprises four essays, by Katy Barnett, Thomas W. Merrill, Lusina Ho, and Pey-Woan Lee and Wei Zhang, which examine bailment, leases, licences, trusts, and security interests, all of which implicate property and contract in some combination.

Part 4, 'Contract and Conveyance', comprises two essays, by Catharine MacMillan and Joshua Getzler, which consider historical understandings of property and contractual aspects of sales of goods.

Part 5, 'Contract, Property, and Beyond', comprises three essays, by William Swadling, Larissa Katz, and James Penner, which focus on the property-contract interface in relation to choses in action and debt.

All of the papers were presented at a workshop at the Faculty of Law, National University of Singapore, from 16 to 18 December 2024. The workshop would not have been possible without the generous financial support of the Singapore Ministry of Education (Academic Tier 1 Research Fund grant No WBS A-8002905-00-00), the Faculty of Law's Centre for Legal Theory, and the EW Barker Centre for Law and Business, which we gratefully acknowledge.

We must also express our gratitude to colleagues in the National University of Singapore Faculty of Law, Lynette Chua, Andrew Halpin, Tan Cheng Han, Hans Tjio, and the Dean, Andrew Simester, for all their encouragement, and also for the invaluable administrative assistance of Jothi Bhavani, Rowena Goh, and Wendy Wee.

Finally, we thank Charlotte Kershaw and Brian Stone at Oxford University Press for making this book a reality.

James Penner
Irina Sakharova
Henry E. Smith
Zhong Xing Tan

Contents

Contributors

Aditi Bagchi is Ignatius M. Wilkinson Chair and Professor of Law, Fordham University Law School, New York, United States.

Katy Barnett is Professor of Law, Melbourne Law School, The University of Melbourne, Australia.

Richard R. W. Brooks is Emilie M. Bullowa Professor of Law, New York University, United States.

Robert Chambers is Professor and Department Chair, Faculty of Law, Thompson Rivers University, Kamloops, Canada.

Joshua Getzler is Professor of Law and Legal History, Faculty of Law, University of Oxford and Fellow of St Hugh's College, Oxford, United Kingdom, and Conjoint Professor of Law, University of New South Wales, Sydney, Australia.

Lusina Ho is Harold Hsiao-Wo Lee Professor in Trusts and Equity, Faculty of Law, The University of Hong Kong.

Larissa Katz is Cecil A. Wright Chair and Professor of Law, University of Toronto Jackman Faculty of Law, Canada

Pey Woan Lee is Professor of Law, Singapore Management University.

Thomas W. Merrill is Charles Evans Hughes Professor of Law, Columbia Law School, New York, United States.

Catharine MacMillan is Professor of Private Law, Dickson Poon School of Law, King's College London, London, United Kingdom.

James Penner is Kwa Geok Choo Professor of Property Law, Faculty of Law, National University of Singapore.

Nick Sage is Associate Professor of Law, London School of Economics and Political Science, London, United Kingdom.

Irina Sakharova is Assistant Professor in Commercial Law, Durham University, United Kingdom.

Henry E. Smith is Fessenden Professor of Law, Harvard Law School, Cambridge, United States.

Rebecca Stone is Professor of Law, School of Law, University of California at Los Angeles, United States.

William Swadling is Professor of Law, University of Oxford, and Fellow of Brasenose College, Oxford, United Kingdom.

Zhong Xing Tan is Associate Professor of Law, National University of Singapore.

Wei Zhang is Professor of Law, Singapore Management University.

I.

THE NATURE OF PROPERTY AND CONTRACT

1

Private Rights

Artificial But Not Instrumental

*Rebecca Stone**

I. Introduction

Contractual rights appear to have the potential to reflect morality precisely, both procedurally and substantively. Procedurally, contracts are formed by agreements through which the parties together define their rights and duties. Substantively, this moment of contracting enables the parties to articulate a just vision for their relationship. In these ways contracts give rise to duties that the parties owe one another, establishing right–duty relationships that are paradigmatically *in personam*.[1]

The right–duty relations that arise from property, by contrast, are created and shaped without the participation of many of the parties to those relations. The rights of owners are *in rem*—constituted by an indefinite number of similar relations between owner and the rest of the world that come into existence simultaneously.[2] When ownership of some property is transferred from A to B, pursuant, say, to a contract between A and B, the duties of C (and everyone else are transformed) without C's say-so: the duty of non-interference that C previously owed to A is now owed to B.[3]

As a doctrinal matter, moreover, the form that property rights can take is constrained. The contrast with contract here is again stark:

> [whereas a] willing buyer and a willing seller can create an infinite variety of enforceable contracts for the exchange of recognized property rights, and can

* For helpful comments, I'm grateful to Jonathan Quong, Tan Zhong Xing, and participants at the workshop on this volume.

[1] Hohfeld 1916, 719.

[2] Ibid, 719, 740.

[3] Penner 1997, 23, 75–76.

Rebecca Stone, *Private Rights* In: *The Property-Contract Interface*. Edited by: James Penner, Irina Sakharova, Henry E. Smith, and Zhong Xing Tan, Oxford University Press. © Rebecca Stone 2026.
DOI: 10.1093/9780198951995.003.0002

> describe these property rights along a multitude of physical dimensions and prices, . . . common-law courts will not enforce an agreement to create a new type of property right.[4]

To the extent that right–duty relations reflect the particularities of parties' relationships, property rights appear underspecified. They look like rights awaiting further (contractual) specification.

Finally, whereas the connection between contractual rights and freedom is direct, the connection between property rights and freedom is indirect. In the realm of contract, freedom is manifested by the parties' creative act of making an agreement that defines the duties they owe to one another contractually. In the realm of property, having a property right, through the concomitant duties of others to respect it, creates spheres of freedom for the rightholder 'to choose among an adequate range of options' and 'to determine [their] own values and interests and to sort through and prioritize these values and interests in deciding how to act'.[5] Those who owe duties to owners generally don't have a say in the shaping of their duties in the way that duty bearers do in the realm of contract. The voluntary transfer of property, for example, is voluntary on the part of the transferor and transferee but not other duty bearers, who, following the transfer, owe duties to the transferee that they previously owed to the transferor without having a say on the matter.

For some or all of these reasons, perhaps, contemporary philosophers have been more sceptical about natural property rights than natural contractual rights.[6] One might wonder if this differential scepticism is indicative of philosophical confusion about the idea of natural contractual rights. There is something prima facie incongruous about natural contractual rights operating alongside conventional property rights, given that the baseline from which contractual agreements begin are set in part by the property rights of the parties. Liam Murphy argues as much in his defence of thoroughgoing instrumentalism about both contractual and property rights.[7]

Here I defend a different position that makes sense of this differential scepticism without endorsing instrumentalism about either kind of right. On my conception, both property and contract are non-instrumentally grounded despite not directly instantiating relational morality. Crucially, there is pervasive moral uncertainty about justice—uncertainty that primarily arises from

[4] Merrill & Smith 2000, 5.
[5] Katz 2008, 311.
[6] Murphy 2020, 457.
[7] Ibid.

the epistemic complexity of matters of justice for limited beings such as ourselves but may be compounded by metaphysical indeterminacy about the applicable principles and their implications. By deliberating in the right way about morally uncertain matters of justice, contracting parties can define morally binding terms of their relationship—terms that they owe it to one another to conform to. Given moral uncertainty, morally valid contractual rights and duties may depart from the true moral duties that deliberating parties seek to approximate, giving them an artificial quality despite instantiating terms that the parties owe it to one another to adhere to: their valid content is determined in part by a determination of the parties.

Property rights, on my conception, are one step further removed from the true moral rights of community members but are nonetheless integral to this process and may be justified accordingly. Property rights function to set the baseline for persons' deliberations with others about what justice between them requires. Because the parties are the ones that ought to define the terms of their relationship, property rights ought not to track relationship-specific considerations of justice. Property rights that are defined without reference to the moral needs and circumstances of the parties leave it to the parties to articulate the relevance of those considerations themselves without putting a thumb on the scale of a particular result. There is a virtue in arbitrariness, because an arbitrary baseline exhibits neutrality with respect to contestable matters of justice between the parties. But the baseline must be fair as well as neutral. Thus, the legal system as a whole ought to ensure that the baseline from which parties begin their deliberations be reasonably just, not only because doing so serves justice at the community level directly, but also because it enables the parties to treat those rights as a reasonable baseline for their deliberations about relationship-specific matters of justice.

While much private law theorizing in the corrective justice tradition foregrounds the equal procedural freedom of each to do as they wish with the means at their disposal,[8] my conception makes substantive justice the foundational value upon which the edifice rests. In this respect, I align myself with consequentialist theorists for whom the ways in which private law structures our rights and duties are justified only insofar as they serve substantive objectives such as the maximization of social welfare. But those accounts accord legal rights only instrumental significance: they are worthy of respect only insofar as they serve those independent objectives. I contend, by contrast, that we can foreground substantive justice without instrumentalizing private law once we

[8] See, eg, Ripstein 2016.

appreciate the moral significance of pervasive moral uncertainty about justice. Drawing on my 'democratic conception' of private law that I have been developing in other work through applications to contract,[9] tort,[10] and remedies,[11] I argue that private legal rights can instantiate claims we have against one another morally speaking, even though they may be artificial in the sense that they depart from the rights that exist at the moral level. They do so when they constitute morally justified responses to moral uncertainty about justice. This means that they have arisen from a process involving the right kind of deliberations about substantive justice by those who are morally authorized to resolve moral uncertainty about it.

II. Foundations

Property and contract regulate conflicts among persons about what is to be done with physical and human resources. Setting aside considerations of justice, persons will answer questions about how resources ought to be allocated differently. In the classical economic model, such differences arise because homo economicus cares only about his self-interest. But they arise even if everyone is a perfect moral agent, where such agents rationally act on partial reasons that others don't share arising from their special relationships.[12]

Call a person's standpoint the balance of such reasons. A's standpoint might dictate that certain resources be put to a use that will benefit a community with which A has special ties while B's might dictate that the same resources be devoted to a use that will benefit a community with which B has special ties. Because they conflict, we cannot figure out what ought to be done with the resources by appealing to either agent's standpoint. We must therefore appeal to moral considerations that transcend the reasons embodied in those standpoints. Because these moral considerations resolve conflicts among standpoints, we can call them considerations of justice.

Justice in the sense that I will use the term here thus has a wide domain. It applies whenever persons' rational standpoints conflict about what is to be done, even when the conflict is a trivial one.

[9] Stone 2024.
[10] Stone 2023 and 2025b.
[11] Stone 2025a.
[12] This assumption is compatible with Samuel Scheffler's argument that morality and partiality are 'inevitable concomitants of certain of the most basic forms of human valuing'. Scheffler 2010.

The economic analogue of justice is the social welfare function, which tells us how resources are to be allocated to maximize social welfare. What matters for the economist is the amount and distribution of preference satisfaction or 'utility'. The amount of utility each person receives doesn't matter, so long as the result is the optimal pattern of preference satisfaction.

In my framework, by contrast, justice assigns persons' standpoints to choices about what is to be done with available resources. In this sense, it creates a system of 'rights' though these rights lack some of the hallmarks standardly associated with rights. Persons have 'rights' that such choices be made in accordance with their standpoints whenever justice assigns their standpoints to those choices. But having a right doesn't entail having decision-making authority. If justice assigns A's standpoint to B's choice, B must make that choice as A's standpoint prescribes even if A told B to do otherwise.

In a world of perfectly morally motivated agents who are willing to set their partial standpoints aside in the name of justice, we have no need for the institutions of property and contract where what justice requires is determinate and known by all. Everyone will simply do as justice requires. If A knows that B's standpoint controls the use of some resource at A's disposal, then A will make choices about that resource in accordance with B's standpoint, because that is what justice requires. While this depends on everyone knowing what resources are available, morally motivated agents will willingly share relevant private information at their disposal insofar as it is relevant to what justice requires. To the extent that empirical uncertainty remains, justice will prescribe an allocation that reflects that empirical uncertainty and allocate associated risk justly.

There is also no need for the institutions of property and contract from an economic standpoint when all agents are motivated to set aside their self-interest to maximize social welfare. Except insofar as the actions of those agents would need to be coordinated, there would be no need for mediating institutions of property and contract because everyone would make social-welfare-maximizing choices anyway.

III. Contract and Property

What then of property and contract? What moral problems do these institutions solve?

1. Economic Model

In the economic model, the combination of information costs and self-interest generates the need for property and contract. Persons' subjective preferences are the inputs into the social welfare function and thus the carriers of moral value. But self-interested actors won't willingly share information about their preferences when they can reap personal advantage by concealing it. Information about available resources is also decentralized, and self-interested actors may not readily give up that information either.

Thus, without more, a social planner attempting to direct resources to maximize social welfare by fiat is unlikely to have the information it needs to do so effectively. The social planner might therefore decide to institutionalize a system of contract to give self-interested actors incentives to act on their private information in socially beneficial ways. If A wants some resources that B controls and B wants some resources that A controls, A and B have reason to exchange those resources. If the exchange can take place simultaneously, they will willingly make the exchange. But if the exchange must take place over time, the first-performing party, A say, needs to be assured that B will perform when it's B's turn despite B's self-interested reasons not to do so. The social planner can provide A with that assurance by enforcing an agreement between A and B to make the exchange, thus making possible the Pareto improvement.

But the institution of contract cannot do this alone, because there must be a stable system of rights over the resources that may be allocated via contract. If A can just take resources from B, A, as a self-interested actor, will do that instead should the opportunity arise, and vice versa. If both successfully take resources from each other, the same Pareto gain may be realized. But absent a stable system of property rights, there is no reason to suppose that mutually beneficial patterns of takings like this will result. Neither party has reason to be attentive to the amount the other values them when they aren't securing the other's assent to the taking. And both will have incentives to take defensive measures to stop resources being taken from them in the first place, thus diverting resources from productive uses.

In the economic model, then, property rights provide a stable baseline against which contractual relationships can form to enable parties to realize Pareto gains and so must exist prior to any relationship, actual or potential, between two parties—thus explaining and justifying property's *in rem* operation. Contractual rights, by contrast, are tailored by the parties enabling them to realize mutual gains against the backdrop of stable property rights. Contract's *in personam* quality thus also makes economic sense. When parties understand what is in their own interests, their mutual assent to the transaction ensures that it is mutually beneficial, and if no non-party is affected, Pareto gains will be the result. The contract must accordingly bind the parties who have assented to it and only those parties.

In a world of epistemically limited beings, the institutionalization of contract and property rights adds further complexity to this picture as Thomas Merrill and Henry Smith explain. For the system to work, parties need to know the contours of everyone's rights and duties both to avoid infringing the rights of others and to figure out whether they might want to acquire others' rights. But there are costs to finding out, which creates pressure on the system to reduce those costs by standardizing rights.[13]

The pressure to standardize tends to be greater in the realm of property than contract. At least in the paradigm case of an agreement formed between parties who are rationally pursuing their own interests with an equal ability to influence the agreement's terms, the tailoring of contractual rights to the situation of the parties is unproblematic, indeed, likely desirable on balance. Tailoring of the terms of the transaction to the parties' particular needs and circumstances makes it more likely that the transaction maximizes the parties' joint welfare. And because the parties did the tailoring and are the only ones bound by the rights and duties they created, they can easily ascertain the content of what they owe one another. (Many contracts, of course, don't fit this paradigm. In a contract of adhesion, for example, one party, aided by their attorneys, offers the other a complex set of terms on a take-it-or-leave-it basis.) By contrast, property rights bind everyone other than the owner including those who have had little or no say in their creation. Thus, tailoring imposes informational burdens on a large and indefinite number of people, making it more likely that standardization is on balance desirable.[14]

2. Democratic Conception

The economic framework makes information costs central—both the difficulties of acquiring accurate information about the empirical world and the burdens associated with identifying the content of persons' legal rights—along with the self-interested motivations of legal subjects. These imperfect motivations are key, because perfectly motivated actors would make the problem of

[13] Merrill & Smith 2001.
[14] Ibid, 777.

information costs disappear by willingly sharing information to which they have special access. Imperfectly motivated actors won't do this when there is advantage to be gained from keeping such information to themselves.

I begin with the contrasting assumption that everyone is motivated to conform to the prescriptions of justice and so will readily share information at their disposal that is relevant to determining what is required for each to act justly. Given this motivational assumption, if everyone also knows what justice determinately requires, they can simply act accordingly, and we won't need the institutions of property and contract at all, except insofar as they serve as coordinating devices.

But a need for those institutions will arise even if everyone is so motivated once we allow for the existence of moral uncertainty about justice. The complexity of many matters of justice in conjunction with our epistemic limitations means that we often won't know what justice requires even if we know all the morally relevant facts. Justice may also be somewhat indeterminate and so fail to offer a singular answer to every question as when competing considerations of justice are incommensurable or on a par.[15]

The economic framework doesn't reckon with the possibility of moral uncertainty because it assumes that we know the operative moral truths that are described by the social welfare function. But what if we don't know what justice prescribes?

Our uncertainty about justice's demands is itself a moral problem for us. Substantive (or first-order) justice, as previously described, prescribes an allocation of standpoints to choices. The standpoint that justice assigns to a choice describes the considerations that ought to be weighed by the person making that choice. But when there is moral uncertainty about justice, we don't know whose standpoint governs each choice, and when there is uncertainty about the balance of reasons that defines persons' standpoints, we don't know what should be done even when we know whose standpoints govern. Because choices must be made in the face of this uncertainty, we need to figure out how, morally speaking, we ought to respond to it. We need to figure out who gets to decide what we should do in the light of the uncertainty and how they must go about deciding. Because the answer will tell us how authority to resolve moral uncertainty about reason and justice ought to be allocated, we can think of this problem as a problem of second-order justice. The main contention of the democratic conception is that we should understand the institutions of private

[15] Chang 2017; Raz 1986, 333–35.

law as centrally concerned with the just management of moral uncertainty about first-order justice.

Consider contract first. Suppose there is moral uncertainty about whether A's standpoint or B's controls the choices to be made with various resources as a matter of first-order justice. What is the just response to that uncertainty? Well-motivated parties can manage uncertainty about empirical facts—the uncertainty that creates information costs in the economic model—through information sharing and contingent arrangements that fairly allocate risk associated with facts that neither party knows. Such risk-management strategies aren't available when it comes to moral uncertainty, because there is uncertainty about the operative principles for evaluating what may or may not have gone wrong. Some authors, inspired by decision theory, nonetheless argue that it is rational to respond to moral uncertainty by hedging across possible principles or theories.[16] But a model of what it may be individually rational for an agent to do when faced with moral uncertainty doesn't speak to what a community of persons ought to do in the face of uncertainty about what justice between them demands, especially when individuals have different views of the problem.

Democratic theorists appeal to second-order principles, like a principle of equal respect for the views of each, to justify decision-making via majoritarian procedures when it comes to community-wide decisions.[17] These theorists are focused on the allocation of authority to resolve matters of collective importance. When it comes to more local matters of justice, such second-order values, I believe, also suggest that authority ought to be decentralized to those whose rights may be implicated by its resolution.[18] Decentralization ensures that those persons have equal input into the rules that will regulate them without outsiders having a say about matters that don't implicate their rights.[19] The point is even clearer when it comes to persons' standpoints. Considerations of personal autonomy seem to confer on each of us exclusive authority to resolve moral uncertainty about our own standpoints. When standpoints are also allocated justly across choices, having each person

[16] For a recent defence of a sophisticated version of such a view, see Horton & Ross (2025).

[17] Eg Christiano 2008, 75–76 (arguing that democratic decision-making is the 'unique way to publicly embody equality in collective decision-making under the circumstances of pervasive conscientious disagreement in which we find ourselves'). For views emphasizing instead the importance of ensuring that citizens stand in relations of equality to one another, see Kolodny 2014; Viehoff 2014.

[18] Stone 2024; Stone 2025a; Stone 2025b.

[19] Cf Shiffrin 2021, ch 2 (emphasizing the democratic value of more decentralized forms of decision-making than legislative decision-making).

resolve moral uncertainty about their own standpoint instantiates a principle of equal respect for agency.

If this is the correct picture of second-order justice, then when it comes to a question of first-order justice that affects the rights of A and B alone, A and B ought to come up with a vision of what justice between them plausibly requires in an egalitarian fashion together, taking the other seriously as an equal partner in the deliberative process. This means that, procedurally, they must deliberate in good faith together about what justice between them requires, while substantively, their agreement must represent a plausible articulation of justice between them given the extant moral uncertainty. When these requirements are met, the parties' agreement has moral validity—and the law has reason to recognize it as a legally binding contract—because it instantiates equal respect for each party as a co-deliberator about matters of justice between the parties, even though, given moral uncertainty, it may only approximate what substantive justice between the parties truly requires.

What then of property? The parties' deliberations must begin from somewhere. The parties need to know, first, that they are morally authorized to determine how the choices that will form the subject matter of their agreement should be made—that one or other of their standpoints, and not the standpoint of a third party, controls those choices. The parties also need to know whose standpoint controls those choices before they begin deliberating, and thus what they owe one another should they fail to reach an agreement. Property law mediated through public institutions of taxation and transfer, in conjunction with tort law's protection of those rights and person's rights over their person, provides the parties with such a baseline.

If there were no clear baseline set of rights from which to begin their deliberations, the set of potentially valid transactions between two parties would be small. The parties would have to be confident absent any legal determination that justice allocated one or other of their standpoints to the choices the transaction might involve; otherwise, others whose rights plausibly might be implicated by any agreement ought to be included in the deliberations.

One can imagine scenarios in which it is obvious that only two parties' rights are implicated by a question of justice in the absence of a legal determination of persons' rights. Suppose A and B find themselves alone in a remote area and stumble upon some goods that will perish if not used immediately. A and B can be confident that justice assigns one of their standpoints to choices about what to do with those goods. It doesn't make sense to assign another person's standpoint to choices about goods they cannot make use of. Thus, all A and B need to decide is whether A's or B's standpoint controls the choices to be made with respect to the goods—a matter that can be validly settled via agreement between them.[20]

But in the very interdependent world we live in, cases like this one will be the exception. Absent a set of legal rights that resolve baseline questions of justice among members of the community, it will usually be hard to identify cases that are amenable to morally valid agreements between two parties. Others will have plausible claims on available resources so long as there is moral uncertainty about the just distribution of those resources among community members. Thus, property (mediated through public institutions of taxation and transfer) must enter the picture to set a reasonably just baseline system of entitlements that resolves moral uncertainty about what members of the community owe one another qua community members. Against this baseline, community members can negotiate to different outcomes via contract, thus defining their own visions of justice for their relationships.

In short, property law assigns persons' standpoints to choices about what is to be done with available resources by resolving moral uncertainty about justice between persons qua community members. This assignment then endows persons with *legal* rights to determine how those choices ought to be made. Because of moral uncertainty, those legal rights generally won't implement perfect justice even among persons qua community members and are thus subject to revision when the community sees need to revise them. Moreover, because those rights reflect a community-wide judgement, they don't resolve moral uncertainty about what parties owe one another qua individuals—they don't speak to justice in particular relationships. Thus, they should be regarded as subject to modification by those who are morally authorized to resolve moral uncertainty about their boundaries on relationship-specific grounds.

Contractual rights also arise from the resolution of moral uncertainty and so are also necessarily provisional. Indeed, on my conception, the parties ought to revise their agreements if they realize they no longer do justice between them. But the provisionality of property rights runs deeper, because those rights embody a resolution that is inherently prior to any contractual resolutions that are premised upon it by defining who is authorized to make those resolutions. This means that the determinations of property rights must reflect substantively plausible community-wide determinations, made through appropriate

[20] It's possible that justice might assign a choice to a standpoint that reflects the interests and commitments of a community of persons rather than an individual. I don't have the space to explore that possibility here and so confine my analysis to situations where individual standpoints control choices.

institutional mechanisms for reflecting the input of all. But it also means that the content of those community-wide determinations ought to reflect the ways in which they will shape the future contractual deliberations of the parties about what justice between them more specifically requires. Few of the affected parties have had a direct say in the right–duty relationships created by property rights, except insofar as they have influenced the community-wide resolution of uncertainty through democratic channels. Thus, those relationships are ripe for revision by contracting parties seeking to reflect more precisely what justice between them requires.

IV. Implications

In this section, I explore implications of the democratic conception for our understanding of the relationships between property and contract and of each with underlying moral rights, illuminating the ways in which private legal rights can instantiate genuine rights and duties despite failing perfectly to reflect substantive justice.

1. The Distribution of Property

According to the democratic conception, morally uncertain questions of substantive justice ought to be resolved by those whose rights may be implicated by their resolution. Questions about the allocation of resources among persons qua community members must be resolved at the community level through procedures that accord equal respect to the good faith views of all concerning how moral uncertainty about such questions ought to be resolved, while local questions of justice should be resolved together in good faith by affected persons through their agreements.

There is a complex interplay between community-wide and local resolutions of moral uncertainty. As we have seen, to know whether a question of justice is a matter for A and B alone, and thus one that they are authorized to resolve together via an agreement, we need to know what rights A and B have and thus what choices A and B are morally authorized to decide, which depends on community-wide determinations about who is entitled to control what resources. But such community-wide determinations represent resolutions of moral uncertainty about community-wide justice that are likely somewhat imperfect and so subject to revision as community understandings evolve. Private resolutions of moral uncertainty like those of A and B that are made against the backdrop of those community-wide resolutions may also alter what justice requires at the community level by altering the overall distribution of resources in ways that may be unjust from the community standpoint.

Suppose the community has resolved moral uncertainty about community-wide justice in such a way as to endow A and B with resources that they'd like to exchange with one another. Because of moral uncertainty about justice, the community might have gotten it wrong. Perhaps C is in fact entitled to control some of the resources choices over which the community has allocated to A or B. But if the community's resolution is reasonable both procedurally and substantively—that is, its allocation of standpoints to choices is plausibly just and arose from a good faith attempt by the community to resolve uncertainty about justice in a way that accords equal respect to the views of all—A and B are entitled to treat their legal property rights as genuine rights in their interactions with one another when deliberating about what justice between them requires. If they then form an agreement that also satisfies the procedural and substantive requirements of the democratic conception, we should regard that agreement as morally valid, articulating what A and B owe one another morally. In making such an agreement, the parties articulate a good faith joint vision of what justice between them requires, thus treating each other as deliberative equals. And because their joint vision must be plausibly just, honouring their agreement is a way of honouring each other's claims to a just share of resources. A and B, however, must appreciate the provisionality of both the community resolution on which their agreement was premised and their agreement. If the community has good reason to revise its resolution notwithstanding any reliance on it by the parties in a way that might disrupt the parties' agreement, the parties must respect the revision. Similarly, insofar as A's and B's agreement is itself a resolution of moral uncertainty about what justice between A and B requires, they ought to revise it if they arrive at a different view about what justice requires.

Thus, although there is artificiality built into the rights that A and B create—both because their starting point depends on a community resolution of moral uncertainty and their agreement reflects their own likely imperfect resolution—they may nevertheless instantiate genuine rights and duties. Contra Murphy, we can allow for some artificiality—the determinations that resolve moral uncertainty—without endorsing general practice-based instrumentalism about contract and property. Persons acquire genuine rights and duties against one another by entering morally valid contracts even when they take as given morally valid property rights that depend on the collective's contingent resolution of moral uncertainty.

This framework can also account for the differential scepticism philosophers have shown towards natural contract rights and natural property rights. Unlike contractual rights, morally valid property rights, on the democratic conception, arise from the community's resolution of community-wide questions of justice. Thus, the contours of those rights don't determine what justice between two persons demands beyond establishing what they owe one another qua citizens. Relational matters of justice are properly determined by the parties through their agreements.

Yet it doesn't follow that there is no relational wrong of any kind when a person infringes another's morally valid property rights. When C forces a transaction upon D instead of entering a morally valid contract with D, C fails to treat D as a deliberative equal. Even if C hasn't wronged D in a substantive sense, because the transaction C imposes on D constitutes a substantively reasonable resolution of what justice between then requires, C has wronged D in a procedural sense by failing to include D in her deliberations.

What happens, though, if the community resolution that determines the property rights that form the baseline for parties' deliberations is morally invalid either procedurally or substantively? If it is procedurally invalid but nonetheless provides a reasonably just starting point for the parties' deliberations, the parties still ought to be able to form a morally valid agreement taking their property rights as given, albeit one that they should accept may be subject to correction should the community fix the procedural problem. Because of moral uncertainty and the democratic importance of community-wide resolutions of community matters, the parties usually won't be able to determine what the morally valid starting point would look like by themselves. Given that the community has thrown its might behind the procedurally invalid resolution, it is reasonable for the parties to treat it as a starting point for their own deliberations. Were the community to subsequently decide to fix the procedural problem, it ought to be attentive to the ways in which contracting parties have reasonably relied on the procedurally problematic resolution to form their own agreements, because it would be unfair on those parties to disrupt those agreements without good reason given that the parties were not individually responsible for the procedurally problematic starting point from which they began. Thus, the morally valid contracts that are premised on a procedurally unsound baseline might even entrench that baseline by making it substantively unreasonable to disrupt it too much as the community resolves moral uncertainty about the baseline going forward.

Substantive invalidity of the community-wide resolution is more of a problem for the parties, because it complicates the substantive matters of justice between the parties. If E is clearly unjustly poor and F clearly unjustly rich, E and F are no longer entitled to view the baseline as a reasonably just starting point for their deliberations. F may, for example, be obligated to deal on more generous terms with E to compensate E for the evident unjust disparity between them. But the existence and content of such an obligation may not be clear to the parties, given that primary responsibility for the unjust disparity lies not with F but with the community at large. Thus, the problem E and F face is a complex one. If they respond reasonably to baseline injustice, I believe we should conclude that their agreement constitutes a morally valid determination of what they owe one another notwithstanding the invalidity of the rights from which they began. But there is a caveat. Conscientious parties seeking to articulate a vision for justice in their relationship in the context of background injustice should recognize that the community is responsible for evaluating and rectifying that injustice. Thus, they should view any agreement as subject to revision should the community become willing and able to do its job.

2. *Numerus Clausus*

A striking feature of the law of property is the way in which it limits property rights to a limited number of standard forms. Under the common law, there are only five general types of possessory interests in land, five basic categories of concurrent interests, four basic forms of right conferring limited rights of use rather than general possession, and when it comes to personal property, there are an even more limited number of forms, for instance, one can't create servitudes in personal property.[21] Parties can fine tune the details of their rights and duties against one another through contract as they see fit. But the *numerus clausus* principle means that they are not free to create new types of property rights.[22]

Through an economic lens, Merrill and Smith argue that the standardization of property rights is a way of limiting information-cost externalities that the further tailoring of rights by parties would impose on third parties—primarily those who won't seek title to the property over which the tailored

[21] Merrill & Smith 2000, 12–19.
[22] Ibid, 5.

right is imposed. Given the *in-rem* character of property rights, everyone needs to know how to avoid infringing the property rights of others. And those acquiring property need to understand the nature of the right that they are acquiring. Thus, there are informational burdens arising from operating in a world of property rights. When one party tailors a right in a novel way, they increase those burdens by complexifying the set of possibilities that third parties must consider when deciding whether to acquire property or avoid infringing the rights of others.[23]

In the ideal world from which the democratic conception begins, however, an appeal to information cost externalities can't do the necessary justificatory work. Ideally motivated actors will readily share information about their rights with potential infringers and successors. They also won't seek legal redress against those who reasonably infringe their legal rights, say because it wasn't reasonable for them to know the exact boundaries of those rights. Legal rights in this world are resolutions of moral uncertainty about what justice requires—not the final word—and ideally motivated actors will recognize this and act accordingly.

But the democratic conception can make sense of the greater standardization of property rights in a different way also related to the *in-rem* character of property rights—thus, explaining why a *numerus clausus* principle is operative even in a world of ideally motivated actors. The justification lies not in information-cost externalities but in an understanding of property rights as specifying the baseline for contractual deliberations between parties about what justice between them requires. On the democratic conception, parties ideally deliberate in good faith together to articulate a joint vision of justice for their relationship that plausibly resolves applicable moral uncertainty. Because the product of their deliberations must represent their own joint vision, it is important that the baseline legal rights from which they begin their deliberations serve as a neutral starting point for those deliberations. Simple rights whose boundaries are transparently arbitrary with respect to the ways parties might tailor them are preferable to more tailored rights that put a thumb on the scale in favour of a particular way of specifying justice for their relationship. Boundaries given by the physical boundaries of objects or lines carving up territorial space, for example, generally won't reflect the way things ought to be used in the context of a relationship and so set neutral baselines for property owners to specify how they will be used through contractual deliberations with others.

[23] Ibid, 26–27.

In principle, the parties might reallocate control of the resources over which they have property rights without regard to the baseline assignment between them. But if the community has done its job well, the initial assignment will represent what the community has determined the parties plausibly owe one another qua members of the community, and the parties accordingly have reason to give it weight in their deliberations. Greater tailoring of those baseline rights thus threatens to intrude on the good faith attempts of the parties to articulate their own joint vision of justice for their relationship, especially where the parties can't easily identify the extent to which the tailoring has gone beyond what was necessary to articulate their rights and duties qua community members. When parties' motivations are less pure, the baseline may intrude even further. Even conscientious agents who are influenced by self-serving biases might inadvertently use the fact that the baseline favours their vision of justice to impose that vision on others.

3. Limits on Transfer

Suppose G and H form a morally valid agreement whereby G will provide a service to H in exchange for H sending money to G a month later as payment. Suppose G provides the service to H and then realizes she needs the money sooner, prompting her to enter an agreement with J transferring to J her right to payment by H in exchange for J sending her money immediately. G does so, however, without obtaining H's assent to the transfer first.

This arrangement might seem innocuous: why should H care whether he makes the payment to J instead of G? The burdensome part of discharging the duty is the relinquishing of the money; it seems irrelevant to whom the money is relinquished. But, as Seana Shiffrin has observed, the transfer of a debt involves not merely the transfer of the right to payment but also the transfer of duties that go with being a creditor: 'the powers and rights of a creditor are informed and constrained by the duties that arise from the relationship of creditor and debtor.'[24] Shiffrin uses these observations to argue that contemporary contract law's permissive treatment of the assignment of contractual debts without the debtor's consent is inconsistent with its less permissive stance towards the delegation of contractual duties.[25]

[24] Shiffrin 2023, 17.
[25] Ibid.

The law's less permissive stance towards the delegation of contractual duties makes sense given that we choose our contracting partners based, in part, on our beliefs about their willingness to do the duties they undertake in contracting with us. It might thus be justified by the imperfect motivations of many to do as duty demands. If everyone were willing to do as duty demands, the free transferability of duties, and the rights to which the duties attach, would be easier to justify.

But we can make sense of the law's less permissive stance towards the delegation of contractual duties without assuming imperfect motivations. Many duties, including those of creditors to enforce their rights in good faith, involve the exercise of judgement and discretion.[26] Creditors who are perfectly motivated to do as duty demands will exercise that judgement and discretion differently in determining how to discharge such duties and their good motivations do not guarantee that they will do so well.

The democratic conception offers a lens on the problem that complements Shiffrin's observations. Rights to a contractual performance are part of a resolution by the parties of moral uncertainty about matters of justice between them. As such, they have been tailored to the parties' joint vision of justice for their relationship. There are thus two important senses in which they constitute the relationship of the parties alone. Procedurally, they arose from the parties' good faith joint resolution of moral uncertainty. Substantively, they are part of a plausible vision of justice for the parties' relationship. Importantly, the parties ought to regard their resolution as a provisional one—subject to revision as their sense of what justice between them requires evolves. For example, if H suffers an unexpected hardship that will make timely payment a more significant burden than the parties anticipated, G and H may be under a duty to renegotiate the terms of the repayment. But this renegotiation will also be particular to the parties—it must reflect their joint vision of justice for their relationship, and given moral uncertainty about what that should look like, even conscientious parties who exercise good moral judgement will arrive at different resolutions of the problem. Thus, even if we don't assume that there are duties that travel with contractual rights to a performance, the centrality of ongoing deliberation to the parties' relationship means that parties will care about the identity of their contracting partner. To the extent that H's dealing with a particular party J isn't clearly compelled by or prohibited by justice, G ought not to be able to dictate that H and J enter into a deliberative relationship on similar terms to the terms to which H and G originally agreed simply

[26] Ibid, 19.

in virtue of having a prior relationship with H and having entered into a new relationship with J. The existence and terms of the relationship between H and J are a matter for H and J alone (insofar as there is moral uncertainty about the terms of their relationship).

Limiting the transferability of contractual rights on these grounds alone, however, leads to counterintuitive results. Suppose that instead of a promise of a future payment of money, H gave property (chattels or money) to G in return for H's performance. Ought G be prevented from transferring the items to J without H's consent? It might, after all, turn out that G and H come to appreciate the injustice of the terms of their agreement after the fact. Perhaps H's circumstances change in such a way that he now really needs the items he transferred to G. The argument I just advanced against the transferability of debt seems to entail that ownership of property acquired through contract would always be provisional and subject to revision when the original parties come to a revised view of what justice between them requires.

Shiffrin finds a limiting principle where chattels are concerned in the fact that the transfer of chattels, unlike a transfer of debt, doesn't create 'an ongoing *relationship* of duty . . . to the prior owner with respect to the object, much less a relationship of substantial vulnerability predicated on how that relationship unfolds.'[27] Yet Shiffrin endorses the ways in which warranties travel with products to non-purchasers, even though they put the manufacturer in a relationship with someone that it didn't enter a contract with. In the case of mandatory safety guarantees, the explanation is simple: 'Those who make artifacts, or food, or who control land have an obligation to render them safe to everyone who may be in contact with them, and everyone has a speech right to review their quality publicly.'[28] In the case of discretionary warranties, contextual features of the relationship do the justificatory work: the central performance [of manufacturing the product] has already occurred; the warranty-holder has limited morally significant discretion; the identity of the warranty-holder won't matter much to the warranty-provider; and the stakes are much lower for a typical warranty-provider given their position in the marketplace.[29]

The domain of application of any principle of non-transferability (absent consent) that arises from the democratic conception cannot be so easily tailored to such circumstantial factors. For that principle, recall, arises from the provisional, relationship-specific quality of the contractual resolution of moral

[27] Ibid, 18.
[28] Ibid, 20.
[29] Ibid.

uncertainty about justice between the original parties. And the provisionality of any such resolution may not vary in ways that track the factors Shiffrin identifies.

An alternative way of setting bounds on the principle can, however, be found in the justification of the *numerus clausus* principle I offered above. If the continuing validity of a transfer of property from to J depends on H and G not validly revising their agreement transferring the property to G, parties could disrupt the standardization of property rights and complicate the deliberations of transferees turned transferors like G with potential successor transferees like J about what justice between them (ie G and J) requires. Agreements between the likes of G and J would have to be made conditional on resolutions of moral uncertainty by the original transferors and transferees (G and H) continuing to hold in the eyes of those parties. But this would mean that G's and J's deliberations about what justice between them requires must depend on their judgements about the ongoing justice of G's and H's joint resolution of moral uncertainty about justice in their own relationship and the likelihood that G and H see the need to revise it. Whenever it appeared likely that the original transfer agreement was no longer valid, there would need to be a deliberation involving all three parties to resolve what justice requires. The picture would become increasingly more complex still were J to transfer the item to K via contract, and K to L and so forth. In short without a simple rule requiring the unconditional transfer of title to property, the possibilities of bilateral resolutions of moral uncertainty about justice between parties would be disrupted.

Does this countervailing rule of finality threaten to swallow the principle restricting the transferability of rights to a contractual performance? I don't think so. When G transfers what was previously H's property to another, H is dutybound not to interfere with the right of the current owner in the same way that any other non-owner of the property owes it to the owner not to interfere. By contrast, when G instead transfers a right to a future contractual performance by H to another (whether that be a promise to render a service, pay money, or transfer other property), H owes a special duty to the current rightholder that no others owe. Thus, only in the latter scenario is there a special deliberative relationship between H and the rightholder, giving rise to a justification to give H a say about the rightholder's identity in the latter but not the former scenario.

What about warranties? There is nothing problematic on the democratic conception about safety guarantees travelling with a product: persons have duties to make their products safe to all who may come into contact with them, not just the purchasers. The distinction I made above does suggest, however, that discretionary or generic but disclaimable warranties ought not to be assignable without the consent of the assignee. But this wouldn't undermine the assignability of mandatory warranty terms, such as the housing merchant implied warranty, which imposes liability for defective construction on a builder of a new house,[30] or the implied warranty of habitability, which imposes upon landlords liability for failing to ensure that the premises are habitable.[31] When terms are mandatory, the community through its legal representatives has determined that a valid contract must contain them, and thus that aspect of the resolution between builder and original buyer or landlord and original tenant ceases to be a matter for the parties. In effect, such terms ensure that a property right to personal property or interest in land always includes a warranty right against the manufacturer or landlord. The community is morally authorized to impose such terms when it reasonably understands that doing so is necessary to achieve community-wide justice.

V. Conclusion

Property and contract are institutions that facilitate the resolution of moral uncertainty about justice between persons understood as equal joint deliberators about matters of justice between them. Property resolves moral uncertainty about community-wide matters while setting a neutral baseline for contractual deliberations between parties. Contract gives legal recognition to successful attempts by parties to articulate a joint vision of what justice between them plausibly requires. The rights created by the two regimes are thus artificial—because they reflect joint or collective judgements about justice—yet non-instrumentally grounded in principles of first- and second-order justice.

References

Chang, R. (2017). 'Hard Choices'. *Journal of the American Philosophical Association* 3: 1–21.

Christiano, T. (2008). *The Constitution of Equality: Democratic Authority and its Limits*. Oxford, Oxford University Press.

Hohfeld, W. N. (1916). 'Fundamental Legal Conceptions as Applied in Judicial Reasoning'. *Yale Law Journal* 26: 710–770.

Horton, J. and J. Ross (2025). 'Evaluative Uncertainty and Permissible Preference'. *Philosophical Review* 134: 35–64.

[30] Eg NY Gen Bus, § 777.
[31] Eg NY Real Prop Acts, § 235.

Katz, L. (2008). 'Exclusion and Exclusivity in Property Law'. *University of Toronto Law Journal* 58: 275–315.
Kolodny, N. (2014). 'Rule over None II: Social Equality and the Justification of Democracy'. *Philosophy & Public Affairs* 42: 287–336.
Merrill, T. W. and H. E. Smith (2000). 'Optimal Standardization in the Law of Property: The Numerus Clausus Principle'. *Yale Law Journal* 110: 1–70.
Merrill, T. W. and H. E. Smith (2001). 'The Property Contract Interface'. *Columbia Law Review* 101: 773–852.
Murphy, L. (2020). 'The Artificial Morality of Private Law: The Persistence of an Illusion'. *University of Toronto Law Journal* 70: 453–488.
Penner, J. (1997). *The Idea of Property Law*. Oxford, Clarendon Press.
Raz, J. (1986). *The Morality of Freedom*. Oxford, Clarendon Press.
Ripstein, A. (2016). *Private Wrongs*. Cambridge, Harvard University Press.
Scheffler, S. (2010). 'Morality and Reasonable Partiality'. *Partiality and Impartiality*. B. Feltham and J. Cottingham. Oxford, Oxford University Press.
Shiffrin, S. V. (2021). *Democratic Law*. Oxford, Oxford University Press.
Shiffrin, S. V. (2023). 'Hidden Delegations: The Assignment of Contractual Rights and Consumer Debt'. *Modern Law Review* 86: 1–30.
Stone, R. (2023). 'Who Has the Right to Enforce Private Rights'. *Oxford Studies in Private Law Theory Volume 2*. P. B. Miller and J. Oberdiek. Oxford, Oxford University Press.
Stone, R. (2024). 'Putting Freedom of Contract in its Place'. *Journal of Legal Analysis* 16: 94–119.
Stone, R. (2025a). 'Rights, Remedies, and Normative Uncertainty about Justice'. *Legal Theory* (forthcoming).
Stone, R. (2025b). 'A Democratic Conception of Tort Law'. Unpublished.
Viehoff, D. (2014). 'Democratic Equality and Political Authority'. *Philosophy & Public Affairs* 42: 337–375.

2

When Contract Makes Property

Aditi Bagchi

I. Introduction

Most of the time, contract and property are like the chicken and the egg. Property rights are usually acquired by contract and most contracts trade existing entitlements, whether property or property-like. But, at least within contract theory, scholars have tended to treat property as prior. 'Starting with' property conveniently outsources many of the normative discomforts associated with justifying a regime of contract law. Most important, contract as an institution takes as its starting point that everyone is entitled to what we have, and further, we are entitled to use imbalances between existing entitlements to extract and expand advantage. To the extent that contract rights flow from property rights as a conceptual matter, it may appear that there is a lot less justificatory work to be done within or for the institution of contract, specifically. I will argue here that the opposite is true. Justifying contractual entitlements as derivative from property rights is impossible. In fact, the best shot at justifying property rights may be their contractual origin, if and when that justification is available. In any event, we should look elsewhere to justify the institution of contract and its allocative effects. We do not have to look far. The bargains that underlie contract give us reason to respect the re-sorting of entitlements that emerge from them.

The high mark of deference to Property within contract theory was will theory, and closely related transfer theories of contract. In their traditional form, these theories suppose that the authority to transfer entitlements by contract derives from each contracting party's property rights. For example, on this view, I can sell my house because I own my house, and the power of alienation is one aspect of my entitlement in my house. Similarly, my buyer can transfer their money to me just because it is *their* money.

Will and transfer theories of contract were eventually displaced by promise theories. While importantly different, promise theories continue to locate a

Aditi Bagchi, *When Contract Makes Property* In: *The Property-Contract Interface*. Edited by: James Penner, Irina Sakharova, Henry E. Smith, and Zhong Xing Tan, Oxford University Press. © Aditi Bagchi 2026.
DOI: 10.1093/9780198951995.003.0003

party's entitlement derived from contract in the other party's will. But instead of recognizing a liberty-right on the part of a promisor to convey an entitlement to another person by contract, promise theory posits only a coincident power to promise and power to contract, both of which create new rights in one's counterparty. Promise theories argue that the state should recognize such a power because of its relational value.

An exchange theory of contract grounds the entitlements that result from contract in the exchange effectuated by contract.[1] We might say, on this view, that I am entitled to a house that I purchased from you not fundamentally because you gave it to me but because I paid you for it. While we have abundant reason to recognize exchange only where it is voluntary, the normative punch of contract lies in the fact of bargain rather than the authority of property rights.

The saga of how the law has treated good faith purchasers nicely puts to test the question of whether property rights traceable to contract depend on the underlying property rights. A buyer who purchases goods, land, or debt from another person who himself lacks good title cannot 'take' good title from her contracting counterpart. With hesitation and inconsistency, many jurisdictions in many situations nevertheless recognize that the good faith buyer acquires good title. Where, then, does her right to the property come from? In this chapter, I will not argue for any particular form of the good faith purchase doctrine. I will argue only that the course of the doctrine, as well as uncertainty about the optimal rule, shows that rights in and from contract may normally depend on existing property rights, but a regime of contract is not essentially an extension of property rights. Our reasons for respecting the bargains that people make are grounded in the normativity of exchange, including its functional advantages, and not the authority of property owners. Attempting to justify the entitlements we acquire through contract by way of the prerogatives of those who transferred them looks backwards rather than forwards. Looking backwards in any meaningful way is unsettling, in more than one sense. The most stable justification for taking the entitlements we bring to contract as given lies in what this approach can do for us going forwards.

In what follows, I will draw out the contrasting approaches to contract in the context of how they frame the problem of the good faith purchaser. In Part I, I will offer a brief history of how the common law has treated the good faith purchaser. In Part II, I will consider the ramifications of competing theories of contract for the good faith purchaser problem. Finally, in Part III, I will

[1] I have elaborated this view of contract in a forthcoming paper, *Contract as Exchange*. Bagchi 2025.

consider how the advantages of an exchange approach to the good faith purchaser dilemma encapsulate its advantages for justifying who ends up with what, not only in weird cases, but also in typical ones.

II. The History of the Good faith Purchase in Common Law

The problem of good faith purchasers arises in a number of distinct contexts. In one typical situation, an owner transfers rights in some property, whether goods or a promissory note, to an intermediary. (We exclude, for now, cases of outright theft.) But there is some defect in the intermediary's claim. For example, they may have procured the transfer by way of misrepresentation or duress. A buyer that is unaware of the defective title then acquires the property interest from the intermediary. In another variation, the original owner's agent sells the property without the owner's permission. A similar problem arises when the original owner transfers real property not once but twice and the first buyer fails to record and the second buyer is unaware of the first buyer's claim (here the two buyers are the two innocent parties with rival claims). In still another scenario, the holder of a security interest fails to authorize sale of secured property. In each case, the last-in-time buyer is 'innocent' in that they have neither notice nor reason to know of a competing claim on the property they have acquired through a good faith purchase. But in each case, there is at least one other party with a compelling competing claim to the same property. Of course, in each case there is also one party whose fault produces the dilemma. The rule around good faith purchases matters only because, in many cases, neither party can secure relief from the actual wrongdoer.[2] Assuming the wrongdoer is unavailable to remedy the situation, the central question at issue is: who gets the property? (I will not address here the further question of whether that person should compensate the other in any way.[3])

There are two simple principles we could invoke to answer the question but they are usually taken to point in different directions. The first principle holds that one has no right to transfer what one does not have (*nemo dat quod non habet.*). Therefore, the second sale cannot transfer good title and the second

[2] Mautner 1991.

[3] A rule that requires the innocent party who ends up with the contested property to compensate the other innocent party who loses out on it would apportion the losses. See Weir 2004 (describing a change whereby modern English courts are more prepared to apportion losses than was traditional common law); see also Code Civil, art. 2280 (Fr.) (requiring the original owner to compensate the good faith purchaser the purchase price when the original owner is allowed to recover).

buyer has no claim to the property beyond what follows from bare possession. This principle is indeed a traditional principle of the common law, but it has been centuries since it was so bluntly applied. This is because categorically denying a robust property claim by the innocent second buyer seems not only inequitable but also jeopardizes commerce with those who worry that they will find themselves similarly situated. Buyers will be reluctant to buy if they may lose the property at any time to someone who had a prior claim, of which they had no notice.

An alternative would be a categorical last-in-time rule, referred to as market overt. The primary principle to support it is pro-commerce. On this view, courts should mimic what we will shortly see was the rule favoured by merchants, on the grounds that the role of courts in managing property and contract is essentially to facilitate commerce.[4] The rule might also be justified to the extent it reflects greater opportunity to avoid the situation, or greater causal responsibility for the situation, on the part of the original owner, who voluntarily placed their property in the hands of an intermediary.[5] But the market overt rule might tend to reward purchasers who meet the technical requirements of good faith purchase but are actually less removed from the underlying wrongdoing than the rival claim-holder. It might also encourage intermediaries to quickly resell property that they have wrongfully procured.

Civil law countries have historically been more receptive to protection of the later purchaser.[6] There is some historical evidence of the market overt rule as far back as custom in the ninth century among German merchants.[7] The common law began with something close to the first principle categorically favouring the original owner but it gradually moved towards the second, ostensibly pro-commerce principle. In the United States, we have returned to an intermediate position. In what follows, I explore that history briefly to observe the deficiencies of either bright line rule.

Protection for good faith purchasers in the common law began with the introduction of the merchant law into the common law.[8] The market overt

[4] Swartz 1962 ('[T]he reason most frequently advanced for favoring the [bona fide purchaser] is that by doing so we are responding to the needs of commerce. That is undoubtedly true.').

[5] Ibid 409 ('Aside from commercial expediency, there is in our Anglo-American jurisprudence yet another principle which is available as support for the position favoring the [bona fide purchaser] . . . [W]here one of two innocent persons must differ for the wrong of another, the loss should fall on him who placed it within the power of the wrongdoer to perpetrate the fraud.').

[6] Ibid 404–405, 407.

[7] Smith 1997, 227.

[8] Swartz 1962, 405; Pease 1908, 381. I do not imply the existence of a uniform medieval merchant law and refer only to relevant local custom at the time of its legal adoption. See Kadens 2015 (debunking the myth of uniform mercantile law in the Middle Ages).

doctrine is so named because it initially protected not all good faith buyers but only those who bought goods in a publicly licensed market or fair. These fairs were not markets as we know them now, which we might associate with local farmer's markets or antiques markets, but were instead the meeting places of merchants from around the country as well as overseas. To these commercial actors, confidence in the transactions at these markets was as essential as the negotiability of promissory notes, which developed doctrinally at the same time.[9] Markets were considered so much in the public interest that people were encouraged to use them.[10] By 1450, common law had absorbed the merchant rule favouring good faith purchasers.[11]

Although initially restricted to markets at discrete times and places, the shops of London were eventually recognized as a 'market' every day of the week.[12] This opened the door to more open-ended treatment of good faith purchasers on the same theory, that is, that commerce depended on their protection. Blackstone opined that protection was necessary or 'all commerce between man and man must soon be at an end'.[13] Similarly, Coke observed that 'the common law did hold it for a point of great policie, and behovefull for the Common-wealth that Faires and Markets overt should be replenished and well furnished with all manner of commodities, vendible in Faires and Markets, for the necessary and sustenation of the people'.[14]

But the link between market overt and a desire to promote commerce proves too much, because the rule did not catch on quickly in the United States, where commerce was presumably also valued. In the first half of the nineteenth century, most US courts had rejected the market overt doctrine.[15] It took root only in the late nineteenth and early twentieth centuries, its rise coinciding with a rise in the 'increased impersonality of commercial activity' and the corresponding difficulty of mitigating risks at time of purchase.[16] American embrace of the doctrine culminated in its codification in the Uniform Commercial Code. While it began as elsewhere in the context of transactions for the purchase of goods, it eventually encompassed debts and other financial instruments, as well as land in certain cases.[17] In twenty-five states, a good faith purchaser of real property is free of a prior unrecorded interest in the property

9 Pease 1908, 377.
10 Weinberg 1981, 4.
11 Smith 1997, 229.
12 Pease 1908, 379.
13 Blackstone 1803, 449.
14 Coke 1642, 713.
15 Weinberg 1981, 7.
16 Balganesh 2016, 279.
17 Sepinuck 2018.

and most remaining states allow a good faith purchaser without notice to do the same.[18] But the doctrine experienced a decline, revival, and in the face of new challenges, is now selectively applied.

Market overt experienced an early decline in the United States when theft became a major problem and the possibility of fast westward movement made it harder for owners to recover improperly procured goods before they were transferred to others.[19] However, by the mid-twentieth century, good faith purchase protection was again associated with vibrant commerce.

Grant Gilmore was one of the drafters of the Uniform Commercial Code in the United States, and he initially described the good faith purchaser doctrine as a kind of pragmatic updating of the law in service to commerce.[20] But Gilmore eventually became more sceptical of the Code's treatment of good faith purchasers. He and other scholars came to see several limitations to the Code's whole-hearted embrace of good faith purchasers, and indeed this protection was increasingly qualified by other statutes and regulations over the years.

One problem was that Article 3 glossed over a growing line of cases that refused to protect those who purchased large amounts of consumer debt from a seller in apparent coordination. Many courts had held that finance companies could not hold consumer notes free of the consumer's contract defences because of their close connection with the dealer-sellers.[21] This was not the situation for which the UCC had been drafted, but its language would have granted broad protection to such finance companies. Until consumer credit became a mass market phenomenon, most cases of good faith purchase involved only commercial parties; the UCC had not contemplated how its rules would apply where the original 'owner' was a consumer.[22] Now that the competing claimants to property, namely consumer paper, were consumer and bank, the rules needed to be adjusted.[23]

More fundamentally, Gilmore also came to regard as tenuous and historically contingent the relationship between the good faith doctrine and the principle of promoting commerce. The doctrine originated in the context of

[18] Ibid, 588.

[19] Weinberg 1981, 8, 11.

[20] Gilmore 1981, 611 ('commercial property must be freely transferable—no restraints on alienation can be tolerated').

[21] Ibid, 619. See, eg, *Commercial Credit Corp v Childs*, 199 Ark 1073, 137 SW 2d 260 (1940) (refusing to allow a finance company closely involved in the original transaction to enjoy the benefits of a holder in due course).

[22] Littlefield 1966, 60. See also Weinberg 1981, 41 (In the antebellum period, 'owners and good faith purchasers were often members of the same commercial community'.).

[23] Littlefield 1966, 49.

distribution of goods from manufacturer to user.[24] It expanded to bank notes and bills of exchange, but in the late eighteenth century, those operated as a kind of unofficial currency to supplement the official currencies, of which there was a shortage.[25] Both contexts became obsolete. With vertical integration and direct retail and franchise-based distribution, the role of intermediate distributor became less important, and 'the principal reason for the protection of good faith purchasers of goods against defrauded owners also disappeared'.[26] Similarly, after currency reform and new forms of bank credit in the nineteenth century, 'mercantile currency' in the form that good faith protection initially contemplated was no longer necessary and was hardly used.[27] The result was that courts lost enthusiasm for good faith purchasers and began pairing back their protections.[28]

In an altogether different context, Deborah DeMott has observed how customary practice surrounding the return of stolen art has evolved in response to the changing role of intermediaries, who are often sophisticated museums and dealers.[29] In that context too, the legal response to two apparently innocent buyers has depended on the market structure in which the legal rule operates, as well as status-specific judgements about social vulnerability and social responsibility.

Just as rules with respect to any class of property have changed with the market in which the property is bought and sold, the rules around good faith purchasers have come to distinguish among different kinds of property. The buyer of secured collateral that has been sold without authorization from the creditor is treated differently than the purchaser of real estate subject to an unrecorded interest, and both are significantly different from a purchaser of goods to which the seller held only voidable title.[30]

We have seen that the courts have rejected either of the two absolutes. That is, they have refused to uphold the broad principle that a party cannot convey a property interest that she does not have. But they have also rejected the contention that commerce requires consistent protection for the good faith purchaser. What they have learned is that it all depends.

[24] Gilmore 1981, 608.
[25] Ibid, 612.
[26] Ibid, 614.
[27] Ibid, 613.
[28] Ibid, 615.
[29] DeMott 2012.
[30] Sepinuck 2018, 601.

III. When Should we Recognize a Good Faith Purchaser?

1. Competing Principles and Where They Point

We have seen that neither of two possible principles that bear on the good faith purchaser dilemma satisfactorily resolved it. We should see this as grounds to reject any theory of contract that would imply a categorical resolution to the dilemma, as well as any theory that fails to explain why there is a dilemma in the first place. Will theorists and their heirs, promise theories, imply a categorial rule that is implausible? Legal economists fail to capture the dilemma at all.

A. Classical Theories of Contract and their Implications for Good Faith Purchase

Common law courts began with the principle that one cannot convey rights one does not have, or, *nemo dat quod non habet*. This principle was not a free-floating commitment; it lies at the heart of a particular conception of contractual authority. Under will theory, the idea that one's right to transfer property derives from one's rights in that property delivers the animating mandate of contract as an institution.

Under will theory, the right to alienate on terms of one's choice flows from one's underlying control interest in the asset. The right to contract is derivative from the right to one's property.[31] On this view, the duty of the state to enforce promises to transfer is just one way in which the state has a duty to protect property.[32] Because the right to transfer was a full-blown liberty-right, will theory supported what became known as 'freedom of contract'. The theory offers principled resistance to any interference in transfers to which a property owner consents. In practice, it called for affirmative state support for any transfer to which a property owner consents. The theory does not on its face necessarily have anything to say about the origins of a property claim but it would be quizzical for the origin to be a contract that did not itself merely effectuate the transfer of an existing property right. That is, will theory appears to favour the original owner over the good faith purchaser in part because it cannot make sense of the good faith purchaser at all. The latter never acquired valid rights in the one mode that will theory recognizes.

[31] Horwitz 1974, 920 ('the most distinctive feature of eighteenth-century contract law is the subordination of contract to the law of property').

[32] Dranias 2008, 289–290.

Will theory and its heirs need not imply that a good faith purchaser has *no* legal right in the contested property at all. Relativity of title can explain the sense in which the good faith purchaser has some ownership interest. If a third party were to wrongfully take the property from the good faith purchaser, the good faith purchaser could sue to get it back. But this would be true even if the good faith purchaser had merely *found* the property. They have a relative claim to the property based on possession alone; their rights would not derive from the purchase.[33] Specifically, it does not protect them against a claim from the original owner.[34] Will theory is not incompatible with recognizing their relative title, but it cannot explain why their purchase from a non-owner generates a distinct moral claim to the property and how such a claim could trump that of the original owner.

More directly, will theory gives us reason to reject the proposition that the original owner could ever be involuntarily divested of their ownership by virtue of a series of events that do not include free exercise of their right of transfer. Even if the original owner handed over their property to an intermediary, once it has been ascertained that this transfer failed to meet the standards of a truly free transfer—for example, because it was induced by fraud—will theory would direct us to restore their original rights in the property. While the theory does not concern itself with the quality of assent to transfer separate from the applicable legal threshold, it does assign overwhelming significance to assent however it may be defined in law because it locates the essence of contract in that assent.

Focused on the wrong to the original owner, we might understand the return of the contested property to them as a kind of restitution. But restitution here is divorced from any unjust enrichment on the part of the defendant (good faith purchaser).[35] Will theory, though, does not have the resources to recognize the good faith purchaser's claim, independent as it is from the fountain of the origin owner's authority.

The focus on assent to transfer in will theory comes at the expense of attention to other potential normative principles that motivate contract as an institution, including positive principles such as reciprocity and planning and negative principles like the avoidance of unjust enrichment, on the one hand, and forfeiture, on the other. I will explore below how these competing

[33] Fox 2006, 332 ('we say the validity of [Purchaser 2's] title is relative, in the void against [Purchaser 1] but generally valid against any third person ('[Purchaser 3]') who interferes with his possession').
[34] Ibid, 344.
[35] See Kull 1995 (arguing that restitution is about unjust enrichment, not restoration).

principles could be relevant, though not dispositive, to the good faith purchaser dilemma.

While will theory is no longer the dominant theory of contract in the United States and other common law countries, it remains influential. Promise theory, its dominant replacement in the philosophy of contract, makes important modifications but maintains the focus on the intentions of each party with respect to their own change of normative position. It is not obvious that promise theories of contract should have a stake in how we resolve the good faith purchaser situation; the mandate either to respect the obligational structure of promise or to promote and protect promise as a moral practice is largely unimplicated. After all, at issue is not whether to coerce any one of the three parties—original owner, intermediary, ultimate purchaser—to keep a voluntarily assumed obligation. Nevertheless, because promise theory sources our contractual entitlements to the promises we have received from our counterparty, its framing of the normative position of a contracting party might suggest that a party's entitlements depend just on the intentions of the other party (whether objectively or subjectively construed). This would lead us to a judgement similar to what we got from will theory.

Promise theory has another feature that frames the situation in a manner even less favourable to the good faith purchaser. Promise theory centres the relational character of contract. It does not take contractual relations to be a by-product of contract, albeit one with important moral implications. It takes the bilaterality to be the whole point: either parties contract in order to effectuate a kind of relationship with each other, or contract recognizes that (promissory) relationship because there is moral value in it. Whether the promissory relation is essentially egalitarian[36] or respectful,[37] the good of contract lies in the relationships that promises create. Given this way of thinking about contract, the two contracts that create the good faith purchaser dilemma are both unworthy of recognition and the best option might appear a return to the original state of affairs. As in will theory, there is nothing in this picture that gives us reason to recognize a claim by the good faith purchaser. It is not that their claim derives from an inferior promissory relationship; the problem is rather that the original owner has a claim to the property that does not depend on the unworthy contracts at all, while the former must depend on contracts that, in the eyes of promise theory, fail as contracts because they do not involve the kind of morally valuable relationships that contracts are supposed to be about.

[36] Shiffrin 2007, 717.
[37] Markovits 2004, 1420.

Classical theories of contract, under the amorphous umbrella of transfer theory, will theory, and promise theory, clearly favour the original owner over the good faith purchaser because they imply that the original owner cannot lose their entitlement without exercise of their own volition, and because they offer no account of what might ground the good faith purchaser's claim. Although those theories remain ascendant among contract theorists, the actual legal doctrine of good faith purchase has rejected their position. This is because, by locating the legal effect of contract entirely in its accompanying mental activity, those theories fail properly to characterize the normativity of contract.

B. Legal Economics and Good Faith Purchase Doctrine

While promise theory has largely displaced will theory and now reigns in the philosophy of contract, it occupies only a small space in the scholarly imagination today in comparison to the prevailing paradigm of legal economics. The functionalism of legal economics seems generally to favour market overt. The legal economic analysis does not strictly speaking set out to 'maximize commerce'; it would maximize utility. But in this context, we could expect these goals to align.

We will turn in a moment to how the economic analysis would play out, and especially the relative precaution costs generated by the doctrinal possibilities, but we might first look to the common law itself as a proxy for the pragmatic analysis that legal economics would offer. After all, legal economists tend to praise the common law for working out the economic analysis incrementally, even if couched in moralistic language intended to placate formal norms of adjudication. But we have seen already that the common law fails to deliver a clear answer in favour of the good faith purchaser. If anything, its embrace of good faith purchaser protection has been more hesitant than in civil law countries.[38] While the common law never fully reverted to categorial protection of original owners, it never definitively embraced market overt either. As Gilmore put it: '"The law" has always been in a constant state of flux as it struggles to adjust itself to changing methods of business practice; what purports to be formal rules of abstract logic are merely ad hoc responses to particular solutions.'[39]

[38] Yale L.J. [No named author] 1963, 1209 ('[U]nless we are willing to assert that America and England have been less fluid and commercial than the Continental societies, we cannot conclude that the greater protection given to the good faith purchaser in the Civil law is a necessary commercial evolution.').

[39] Gilmore 1954, 1069.

Perhaps in this instance, the natural forces of legal evolution failed the common law. We will consider now whether a direct economic analysis would give us a less equivocal doctrinal answer.

Several scholars have observed that whether the original owner or the last purchaser should be recognized as the valid owner turns on whether the selected rule incentivizes the optimal level of precaution and disclosure from each of the parties involved.[40] However, this analysis may point in different directions. Alan Schwartz and Robert Scoot argue for a negligence standard to be applied to owners with respect to precautions and search, which may favour good faith purchasers but does not, of course, when the original owners were not negligent.[41] Omri Ben-Shahar considers a variety of incentives, including 'incentives to protect assets before the theft occurs, and to search and trace their assets after theft occurs, and . . . thieves' incentives to engage in theft'.[42] But Ben-Shahar concludes that the buyer's incentives are unlikely to be moved by the rule in most cases, given the low frequency of recovery and costs of diligence, and so he ultimately focuses only how priority rules affect owners' incentives rather than buyers' incentives.[43] His nuanced analysis does not definitely favour any particular rule but would appear to depend for its upshot on the market context of particular transactions. For example, Ben-Shahar observes that 'if it is easier for owners to insure against theft than for buyers to insure against buying stolen goods . . . one could expect a stronger dilution of incentives at the protection stage'.[44]

Given that even an embrace of the principle of promoting commerce does not dictate in favour of good faith protection,[45] we cannot take a pro-commerce principle to support a market overt principle in the way that a property rights focus favours the original owners.[46] Instead, a functional analysis can lead to different treatment of good faith purchasers depending on specific features of

[40] Merrill & Smith 2001, 840 (rules on good faith purchasers are 'designed to protect parties with incomplete information and to create incentives for informationally advantaged parties to provide notice'); Medina 2003 (optimal rule 'maximizes the value of the ownership right' by taking into account both the effect of the rule on trade and its effect on the risk of rights violations).

[41] Schwartz & Scott 2011.

[42] Ben-Shahar (1999), 2.

[43] Ibid, 3.

[44] Ibid, 30.

[45] Given different assumptions about the cost of preventing theft and investigating title, economists disagree on the optimal rule. See Ogus 2006, 45–47; Ogus 2004, 394–395 (arguing that good faith purchase protection is superior); Landes & Posner 1996 (favouring the original owner in the context of art theft).

[46] See Levmore 1987 (jurisdictions may all be trying to achieve similar functionality through the good faith purchaser rule but disagree on the optimal rule).

the market in which they operate. This tracks the disparate treatment we observe across transactional categories in the law, as well as across jurisdictions.

While the pro-commerce principle responds to varying fact patterns and is, in this respect, consistent with the diversity of legal rules we observe, it is nevertheless deficient in an important respect: it does not account for the basic fact that the good faith purchaser dilemma is a *dilemma*. That is, it does not capture the sense in which both the original owner and the final purchaser have legitimate moral claims and it does not show either of their claims ever to be morally superior. On a legal economic analysis, the rule that favours commerce will take into account the relative costs of preventing theft and fraud, on the one hand, and checking for good title before purchase, on the other. The parties' entitlements depend just on the outcome of this analysis and the 'loser' has no residual or forfeited claim to the property. The simple pro-commerce principle drains the situation of its defining moral anxiety. This might be useful but it is too much at odds with how people tend to think about the scenario to make sense of it.

2. An Alternative Principle: Contract as Exchange

I now want to explore another normative account of contract that might allow us to avail ourselves of the functionality of the legal economic narrative while providing a more satisfying account of the normative problem that the good faith purchaser presents. Understanding contract as essentially exchange suggests that we should care about more than either the chain of valid title or the quality of contractual relationships. It indicates that contracting parties have morally significant claims arising from their bargains, even if the rules surrounding enforcement of those bargains are indeed designed to promote public ends like commerce. In particular, understanding contract as exchanges that are morally significant *for the parties* directs our attention to four principles that contract law usually upholds.

On the positive side, contract law promotes reciprocity and enables planning. To be sure, contract law's commitment to reciprocity is rather minimalist. It does not, for example, demand equivalence of exchange in each transaction. We can understand reciprocity in contract to manifest at two interconnected levels. First, as a foundational element of the market, which is in turn a basic feature of our social structure, contract as an institution must be defensible to all members of the political community. It must, therefore, meet minimum demands of justifiability that reflect a systemic norm of reciprocity;

the institution must work for all its participants. It cannot be useful in securing people the resources they need to pursue their projects, however, if it aims to ensure that each bargain works out well. In that case, contracts would fail as tools for managing uncertainty and risk.

Instead, contract requires reciprocity at the micro level only by requiring assent to an exchange of obligations. The fact of mutual assent provides some assurance that parties have reason to believe the transaction will improve their situation relative to other available options. The requirement of consideration, or of an exchange, demands that each party assume at least some irrevocable obligation to the other. This is also reflected in the doctrine of mutuality of obligation.

The norm of reciprocity helps locate some of our discomfort with the good faith purchase situation. Either the original owner's or the final purchaser's loss of title to the property would represent an asymmetric result to which neither assented. The original owner would lose something without having gotten something they agreed to in return (or on terms to which they meaningfully agreed). The final purchaser would have handed something over to the intermediary without getting anything in return. Note, however, that with respect to the norm of reciprocity, the two parties are not equally situated. While we have seen that there are other normative considerations that may favour the original owner, the good faith purchaser more clearly fails to get the benefit of a bargain when property that they secured by contract is taken away because of some fault that is neither theirs nor even related to their transaction.

The other affirmative principle implicit in contract is the principle that contracts should facilitate individual plans. While an apparently modest principle, it serves the deeper commitment of a liberal state to enabling individuals to pursue their various conceptions of the good. One of the problems with the good faith purchaser situation is that, by virtue of the wrongdoing of an intermediary, plans that were to be advanced through contract are instead upended. Again, we can ask whether the well-laid plans of either the original owner or the final purchaser were more disrupted. It is not clear that we can say, but one way of understanding the normative significance of precaution is that it not only speaks to fault but also indicates how well-formed and executed were the plans that were disrupted.

Contract law also has two complementary negative commitments that help explain the unfairness of good faith purchaser situations. Both of these can be understood as derivative from the affirmative commitment to reciprocity. First, contract avoids unjust enrichment. While contract does not prevent asymmetric results that are consistent with terms that the parties have agreed to (if only because of asymmetric initial holdings), lopsided returns to a bargain are considered 'unjust' when one party gains at the expense of the other and that transfer is uncompensated or nonconsensual. We can describe gains as meeting these criteria when they were not within the contemplation of the parties, and therefore not part of the two-way bargain that the parties struck. Neither the original owner nor the final purchaser is unjustly enriched should they prevail in a contest for the disputed property.

However, contract law also disfavours forfeiture. Forfeiture is the flipside of unjust enrichment, and is likewise a corollary of the principle of reciprocity. It occurs when a party loses value without compensation in a way that was outside the contract's plan, even its more remote contingencies. Of course, whoever loses out in the contest for property in the good faith purchaser situation experiences forfeiture. That is why the mere efficiency of a rule that allocates the property to one over the other does not suffice to render the outcome satisfactory. The fact of forfeiture remains.

Thinking about contract in terms of exchange highlights the demands of reciprocity, including its disfavour of unjust enrichment and forfeiture, and the value of contract to individual planning. It directs us away from the focus on the chain of title that we get from will theory, and on the integrity of the contractual relationships that we get from contract as promise. Contract as exchange does not direct us to a more definitive result than a legal economic approach. But it adds to the analysis of incentives for precaution and diligence the normative dimension that explains why the good faith purchaser dilemma is morally fraught.

IV. Contract (Usually) Makes Property

I have argued thus far that understanding contract as exchange helps us understand the good faith purchase dilemma better than thinking about contract as essentially derivative from property. Taking a step back, the theories I have put in contest with one another are all 'last mile' theories for justifying legal rights to property. Will or transfer theories of contract would respect the transfer of a contractual entitlement because the previous holder of the property had the right to transfer it. We recognize the right of transfer by recognizing the rights of the current holder. Promise theories are invested only in contractual relationships and how those relationships go, not what preceded the encounter between the parties or what befalls the parties after they part ways. These traditional views of contract have difficulty accounting for the reality of the good faith purchase exception. They do not give us any reason to worry about the good faith purchaser. The lens of exchange, by contrast, allows us to see the dilemma and would resolve it by reference to contingent facts.

Each of these accounts justifies the 'last mile' because it does not purport to justify either the distribution of assets or the particularities of who has what, that any trade or transfer account presupposes. Contract as exchange posits that exchange may justify a holding without inquiring whether either the asset that was procured or the asset that was given up in exchange for it were justly held. Similarly, will theory (and its cousin, promise theory) presuppose that the property rights of the original owner were just, such that exercise of their right to alienate would justify recognition of property rights in the new owner.

While traditional and exchange theories are both 'last mile' accounts, they are not equally demanding with respect to the justification of background entitlements. If the normativity of contract is grounded in exchange, then we recognize property rights acquired in contract because they flow from and then support a valuable practice of exchange and not fundamentally because someone who previously had rights to the property chose to transfer those rights—and had a moral right to do so. We might separately require that people ordinarily offer in exchange only those assets in which they have a recognized legal interest. But this requirement only serves the practice: allowing people to control what they have, including trading what they have for what they want more, enables exchange to direct resources to those who value them and empowers people to acquire what they need and want using what they have. Such a justification rests on present possession but not any normatively thick conception of property as authority, or property as moral *right.*

To be sure, contract does not perfectly serve the end of empowerment through trade, but there is basically no function we could devise that the institution of contract performs perfectly. It does it pretty well, though, and the goal of regulating contract should be that it perform its function better. Still, our doubts about whether exchange, starting as it does with grossly unequal entitlements, is the best way to empower people to pursue their various ends are the most significant gaps in the picture of contract that I have painted here with only broad strokes.

The alternative picture, though, has bigger problems. A picture of contract in which it is the mere by-product property, must explain why the fact that people have various things should give them rights to control future transfers, without referring to the functional value of recognizing such a power. While the exchange account of contract treats existing possessions as controlling for forward-looking reasons, a theory in which property conceptually and normatively precedes contract must argue one of the following: possession inherently entails rights of disposition; property rights inherently entail rights of disposition; or, rights of disposition can be justified in a backward-looking fashion.

The first possible way to explain the authority to transfer is to argue that it inheres in the facts—the fact of possession. The argument might be that people should be able to control the disposition of whatever they have because dispossession and forced possession are both wrongful. There is something to the idea that treating 'is' as 'ought' brings stability because contests over authority are disruptive and tend to result in deadweight losses. But the argument proves too much because, clearly, we do not defer to the bare fact of holding as giving right to a property right against all; we could not otherwise account for why someone who has lost possession could have a claim against someone who has taken possession. Restrictions on alienability also do not implicate the risk of forced possession, given the possibility of abandonment for many forms of property. Any interest we have in the stability of possession is inadequate to explain why some holdings give rise to full-blown property rights, while others do not. The bare fact of possession does not explain authority to transfer.

Instead of appealing to the natural law of possession, one could argue that the right to transfer is a necessary feature of a concept of property rights. This argument is even less promising, since there are property rights that are inalienable and others that cannot be alienated for consideration. Property rights as such are not at stake in the question of whether they include the right of transfer through contract. While most property rights do include such a right, this is the (malleable) legal fact to be explained.

A different way to extract a right to control the movement of an asset from the fact that one has it now, without invoking the functional value of such a right, is to trace the history of the entitlement. On this account, an owner has the right to transfer their property because such a right was among the rights to the property that were earlier transferred to them. Recognizing the authority to control the disposition of an entitlement is then often a matter of circular procedural justice; we respect the rights of transfer with respect to some property because they were transferred through the exercise of a right to transfer that property. This is probably the best way to understand how will theory can assume that property rights are authoritative in the way the theory must assume. It is the one mode of acquisition that will theory has the internal resources to recognize. But this strategy is doomed not because there is an infinite regress but because eventually we arrive at an acquisition that was not willed by a rightful owner. For most (but not all) property, there was a moment when initial property interests were recognized, and it almost certainly took place within the context of an unjust social order that cannot operate as an eternal fountain of legitimacy. While procedural justice can explain the last mile, it cannot go all the way back. Given familiar histories of radical injustice almost everywhere, it is unlikely that we can look backwards to justify who has what today.

To clarify, my aim here is not to argue for any theory of property. My claim is that the advantages of conceiving contract as exchange over an account that understands contract as derivative of property for understanding the good faith purchase dilemma reveals a deeper advantage, that is, an independence from backwards-looking justifications of property more generally. Even theories that do not assume the liberty-rights we associate with will theory, like promise theory, tend to valourize the control interest of those who transfer property in contract rather than the bargained-for or reciprocal interest of the party receiving property by way of contract. The weakness of these theories that ground contractual entitlements in the intentions of the those who grant them is that they attribute an important moral power to those with legally recognized property interests without justifying why they should have such powers over the property in their possession. There are plenty of forwards-looking reasons to recognize those powers, but traditional theories of contract are backwards-looking and they cannot help themselves to the pragmatic reasons we have for recognizing existing entitlements.

Contract is the primary means by which we can justify why particular people have what they do. It is a form of procedural justice that accounts for the last move. Property rights acquired by other means face a greater burden in meeting the last mile of explanation, that is, not just why property exists but why particular people should have what they do. Last-mile accounts are oriented to solving the immediate adjudicatory question of who should get what now. But they should be judged too by the availability of a plausible, complementary account of the distance that comes before. That is, we should justify how we move entitlements by contract—including how we resolve competing claims, when contracts go wrong—in a way that lends itself to justifying the entire edifice.

If contract depends on the authority of property, we need to supplement our theory of contract with a story about why present holdings give rise to just claims of authority in order to validate each move forwards. It will be hard to write a nonfiction story that serves that need. If, instead, we defer to the terms of contracts because the bargains that we make in contract harness reciprocity and enable planning, we need to supplement our theory of contract with something more like a plan, a forwards-looking account of how we can collectively use trade to advance our individual life projects.

V. Conclusion

Unlike most essays on the good faith purchase doctrine, this chapter has not aimed either to celebrate or bemoan its development or current form. Instead, I have tried to show that the rules have diverged among transactional categories and have been unstable because the optimal rules depend on evolving facts that vary among transactional categories. The optimal rule is not a clear, categorial rule because there are competing normative considerations that give rise to legitimate moral claims by both the original owner and the good faith purchaser.

All of that should be intuitive—and is reflected in the law. But the inconsistent doctrine and the dilemma itself cannot be explained by dominant theories of contract, which would defer to property as conceptually and morally prior to contract. Philosophical accounts of contract cannot explain why the good faith purchaser has a legitimate claim against even the original owner to property acquired from a fraudulent intermediary. Economic theories cannot explain why whoever does not get the property—given whichever rules turn out to be best in a given setting—has any grievance such that we face a dilemma at all.

A theory of contract that locates a buyer's claim to the property they acquire in the bargain through which they acquired it handles the problem of good faith purchases better than dominant accounts of contract. It explains why both parties have real claims, and it helps explain too why we will often defer to the claims of the good faith purchaser.

The case of the good faith purchaser turns out to encapsulate some of the deeper theoretical advantages of an exchange theory of contract. Deriving contract rights from property rights makes contract claims vulnerable to the history of property entitlements. In cases of good faith purchase, the immediate history is faulty; the seller to the purchaser did not have good title to convey. But the problem of faulty origins to property is more pervasive that that. Rather than looking backwards to the long history of property entitlements to explain who holds those entitlements now, we do better to justify rules of exchange by what those rules can do for all of us going forwards.

References

Bagchi, A. (2025). 'Contract as Exchange'. *California Law Review* 113: 1661–1621.

Balganesh, S. (2016). 'Copyright and Good Faith Purchasers'. *California Law Review* 104: 269–322.

Ben-Shahar, O. 'Property Rights in Stolen Goods: An Economic Analysis'. Working paper available at https://home.uchicago.edu/omri/pdf/articles/Buyer_In_Good_Faith.pdf.

Blackstone, W. (1803). *Commentaries on the Laws of England II, 14th edn.* Chicago, University of Chicago Press.

DeMott, D. (2012). 'Artful Good Faith: An Essay on Law, Custom, and Intermediaries in Art Markets'. *Duke Law Journal* 62: 607–644.

Dranias, N. (2008). 'Consideration as Contract: A Secular Natural Law of Contracts'. *Texas Law Review* 12: 267–328.

Fox, D. (2006). 'Relativity of Title at Law and in Equity'. *Cambridge Law Journal* 65: 330–365.

Gilmore, G. (1954). 'The Commercial Doctrine of Good Faith Purchase'. *Yale Law Journal* 63: 1057–1122.

Gilmore, G. (1981). 'The Good Faith Purchase Idea and the Uniform Commercial Code: Confessions of a Repentant Draftsman'. *Georgia Law Review* 15: 605–29.

Horwitz, M. (1974). 'The Historical Foundations of Modern Contract Law'. *Harvard Law Review* 87: 917–56.

Kadens, E. (2015). 'The Medieval Law Merchant: Tyranny of a Construct'. *Journal of Legal Analysis* 7: 251–289.

Kull, A. (1995). 'Rationalizing Restitution'. *California Law Review* 83: 1191–1242.

Landes, W. and R. Posner, (1996). 'The Economics of Legal Disputes Over the Ownership of Works of Art and Other Collectibles'. *Handbook of the Economics of Art and Culture* V. Ginsburgh and P. Menger. Amsterdam, Elsevier: 211–51.

Levmore, S. (1987). 'Variety and Uniformity in the Treatment of the Good-Faith Purchaser'. *Journal of Legal Studies* 16: 43–65.

Littlefield, N. (1966). 'Good Faith Purchase of Consumer Paper: The Failure of the Subjective Test'. *Southern California Law Review* 39: 48–77.

Markovits, D. (2004). 'Contract and Collaboration'. *Yale Law Journal* 113: 1417–1518.

Mautner M. (1991). '"The Eternal Triangles of the Law": Toward a Theory of Priorities in Conflicts Involving Remote Parties'. *Michigan Law Review* 30: 95–154.

Medina, B. (2003). 'Augmenting the Value of Ownership by Protecting It Only Partially: The "Market-Overt" Rule Revisited'. *Journal of Law, Economics & Organization* 19: 343–372.

Merrill, T. W. and H. E. Smith (2001). 'The Property/Contract Interface'. *Columbia Law Review* 101: 773–852.

Ogus, A. (2006). *Costs and Cautionary Tales: Economic Insights for the Law.* Oxford and Portland, Hart.

Ogus, A. (2004). 'What Legal Scholars Can Learn from Law and Economics'. *Chicago-Kent Law Review* 79: 383–402.

Pease, J. G. (1908). 'The Change of the Property in Goods by Sale in Market Overt'. *Columbia Law Review* 8: 375–383.

Schwartz, A. and R. Scott (2011). 'Rethinking the Laws of Good Faith Purchase'. *Columbia Law Review* 111: 1332–1384.

Sepinuck, S. (2018). 'The Various Standards for the "Good Faith" of a Purchaser'. *Business Law* 73: 581–626.

Shiffrin, S. (2007). 'The Divergence of Contract and Promise'. *Harvard Law Review* 120: 708–753.

Smith, P. (1997). 'Valediction to Market Overt'. *American Journal of Legal History* 41: 225–249.

Swartz, E. (1962). 'The Bona Fide Purchaser Revisited: A Comparative Inquiry'. *Boston University Law Review* 42: 403–411.

Weinberg, H. (1981). 'Markets Overt, Voidable Titles, and Feckless Agents: Judges and Efficiency in the Antebellum Doctrine of Good Faith Purchase'. *Tulane Law Review* 56: 1–41.

Weir, T. (2004). 'All or Nothing'. *Tulane Law Review* 78: 511–52.

[No Named Author] (1963). 'The Owner's Intent and the Negotiability of Chattels: A Critique of Section 2–403 of the Uniform Commercial Code'. *Yale Law Journal* 72: 1205–1226.

3

Property, Contract, and Normative Powers

*Irina Sakharova**

I. Introduction

Are contractual obligations created by the prospective contracting parties exercising the normative power to transfer (a right)? This chapter gives a negative answer to this question by revealing some problems with approaches that suppose a reduction of the normative power that persons exercise in order to enter into contractual relations to the normative power to transfer.

An idea that is central to different versions of the transfer thesis is that contract formation effects, and indeed manifests itself in, a transfer of some entitlement between the prospective contracting parties or between the promisor and the promisee, which entitlement is compared to, although not necessarily analogised with, a property right. This thesis can be found in some form in different contract theories, as well as in different moral theories of promising, but is certainly central to what could be referred to as *transfer theories* of contract or of promising. It might be apposite to emphasise that although the term 'transfer theory' is sometimes, or even often, used in the literature,[1] it seems more appropriate to speak about 'transfer theories',[2] as different theoretical approaches can be grouped under this name.[3]

This chapter focuses on two versions of the transfer thesis. One approach places an emphasis on a supposed transfer of *(decision-making) authority* from the promisor to the promisee as an explanation of promising (and, by

* I am grateful to James Penner, Nick Sage, and the participants of the Property-Contract Interface Workshop at the National University of Singapore (December 2024) and the Society of Legal Scholars Annual Conference at Bristol University (September 2024) for their helpful comments and questions.

[1] See, eg, Dagan & Heller 2017, 10.

[2] See, eg, Smith 2004, 97.

[3] For some of the most prominent examples of the theories putting forward (some version of) the transfer thesis as an explanation of contract formation, see Barnett 1986; Barnett 2014; Gold 2009; Benson 2019. For earlier statements of Peter Benson's thesis, see also his works listed in note 23 below. For Seana Shiffrin's transfer explanation of *promising* and application of her ideas about the moral practice of promising to the (legal) practice of contracting, see Shiffrin 2012; Shiffrin 2008; Shiffrin 2011.

Irina Sakharova, *Property, Contract, and Normative Powers* In: *The Property-Contract Interface*. Edited by: James Penner, Irina Sakharova, Henry E. Smith, and Zhong Xing Tan, Oxford University Press. © Irina Sakharova 2026.
DOI: 10.1093/9780198951995.003.0004

extension, contracting);[4] within this approach, an obligation under which the promisor comes is (still) regarded as a duty to do as promised (or a duty to perform). Another approach puts an emphasis on a supposed transfer, from the promisor to the promisee, of *(exclusive) control* over the promisor's performance or over the 'promised consideration'; while the language of promising is still deployed, an idea of transferring *ownership* is crucial to this approach, and a contractual duty is regarded as a *duty of non-interference* with the promisee's supposed ownership of the promisor's performance or the 'promised consideration'.[5]

As can be seen from this brief description, the two theoretical approaches share some similarities, but they also represent very different versions of the transfer thesis. The first version does not make any explicit reference to *proprietary* entitlements, with which reference transfer theories are often associated, but rather focuses on promising and 'distribution', between the parties, of (decision-making) *authority*; in this respect, some affinity with promissory theories more generally could be registered, as even if promissory theories do not typically place any special emphasis on transfer (ie they regard promissory, and contractual, rights and duties as *created* and not *transferred*), they still utilize some idea of *giving* by the promisor some (decision-making) authority to the promisee. In contrast, the second version of the transfer thesis explicitly focuses on transferring *ownership* between the contracting parties at contract formation and, thus, engages more directly with an idea of transferring entitlements.

Focusing on these two different versions of the transfer thesis (in sections II and III), both of which are elaborated within two rich and intellectually stimulating theoretical approaches, allows this chapter to explore whether the *normative power to transfer* (a right) is key to explaining contract formation.

The argument that it is not provides a novel critique of transfer theories of contract and reveals previously overlooked avenues for challenging other reductionist conceptions of the power to contract, advanced, in particular, by promissory theories of contract; it also opens a path to a more 'positive' argument substantiating a non-reductionist account of the power to contract.[6]

It should, however, be emphasized that given that this chapter is interested in normative powers that persons exercise in order to enter into contracts, rather than in contract theories (that might be relying on various normative

[4] See Shiffrin 2012; Shiffrin 2008; Shiffrin 2011.
[5] See Benson 2019.
[6] See Sakharova 2024b.

powers) as such, the chapter only focuses on selected propositions put forward by the two theoretical approaches with which it engages, without discussing these approaches in their entirety.

II. Does a Contract Transfer (Decision-Making) Authority?

The central idea of transfer theses is that contract formation effects, and manifests itself in, a transfer of *some* entitlement between the prospective contracting parties or between the promisor and the promisee. The idea is rather simple; what has, however, proved to be much more difficult is pinpointing what exactly it is that is supposedly transferred from one party to another.[7] This section focuses on one understanding of what is supposedly transferred from the promisor to the promisee, which (at the highest level of generality) can be labelled as some *(decision-making) authority*; this understanding can be found in Seana Shiffrin's explanation of promissory (and, by extension, contractual[8]) obligations. She writes:

> [A] promise is a voluntary commitment to perform (or to omit) an action the promisor has the authority to perform, a commitment qualified (sometimes explicitly) by apt conditions of performance, that works by transferring some form of the promisor's right to decide whether or not to perform that action to the promisee. In light of this transfer, the promisee has a right to expect (and often demand) performance and has the concomitant power to use her transferred power or decision to waive or excuse the promisor's obligation of performance.[9]

In this passage, Shiffrin identifies the object of a supposed transfer as *the promisor's right to decide whether or not to perform*, but elsewhere in her work, she also suggests some other formulations of what is supposedly transferred from the promisor to the promisee, such as *the right to act otherwise*,[10] which formulations might point to somewhat different versions of the transfer thesis.

[7] See eg Owens 2014 (discussing Shiffrin's transfer theory).

[8] Shiffrin focuses on the moral practice of promising but sees contracts as legally enforceable promises and argues for a closer convergence of the two (see, in particular, Shiffrin 2007).

[9] Shiffrin 2012, 243–244. Shiffrin adds that 'upon making a promise, contracts have the same elemental features of promises. The recipient of a contractual commitment has a right to expect performance [. . .]. Further, just as with a promise, the recipient of a contractual commitment has the power to waive or excuse performance.' Ibid, 244.

[10] See Shiffrin 2008, 517 (another similar formulation is *the right to decide to act otherwise*. See Shiffrin 2011, 156).

This chapter mainly focuses on the *right to decide whether or not to perform*, trying to understand (by deploying the language of the Hohfeldian *jural* relations and the categories of deontic logic) whether contract formation could be a transfer of something like the 'right' to decide whether or not to perform (or the 'right' to decide whether or not to ϕ).

How is it to be understood, in legal (or normative) terms, that the promisor transfers to the promisee the 'right' to decide whether or not to perform (whether or not to ϕ)? If the conventional idea of *transfer* is to be taken seriously, the promisor must have a 'right' to decide whether or not to ϕ before contract formation (before promising) so that he[11] could possibly transfer exactly this right to the promisee at contract formation (by promising/exercising the normative power to transfer) and so that, synonymously, the promisee could acquire exactly this right in the result of the transfer.[12] A series of related questions can be raised.

To begin with, what is precisely this '*right*' to decide whether or not to ϕ? It would seem that with respect to a contract between A (the promisee) and B (the promisor) according to which B undertakes to ϕ, the requisite 'right' to *decide* whether or not to ϕ by B should translate into B's right to ϕ or not to ϕ. In Hohfeldian terms, this right should mean B's *liberty* (or privilege) to ϕ, and it has to be a *full liberty,* meaning that B should have both *liberty* to ϕ and *liberty* not to ϕ. In terms of deontic logic, the 'right' to decide whether or not to ϕ should mean that B has an *option* to ϕ or not to ϕ. Does B *necessarily* (or even *typically*) have such *full liberty* or *option* before entering the contract with A, and can A have it afterwards (as the result of the supposed transfer)?

It would seem that there is inherent ambiguity in saying that a person is at liberty (has an option) to decide whether or not to do something. Two types of scenario can be contrasted to illustrate this point. In the first scenario, I own Blackacre, *decide* to enter it, and actually enter it. In the second scenario, you own Whiteacre, and I *decide* to enter it and actually enter it. Am I at *liberty* to decide whether or not to enter Blackacre and Whiteacre, or, in other words, do I have an *option* to do so? In one sense, I *am* at such liberty (or I have such an option) in both types of scenario—in the sense that I can *actually* make a decision to enter (and I can *actually* enter) both Blackacre and Whiteacre (this might be called '*factual liberty*' or a '*factual option*' (to ϕ or not to ϕ), even if

[11] To simplify the exposition, throughout the chapter the promisee (or any other rightholder) is gendered female and the promisor (or any other duty-bearer) male, unless otherwise specified.

[12] For a possible alternative perspective on the nature of transfer, see Hohfeld 1917. For a criticism, see Penner 2013; Penner 2020, chapter 6.

the term 'liberty' might not be entirely appropriate in such a 'factual' context). In the second scenario, entering Whiteacre (without your consent) would, of course, make me a trespasser, but this does not deny the fact that factually I did decide to enter Whiteacre, although I could have decided not to enter, that is, I realized an option that I have. I would be a trespasser, however, because I am not *entitled* to decide whether or not to enter Whiteacre, meaning that I do not have what might be called '*normative liberty*' or a '*normative option*' (to ϕ or not to ϕ). In contrast, I clearly do have normative liberty (to ϕ or not to ϕ) when it comes to deciding whether or not to enter Blackacre, or I have a normative option to do so, in addition to 'factual liberty' or a 'factual option', which I also have.[13] Does entering into a *contractual* relation always or at least typically resemble the first or the second type of scenario described above?

A simple example may be considered first. B enters into a contract with A to paint A's wall. Before entering into the contract with A, as well as after entering into this contract, B has normative liberty to do whatever B likes as long as 'whatever B likes' does not include something B is under a duty not to do. Returning to the land example above, although it can be said that I have normative liberty to walk wherever I like, this can only be a qualified proposition, as I do not have normative liberty to enter your Whiteacre because I am under the duty not to do so (without your consent); if I fully realize my 'factual liberty' to enter Whiteacre, I will commit a wrong. Similarly, before entering into the contract with A, B may have 'factual liberty' to paint A's wall (which liberty, it might be observed, also remains with B after entering into the contract with A) and B can actually do it. However, painting A's wall in such circumstances would constitute a wrong, as B does not have normative liberty to paint A's wall; B is under the duty of non-interference with A's title to the wall. In terms of deontic logic,[14] before entering into the contract with A, B's painting A's wall is not optional (OP p or OP $\sim p$, which are equivalents), because an action can only be optional (OP p or OP $\sim p$) when there is neither obligation to perform this action (OB p) nor obligation not to perform this action (OB $\sim p$), but the fact that B does not have permission to paint A's wall (PE p) necessarily means that B is under obligation not to paint A's wall (OB $\sim p$), as PE p and OB $\sim p$ are contradictories.

[13] Neil MacCormick makes a similar point to illustrate the proposition that the court has no choice but to enforce a properly made contract: '[i]t may, of course, be said that if trial judges and appellate judges choose to flout the law, no one can stop them; but that is as irrelevant to the existence of an obligation on their part to enforce the law as is the manifest truth that murders are committed to the equally plain truth that citizens have an obligation in law not to murder each other.' See MacCormick 1972, 76.

[14] See Figure 3.1 for (a version of) the standard deontic hexagon. Such an approach to drawing the hexagon can be found in Hurd & Moore 2018, 309ff. See also Sakharova 2024a.

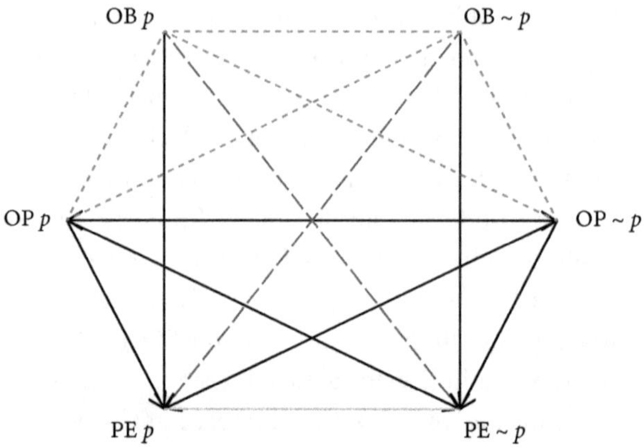

Figure 3.1 Standard deontic hexagon

It might be reiterated that even if the promisor does not have the promisee's permission to ϕ before contract formation, that is, he does not have normative liberty to ϕ, the promisor may, and normally does, have 'factual liberty' to ϕ or not to ϕ (he can actually decide whether or not to ϕ), but this 'liberty', once again, *stays with the promisor after contract formation.* In other words, both before contract formation and after it the promisor can normally actually decide to ϕ or not to ϕ, even though before contract formation *ϕ-ing* would constitute a tort, and after contract formation *not ϕ-ing* would constitute a breach of contract; in other words, it is only the promisor who can *decide* whether *to comply* or *not to comply* with either a duty to ϕ or a duty not to ϕ. It would follow that it must be *normative* liberties that any transfer thesis should be interested in, but as far as typical contractual scenarios are concerned (of which painting A's wall by B would be a clear example), this is precisely a kind of liberty that the promisor normally or even (almost) never has before contract formation (B needs to obtain A's permission to paint her wall or her consent to painting her wall, which would remove B's duty of non-interference with A's title to the wall).[15]

It might, however, be objected that at least as far as moral theory of *promising* is concerned, the predicament discussed in the preceding paragraphs might not be so relevant, and that regardless of whether moral theory of promising or (legal) practice of contracting is in question, it might be possible to find a way

[15] It might be apposite to mention here Shiffrin's emphasis on the promisor's 'authority to perform'. See Shiffrin 2012, 243–244. The promisor's 'authority to perform' could, of course, be understood in different ways, but if it is taken to mean his normative liberty to ϕ, most (or even all) *contracts* would prima facie be outside of Shiffrin's theory.

out of such a predicament. In other words, we could either focus on such cases in which the promisor does have normative liberty to ϕ (which can often be the case as far as many moral promises are concerned), or we could try to account for how such normative liberty arises (whether moral promises or contracts are concerned). It might be observed that focusing on such cases in which the promisor has normative liberty to ϕ (or 'authority' to ϕ) is what a moral theory of promising not infrequently does, as it often contemplates promises the fulfilment of which by the promisor would not involve any (serious) 'cooperation' on the part of the promisee (such as a promise to turn up at a certain place on a certain day and at a certain time). In other cases, where the promisor is not at liberty to ϕ, when it comes to accounting for *how the promisor's normative liberty to ϕ might arise*, the idea of *accepting* a promise by the promisee (and by so doing giving to the promisor the requisite permission to ϕ) would be central.[16] Whatever the success and relevance of this idea to contracts is,[17] for the present purposes (of discussing the transfer thesis), it is more important to ask the following question: even if it were possible to account, within the transfer thesis, for the promisor's normative liberty to ϕ or his (decision-making) authority, could the promisor be seen as transferring *this* normative liberty or authority to the promisee?

A difficult thing to grasp is how the *promisee* could be regarded as holding the promisor's 'right' to decide whether or not to ϕ; holding *somebody else's* 'right' to decide whether or not to ϕ appears to be a rather mysterious notion. How could this be conceptualized or represented in legal (or normative) terms? It seems that it makes more sense to focus on the promisee's *own* (putative) 'right' to decide whether or not the promisor performs, rather than on the promisee's holding *the promisor's* 'right' to decide this. Obviously, the promisee's (putative) 'right' to decide whether or not the promisor performs should also correspond to an option that the promisee would have. In other words, the promisee's 'right' to decide whether or not the promisor performs should translate into her right that the promisor perform *and* her right that the promisor not perform (between demanding the fulfilment or the enforcement of which two rights she would be able to choose).[18] However, it is not the case that the promisee

[16] It might be mentioned that Shiffrin herself finds the 'often-posited' requirement of acceptance of a promise by the promisee questionable. As she explains, '[p]romisees have a clear interest in being able to avoid the sometimes charged relation of moral debtor to the promisor. But protecting this interest entails only that the potential promisee have a right (and a low-cost opportunity) to reject the promise or to waive performance.' See Shiffrin 2008, 491.

[17] For a discussion, see Sakharova 2024b; Sakharova 2025.

[18] This understanding appears to be also confirmed by the language that Shiffrin sometimes uses. In particular, she argues that 'it is appropriate and illuminating to begin by conceiving of the relevant

has such an option, as she only has the right that the promisor perform, and she has no right that he not perform; she is under the duty to accept the promisor's performance.[19] It might also be noted here that even if the promisee had such a right, this would be a claim-right, whereas the right that the promisor had before contract formation (ie not to ϕ) was a liberty (not to ϕ). This would mean that the supposed transfer of the promisor's *liberty* to the promisee would result in her obtaining a *claim-right*, which, it seems, would negate the idea of a 'transfer'—the two are not the same jural conception. However, this is an aspect of a more general objection to transfer theories, stating that it is difficult to establish equivalence between something that the promisor could possibly have before contract formation and something that the promisee could possibly acquire as a result of contract formation,[20] and elaborating on this point is not, strictly speaking, necessary for the argument of this chapter. It might also be emphasized (for the sake of completeness) that even if the promisor's full liberty (to ϕ or not to ϕ) exists or existed before contract formation, after contract formation no such *jural* conception (no such 'normative entity') exists in the normative world, meaning that it cannot be 'held' by anyone, including the promisee: after contract formation, the promisor is under the duty to ϕ, which excludes his full liberty in this regard (Hohfeldian opposites), or (in terms of deontic logic) the promisor's obligation (OB p) excludes any option on his part (OP p or OP $\sim p$), and the promisee, as has already been mentioned, does not have any right that the promisor not perform.

It is, of course, not possible to deny that the promisee's right that the promisor *perform* places a certain restriction on the promisor, who is under the duty to perform, and if the expression that the promisee 'holds' the promisor's 'right' to decide whether or not to perform were merely a metaphorical reference to the restriction in that sense, this metaphor could, perhaps, be accepted were it not misleading; the *contract* does place a certain restriction on the promisor, who has the duty to perform, but the contract *also* places a similar restriction on the promisee, who has the duty to accept the promisor's performance, which duty protects the promisor's own right to perform.

right as the right between the promisor and the promisee, *to be the one to decide whether to act, how to act, and on what grounds*'. Shiffrin 2011, 156 (emphasis added). See also Shiffrin 2012, 244 (observing about a transfer that '[i]n light of this transfer, the promisee has a right to expect (and often demand) performance and has the concomitant power to use her transferred power or decision to waive or excuse the promisor's obligation of performance.'). Referring to contracting parties, Shiffrin emphasizes A's 'right to make the decision *whether* B performs or not (without B's further consent)'. Shiffrin 2023, 11 (emphasis in original).

19 See Sakharova 2024a; Sakharova 2025.

20 See, eg, Smith 2000, 119–120; Smith 2004, 101–102.

In conclusion, it might be emphasized that the analysis in this section has highlighted, inter alia, two interconnected problems with the transfer thesis (that focuses on transferring *(decision-making) authority*).[21] First, there is no *prior* 'right' (of the promisor) that could be transferred (to the promisee) at contract formation. Second, seeing the promisor as exercising the normative power to transfer something that supposedly already exists does not account for the *transformative* role of contract formation. Could these two problems be addressed (and ultimately resolved) within a transfer thesis? One attempt to do so is Peter Benson's recent reiteration of his 'contract as a transfer of ownership' theory (focusing on transferring *(exclusive) control* over the performance); it appears that he purports to solve the first problem explicitly and the second one at least implicitly; the next section will look at this intriguing approach.

III. Does a Contract Transfer (Exclusive) Control over the Performance?

This section focuses on the thesis that some *(exclusive) control* over the promisor's performance or the 'promised consideration' is transferred at contract formation. This version of the transfer thesis engages most directly with the idea of ownership and applies this idea not only to proprietary rights (and duties) but also to contractual rights (and duties). A clear and particularly well-articulated statement of this thesis can be found in Peter Benson's most recent book on the subject,[22] which develops ideas expressed in some of his earlier works.[23] This section highlights some aspects of Benson's comprehensive and nuanced transfer thesis to examine the question of whether this thesis can address (and ultimately resolve) the problems with the version of the transfer thesis considered in the previous section.

Before attending to the version of the transfer thesis that this section considers, it is important to highlight what motivates, at least in part, Benson's transfer theory. By *explaining* the power to enter into a contract as essentially the power to transfer, the transfer theory attempts to *justify* the change in the normative landscape that contract formation brings about by supposing that in virtue of the transfer occurring at contract formation the promisee acquires an entitlement the protection of which is consistent with the *harm principle*[24]

[21] At least in some form, these problems have been raised in the literature, albeit in different contexts.
[22] See Benson 2019.
[23] See, in particular, Benson 2007. See also Benson 2011; Benson 2010; Benson 2001; Benson 1996; Benson 1995; Benson 1989.
[24] See Mill 2003, 88.

in the sense that a breach of contract would represent *misfeasance*, and not *nonfeasance*, yielding the contractual remedial regime; without such an *explanation* of the power to enter into a contract, the *justification* of this power is regarded as difficult or even impossible, as per a challenge put forward by Fuller and Perdue.[25] Benson suggests a way of answering the challenge— for Benson, the *only* decisive way:

> If expectation damages and specific performance are to qualify as compensatory in the way assumed by contract law, it must be possible to understand contract formation as itself effectuating between the parties a kind of *transactional acquisition* that vests in them exclusive entitlements with respect to what they have promised one another. And since the acquisition of each party is from the other, it is constituted by a transfer between them. This acquisition must be juridically complete and effective just on the basis of their mutual assents alone, prior to and independent from actual performance and irrespective of whether either party detrimentally relies on the other's promise. If contract formation can be so conceived, breach of contract can now plausibly be viewed as an injury to the rights already vested at formation. Breach becomes the equivalent of attempting to 'take back' or 'withhold' what, as a matter of rights, one has *already* given over to the other. It interferes with the other's ability to take or receive in fact what, in accordance with the terms of the agreement, is rightfully already hers. By aiming to put the promisee in the position that she should have been in had the promisor not breached, the law can now be understood as correcting a loss that the promisee has suffered with respect to rights.[26]

Benson concludes by expressing his contention that 'the Fuller and Perdue challenge can be answered and its theoretical consequences avoided *if—and only if*—something like this view of contract formation as transfer is plausible'.[27]

A central claim that the transfer thesis puts forward is that 'contract can be understood and justified as a form of acquisition'.[28] Contract as transactional acquisition involves a transfer of ownership between the parties,[29] and 'this is how [. . .] contract is best understood as a morally defensible interpretation of the law';[30] 'what a contractual transfer of ownership entails [. . .]

[25] See Fuller & Perdue 1936; Fuller & Perdue 1937.
[26] Benson 2019, 8 (emphasis in original).
[27] Ibid, 9 (emphasis added).
[28] Ibid, 21.
[29] Ibid.
[30] Ibid.

is wholly anchored in and developed from the transactional analysis of the basic promise-for-consideration relation'.[31] Two aspects of this version of the transfer thesis should be specifically highlighted.

First, the transfer thesis emphasizes that it is not some *prior* right that is transferred from the promisor to the promisee at contract formation:[32]

> A contractual transfer should not be understood as vesting anything as it may be *prior* to or apart from the promise-for-consideration relation: the transfer is never of some *preexisting* right. This does not properly model the purely transactional and representational contractual transfer at formation. Nor does it vest something that, properly viewed, is the normative consequence of the transfer.[33]

In particular, 'what is acquired or transferred is not a right to *x* but always some substantive content that can be rightfully and exclusively held and transferred';[34] 'the right to performance is the normative *consequence*, not the object, of the promisee's base entitlement at formation'.[35] What *is* transferred is 'the represented substance of the consideration as promised'.[36] More specifically, on the view 'which takes the parties' promises as the mutually related acts that effectuate or cause the transfer, the *objects* of the transfer are *the substantive considerations as mutually promised*, not the promises or the substantive contents viewed independently from the other'.[37]

Second, and relatedly, the transfer thesis emphasizes a specific *interaction* between the parties at contract formation in virtue of which exclusive control over, or ownership of, the promisor's performance or the 'promised consideration' is transferred:

> [T]o satisfy the consideration requirement, each party's promise must be specified in relation with the other's, making both sides intrinsically and identically relational. The promise-for-consideration relation is itself a transactional process consisting in each party reciprocally and identically moving a substantive content from its side to the other—all in and through

[31] Ibid, 320.
[32] It must be emphasized that Benson understands the notion of transfer itself in a conventional way: in particular, the transferee must get exactly the same right that belonged to the transferor. See Benson 2019, 322, 227, 335; Benson 2007, 1725.
[33] Benson 2019, 324 (emphasis added, footnotes omitted).
[34] Ibid, 323 (footnote omitted).
[35] Ibid (emphasis in original, footnote omitted).
[36] Ibid, 324.
[37] Ibid, 322 (emphasis in original).

> the representational medium of mutual promises. Thus, necessarily, each party's promise represents the content as on his or her side, as actually or potentially under his or her exclusive control, and as moving into the recognized rightful exclusive control of the other side in return for the very same movement of a second content from that other party. Each side gives up only insofar as the other gains, and the substance that the first gives up is precisely what the second gains. [. . .] This is the process that constitutes the promise-for-consideration relation in which cause—the reciprocal moving of considerations in return for each other—and effect—the vesting of each party's consideration with the other—are inseparable.[38]

In this way, 'contract formation may properly be viewed as a form of transactional acquisition that is effectuated in and through the purely representational medium of the parties' mutual assents, prior to and independent of actual performance'.[39]

Highlighting these two aspects of the transfer thesis does not do justice to this thesis, which is admirably comprehensive and nuanced, and which substantially develops many aspects of prior reiterations of the transfer theory.[40] Much could be said, in particular, about the (novel) conception of *ownership*, which on the transfer thesis is transferred only as between the parties, while ownership is normally taken to be a right as against the whole world, as well as about what precisely is supposed to be the object of such ownership. Instead, without considering this version of the transfer thesis in detail, this section focuses on the two highlighted aspects in order to address the question of whether the normative power to transfer, on this version of the transfer thesis, is the key power that operates at contract formation and generates a contractual relation (and whether this version of the transfer thesis solves the problems identified in the previous section with respect to (decision-making) authority).

It is an important idea in Benson's transfer thesis that it is not a *prior* right that is transferred between the parties at contract formation resulting in the promisee's entitlement. Two points can be made with respect to this idea.

First, it appears that by introducing this idea Benson makes a serious concession. As already mentioned, his transfer theory is explicitly presented as a 'complete answer' to the challenge put forward by Fuller and Perdue,[41] and it can also be said that the perceived need to address this challenge is what motivates,

[38] Ibid, 320–321.
[39] Ibid, 20.
[40] See note 23 above.
[41] See note 25 above.

at least in part, Benson's transfer theory. Benson sees it as one of the main tasks of a contract theory to explain contractual rights in such a way that the contractual remedial regime could be regarded as protecting some entitlement belonging to the promisee; Benson considers it problematic to regard such an entitlement as generated by the promisor's contractual undertaking (or by his promise), as it would mean that contractual right (and duties) would arise out of nothing, which would make protecting these rights either by specific enforcement or by expectation damages inconsistent with the harm principle, which demands that private law liability can only be imposed for misfeasance and not for nonfeasance. A lot could be said on the question of whether contract theory, as well as moral theory of promising, should be so concerned with answering the Fuller and Perdue challenge.[42] However, putting this question to one side, it appears that given the concession that Benson's transfer theory makes, the theory can hardly be a 'decisive' answer to Fuller and Perdue. If the right that is supposedly transferred to the promisee at contract formation does not exist before contract formation and therefore, it would seem, must be *created* at contract formation as a result of specific interaction between the contracting parties and then, apparently, (almost) simultaneously *transferred* from the promisor to the promisee, it is not clear how the emphasis on the supposed (subsequent) transfer of entitlement answers the challenge.

Second, and more importantly for the present discussion, it seems that the concession that Benson's transfer theory makes does not allow the transfer thesis to explain contract formation (only) with reference to the normative power to transfer. Even if it were accepted that the normative power to transfer does operate at contract formation in the way that the transfer theory supposes that it does, it would seem that if before transferring anything, the parties must first *create* what will be transferred, the power to transfer is not the *only* normative power that operates at contract formation. There must also be some *primary* normative power—the one that *first* creates (apparently for the promisor), at contract formation, the entitlement that is *thereafter* transferred (to the promisee), apparently almost simultaneously; this power remains unexplained in the transfer theory, but it appears that accounting for *this* primary

[42] As has been aptly remarked, '[e]ver since Fuller and Perdue wrote "The Reliance Interest in Contract Damage" concern with the justifiability of the expectation measure of damages is such that it might be regarded as the test of any acceptable theory of contract that it reproduces the "problem of expectation damages" but also finds some means to deal with it, so that the law's expectation measure of damages is, while theoretically problematic, somehow right after all.' Penner 1996, 346–347. It has also been observed about promising that '[s]ince promissory powers are only some among many types of volitional power, it is very curious that promising has been the main target of skepticism. If promising involves magic, then moral (or normative) transubstantiation appears to be rampant.' Watson 2009, 160.

power creating an *initial* contractual entitlement at contract formation should be more important than explaining how any transfer of this contractual entitlement could *thereafter* be possible at contract formation.[43]

A couple of points could also be made about a related idea one finds in Benson's transfer thesis that as the result of a specific interaction between contracting parties at contract formation, *(exclusive) control* over, or ownership of, the promisor's performance is transferred to the promisee. It must be acknowledged that Benson's thinking about contract formation (and about the role of the doctrine of consideration) is very insightful. He places a special emphasis on the interaction between the contracting parties in virtue of which a contractual relation arises and, in particular, in distinguishing this interaction from that which would obtain in the case of (accepted) gratuitous promises; in doing so he highlights different senses of what it means for a relation to be bilateral (a contractual relation is bilateral in a stronger sense, while a gratuitous relation is bilateral in a weaker sense) and acknowledges some implications of making such a distinction for explaining *contract* formation. However, despite maintaining that a contractual relation is 'fully and intrinsically' or 'robustly' bilateral, he, as many others, still ends up focusing on the correlation between the (promisee's) contractual right and the (promisor's) contractual duty in his explanation of contractual rights and duties, how they arise, and how they can be performed and breached. Two aspects of this version of the transfer thesis can be highlighted. First, Benson represents the promisor's performance, or what he conceptualizes as the 'promised consideration' in the 'promise-for-consideration relation', as being in the *(exclusive) control* of the promisee (or as being something that she own); such representation obviously demands an explanation of how such control (or ownership) is vested in the promisee at contract formation, and the 'transfer explanation', which this chapter challenges, comes naturally. Second, and consistently with Benson's representation of a contractual right as an ownership right, he conceptualizes the promisor's contractual duty as that of *non-interference*, and a breach of contract as interference, with the promisee's ownership entitlement or with her (exclusive)

[43] It can be observed that it might also be possible to read Shiffrin's transfer thesis with a similar modification (or at least to supply her transfer thesis with such a modification). In other words, it might also be said that contract formation first creates (for the promisor) the normative liberty to perform the action that the promisor undertakes to perform, and that this normative liberty is thereafter transferred (to the promisee). However, quite apart from the difficult question of what right it is, precisely, that the *promisee* would acquire (it can hardly be the promisor's liberty to do what he undertakes to do), if Shiffrin's transfer thesis so qualified, the idea of transferring decision-making authority would not be central to explaining how a contractual relation is created.

control over the promisor's performance or the 'promised consideration'.[44] This chapter challenges such conceptualization. Most fundamentally, it maintains it is not the case that contract formation transfers to the promisee some (exclusive) control over, or ownership of, the promisor's performance or the 'promised consideration'.[45]

Pressing these points further, seeing the promisor's performance as being in the promisee's (exclusive) control does not account for, or simply misses, the fact that the promisee is under the *duty to accept* the promisor's performance and the promisor has the *right to perform*, and the *right that the promisee accept* his performance. It might be briefly observed that Benson's conception of *what* it is that is *transferred* from the promisor to the promisee is susceptible to criticism. In most basic terms, he has relied on the idea of *externalising* some promisor's *liberty* at, and as the result of, contract formation, which liberty, in an externalised form, can become an object of *ownership*, but as has been aptly remarked, '[j]ust because something is the subject of an agreement does not obviously suggest that it is being conceived of in some special way that serves to externalise what is previously internal'.[46] By claiming that it is not a *prior* right that is transferred to the promisee (suggesting that such a right is created at, and is the result of, contract formation), Benson avoids, at least to some extent, the problems with the absence of the requisite full liberty (to ϕ or not to ϕ) on the part of the promisor *before* contract formation, but other problems remain; some of these problems will be similar to those identified in the analysis of Shiffrin's transfer thesis in the previous section. However, an important point is that even if we disregarded such problems and analysed contract formation on the assumption that some promisor's liberty can be 'externalized' and become an object in the sense that the transfer theory supposes—an object (in the form of the promisor's performance or the 'promised consideration') that could be an object of somebody's (exclusive) control or ownership, it is not the case that as a result of contract formation, the promisee ends up with (exclusive) control over, or ownership of, the promisor's performance or the 'promised consideration'. The transfer thesis postulates that the promisor's performance or the 'promised consideration' *belongs* to the promisee and

[44] See, eg, Benson 2019, 251 (observing that '[f]rom a contractual point of view, failure to perform is [. . .] conceptualized as an interference with the plaintiff's exclusive right to an asset—the substance of the consideration—that has already been moved to her at formation in the promissory medium of representation.').

[45] See Sakharova 2024a.

[46] See Penner 1997, 178. The observation quoted in the main text was made with respect to Hegel's work (Hegel 1942), on which Benson's discussion of contracts draws, as he himself emphasized with respect to his earlier discussion of contracts for services. See Benson 2007, 1728, fn 88.

constitutes her ownership entitlement, but if so, it is difficult to understand how the promisee—the owner—can be so restricted by the contract in respect of her ownership. It is surely not the case that the promisee can do anything she likes with what she supposedly owns, that is, with the promisor's performance or the 'promised consideration'; more specifically, the promisee's duty to accept the promisor's performance does not allow us to say that she is in *(exclusive) control* over the promisor's performance, and the promisor's right to perform, as well as his right that the promisee accept his performance, does not allow us to say that the promisor *gives up* his (exclusive) control over, or ownership of, his own performance (whether by way of a transfer or otherwise, it might be added).

Conceptualizing breach of a contractual duty as interference with the promisee's exclusive control over, or ownership of, the promisor's performance or the 'promised consideration' and conceptualizing the promisor's duty as that of non-interference with such exclusive control or ownership is consistent with the transfer theory's understanding of contractual rights as ownership rights, but also reflects the problems outlined earlier. A central problem is that this outlook assumes a merely *passive* role of the promisor in a contractual relation. A basic idea is, once again, that through a transfer at contract formation, the promisor gives up his exclusive control over, or ownership of, his own performance (or in other words, over/of what he promises, which, on the transfer theory, constitutes the 'promised consideration') and comes under the duty of non-interference with the promisee's ownership entitlement to the promisor's performance or the 'promised consideration', which duty can be breached by *interfering* with the promisee's ownership entitlement so described. Even though the transfer theory distinguishes contractual and property rights, both of which fall into the category of ownership as understood by the transfer theory, the promisor's contractual duty is compared, if not strictly analogized, to the duty of non-interference with a property right, such as an owner's right to land. However, it is difficult to draw such a comparison precisely for the reason that seeing the promisor's contractual duty as that of non-interference does not take into account the promisor's *active* standing in performing his duty.

It might be mentioned that Benson himself may be said to be foreseeing a possible objection to his approach, but he seems to associate any potential criticism primarily with the fact that contractual duties are typically, or at least often, duties *to do* something rather than duties *not to do* something, but for Benson, it does not appear to be important that contracts typically or often are about doing something, and a duty to do something can also be constructed as a duty of non-interference. Additionally, he points out that there are also contracts in which the duty is to refrain from doing something.[47] However, it is objectionable to construct contractual duties as duties of non-interference not *merely* because contracts typically or often are about doing something (although, it might be remarked, the very fact that contracts typically or often are about doing something tells us a lot about the nature of contractual relations); rather, conceptualizing contractual duties as duties of non-interference is objectionable for at least two further reasons.

First, it is difficult not to notice that the moment we try to construct the promisor's duty to do something negatively, that is, as a duty to '*refrain*' from *not* doing something, a problem of double negation arises. In the familiar example of a duty to paint a wall, not interfering with painting the wall by painting it means not not painting it, which simply means painting it, the failure to do which could only be conceived as a case of non-feasance. However, even if this problem were put to one side, or even if we focused, for the sake of argument, only on those contracts in which the actual contractual duty is to *refrain* from *doing* something, what the bearer of a contractual duty is 'doing' or 'not doing' would still be very different from what the bearer of the duty not to interfere with a property right, for example with the owner's right to land, is 'doing' or 'not doing'; to put it differently, what the contractual duty demands of a contracting party is not the same as what a duty of non-interference demands of its bearer, or to put it in a different way still, there is a difference in what it takes to comply with the respective duties and what suffices to breach them. Even if the promisor has undertaken to refrain from doing something, the promisor's role is active and not comparable with non-interference with property rights.

Second, regardless of how the promisor's duty is constructed, focusing on a breach of *this* duty *only* in explaining how a contractual relation may go astray disregards the ways in which the *promisee* herself may become a breaching party not with respect to her own reciprocal duty to perform but with respect to the *promisor's performance* or the 'promised consideration' that she supposedly owns (or over which she has exclusive control). On the transfer theory, the promisee has exclusive control over, or ownership of, the promissor's performance or the 'promised consideration', and consequently, any contractual breach is understood as merely interference with the promisee's ownership entitlement. However, to construe a contractual breach as merely the promisor's interference with the promisee's ownership entitlement is to adopt a rather narrow conception of a contractual breach. Such a conception supposes that

[47] See Benson 2007, 1725–1726.

it is only the promisor who can possibly be in breach as far as his performance or the 'promised consideration' is concerned, as only he can breach the duty of non-interference with the promisee's ownership entitlement (or his duty to perform). A major problem is that this outlook misses the situation in which the promisee can also be in breach *not* by breaching her own reciprocal duty not to interfere with the promisor's reciprocal ownership entitlement (or with her own duty to perform whatever it is that she has undertaken to perform in return for the promisor's performance), but by refusing to *accept* the promisor's performance or the 'promised consideration' or, in other words, by breaching her own *duty* to accept the promisor's performance or the 'promised consideration'; for example, if B is to paint A's wall and A is to pay B, A can be in breach not merely by not paying, but also by preventing B from painting. It appears to be remarkable that the promisee may be in breach with respect to the promisor's performance or 'promised consideration' which, on the transfer theory, is supposed to be in her exclusive control or in her ownership. Fully accounting for the promisor's right that the promisee accept the performance and his right to perform protected by the promisee's duty to accept (or, in other words, the promisor's *active* standing in performing his duty and his equal (with that of the promisee) position in a contractual relation) precludes conceptualizing the promisor's duty as that of non-interference and a contractual breach as interference with the promisee's exclusive control over, or ownership of, the promisor's performance.

IV. Conclusion

In conclusion, it might be reiterated that the *idea* that contract formation effects, and indeed manifests itself, in a transfer of some entitlement from the promisor to the promisee appears to create a misleading metaphor, while the *normative power* to transfer is not the power that generates a contractual relation. It could hardly be said that the promisee has exclusive control over, or ownership of, the promisor's performance or the 'promised consideration'. Moreover, to the extent that it is not possible to pinpoint some *prior* right—the right that the promisor would have *before* contract formation—that could be transferred to the promisee at contract formation resulting in her *contractual* right, the normative power to *transfer*, even if it were taken to be relevant and operating at contract formation in the first place, would not suffice to explain what is happening at contract formation; some *other* power that would initially *create* some *new* right for the *promisor* at contract formation—the right that would be (almost simultaneously) transferred to the promisee resulting in her *contractual* right—would have to be identified and explained.

References

Barnett, R. E (1986). 'A Consent Theory of Contract'. *Columbia Law Review* 86(2): 269–321.

Barnett, R. E. (2014). 'Contract is Not Promise; Contract is Consent'. *Philosophical Foundations of Contract Law.* G. Klass, G. Letsas, and P. Saprai. Oxford, Oxford University Press: 42–57.

Benson, P. (1989). 'Abstract Right and the Possibility of a Nondistributive Conception of Contract: Hegel and Contemporary Contract Theory'. *Cardozo Law Review* 10(5–6): 1077–1198.

Benson, P. (1995). 'The Idea of a Public Basis of Justification for Contract'. *Osgoode Hall Law Journal* 33: 273–333.

Benson, P. (1996). 'Contract'. *A Companion to Philosophy of Law and Legal Theory.* D. Patterson. Cambridge, Blackwell Publishers: 24–56.

Benson, P. (2001). 'The Unity of Contract Law'. *The Theory of Contract Law: New Essays.* P. Benson. Cambridge, Cambridge University Press: 118–205.

Benson, P. (2007). 'Contract as a Transfer of Ownership'. *William and Mary Law Rev* 48: 1673–1731.

Benson, P. (2010). 'Contract'. *A Companion to Philosophy of Law and Legal Theory.* 2nd edn. D. Patterson. Malden, Wiley-Blackwell: 29–63.

Benson, P. (2011). 'The Idea of Consideration'. *The University of Toronto Law Journal* 61(2): 241–278.

Benson, P. (2019). *Justice in Transactions: A Theory of Contract Law.* Cambridge, Harvard University Press.

Dagan, H. and M. Heller, (2017). *The Choice Theory of Contract.* Cambridge, Cambridge University Press.

Fuller L. L. and W. R. Perdue, Jr (1936). 'The Reliance Interest in Contract Damages: 1'. *Yale Law Journal* 46(1): 52–96.

Fuller L. L. and W. R. Perdue, Jr (1937). 'The Reliance Interest in Contract Damages: 2'. *Yale Law Journal* 46(3): 373–420.

Gold, A. S. (2009). 'A Property Theory of Contract'. *Northwestern University Law Review* 103(1): 1–62.

Hegel, G. W. F. (1942). *The Philosophy of Right.* T. M. Knox, tr. Oxford, Clarendon Press.

Hohfeld, W. N. (1917). 'Fundamental Legal Conceptions as Applied in Judicial Reasoning'. *Yale Law Journal* 26: 710–770.

Hurd, H. M and M. S. Moore, (2018). 'The Hohfeldian Analysis of Rights'. *The American Journal of Jurisprudence* 63(2): 295–354.

MacCormick, N. (1972). 'Voluntary Obligations and Normative Powers'. *Proceedings of the Aristotelian Society* 46: 59–78.

Mill, J. S. (2003). 'On Liberty'. *Utilitarianism and On Liberty: Including Mill's 'Essay on Bentham' and Selections from the Writings of Jeremy Bentham and John Austin.* 2nd edn. M. Warnock. Malden, Blackwell Publishing: 88–180.

Owens, D. (2014). 'Does a Promise Transfer a Right?' *Philosophical Foundations of Contract Law.* G. Klass, G. Letsas, and P. Saprai. Oxford, Oxford University Press: 78–95.

Penner, J. E. (1996). 'Voluntary Obligations and the Scope of the Law of Contract'. *Legal Theory* 2(4): 325–357.

Penner, J. E. (1997). *The Idea of Property in Law.* Oxford, Clarendon Press.
Penner, J. E. (2013). 'On the Very Idea of Transmissible Rights'. *Philosophical Foundations of Property Law.* J. E. Penner and H.E. Smith. Oxford, Oxford University Press: 244–271.
Penner, J. E. (2020). *Property Rights: A Re-Examination.* Oxford, Oxford University Press.
Sakharova, I. (2024a). '(Mis)Understanding Correlativity in Contractual Relations'. *Ratio Juris* 37: 48–66.
Sakharova, I. (2024b). 'The Power to Contract and the Offer-and-Acceptance Analysis of Contract Formation'. *Canadian Journal of Law and Jurisprudence* 37: 261–285.
Sakharova, I. (2025). 'The Bilaterality of Contract'. *Research Handbook on the Philosophy of Contract Law.* M. Chen-Wishart and P. Saprai. Cheltenham, Edward Elgar: 178–191.
Shiffrin, S. V. (2007). 'The Divergence of Contract and Promise'. *Harvard Law Review* 120(3): 708–753.
Shiffrin, S. V. (2008). 'Promising, Intimate Relationships, and Conventionalism'. *Philosophical Review* 117(4): 481–524.
Shiffrin, S. V. (2011). 'Immoral, Conflicting, and Redundant Promises'. *Reasons and Recognition: Essays on the Philosophy of T.M. Scanlon.* J. R. Wallace, R. Kumar, and S. R. Freeman. Oxford, Oxford University Press: 155–178.
Shiffrin, S. V. (2012). 'Is a Contract a Promise?' *The Routledge Companion to Philosophy of Law.* A. Marmor. New York, Routledge: 241–257.
Shiffrin, S. V. (2023). 'Hidden Delegations: The Assignment of Contractual Rights and Consumer Debt'. Modern Law Review 86(1): 1–30.
Smith, S. A. (2000). 'Towards a Theory of Contract'. *Oxford Essays in Jurisprudence: Fourth Series.* J. Horder. Oxford, Oxford University Press: 107–129.
Smith, S. A. (2004). *Contract Theory.* Oxford, Oxford University Press.
Watson, G. (2009). 'Promises, Reasons, and Normative Powers'. *Reasons for Action.* D. Sobel and S. Wall. Cambridge, Cambridge University Press: 150–178.

II.

PROPERTY, CONTRACT, AND THE STRUCTURE OF PRIVATE LAW

4

Combining Property and Contract

*Henry E. Smith**

I. Introduction

Property and contract are traditionally taken to be distinct but related. However, both their distinctness and the nature of their relation have engendered increasing controversy. Many have questioned whether there is really any important difference between property and contract. And developments old and new—from the trust to equitable servitudes to new intangibles—lead many to believe that contract and property can be combined in any way that produces some benefit to someone. At the same time, others have voiced caution over breaking down the distinction between property and contract and have refused to bless the open-ended blending of contract and property elements.

On the most plastic versions of the bundle-of-rights picture of property, contracting could be used to package and repackage sticks in the bundle at will, leading to whatever collection of 'entitlements' or sticks would further party preferences, policy, or whatever external standard one might adopt.[1] This is in tension with the traditional idea that, in contrast to contract where customization is the name of the game, property comes in a limited set of forms and is standardized in many ways. This feature of property is mostly implicit in the common law and was first associated with the civil-law term *numerus clausus* by Bernard Rudden.[2] Standardization of property prevents contract rights from receiving property treatment and maintains the traditional distinction between property and contract, the in rem and in personam. Various

* For helpful questions and comments, I would like to thank Aditi Bagchi; Zhong Xing Tan; participants at the Conference on the Property Contract Interface at the National University of Singapore Faculty of Law; faculty workshops at Fordham Law School, Tel Aviv University Buchmann Faculty of Law, and Yale Law School; a law and economics workshop at the University of Toronto Faculty of Law; the American Law and Economics Annual Meeting at NYU Law School; and the Obligations XI conference at Harvard Law School.

[1] Penner 1996; 2020b; Symposium 2011.

[2] Rudden 1987.

Henry E. Smith, *Combining Property and Contract* In: *The Property-Contract Interface*. Edited by: James Penner, Irina Sakharova, Henry E. Smith, and Zhong Xing Tan, Oxford University Press. © Henry E. Smith 2026.
DOI: 10.1093/9780198951995.003.0006

rationales have been offered. From a doctrinal point of view, the in personam/in rem distinction matters: because in rem rights bind people generally, allowing contract rights to bind third parties would illicitly subject them to non-consensual legal liability.[3] Contracting for new kinds of in rem rights violates this principle, giving such non-consenting people more to be on the lookout for in order to avoid liability. This more functional worry about 'externalities' in terms of third-party impact or the costs of its avoidance was at the heart of the economic theory of the *numerus clausus* and standardization that Thomas Merrill and I offered to explain and justify it.[4]

On our theory, the *numerus clausus* principle serves to standardize legal relations where they impact large and indefinite groups of people, who are least suited to evaluating information about such rights. Very prominently, in the so-called catalogue of estates, parties and courts are not supposed to create new types of property rights.[5] Such rights would impose liability on non-consenting third parties, who would either risk liability or invest in costly measures to decipher their content. Idiosyncratic rights—or 'fancies'—can require costly evaluation not just of the rights in question but of all rights (even to assure their absence), and these costs are not internalized to those creating the idiosyncratic rights (who reap all the benefits).[6]

This theory of the *numerus clausus* included a functional account of aspects of the law that straddle in rem and in personam, or property and contract.[7] There are situations intermediate between in rem and in personam, where the set of duty holders is large but definite or small but indefinite. Here we tend to find an intermediate degree of standardization, which served as suggestive evidence for our 'information cost' theory of standardization in property law. Where the 'audience' for property rights (duty bearers, successors) is intermediate in either numerosity or definiteness, the need for standardization is also intermediate. Examples were drawn from bailments, leases, security interests, and trusts. In those areas, there are aspects that are in rem, in personam, or in between. In the 'intermediate' situations, we found a spectrum of stricter

[3] McFarlane 2010. In civil law jurisdictions, the *numerus clausus* is variously treated as a logical necessity, a matter of requiring state sanction to bind parties without their consent, and as reflecting the need for in rem rights to be determinate and recognizable to third parties. Akkermans 2008, 169-252; von Bar 2023, § 2.44. See generally Chang 2023, 62–100.

[4] Merrill & Smith 2000.

[5] Bergin & Haskell 1984, 19–55.

[6] Merrill & Smith 2000, 26–34; Merrill & Smith 2020; Smith 2011b. The term 'fancies' is taken from the leading case of *Keppell v Bailey*, 2 My & K 517, 39 Eng Rep 1042 (Ch 1834).

[7] Merrill & Smith 2001a. We noted that Kocourek (1920) objected to the emphasis in Hohfeld 1917 on numerosity as capturing in rem: in contrast, Kocourek thought that indefiniteness was the key variable. Kocourek was in turn inspired by Austin and the civil-law tradition. The idea of indefiniteness is related to social distance. See, eg, Rose 1999; Smith 2003.

to looser standardization based on protection strategies and notice-giving requirements.

Concerned as we were with providing a functional explanation, we focused more on the similarities than the differences in our four areas of law. On closer look, they are quite different. In bailment, contract and property come together in a simple (but often overlooked) way, whereas in leases of real property, contract and property elements are intertwined. Generally speaking, the property-contract interface is far from homogeneous. Property and contract elements are components—modules—in a complex system of legal relations. As in complex systems generally, the action is in the interaction of the elements, which produces emergent effects and creates information costs at the same time.[8]

This pushes the puzzle up one level. We could imagine a law that produces the pattern of standardization—more for in rem, least for in personam, and intermediate for intermediate legal relations—by simple fiat. And we could imagine such a law combining property and contract in many ways as long as this external 'constraint' were satisfied. I will argue that that is not our law. Instead, standardization, including differential standardization, is a by-product of the architecture of private law. It is built into the interface of property and contract but not as an external constraint. Instead, property and contract law are themselves shaped in such a way that they come together to produce (differential) standardization. To take the simplest example, in a bailment by contract, the contract creates a possessory relationship and can modify some if its features, but the 'bailment effect' is the result of the simple mode of combining contract and possession. In our other areas—leases, security interests, and trusts—the interface is not as simple but is quite constrained. To produce beneficial emergent effects at reasonable cost, the interface between property and contract is highly structured, with modular property and contract elements being only allowed to combine in particular ways. Thus the *numerus clausus* effect is produced by a general feature of private law: the relative invariance of higher-order structures. And that invariance is in turn protected by its being structural rather than stipulated.[9]

This chapter begins in section I by revisiting the property-contract interface to set out the nature of the problem of combining property and contract and offering a theory of how the law heads off this kind of complexity by building structure into the modes of combining legal relations. In section II, I show that

[8] See, eg, Mitchell 2009; Simon 1981; see also Smith 2025.
[9] On the architectural approach, see Merrill & Smith 2020; Smith 2025.

the differential level of standardization in various institutions at the property-contract interface is the product of different modes of combining property and contract that all involve a modular structure separating the property and contract elements. Section III links the property-contract interface to the way that high-order structures of the law are standardized in a robust fashion, not least through the combinatorial possibilities built in the modules of property and contract law. I conclude with some thoughts on how such an architectural account points to the need to combine internal and external perspectives on the law, and how this fits into the New Private Law.

II. The Interface Problem

The focus of the literature so far has been on whether the property-contract interface is constrained and less on how this comes about. This section argues that some very 'built in' features of the law serve to manage the benefits and costs of this complexity at the property-contract interface.

What is the property-contract interface? In systems theory, an interface between modules is the limited way that modules are allowed to communicate (interact). In Carliss Baldwin's hypothetical example of modularity, a team of smiths makes an iron pot hook for a team of cooks in return for payment.[10] Each team is a highly interactive module inside. Between them, the two teams communicate much less: neither needs to know much about the other, and their actions do not affect the other, except in a limited way. The pot hook needs to have a certain shape, tensile strength, etc. How it is made and what other features it has (colour) are less relevant (or not at all).

An interface is thus a set of conditions for modules to come together. The conditions can take a number of forms. They can be spelled out as a set of design requirements (as in the cook-smith example) in an exogenous fashion. They could also be built into the modules themselves, as in smiths by definition working with metal and therefore producing a certain kind of product (which will be attractive to cooks). Likewise, the interface conditions can be more or less subject to revision over time. The more they are built into the modules, the more difficult it is to revise them.

We can see something similar in law. The different areas of private law can themselves be regarded as modules in a system.[11] Each area of law has rules,

[10] Baldwin 2007:167–169.
[11] Gold 2024; Smith 2021c.

principles, and doctrines that interact more with each other than with rules, principles, and doctrines in other areas of law. This allows for the law to be much easier to track and to avoid ripple effects and complexity cascades. For example, if liability in tort could depend on the complex interaction of many rights, including contract rights, whether a person would be liable could be hard to discover, could depend on apparently far-flung and unrelated matters, and could quickly become highly complex (even chaotic). The economic loss rule is an example of an attempt to keep tort, property, and contract from interacting in an overly intense way: someone negligently damaging property is liable to the possessor or owner but not to those non-possessors who have contracted for use of the property and have suffered economic loss.[12]

We could imagine the interface conditions being a set of propositions about the areas of private law and their interrelations. One could see the economic loss rule in this way, as an exogenous constraint on tort liability that makes reference to contract. In a similar manner, the general principle that people cannot be bound without their consent except through approved acquisition methods could be seen as an external constraint on property law and any combination of property and contract.

The interface conditions might, however, be more built into the system. That is, instead of being purely exogenous constraints, they can be an implication of the definition of various areas of law themselves. That is, the external face presented by the module of an area of law combines in only certain ways with other areas of law. Thus, if being in personam is characteristic of contract rights, then when contract comes together with property, the result will not be in rem.

When property and contract come together, results can be achieved that cannot be handled easily by property or contract alone. As we will see in the next section, in areas like bailments, leases, security interests, and trusts, the objectives served partake of the purposes of both property and contract. And in previous work, Merrill and I showed that the degree of standardization tracked the kind of audience reached, with the most standardization for in rem aspects, the least for in personam, and an intermediate level of standardization for audiences that are intermediate.[13] 'Intermediate' could mean that a relation avails against a set of duty bearers that is large but definite, as in mass contracts

[12] *Robins Dry Dock & Repair Co v Flint*, 275 US 303 (1927) (Holmes, J); *Ultramares Corp v Touche*, 174 NE 441 (NY 1931) (Cardozo, J); Restatement of the Law Third, Torts: Liability for Economic Harm § 7 (Am L Inst 2020) (Economic Loss from Injury to a Third Person or to Property Not Belonging to the Claimant) For an analysis of the economic loss rule in terms of modularity, see Smith 2011a: 25–28.

[13] Merrill & Smith 2001a.

('compound-paucital' in our neo-Hohfeldian terminology);[14] or the set of duty bearers could be small but indefinite, as in transfer situations ('quasi-multital').[15] When the number of duty holders starts to increase, as with mass contracting, the tendency is to use a protective strategy through mandatory or penalty default rules.[16] In other situations, especially those of transferees, indefiniteness was the main problem, and the law tends to use notice-providing strategies, like recording requirements or exempting parties without notice from liability.[17]

Returning to the generalization that intermediate aspects of legal institutions—intermediate between in personam and in rem—show an intermediate level of standardization, we can now ask how this is achieved. There might be a principle that dictates that when one is trying to reach an audience for a duty that is intermediate (numerous but definite or indefinite but non-numerous), some strategy to lower information costs, through notice or protection, would be required. Or this very effect might be achieved by the limited ways that contract and property are allowed to come together. That is, when contract and property affect intermediate audiences, the intermediate standardization will be the effect produced by the way that property and contract come together. And to a large extent, the way they come together will be a feature of their properties, like atoms bonding to form a molecule.

To see whether the interface conditions are more exogenous or built in, let us return to the institutions along the property-contract interface—bailments, leases, security interests, and trusts.

III. Institutions along the Property-Contract Interface Revisited

In this section, I revisit some devices that partake of both property and contract to show that the information-cost management and standardizing role of law is built into the combinatory potential of the contract and property elements, supplemented by devices that regulate this interface. In all such areas, the interstitial law in this area has a modular architecture that manages complexity in light of its benefits and its costs.[18]

[14] Ibid, 785. See Hohfeld 1917.
[15] Merrill & Smith 2001a.
[16] Ibid, 806–807. On penalty default rules, see Ayres & Gertner 1989.
[17] Merrill & Smith 2001a, 805, 807–808.
[18] Smith 2024.

Before turning to the interfaces, it is worth emphasizing what they are for. Each of the areas in question is called upon to serve the purposes of property and contract, but in different ways. Bailment uses contract to set up a possessory relationship, and while an agreement may tailor its scope, the relation is a relatively simple one. By contrast, leases typically need to cover longer periods with many more interacting activities by the lessor and the lessee.[19] As we will see, it is a more integrated institution than is bailment. Security interests provide for a contingency of non-payment and help give notice to future creditors of the current situation. Trusts are highly complex institutions, which deal with an especially wide variety of situations with extreme agency problems through a structure that is not only modular but hierarchical.[20] One might think that the different structures we will see in these areas are dictated by these different purposes. That is only half true. In all of these devices, we do indeed need to combine property and contract. However, the focus in this section will be on how heavily constrained that combination is. These limits on how property and contract can combine stem from the need to manage complexity and prevent various forms of information costs to non-consenting parties.

1. Bailments

Bailment combines contract and property in a simple way, with a contract to establish a possessory relation as the interface across which the contract and possession parts act as separate modules. However, there has been a tendency to reduce bailment to one of its components, especially contract, with problematic results.

There are two theories of bailment, both of which have a distinguished line of defenders. Some see bailment as a contract, which captures how easily tailored it is.[21] The problem with this view is that it downplays the possessory aspect of bailment. And some situations do not fit comfortably under the rubric of contract. Gratuitous bailments do not involve consideration (but do involve possession), and involuntary bailments, as in finder situations, involve no contract at all (but again are centrally about possession). One can try to

[19] Merrill 2020.
[20] On the agency problem in trust law, see Sitkoff 2004.
[21] Blackstone 1766, 452 ('A delivery of goods in trust upon a contract express or implied, that the trust shall be faithfully executed on the part of the bailee.'); Story 1846, 4 ('[A] bailment is a delivery of a thing in trust for some special object or purpose, and upon a contract, express or implied, to conform to the object or purpose of the trust.').

craft notions of implicit or constructive contract to cover such situations, but it is a stretch.

The second view is that bailment is the rightful possession of an item of personal property by someone other than its owner.[22] This puts possession front and centre and covers the cases of gratuitous and involuntary bailment. Of course, many bailments are created by contract, but the bailment is distinct from the contract that creates and governs it. Many aspects of bailment relate to the problem of ostensible ownership created by separating possession by the bailee from ownership (including the right to possess) by the bailor. Generally, the law prevents contractual detail from mixing into the possessory side of bailment. Thus, from the point of view of third-party trespassers, the bailee has possessory rights and standing to sue: the internal bailment structure created by contract should not matter. For example, in *The Winkfield*, a tortfeasor was liable to a bailee for destruction of property (mail on board a ship), even if the bailee (the postmaster) would not have been liable to the bailors (customers).[23] Possession is modular with respect to third-party duty bearers, and the liability of the bailee to the bailor does not affect tort liability at all.[24]

The effect in bailment is produced by the simple interaction of contract and property. To say it is simple does not mean that it is not easy to overlook. Much of the confusion surrounding bailment law stems from not keeping the contract and property elements of bailment separate. Most of the time, though, focusing on the contractual aspect works as between the parties. Contract can be used to govern duties of bailees as long as they do not impact third parties. Nevertheless, one cannot change the nature of possession itself and its implications by contract, especially when that would impact third parties. And even between the parties to a bailment, the fact that possession is involved matters: boilerplate disclaimers are less effective in bailment situations like parking garages than they are in consumer law generally.[25] In this intermediate situation, a notice strategy shades into a protection strategy.

[22] Restatement of the Law Fourth, Property Vol 3, Div III, § 1.1 (Am L Inst, Tent Draft No 2, April 2021). See, eg, Palmer 2009, § 1-012 ('[I]t is now well established that the existence of claims in bailment does not depend on contract. What is fundamental is not contract, but the *bailee's* consent. The duties of a bailee arise out of the voluntary assumption of possession of another's goods[.]') (quoting *East West Corp v DKBS AF 1912* [2003] QB 1509 at para 24); Williston and Lord (2025), vol 19, § 53:1 (A bailment 'may be defined as the rightful possession of goods by one who is not the owner'.).

[23] On how the principle in *The Winkfield* has been elaborated in intermediate situations, see Barnett forthcoming.

[24] [1902] P 42, [1902–1903] All ER 346 (Ct App 1901) (Eng). Under modern law the bailor can also sue, but double recovery will not be allowed.

[25] See, eg, *Allen v. Hyatt Regency-Nashville Hotel*, 668 SW 2d 286 (Tenn 1984); Restatement of the Law Fourth, Property Vol 3, Div III, § 15 (Tent Draft 3 Am L Inst 2022); Dickerson 1988:149–155.

2. Leases

The most integrated institution at the property-contract interface is the lease of real property. One could imagine leases as being contracts to establish a possessory relation, with the contract and the possessory relationship being separate, as in bailments. Each would contribute to the overall effect but could be analysed in isolation. That is not how real property leases work. Because leases elaborate the relations between the parties, the property and contract elements are much more intertwined, but the strands of contract and property are kept distinct for many purposes. The interface between contract and property in leases is itself more elaborate than in bailment, but a modular distinction between the two elements is still discernable.

Leasing law in the realm of real property is a unitary body of law with two aspects, contractual and proprietary. Over time, the balance between these two has shifted: according to the conventional wisdom, leasing became more contractual during the landlord-tenant revolution.[26] Alternatively, some have said that leasing in its contract-law aspect has simply lagged contract law itself.[27] Either way, when courts were asking whether covenants should be regarded as independent or as mutually dependent or whether mitigation doctrine should apply, they treated the lease as a contract.[28] And yet courts implementing this shift to dependent covenants were quite aware that property and contract even in leasing are distinct. As the California Supreme Court explained in its landmark decision in *Medico-Dental Building Company of Los Angeles v Horton and Converse*, it was taking what could be considered a modular approach:

> While it is true that a lease is primarily a conveyance in that it transfers an estate to the lessee, it also presents the aspect of a contract. (Pollock on Contracts, Third Am. ed., p. 531.) This dual character serves to create two distinct sets of rights and obligations—'one comprising those growing out of the relation of landlord and tenant, and said to be based on the "privity of estate," and the other comprising those growing out of the express stipulations of the lease, and so said to be based on 'privity of contract.' (Samuels v. Ottinger, 146 P. 638, 638–39 (Cal. 1915).) Those features of the lease which are strictly contractual in their nature should be construed according to the rules for the interpretation of contracts generally and in conformity with the

[26] For general discussion, see, eg, Cunningham 1979; Glendon 1982.

[27] See generally Orth 2008.

[28] See, eg, *Medico-Dental Building Company of Los Angeles v Horton and Converse*, 132 P 2d 457 (Cal 1942); *Sommer v Kridel*, 378 A2d 767 (NJ 1977).

fundamental principle that the intentions of the parties should be given effect as far as possible.[29]

While not always emphasized, tenants are recognized as possessors of the leased premises, with possessory rights against the world including the landlord. Within the law of leasing, there are subtle ways in which the property and contract aspects are distinguished: privity of contract is distinguished from privity of estate for the purposes of determining liability on transfers of leases.[30] Transferees are in privity (a direct property-based relationship) with the lessor in assignments, but not in subleases. The separate but intertwined aspects of property (possession and the right to use) and contract (requirement of consideration, warranties, tailorability, and remedies) are brought to the fore in the Restatement Fourth of Property.[31]

The constraints on the property-contract interface in the area of leasing come from the way leasing law itself is built. The privity doctrines and touch and concern serve as mechanisms to manage the contract aspect. Overall, much effort has been put into making leasing a freestanding institution. As such, it can be treated as a whole, without worrying that changes in leasing doctrine will ripple throughout property law and private law more generally. For example, adopting an implied warranty of habitability (IWH) is not as interconnected to other doctrines as is possession itself. And we see more changes over time in the IWH and other contractual aspects of leasing than in property aspects like possession.[32]

3. Security Interests

Security interests combine contract and property by employing a different and very productive form of encapsulation based on a single purpose, which is of overriding importance: to secure an obligation. A security interest itself is an

[29] 132 P2d at 462.

[30] See Restatement of the Law Fourth, Property § 12.4 (Effect of an Assignment by the Lessee and Relations with the Lessor); Ibid, § 12.5 (Effect of a Sublease by the Lessee on Relations with the Lessor) (Am L Inst Tent Draft 6, 2025).

[31] Restatement of the Law Fourth, Property Vol 4, Div. III as reflected currently in Tentative Draft 5 (2024) and Tentative Draft 6 (2025). I am the Reporter for this project, and Tom Merrill is the Associate Reporter working in this area. He explores the Restatement and the intertwining of property and contract in Merrill forthcoming.

[32] Chang & Smith 2019. The civil law takes as its starting point the lease as a contract and adds property features. It too shows a modular structure, and Chang and Merrill analyse both styles of lease in terms of systems theory. Chang & Merrill 2025.

interest in property but a very minimal one. Security interests—personal property security interests and mortgages—can be (and typically are) created by contract, but they are distinct from the contract and from the obligation they secure.

There is another sense in which a mortgage is constrained at the property-contract interface. There are various ways that people might (and have) taken security, and these methods combine contract and property in different ways. A traditional method was to give title to another and only be able to demand it back after the obligation secured by the mortgage was paid off. Equity treated this transfer of title as different from a regular transfer of title and made sure that for most purposes the borrower was treated as the owner. The idea was that security would be the effect, and the only effect, of the title transfer. As procedural protections grew up around mortgages, lenders resorted to other devices. In the installment sales contract, the contract was stretched out to provide the security: such contracts for the sale of land would delay the transfer of definitive title until the installment sale contract was paid off. The modern view of mortgages treats the mortgage as a lien, a mini-property interest. Who is bound depends on notice, and these rules keep the information contained. Good faith purchasers can take free of security interests. Moreover, under modern law, other devices that function as a mortgage are treated as mortgages under the lien theory, even if they are couched as, for example, installment sales contracts.[33]

Security interests in personal property work similarly, and the security interest concept is if anything clearer (and has had an influence on mortgages in real property). The Uniform Commercial Code (UCC) defines 'security interest' to mean 'an interest in personal property or fixtures, which secures payment or performance of an obligation.'[34]

In mortgages of real property and in personal property security interests under the UCC, the purpose of providing security is used directly to contain the information and complexity of the security interest. If the purpose is to secure an obligation, then whatever the device used, it will work as a security interest. And in modern law, this means that the interest will be treated

[33] Restatement of the Law Fourth, Property, Vol 5, Div V, § 1.1 (Am L Inst Council Draft No 12, 2025) ('A mortgage is an interest in real property conveyed or retained as security for performance of an obligation.'); Restatement of the Law Fourth, Property, Vol 5, Div V, § 3.4 (Am L Inst Prelim Draft No 12, 2025) (A Contract for Deed Creates a Mortgage); Restatement of the Law Third, Property (Mortgages) § 3.4 (Am L Inst 1997).

[34] UCC § 1-201(35) ('"Security interest" means an interest in personal property or fixtures which secures payment or performance of an obligation.').

as a lien. The category of security is defined by its function—to secure an obligation.[35]

4. Trusts

More integrated than the bailment is the trust, which combines obligation and property in yet another way: by layering obligation on property. As I have argued elsewhere, the trust manages to improve on the tradeoff between reaching a broad and impersonal audience and providing detail relevant to specified persons by making the detail of the arrangements internal to the trust.[36] The method for accomplishing this is to use a two-tier structure: the trust consists of a module of regular title in the trustee (in rem property) overlaid by a contractual/obligational module regulated at their interface by equity and fiduciary law. This two-tier mode of combining property and contract extends to the outgrowths of the trust like the corporation.[37]

Whether the trust is more like contract or property is the subject of a perennial debate,[38] but one we can now transcend. The trust is a hybrid institution on the property-contract interface, and recent private law theory has broken the trust open and analysed how obligation and property combine to produce the effect of the trust.

What many analyses of the trust have in common is that the obligational part of the trust applies in such a way that it is encapsulated. The content of the obligational element is not allowed to bind third parties or interact with information outside the dyad of trustee and beneficiary. Ben McFarlane and Robert Stevens propose that the trustee has the right to the property and the beneficiary has a right to the right, a second-order right.[39] If the beneficiary holds a right to a right, that furnishes no standing to sue for trespass. However, following the right into the hands of a good faith purchaser is to assert the right to the right—not based on the content of the right but based on who (wrongfully)

[35] In earlier US law there were more forms of security, as there still are in English law. McFarlane 2008, 583–587. These other forms of security correspond to various institutions at the property-contract interface. A pledge involves taking possession of as asset to secure a debt and so resembles bailment. A mortgage historically (and in some jurisdictions currently) involves taking title for purposes of security, which resembles the trust in some ways.

[36] Smith 2021b, 31–32.

[37] Corporations grew out of the trust and a similar analysis of the property and contract elements could be given for the corporation and other organizational forms. See, eg, Hansmann & Kraakman 2000; Armour & Whincop 2007; Getzler 2009; Gold & Smith 2025a.

[38] Compare Maitland 1936, 29 (contract) and Scott 1917, 289 (property), and more recently Langbein 1995, 669 with Hansmann & Mattei 1998, 454–559.

[39] McFarlane & Stevens 2010; 2019.

holds it. A similar distinction is natural (if not deduced) on the more traditional analysis of James Penner, in which the trustee holds the property and is subject to duties to use the powers of title for the benefit of the beneficiary.[40] When there is a wrongful transfer to a third party, the rights obtained are subject to an equitable hook allowing the beneficiary to impose a constructive trust for its return. What these analyses have in common is that the management of information costs is a by-product of structure—in some sense a two-tier structure—and need not be imposed exogenously.[41] This would be very different if the trust were a homogenous bundle of sticks, some labelled legal and some equitable.

Other features of the trust also benefit from this two-tier structure. The trustee can deal with the property as any owner would, up to the limits of good faith purchase law, because generally it is legal title that matters for the in rem set of duty bearers. The same goes for trespass: potential trespassers have nothing more or different to worry about if property they encounter is impressed with a trust. By contrast, fiduciary duties can be customized (up to a point) as this information is contained with the trust module.

Much of the management of information costs here simply emerges from the two-tier trust structure. As Jessica Hudson and Charles Mitchell argue, the effect of the trust is the joint product of many trust rules,[42] and the complexity-management function of the trust is a prime example. Complexity can be beneficial or harmful, useful or useless. In the trust, by having the obligation bind the trustee, the interactions with third parties are kept to a minimum.

Two-tier structure is characteristic of equity, and as I have argued elsewhere, equity itself can serve as a module of the law contributing the benefits of complexity and containing its costs.[43] And equitable property rights are equitable in more than a historical sense: the residue of two-tier structure, with its characteristic good faith purchaser and notice rules, generally manages information costs in a way intermediate between property and contract.[44]

[40] Penner 2010. See also Ho forthcoming. For an analysis of the trust as 'semi-property', see Chang forthcoming.

[41] See Restatement of the Law Fourth, Property Vol 4, Div I, § 1.3(b) (Tent Draft No 3, 2022, Am L Inst) ('An equitable interest is an indirect entitlement in a thing that is effected through a right against another and that entitles its holder: (i) to secure a beneficial use or other benefit or recourse in derogation of the full powers of legal title or another lesser interest, legal or equitable; or (ii) to acquire legal title.').

[42] Hudson & Mitchell 2023.

[43] Smith 2021a.

[44] Smith 2023.

5. Combinatory Principles at the Property-Contract Interface

In revisiting bailments, leases, security interests, and trusts, the claim is not that these are the only institutions that combine property and contract. There are to be sure others, including those that are related to the ones covered here, including forms of organization like the corporation.[45] The corporation in particular grew out of the trust and exhibits a similar if elaborated modular structure.[46] And this trust structure was not equity's sole contribution. In many ways, equity has served to modulate the interface between areas of law; for example, by tweaking the law of privity and through the doctrine of good faith purchase.[47]

There are thus several kinds of property-contract interface. They correspond to the different ways that contract and property combine, and these different structures achieve standardization of the property-contract interface in characteristic ways that reflect the architecture of private law.

Some standardization is built into the combinatory potential of the law. If contract and property come together as in bailments, one way to make sure that information costs are not too burdensome on third parties is to keep these elements separate as modules. If one were to view bailment as all contract or all property, one might allow too much or too little information costs in light of the benefits one is trying to achieve. In particular, the risk is that the content of the contract will become relevant to in rem duty bearers.

By way of further comparison, consider the situation with licenses. A license is often created by contract, but it is distinct.[48] Thus, if someone buys a ticket to see a movie, the strictest separation between contract and property would hold the licensor liable in contract but a patron who refused to leave would be a trespasser.[49] Identifying licenses with contracts threatens to create new categories of easement outside the usual channels.

Modular structure operates in the law at multiple levels. The structure of rights is as simple as it is because rights can combine in productive

[45] Smith 2013. The asset partitioning framework of Hansmann & Kraakman (2000) brings out what could be considered a modular property element in organizational law, which importantly accounts for the nexus in the 'nexus of contracts'.

[46] Hansmann & Kraakman 2000, 405, 416–417; Sitkoff 2013.

[47] Smith 2021a, 1090–1092, 1094–1098.

[48] Newman 2013.

[49] While there is much confusion, the tendency in the United States is to hold that, to the extent the common law baseline is not displaced by statute, a ticket provides a revocable license, even if the revocation might be a breach of contract. *Marrone v. Washington Jockey Club of the District of Columbia*, 227 US 633, 636 (1913). This was the approach in England, *Wood v Leadbitter*, 153 Eng Rep 351, 13 M & W 838 (Exch Pl 1845), until *Hurst v Picture Theatres, Ltd* [1915] 1 KB 1 (CA 1914).

ways.[50] The estate system has rules that feed themselves (recursively) to produce complex structures (eg multiple remainders). At a higher level, trusts allow for fine-grained divisions of rights and a special effect on third parties. The structure of combinatorial potential—again, compare atoms bonding together—achieves much of the *numerus clausus* effect in property. At the level of areas of law, like contract and property, we see modules whose interfaces are highly structured based on the limited combinatory potential built into those areas.

IV. Further Implications

The property-contract interface is not totally fluid. In order to manage complexity and achieve needed standardization for far-flung audiences, the law provides modular structures that contain complexity. Revisiting the property-contract interface has confirmed the hypothesis that the pattern of standardization is more built in than exogenously imposed through an independent constraint (whether called '*numerus clausus*' or not). We are now in a position to see why.

The purpose of modularity is to manage complexity. Higher-order aspects of the law impinge on many different and disparate areas and thus are a potential source of complexity and information cost. Thus, one way to implement differential standardization in the law is to make higher-order aspects of law more invariant. Thus, the interface between property and contract is difficult to change. Parties are not allowed to tailor higher-order structures. Even in contract, one can customize the substance of the contract, but one cannot change the law of offer and acceptance or the third-party effects of the contract. Powers generally have ripple effects and are more constrained and less tailorable than first-order legal relations like rights.

These structures themselves are taken more or less as given. Allowing them to be varied by parties or easily altered by judicial opinions would undermine their role in managing complexity, because parties and even courts can easily make a change that will have ripple effects. That is the cost side. On the benefit side, parties and judges are likely to be able to achieve their objectives without recourse to structural change of this sort.[51]

[50] This is true of the kind of property rights that are recursive (ie, self-feeding and iteratively applicable), which is especially true in common law systems. Smith 2011b, 152–153; see also Shrutarshi, Foster, & Grimmelmann 2019.

[51] On 'architectural fit', see Gold & Smith 2023.

The robustness of structures at the higher level could be thought of as built into the combinatorial potential of property and contract law themselves. Rather than having a set of exogenous constraints that could be otherwise and could easily be more detailed and subject to exceptions, it is as if property and contract are designed to combine in certain ways. Hohfeld's scheme of jural relations is sometimes likened to a periodic table, but what it does not do is what the periodic table does: organize elements in a way that captures their combinatorial potential.[52] Property and contract are themselves built in a way that leads to limited but generative—and purposeful—combinations.

These questions raise perennial philosophical issues about where the robust structure for managing complexity comes from. These structures make their way into caselaw and legislation, and there needs to be some norm protecting that structure from constant revision, especially by contracting parties. Again, the fact that it is so deeply engrained in the law may make it intuitively hard to touch. Various perspectives on the law may reinforce this sense. On a natural law account, some of the principles involved, like avoidance of binding parties non-consensually outside approved channels, might be a candidate for something beyond social convention.[53] Or certain presuppositions about the law have an inherent pull.[54] For example, it is in the nature of a promise to create an obligation and in the nature of a waiver to extinguish a claim. Similarly, we might say that certain basic forms of privity or encapsulation of claims are robust presuppositions in the law. There is some convergence between ordinary ontology (what is a thing), basic moral norms, and human psychology.[55]

Perhaps if the world worked differently, there would be no need for complexity-containing structures at the property-contract interface or elsewhere in the law. One could adapt the Coase theorem to state that in a world of zero institution costs we could let complexity run wild.[56] That is not our world, and even the science of complexity points to how infeasible it is to compute many problems.[57] (Even the Coasean zero-transaction-cost thought experiment becomes problematic at some point.)

One can achieve 'complex' results from simple parts and a few interconnections. The realist-inspired idea that complexity in the world must be mirrored in complexity in the law is only half right, as is the hyper-formalist idea that

[52] Hohfeld 1913. See, eg, Dowty, Wall, & Peters 1980; Steedman 2001; Hopcroft, Motwani, & Ullman 2007 (chs 5, 7).
[53] See Klimchuk 2020; see also Claeys 2025; MacLeod 2015.
[54] Reinach 2012; Gold & Smith 2025b.
[55] See, eg, Toomey 2022; Smith 2012, Wilson 2020.
[56] Coase 1960. For an application to property rights themselves, see Lee & Smith 2012.
[57] Hopcroft, Motwani, & Ullman 2007.

simplicity is always up to the job. Often what is required are simple parts that combine in the right way.[58] Thus, the property-contract interface from one point of view looks complex. As Ben McFarlane and Andreas Televantos point out, the various ways of acquiring rights—property, contract, and equity—and the various areas of law—like agency trusts and partnership—combine to produce very subtle effects.[59] How complex is this? The effects are multifarious and subtle indeed. The connections produce this complexity. However, we could imagine a property-contract interface that is much more complex. There could be more modes of acquisition, and they could be combined in far more ways than they are. And the techniques for encapsulation we have reviewed above could be absent. Indeed, one could imagine a property-contract interface that is so complex it would take impossibly long to compute its results. The property-contract interface is constrained in just the ways needed to head this off.

The architectural approach to the property-contract interface also points to the inseparability of the so-called internal and external perspectives on law. An external account holds the law up to external criteria, whereas an internal perspective takes the law seriously on its own terms, up to a point.[60] On the architectural account of the property-contract interface and the modular structure of property and contract, the external information-managing aspect of the law is inseparable from its internal aspect. Something deep and robust shapes the way that the law can manage information cost in achieving its purposes. And if these architectural features were not so ingrained—so integral a part of the law's architecture—they would not function the way they do. Among other things, they would permit a lot more complexity and of the wrong kind. If the internal and external are this integrated, the property-contract interface illustrates the need for the perspectives offered by the New Private Law.[61]

V. Conclusion

The property-contract interface is a crossroads not just of doctrine and theory but of the deeper structures of the law itself. When in personam and in rem are mixed, the law responds in the ways we should expect if complexity and

[58] Gold & Smith 2022.

[59] McFarlane & Televantos 2020. US law treats the partnership and even the trust as more like an entity, a different kind of interface, than the law of the UK which is the focus of their chapter.

[60] See Gold 2021; see also Miller & Pojanowski 2022; Khaitan & Steel 2022.

[61] See Gold et al 2021; Goldberg 2012; Hosemann 2014; Miller 2021.

information costs are among its concerns. When it comes to mixed situations like bailments, leases, security interests, and trusts, in personam aspects are tailorable, in rem aspects are standardized, and intermediate aspects show a mix of protection and notice strategies that are somewhere in between.

This pattern arises from the law's employment of modular structures to achieve the benefits of complexity at a manageable cost. In combining property and contract, the law does not mix elements of each in a homogeneous fashion. Property and contract are kept more or less distinct as modules and only allowed to interact in circumscribed ways at their interface. They can be combined simply (contracting for a possessory relationship as in bailments), or they can be combined in a cross-cutting but still distinct fashion (real property leases). Moving beyond the first-order level of law, property and contract can be encapsulated by purpose into a module (security interests), or contract can be a second-order tier that fits into a property right in a modular fashion (trusts). These simple modular modes of combining property and contract can achieve great complexity and subtle results without imposing large information costs where audiences are not well-suited to bear them.

Because the information-cost management in the law is an effect produced by deeply engrained structures of the law, in the faces that property and contract present each other, the property-contract interface is a diagnostic about the nature of law itself. The need to manage information costs is served better by modular structures in the law that are not constantly up for grabs. This robustness could stem from dynamic feedback and evolutionary pressures, from human cognitive psychology, or a basic and widely shared set of moral or legal presumptions. This does not mean that the law is or should be frozen. Given the constrained but productive combinatorial potential of property and contract, there has been great innovation at the property-contract interface. And from the major changes in lease law and the rise of the trust and its development, innovation can occur without slipping the bounds of the structures that preserve the law from a flood of information costs and runaway complexity. Here, as elsewhere, deeply internal aspects of the law have important external consequences.

References

Akkermans, B. (2008). *The Principle of Numerus Clausus in European Law*. Antwerp, Intersentia.

Armour, J. and M. J. Whincop (2007). 'The Proprietary Foundations of Corporate Law'. *Oxford Journal of Legal Studies* 27: 429–465.

Ayres, I. and R. Gertner (1989). 'Filling Gaps in Incomplete Contracts: An Economic Theory of Default Rules'. *Yale Law Journal* 99: 87–130.

Baldwin, C. Y. (2007). 'Where Do Transactions Come From? Modularity, Transactions, and the Boundaries of Firms'. *Industrial and Corporate Change* 17: 155–195.

Barnett, K. (forthcoming) 'Bailment and the "Three Body Problem"'. *The Property-Contract Interface*. J Penner et al, Oxford, Oxford University Press.

Bergin, T. F and P. G Haskell (1984). *Preface to Estates in Land and Future Interests*. 2nd edn. Mineola, NY, Foundation Press.

Blackstone, W. (1766). *Commentaries on the Law of England*, Vol 2.

Chang, Y. C. (2023). *Property Law: Comparative, Empirical, and Economic Analyses*. Cambridge, Cambridge University Press.

Chang, Y. C. (forthcoming). 'A Complex Systems Theory of Trust'. *George Mason Law Review*.

Chang, Y. C. and T. W. Merrill (2025) 'The Nature of Leasing'. *Cornell International Law Journal* 58: 1–36.

Chang, Y. C. and H. E. Smith (2019). 'Convergence and Divergence in Systems of Property Law: Theoretical and Empirical Analyses'. *Southern California Law Review* 92: 785–808.

Claeys, E. R. (2025). *Natural Property Rights*. Cambridge, Cambridge University Press.

Coase, R. H. (1960). 'The Problem of Social Cost'. *Journal of Law & Economics* 3: 1–44.

Cunningham, R. A. (1979). 'The New Implied and Statutory Warranties of Habitability in Residential Leases: From Contract to Status'. *Urban Law Annual* 16: 3–153.

Dickerson, A. D. (1988) 'Bailor Beware: Limitations and Exclusions of Liability in Commercial Bailments'. *Vanderbilt Law Review* 41: 129–172.

Dowty, D. R., R. E. Wall, and S. Peters (1980). *Introduction to Montague Semantics*. Dordrecht, D. Reidel.

Getzler, J. (2009) 'Plural Ownership, Funds, and the Aggregation of Wills'. *Theoretical Inquiries in Law* 10: 241–270.

Glendon, M. A. (1982). 'The Transformation of American Landlord-Tenant Law'. *Boston College Law Review* 23: 503–576.

Gold, A. (2021). 'Internal and External Perspectives: On the New Private Law Methodology'. *The Oxford Handbook of the New Private Law*. A. S. Gold et al. Oxford, Oxford University Press: 3–19.

Gold, A. S. (2024). Private Law's Choice of Private Law. *Interstitial Private Law*. S. Bray et al. Oxford, Oxford University Press: 111–133.

Gold, A. S. and H. E. Smith (2022). 'Sizing Up Private Law'. *University of Toronto Law Journal* 70: 489–534.

Gold, A. S. and H. E. Smith (2023). 'Restatements and the Common Law'. *The American Law Institute: A Centennial History*. AS Gold and RW Gordon. Oxford, Oxford University Press: 441–462.

Gold, A. S. and H. E. Smith (2025a). 'The Equity in Corporate Law'. *Notre Dame Law Review* 100: 789–870.

Gold, A. S. and H. E. Smith (2025b). 'Legal Concepts as a Deep Structure of the Law: Reinach's A Priori in Action'. *Reinach and the Foundations of Private Law*. Marietta Auer et al. Cambridge, Cambridge University Press.

Gold, A. S. et al (2021). 'Introduction'. *The Oxford Handbook of the New Private Law*. A. S. Gold et al. Oxford, Oxford University Press.

Goldberg, J. C. P. (2012). 'Introduction: Pragmatism and Private Law'. *Harvard Law Review* 125: 1640–1663.

Hansmann, H. and R. Kraakman (2000). 'The Essential Role of Organizational Law'. *Yale Law Journal* 110: 387–440.

Hansmann, H. and U. Mattei (1998). 'The Functions of Trust Law: A Comparative Legal and Economic Analysis'. *New York University Law Review* 73: 434–479.

Ho, L. (forthcoming) 'The Nature of the Interest of an Object of Trust or Power'. *The Property-Contract Interface.* J. Penner et al. Oxford, Oxford University Press.

Hohfeld, W. N. (1913). 'Some Fundamental Legal Conceptions as Applied in Judicial Reasoning.' *Yale Law Journal* 23: 710–770.

Hohfeld, W. N. (1917). 'Fundamental Legal Conceptions as Applied in Judicial Reasoning.' *Yale Law Journal* 26: 16–59.

Hopcroft, J. E., R. Motwani, J. D. Ullman (2007). *Introduction to Automata Theory, Language, and Computation.* 3rd edn. Boston, Addison Wesley.

Hosemann, E. G. (2014). '"The New Private Law": Die neue amerikanische Privatrechtswissenschaft in historischer und vergleichender Perspektive ("The New Private Law": A Historical and Comparative Perspective on the Emerging New Private Law Scholarship in the United States)'. *Rabel Journal of Comparative and International Private Law (RabelsZ)* 78(1): 37–70.

Hudson, J. and C. Mitchell (2023). 'Justificanda'. *The Philosophical Foundations of the Law of Express Trusts.* S. Degeling, J. Hudson, and I. Samet. Oxford, Oxford University Press 12–43.

Khaitan, T. and S. Steel (2022). 'Theorizing Areas of Law: A Taxonomy of Special Jurisprudence'. *Legal Theory* 28: 325–351.

Klimchuk, D. (2020). 'Natural Rights and Natural Law'. *The Oxford Handbook of the New Private Law.* A. S. Gold et al. Oxford, Oxford University Press.

Kocourek, A. (1920). 'Rights in Rem'. *University of Pennsylvania Law Review* 68: 322–336.

Langbein, J. H. (1995). 'The Contractarian Basis of the Law of Trusts'. *Yale Law Journal* 105: 625–75.

Lee, B. A. and H. E. Smith (2012). 'The Nature of Coasean Property'. *International Review of Economics* 59: 145–155.

MacLeod, A. J. (2015). *Property and Practical Reason.* Cambridge, Cambridge University Press.

Maitland, F. W. (1936). *Equity: A Course of Lectures.* A. H. Chaytor and W. J. Whittaker. Cambridge, Cambridge University Press.

McFarlane, B. (2008). *The Structure of Property Law.* Oxford, Hart.

McFarlane, B. (2010). The *Numerus Clausus* Principle and Covenants Relating to Land. *Modern Studies in Property Law*, Vol. 6. S. Bright. Oxford, Hart.

McFarlane, B. and R. Stevens (2010). 'The Nature of Equitable Property'. Journal of Equity 4: 1–28.

McFarlane, B. and R. Stevens (2019). 'What's Special About Equity? Rights about Rights', *Philosophical Foundations of The Law of Equity.* I. Samet, D. Klimchuk and H. E. Smith. Oxford, Oxford University Press: 191–209.

McFarlane, B. and A. Televantos (2020). 'Third Party Effects in Private Law: Form and Function'. P. B. Miller and J. Oberdiek. *Oxford Studies in Private law Theory: Volume 1.* Oxford, Oxford University Press.

Merrill, T. W. (2020). 'The Economics of Leasing'. *Journal of Legal Analysis* 12: 221–272.

Merrill, T. W. (forthcoming). 'The Property/Contract Interface: Hybrid Leases'. *The Property-Contract Interface.* J. Penner et al. Oxford, Oxford University Press.

Merrill, T. W. and H. E. Smith (2000). 'Optimal Standardization in the Law of Property: The *Numerus Clausus* Principle'. Yale Law Journal 110: 1–70.

Merrill, T. W. and H. E. Smith (2001a). 'The Property/Contract Interface'. *Columbia Law Review* 101: 773–852.

Merrill, T. W. and H. E. Smith (2020). 'The Architecture of Property'. *Research Handbook on Private Law Theories*. H. Dagan and B. Zipursky. Cheltenham, Edward Elgar: 134–154.

Miller, P. B. (2021). 'The New Formalism in Private Law'. *American Journal of Jurisprudence* 66: 175–238.

Miller, P. B. and J. A. Pojanowski (2022). 'The Internal Point of View in Private Law'. *American Journal of Jurisprudence* 67: 247–277.

Mitchell, M. (2009). *Complexity: A Guided Tour*. Oxford, Oxford University Press.

Newman, C. M. (2013). 'A License is Not a "Contract Not to Sue": Disentangling Property and Contract in the Law of Copyright Licenses'. *Iowa Law Review* 98: 1101–1162.

Orth, J. V. (2008) 'Leases: Like Any Other Contract?'. *Green Bag 2d* 12: 53–65.

Palmer, N. (2009). *Palmer on Bailment*. 3rd edn. London, Sweet & Maxwell.

Penner, J. E. (1996) 'The "Bundle of Rights" Picture of Property'. *UCLA Law Review* 43: 711–820.

Penner, J. E. (2010). 'An Untheory of the Law of Trusts, or Some Notes Towards Understanding the Structure of Trusts Law Doctrine'. *Current Legal Problems* 63: 653–675.

Reinach, A. (2012). 'The Apriori Foundations of the Civil Law'. JF Crosby tr. Frankfurt, ontos verlag. Originally published as Reinach, A (1913). 'Die apriorischen Grundlagen des bürgerlichen Rechtes'. *Jahrbuch für Philosophie und phänomenologische Forschung* 1(2): 685–847.

Rose, C. M. (1999). 'What Government Can Do for Property (and Vice Versa)'. *The Fundamental Interrelationships Between Government and Property*. N. Mercuro and W. J. Samuels. New York, Routledge: 209–222.

Rudden, B. (1987). 'Economic Theory v. Property Law: The *Numerus Clausus* Problem'. *Oxford Essays in Jurisprudence, Third Series*. J. Eekelaar and J. Bell. Oxford, Oxford University Press: 239–263.

Scott, A. W. (1917). 'The Nature of the Rights of the *Cestui Que Trust*'. *Columbia Law Review* 17: 269–290.

Shrutarshi, B., N. Foster, and J. Grimmelmann (2019). 'Property Conveyances as a Programming Language', in *Proc 2019 ACM SIGPLAN Int'l Symposium on New Ideas, New Paradigms, & Reflections on Programming and Software (Onward!)*: 128–142.

Sitkoff, R. (2004). 'An Agency Costs Theory of Trust Law', *Cornell Law Review* 89: 621–84.

Sitkoff, R. H. (2013) 'Trust Law as Fiduciary Governance Plus Asset Partitioning'. *The Worlds of the Trust*. L. Smith. Cambridge, Cambridge University Press: 428–453.

Simon, H. A. (1981). *The Sciences of the Artificial*. 2nd edn. Cambridge, Mass, MIT Press.

Smith, H. E. (2003). 'The Language of Property: Form, Context, and Audience'. *Stanford Law Review* 55: 1105–1191.

Smith, H. E. (2011a). 'Modularity and Morality in the Law of Torts'. *Journal of Tort Law* 4(2): 1–32.

Smith, H. E. (2011b). 'Toward an Economic Theory of Property in Information'. *Research Handbook on the Economics of Property Law*. K. Ayotte and H. E. Smith. Cheltenham, Edward Elgar: 104–124.

Smith, H. E. (2012). 'Property as the Law of Things'. *Harvard Law Review* 125: 1691–1726.

Smith, H. E. (2013) 'Property as Platform: Coordinating Standards for Technological Innovation'. *Journal of Competition Law & Economics* 9: 1057–1089.

Smith, H. E (2021a). 'Equity as Meta-Law'. *Yale Law Journal* 130: 1050–1144.

Smith, H. E. (2021b). 'Property beyond Flatland'. *Brigham-Kanner Property Rights Journal* 10: 9–56.

Smith, H. E. (2021c). 'Systems Theory'. *The Oxford Handbook of the New Private Law*. A. S. Gold et al. Oxford, Oxford University Press: 143–158.

Smith, H. E. (2023). Equitable Meta-Law: The Spectrum of Property. *Equity Today: 150 Years After the Judicature Reforms*. B. McFarlane and S. Elliott. Oxford, Hart: 319–338.

Smith, H. E. (2024). 'Introduction: Why Interstitial Private Law?'. *Interstitial Private Law*. S. L. Bray et al. Oxford, Oxford University Press: xiii–xviiii.

Smith, H. E. (2025). 'The Complex Architecture of Property Rights'. *Handbook on Institutions and Complexity*. Eric Alston, Lee Alston, and Bernardo Mueller. Cheltenham, Edward Elgar: 241–262.

Steedman, M. (2001). *The Syntactic Process*. Cambridge, Mass, MIT Press.

Toomey, J. (2022). 'Property's Boundaries'. *Virginia Law Review* 109: 131–191.

Symposium (2011). Property: A Bundle of Rights? *Econ Journal Watch* 8(3): 193–291.

Von Bar, C. (2023). *Foundations of Property Law: Things as Objects of Property Rights*. J. G. Allen tr. Oxford, Oxford University Press.

Wilson, B. J. (2020). *The Property Species: Mine, Yours, and the Human Mind*. Oxford, Oxford University Press.

Williston, S. and R. A. Lord (2025). *Williston on Contracts*. 4th edn. St Paul, Minn, West.

5

The Basic Stuff of Private Law

Nick Sage

I. Introduction

Here I first set out a view on which some of the main domains of private law—property, contract, and tort—are pervaded by a plurality of thickly characterized forms of relationship that are normatively basic. To see why the law might vindicate or disapprobate each relational form, we merely have to remind ourselves of the kind of relationship it is and situate it within its broader social context. I resist the temptation to look for an understanding of private law deeper or more unified than this.

Next I turn to the question Bernard Rudden famously posed, which motivates much of Henry Smith's work (together with Thomas Merrill). Why are some domains of private law more generous and flexible in recognizing relational forms? Roughly speaking, contract law seems most generous, property least, and tort law in between. My answer will in part deliberately vulgarize Smith's penetrating account of the structure of contract and property law. I link contract's expansiveness and property's restrictedness to an economic ideology, influential in our society, which esteems impersonal transacting and private decision-making about commerce and resource use. The economic ideology is largely agnostic as to the number of forms in tort. But tort is shaped by the common law's stance with respect to a certain politico-philosophical ideology, less influential in our society than in others, which might be labelled rationalism.

II. Private Law as a Law of Forms

Tort, property, and contract law are pervaded by a plurality of thickly characterized relational forms or 'transaction types' that are normatively basic. The forms are *pervasive*: they appear throughout these areas of private law and are

Nick Sage, *The Basic Stuff of Private Law* In: *The Property-Contract Interface*. Edited by: James Penner, Irina Sakharova, Henry E. Smith, and Zhong Xing Tan, Oxford University Press.
DOI: 10.1093/9780198951995.003.0007

indispensable to a full understanding. The forms are *basic*: they cannot be explained by a reductive appeal to other norms or values. Relatedly, the forms are best understood through '*thick*' characterizations: to understand why the law might valorize or disapprove of each, we should give a characterization that brings out the kind of thing that it is. It may also help to situate the form in the context of a certain sort of society—a society like ours. Finally, the forms are *plural*: there are at least a dozen and sometimes many more in each domain of private law. We cannot give a highly unified account of all the forms in any domain, let alone across private law as a whole. There is no essence of property, tort, or even contract, let alone a unified 'idea of private law'. However, the forms within each domain share family resemblances.

1. Tort

Bernard Rudden's best-known paper on tort law 'attempts something not, apparently, done before: an alphabetical list of known torts'.[1] The list has seventy main entries ranging from abduction, abuse of process, and assault, to trespass, unfair competition, and vexatious litigation. Rudden seeks to prompt reflection on why the common law persists with 'a pigeonhole system of nominate torts'.[2] Contrast the French Civil Code, which famously articulates more general principles, prima facie imposing liability for any damage caused deliberately or carelessly.[3]

A list of named wrongs along Rudden's lines could, if suitably developed, supply an adequate understanding of tort law. This suggestion runs against the grain of much modern legal scholarship. Some of the most ambitious academic common lawyers—for example Pollock in the nineteenth century and Winfield in the twentieth—have sought to discover general principles of liability.[4] More recently, legal theorists who have felt the impulse to generalize include economic analysts, who understand tort in terms of the costs and benefits of inflicting damage and taking precautions,[5] and Kantian theorists, who apply a stark conception of human agency to private law's interpersonal transactions.[6]

[1] Rudden 1992, 105.
[2] Ibid, 105.
[3] Ibid, 105–106.
[4] Ibid, 108.
[5] Calabresi 1970.
[6] Weinrib 1995.

The leading contemporary counterexample is Goldberg and Zipursky's 'civil recourse theory'. Those authors sometimes characterize tort law as a 'gallery of wrongs',[7] irreducible to a single pervading principle or set of principles. The authors provide thumbnail sketches of the various culprits in the gallery, designed to bring out why they attract the law's disapproval. They note it is wrong, for example,

> for one person to intentionally touch another's body in a manner that is harmful or offensive (battery), to act carelessly toward them so as to cause them physical injury (negligence), or to place a dangerously defective product in the stream of commerce so as to injure someone (products liability) . . . to invade physically another's land (trespass), to steal or intentionally destroy property (conversion), to temporarily deprive or carelessly damage or destroy property (trespass to chattels, negligence), and to create an unreasonable interference with another's use and enjoyment of her real property (nuisance).[8]

Yet most contemporary theorists of private law will find this understanding of tort wanting. These theorists tend to seek a *deeper* or more *unified* understanding. First, one might worry that a mere catalogue of wrongs is too superficial for a genuine understanding of tort—surely something deeper must be going on?[9] This worry might manifest in various ways. One might say that a catalogue of wrongs merely 'describes' the law without 'justifying' it; or that the list tells us 'what' the law is but not 'why' we have it; or is mere 'positive law' that does not identify the underlying 'reasons'.

This objection may be met by an approach hinted at, though not fully pursued or elaborated, by Goldberg and Zipursky. Rather than abandoning our focus on tort law's gallery of wrongs and pursuing deeper 'justificatory reasons' (etc), we should more 'thickly' characterize each wrong.[10] A 'thick' characterization is designed to bring out why each wrong might be a bad thing, intertwining a 'descriptive' and an 'evaluative' component. The characterization should be concrete, bringing out the particular wrongful conduct involved, yet also simple, ideally calling to mind the gist of the wrong in a word or short phrase (such as *cheating* or *slandering*) without distracting detail. Finally, to dispel any remaining mystery about why each wrong could be

[7] Goldberg & Zipursky 2010b, ch 3.
[8] Goldberg & Zipursky 2010a, 917, 937.
[9] Wittgenstein 1953 §§ 89, 91–92, 126–129, 435–436.
[10] Murdoch 1970, 22, 40–41; Williams 1985, 129.

worthy of legal disapproval, we can situate it in the broader context of our kind of society.[11]

Consider briefly three well-known torts: nuisance, negligence, and trespass. A nuisance, in everyday language, is an annoyance, and the tort paradigmatically occurs where someone seriously annoys their neighbour. So we might roughly characterize it as *unneighbourly annoyance*. We can intuitively recognize this might be a bad thing—it is unfortunate to have an unhealthy relationship with one's neighbour involving fairly egregious annoying on the part of one party and being annoyed on the part of the other. The misfortune might be especially frequent and afflicting in a society, like ours, where people live and work close to strangers who may make disruptive noises and other kinds of pollution. We need no deeper explanation or justification for the tort of nuisance to make sense. If someone asks why, say, a neighbour's continual egregious noise-making is wrongful, the answer might just elaborate the basic idea: 'because it is a nuisance'.[12] If our interlocutor remains puzzled, we might ask them to reflect further on unneighbourly annoyances they have experienced, or upon how our society might look if such annoyances were legally tolerated, etc.

Negligent, in everyday language, means careless, and the tort, or at least a paradigm case, occurs where someone carelessly or dangerously injures another in a serious way. So we might roughly characterize the wrong as *careless injury*. Again, a sensitive or thoughtful member of a society likes ours can grasp why careless injuries are wrongful. That is, a society in which powerful but dangerous vehicles and machines and other industrial processes and products mean that people often have the capacity to injure, and be injured by, each other in unintentional but foreseeable and grave ways.

Trespass is harder to capture, with its three species—to the person, chattels, and land—and uncertain number of sub-species—battery, false imprisonment, conversion, etc. Rehearsing these would produce a lengthy catalogue that would not illuminate the gist of trespass. Consider instead a few paradigm cases: touching another person in an unwanted way, taking their goods, or entering onto their land. With those in mind we might say a trespass is, roughly: an *occupation* of another's body or property. Everyone in our society has a body, and most enjoy some property, and would readily recognize the sense of injury that comes from having these occupied by uninvited others.

[11] Given the law's complexity, a simple characterization of each wrong will inevitably be contestable and even inaccurate in some respects.
[12] Williams 1981, 18.

Second, one might object that my proposed account of tort is insufficiently unified. Kantian tort theorists explicitly seek 'unifying' abstractions that 'pervade[]' the whole of the law.[13] Other theorists do not press such an extreme demand for unity but still seek an integrated account rather than a mere list, or 'hodgepodge', of various wrongs.[14] It would seem that my view, which does not identify any factor common to all of tort law's wrongs, cannot possibly meet the theoretical demand for unity.

Is there an antidote to the theoretical craving for a criterion (or set of criteria) that unifies the various tortious wrongs (and distinguishes them from other wrongs)? Consider Wittgenstein's model of 'family resemblances'. '[T]he various resemblances between members of a family—build, features, colour of eyes, gait, temperament, and so on and so forth—overlap and criss-cross' in various ways.[15] There need be no common trait that appears in all members of a family (and distinguishes them from non-members). Still, we can give an account of a family's traits by proceeding from member to member, seriatim and by analogy, pointing out what each has in common with some of their kin. Similarly, we might consider each tort in turn, seeking to show what each has in common with some others though no single feature pervades all. We might begin, for example, by noticing that unneighbourly annoyances share much in common with occupations of land. (Indeed, they are sometimes difficult to distinguish, as when a sagging fence or significant debris regularly crosses the boundary line between two properties.) Both nuisances and trespasses to land tend to prevent people controlling and using their real estate; they tend to diminish the land's value—economic, aesthetic, or other; and so on and so forth.

2. Real Property

In his best-known property paper Bernard Rudden tells us that, '[i]n all "non-feudal" systems with which I am familiar . . . there are less than a dozen sorts of property entitlement' over land.[16] Rudden's list begins with the broadest entitlements to possess land and exclude others—full *ownership* ('fee'), the *life estate*, and the *lease* or landlord–tenant relationship; next come the servitudes, which allow or restrict the use of land another owns—for example *easements*, *profits*, *covenants* running with the land; finally security interests over

[13] Weinrib 1995, 29, 87.
[14] Goldberg and Zipursky 2010b, 936.
[15] Wittgenstein 1953, § 67; see too §§ 65–72, 75–80, 83–88.
[16] Rudden 1987, 241.

land—for example *mortgages* and *charges*. Merrill and Smith supplement the list with various concurrent interests—such as tenancies in common and joint tenancies, marital property; trusts; condos, co-ops, and time-shares.[17]

Rudden's list could, if suitably developed, supply an adequate account of the law of real property. Again this suggestion runs counter to a prominent strand in property theory. Contemporary Kantian theorists, to take perhaps the clearest example, expound very general, abstract accounts of the idea of property conceived as an individual's exercise of exclusive control over things.[18] Similar lines of argument appear in accounts from Blackstone through to James Penner[19] and Merrill and Smith.[20] The latter scholars are reacting against the extremely disaggregative and particularistic 'bundle of rights' theory of property, which holds that each so-called property right is in fact a complex manifold of Hohfeldian jural relations (claim-rights, liberties, powers, and their correlatives) concerning an enormous variety of specific potential actions and omissions, holding against often very numerous sets of persons who owe the correlative duties (etc).[21] My proposed view is far less general and integrated than property-as-exclusive-control theories, but also resists the bundle-of-rights disaggregation. We should focus on the plurality of property forms of the kind Rudden lists—ownership, easement, mortgage, co-op, etc—without decomposing them into Hohfeldian jural bundles. Indeed, we should keep our eye on the surface of each property form and not attempt to go behind it with any sort of analysis.

This approach is hinted at, though not fully elaborated, by Joseph William Singer.[22] Rejecting property theories based on the right to exclude, while also resisting analytical decomposition, Singer proposes a 'social relations model'.[23] Property is a 'system of entitlements that shape'—and are shaped by—'the contours of social relationships'.[24]

> Typical situations include relations between landlords and tenants, mortgagors and mortgagees, homeowners and lien holders, servitude or easement owners and servient estates, present and future estate owners, parents and children, husbands and wives, testators and heirs, homeowners associations

[17] Merrill & Smith 2000, 15.
[18] Weinrib (2003).
[19] Penner 1997.
[20] Merrill & Smith 2001.
[21] Especially Penner 1996.
[22] Dagan 2021 stresses the plurality of property forms but ultimately rests his account on a conception of autonomy.
[23] Singer 1996, 1461.
[24] Ibid.

> and unit owners, shareholders and managers, trustees of charitable foundations and their beneficiaries, . . . creditors and debtors, . . . bailors and bailees.[25]

Many legal theorists will find this kind of catalogue of property relationships wanting. First, it appears to lack intellectual depth. A desire for depth surely helps motivate, for instance, Kantian theories of property—which try to deduce the possibility of exclusively controlling things from abstract propositions about human agency and interpersonal freedom. Arguably it also motivates Penner, who seeks to link property to a 'fundamental human interest' which supplies 'the basic operative reasons for action recognised by the law': the interest in 'exclusively determining the use of things'.[26]

But an adequate understanding of real property might just consider each of the recognized forms in turn and give it a 'thick' characterization in its social context. Consider a few prominent forms—the lease, easement, and full ownership—and some rather obvious things one might say. A *lease* is a relationship between a landlord and tenant, in which the landlord remains the ultimate controller of the property but gives the tenant temporary enjoyment of it. (To the exclusion of everyone else and even the landlord herself—with limited exceptions.) The tenant must pay rent and take care of the property and the landlord maintain it in a good and fit condition. Other obligations may concern, for example, removing or altering things on the property, and ending the lease.[27] Many of these obligations address (and some may perpetuate) frequent power imbalances between landlord and tenant that create a potential for tyrannical behaviour. Despite that potential, the landlord–tenant relationship might be valuable—at least in a society like ours, where virtually all land is owned, but some own more than they can use themselves while others cannot afford (or do not want) to own it but nevertheless seek a relatively stable location to cook, eat, and sleep, work, run a business in, etc.

An *easement* allows one person to use or enjoy land owned by another. (Either by doing something on that land (eg walking over it) or by preventing the owner from doing something (eg building so substantially as to block sunlight).)[28] Classically the easement connects two landholders and their land, the restricted 'servient tenement' and the benefiting 'dominant tenement', though sometimes the dominant party may not own any land at all (eg an electric utility). Why is the easement a valuable relational form in a society such as

[25] Ibid, 1456 (more controversial examples pruned).
[26] Penner 1997, 49.
[27] Merrill & Smith 2001, 820–833.
[28] Merrill & Smith 2000, 16.

ours? Well, people often want to use or prevent the use of land that others own in a limited way, rather than fully controlling it. Such rights may aid the enjoyment or value of connected ('appurtenant') land—for example property which would otherwise be landlocked, too dark, etc.

Finally consider full *ownership* of land, as exemplified by the fee simple absolute or 'free-hold'. This form, as scholars from Blackstone have observed, comes closer than any other to the lay idea of 'property'.

> When most people think of property, they have an image in their minds of an individual owning a plot of land with a house on it. The land has clear borders, and no doubt exists about who the owner is. Only one person is involved. Others enter the picture only if the owner invites them in or voluntarily transfers some of his rights to them.[29]

The holder of the fee simple has unconditioned exclusive possession of the land for an unlimited time, and can transfer it to others of their choosing or pass it to their heirs when they die. How could all this be a good thing? Penner no doubt comes close to the truth when he identifies an interest in 'exclusively determining the use of things'. I doubt this is a 'fundamental human' interest—something all humans might want or benefit from irrespective of the kind of society in which they live. But in our highly individualistic society,[30] it is unsurprising that individuals might seek legally secured and recognized control of real estate to the exclusion of all others, engendering a certain sense of security, predictability, power, and associated opportunities for enjoyment and profit and privacy.[31] Many of us aspire to lord it over houses and other buildings and grounds, perhaps with something like Singer's lay image of property in mind.

Still, some theorists will remain unimpressed by my account of real property for a second reason: it appears too disunified. As we have seen, theorists such as Penner oppose the extreme disaggregation threatened by the 'bundle of rights' picture of property. Penner responds by proposing a paradigmatic 'idea of property' and associated fundamental human interest in exclusively determining things. In my view, while this idea of property and associated

[29] Singer 1996, 1462; also 1459.
[30] MacFarlane 1978.
[31] Penner 1996, 787.

human interest do illuminate the most culturally prominent property form—the fee simple absolute—it is less obvious that other property relationships are similarly illuminated—for example servitudes, mortgages, and other security interests, and concurrent interests such as joint tenancy.

Since Penner is fully aware that his paradigm does not easily fit all property law, he appeals to 'family resemblance'. We may want to use a concept such as 'property', Penner observes, even if we cannot define it by specifying necessary and sufficient conditions.[32] Sometimes we can only identify various sets of criteria for a concept's application, with different instances satisfying slightly different sets.[33] The criteria may be defeasible: 'Criteria *x*, *y*, and *z* may serve to support the application of an expression in one circumstance, but not in others'.[34] Perhaps 'a complete set of criteria . . . normally indicates the ownership of a fee simple, but the imposition of various duties following, say, its historical listing, . . . render absent the consequences of having that "property right" '.[35] Penner notes that seeing family resemblances often involves a sort of 'negative recognitional ability (recognizing when a term does *not* apply)' rather than a positive ability to list all the criteria for a concept's application.[36] 'In the case of property, the "items" which show this family resemblance are the various normative situations, or legal relations, to which property "applies".'[37]

I endorse Penner's appeal to family resemblance but would take it a step further, and abandon the search for any unifying idea or paradigm of (real) property. In my view, 'the most we can do to determine that something does or does not fall under the concept [real property] is to assess its likeness to other kinds of [real] property'.[38] There is no overall 'index of relevance to features of comparison'; each relationship must be considered on its own terms in connection with another particular relationship or relationships.[39] We need not regard the exclusive determination of things as a constant theme running across this legal domain. We can, if we like, define real property as a set of legal relationships that closely concern land—but the vagueness of this betrays the fact that it is only a label for a set of family resemblances.

[32] Ibid, 769.
[33] Ibid, 780.
[34] Ibid, 781.
[35] Ibid, 787.
[36] Ibid, 789.
[37] Ibid, 788; also 799
[38] Ibid, 773.
[39] Ibid, 773.

3. Contract

Throughout his famous tort and property papers Bernard Rudden gestures towards a certain picture of contract, which appears for him mainly as a general-purpose facility that allows parties to create idiosyncratic or fanciful transactional forms:

> as a matter of contract, the seller may seek to impose any number of fancy obligations. [T]here is no numerus clausus of contract. On the contrary, freedom of contract means that so long as we stay licit we can have any contractual figure custom-built, not to say boiler-plated.[40]

Only briefly does Rudden concede that nominate categories of transaction play an important role in the common law:

> It is true, of course, that there are the great contractual figures and that they have names: sales, hire, loan, partnership, and the like.[41]

My proposed view of contract law begins with these particular nominate forms. Contrast most contemporary contract theory from Charles Fried onwards. Influential theorists have tended to invoke quite general concepts that they claim illuminate the whole or most of contract law: promise, reliance, transfer, autonomy, economic efficiency, and so on. But some contract scholarship has highlighted the so-called contract 'types'. Roscoe Pound, reacting against nineteenth-century will theories, argued that the common law consists fundamentally of a series of particular relations:[42]

> [O]ur private law is the field where the idea of relation is most conspicuous as a staple juristic conception. . . . We say law of landlord and tenant, not of the contract of letting. We say master and servant, not *locatio operarum*. . . . We say principal and agent, not contract of mandate, principal and surety, not contract of suretyship; vendor and purchaser, not contract of the sale of land. We think and speak of the partnership relation and of the agency, liabilities, claims and duties which it involves—which give effect to it as a relation of good faith—not as a contract of *societas*. We think of the claims and

[40] Rudden 1987, 256.
[41] Rudden 1992, 126.
[42] Pound 1923, 57–58.

> duties involved in a fiduciary relation and of the legal incidents that give effect to trusteeship or executorship as a relation of good faith . . . We do not ask what are the logical deductions from the will of the parties involved in a sale of land.

This line of thought influenced the great realist contract lawyer Karl Llewellyn, who stressed the importance of particular 'transaction types' over general contract law.[43] Others followed suit in the twentieth century.[44] More recently, Hanoch Dagan and Michael Heller seek to reorient law teaching and theorizing around the thought that we have a law of *contracts* rather than *contract*.[45]

Similarly, I maintain that to understand contract law we may begin with relations such as that between a seller and purchaser of goods, a pledgor and pledgee, an insurer and insured, or a master and servant (employer/employee). These are important and generally valuable forms of human activity the law may seek to vindicate. To say why they are important and potentially valuable we can give a thick characterization of each contract type situated in social context.

Goods—roughly, things you can touch and carry off as they are not fixed to land—are hugely important in a mercantile and consumer society like ours, and have been for a long time. Most of us spend much of our lives using or trying to acquire them; many earn their livelihoods producing or trading them. In our society money is also very important, as a nigh-universal medium of exchange with which one can acquire almost anything. Consequently, one person often wants to receive goods from another person, who is willing to provide them in return for money. Unsurprisingly, then, the law will uphold 'a contract by which the seller transfers or agrees to transfer the property in goods to the buyer for a money consideration, called the price'—a sale of goods.[46]

In a pledge, one person takes possession of a good belonging to another so that the first can have recourse to the good as security (eg by selling it and keeping the money) if they do not receive some other satisfaction that is due, such as repayment of a loan. The importance and value of this transaction are obvious once we connect it to familiar facts of social life in a credit and investment based economy like ours. People sometimes want to loan money to others, especially in order to profit by receiving interest. But it is not always

[43] Llewellyn 1931, 705–706, 710.
[44] Kessler 1943, 629–630.
[45] Dagan & Heller 2017. Though they maintain contract law's 'ultimate value' is individual autonomy.
[46] Sale of Goods Act 1979 (UK), s 2(1).

easy to gauge others' creditworthiness or trustworthiness. One can often have relative confidence in the value of a good and ability to sell it to realize that value.[47]

Finally consider insurance. No less an authority than Blackstone, in the course of distinguishing marine insurance from mere wagering, notes insurance is a valuable commercial enterprise because it allows 'adventurers' to spread potentially catastrophic losses across a group rather than bearing their losses individually. At least in Blackstone's day, the law sought clearly to distinguish legitimate insurance from mere gambling or speculation. For instance, one could not insure a merchant ship in which one had no ownership or other similar interest, nor over-insure one's interest (only indemnify losses). Insurance could therefore be seen, not as mere gambling or betting on risk, but as a useful method of managing risk—an obviously valuable commercial enterprise. Insurance, as Blackstone puts it, has clear 'advantage to commerce'.[48]

In this manner we might understand our contract law by bringing out the significance of each transaction type, reminding ourselves of its character and the context of our broader ways of life, noting the judgements of value the type instantiates and the social practices in which it plays a part. Still, we must confront one key fact about contract that impresses Rudden and many other theorists—and which seems to distinguish contract from tort and property. Although contract law includes many nominate forms,

> common lawyers are quite happy to reason within the 'general part' of the law of contract and, indeed, are much less likely than the civil lawyer to make use of its nominate categories.[49]

The 'general part' roughly coincides with the coverage of first year contract courses. Rules of offer and acceptance ensure mutual assent. The infamous doctrine of consideration requires the parties to cast their transaction in the form of a quid pro quo bargain or exchange. Rules of incorporation, interpretation, and implication determine what terms are included in contracts. 'Vitiating' doctrines such as misrepresentation, duress, and unconscionability ensure that exchanges are procedurally and perhaps to some extent substantively fair. Doctrines such as illegality and the rule against penalties proscribe certain exchanges as unworthy of legal vindication. We might very roughly

[47] Of course pledges may be exploitative or otherwise objectionable.
[48] Blackstone 1979, 461. Quoted in O'Malley 2003, 238.
[49] Rudden 1992, 126.

sum up the effect of these doctrines as follows: they require an exchange that is voluntary and falls within certain broad ethical bounds.

Contract law's general part, which abstracts from particular transaction types, means parties can—within broad bounds—enter whatever exchanges they like. They may create idiosyncratic 'fancies', modifying old transaction types or creating new ones. Impressed with this potential for 'free customisation'[50] of the contractual relation we may even say it is 'infinite'.[51]

Yet we should not over-emphasize the abstraction and generality of contract law. An enormous amount of the law in practice is oriented around particular transaction types. A rough list of fifty types should give a flavour of their importance and pervasiveness: arbitration, apprenticeship, auction, banking, bill of exchange, carriage (by road, rail, sea, or air), charterparty, construction, consumer credit, consumer sale, derivative, distribution, doctor-patient, employment, franchise, gambling, hire-purchase, insurance (life, property, marine), joint venture, letter of credit, loan, long term supply, merger/acquisition, public procurement, restraint of trade, sale of goods, sale of land, salvage, schooling, settlement, solicitor–client, supply of service, suretyship, surrogacy, telecommunications, tender, and website terms.

Moreover, the content of virtually all contracts is heavily structured by industrial customs and compromises concerning how various types of exchange are and ought to be carried out. Legislation crystallizes commercio-legal practices or creates new ones. So does official or semi-official industry convention, as established by business groups, NGOs, or governments. The common law is an enormous, evolving repository of the norms of contract types. Finally, much contractual content arises through boilerplate: even where no official industry form exists, customary industrial norms enter contracts through lawyers' and businesspersons' use of 'precedent' transactions, so that a clause initially drafted for one contract may appear in almost all subsequent deals of the same type. A truly bespoke contract not heavily based on some existing customary type or transactional form must be rare indeed.

Still, it is true that systems of contract law—at least in relatively sophisticated commercial societies—tend to feel practical and intellectual pressure to go beyond a mere list of various important substantive relations—sales, leases, employments, pledges, etc—and articulate a more general approach. The common law notoriously decided that simple contracts must partake of a quite

[50] Merrill & Smith 2001, 776.
[51] Merrill & Smith 2000, 1, 5.

general transactional form: *exchange*.[52] This is a not wholly unconvincing way of capturing what certain core forms of contractual relationship—such as sales, leases, employments, pledges, and others—have in common. And the decision to orient the law of contract around exchange should not be wholly surprising given the character of the society that made it: a burgeoning mercantile civilization, in which exchange was widespread and hugely important.

The exchange criterion begets many complexities and difficulties. Consideration doctrine is regularly subjected to calls for abolition, riddled with exceptions, and undermined by legal sleight of hand. Some types of recognized contractual transaction are arguably not true exchanges because there is no clear quid pro quo. (Eg letters of credit, bills of exchange, suretyship arrangements, and (in the United States) firm offers.) Thus, the law of contract admittedly extends beyond exchange in the strict sense to reach transactions that resemble exchange and which tend to have a significant commercial aspect. Put another way, various types of transaction and relationship sit at contract's borderlines. I will not police the borderlines. The theoretical temptation to do so should dissipate if—as PS Atiyah recommended—we view 'contract' as a family resemblance concept.

> [W]e should not think of contract law as 'about' *one* central paradigmatic type of conduct, but about clusters of typical *situations*. So we are looking for situations rather than simple transactions. There are *families* of situations, related to each other, much as there are 'family' resemblances among games, in Wittgenstein's famous example.[53]

III. The Number of Forms

As we have seen, real property law recognizes a relatively limited number of forms: about a dozen by Rudden's count. Tort law has more: at least seventy. Contract law approximates or perhaps even surpasses tort with respect to the number of particular forms, but also confers a general freedom to customise existing forms or even invent new ones. Why the different approaches?

My answer to a large extent tracks Henry Smith's account of the structure of contract and property law, but is both more sceptical and more simple-minded.

[52] In his striking treatment Lewinsohn 2020 conceives it as reciprocal 'payment', whereby what each side provides is regarded as *satisfying the debt* incurred by what the other provides.
[53] Atiyah 1986, 5.

Smith's account presents as straight economic analysis: he considers the 'characteristic costs and benefits'—especially 'information costs'—of various 'functional' 'strategies' for controlling resources, and assumes that the law will 'tend towards cost effective use of each strategy' over time.[54] Smith believes the law approximates an optimal design scheme embodying a cost-benefit analysis. I will not claim that the common law is economically rational in that sense. I will merely claim it instantiates a certain economic ideology or mercantile ethic—an ideology endorsed by lawyers of past ages who never carried out complex cost-benefit analyses in the manner of contemporary economic analysts.

Contract law's recognition of manifold forms of commercial exchange, and broad freedom to modify the terms of exchanges, will seem desirable if one endorses an economic ideology that prizes impersonal, private decision-making about commerce. Real property law is in a way the opposite of contract: it tightly constrains the recognized legal forms allows no general freedom to modify or innovate. Still, this constraint is motivated by essentially the same economic ideology that undergirds contract: the perceived need to assist, in an impersonal mass society, largely unconstrained individual decision-making about productive land use. To bring out these points I draw upon the leading case of *Keppell v Bailey* (1834).[55] Between property and contract, in terms of expansiveness and flexibility, lies tort. Here the economic ideology does not produce the same contractionary pressure as in real property law, nor the same expansionary pressure as in contract. Pressure to formulate general principles of tort law could arise from a different source: the politico-philosophical ideology, sometimes called rationalism, that animates civilian tort codes such as France's. But that ideology rarely tempts common lawyers.

1. Contract

'It is easy to see', Bernard Rudden says, 'why [a general law of] contract develops once the market becomes an important institution'.[56] I find this not entirely easy. Does Rudden mean mass, public markets, such as modern markets for consumer goods or widely traded commodities, or would he include the medieval town fair, or even more rudimentary forms? Does not the arrival of

[54] Merrill & Smith 2001, 789–790.
[55] 2 My & K 517; 39 ER 1042.
[56] Rudden 1987, 254.

certain kinds of market, at least, presuppose a fairly well-developed law of contract?[57] The development of contract law and markets should at least go hand in hand. Perhaps that is what Rudden had in mind.

I find it easier to see that the common law's facility of contracting—which tolerates an enormous proliferation of particular transaction-types, and grants a quite general power to craft novel terms for exchanges—makes sense if one endorses a certain economic worldview with two major features. First, a generalized legal facility of enforceable exchange will seem especially valuable if one prizes *impersonal* commercial transacting. That is, commerce between strangers, or at least, between persons who are not assured of contractual performance by relationships of trust, reputational sanctions, or other social or normative bonds (eg the emotional ties of a family or the rules of a guild). The motivation will be stronger still if one seeks to facilitate commercial transactions with significant intertemporal aspects (eg payment now, delivery next month) where assurances of performance may be important. In an impersonal society it will make sense for the law to step in to supply the needed reassurance.

Second, an expansive and flexible contract law will seem desirable if one valorizes private decision-making and innovation in matters of commerce. It will allow private citizens to make whatever commercial decisions they want (within broad bounds) so long as they mutually assent to an exchange.[58] The private citizens making the decisions may be individuals or pairs of individuals, or corporations, trade, and lobby groups and so forth that create standardized contractual forms for themselves or their industries.

To be sure, the recognition of a broad freedom of contract comes with negative consequences. However, one can be largely blind to or unconcerned about these downsides, if one hews to the economic ideology I am sketching and assumes a fairly simplistic conception of contract. One might even be tempted to say:

> There can be no harm in allowing the fullest latitude to men in binding themselves and their representatives . . . to answer in damages for breach of their obligations. This tends to no mischief, and is a reasonable liberty to bestow . . .

Those are the words, in *Keppell v Bailey*,[59] of the Lord Chancellor Lord Brougham—the committed free trader who helped found the *Edinburgh*

[57] See further Oman 2016.
[58] Whether the same freedom should extend to gift promises is a difficult question.
[59] *Keppell v Bailey*, 1049 (emphasis added).

Review and wrote extensively for it 'on the new political economy', opposed the Corn Laws, and helped Ricardo get into parliament.[60] To be fair, Brougham was not reflecting generally on the impact of extensive freedom of contract on the conditions of nineteenth-century England, but comparing the jural schemes of contract and real property law. Brougham thinks there is no harm in recognizing new contractual forms because contracts are self-imposed by parties through their mutual assent and do not directly affect third parties. In contract, as he puts it, 'men . . . bind[] themselves'. Relatedly, contracts, unlike real property rights, are (in Rudden's phrase) 'born to die':[61] they bind persons (and sometimes their legal 'representatives', eg executors) rather than attaching to physical resources potentially for long periods of time, thereby constraining future choices about resource use.

The reality of contract law, especially today, is of course more complex than this ideological picture assumes. For one thing, contracts may have third-party effects. They may create rights in third parties under exceptions to the privity rule. Contractual rights are frequently assigned, and duties delegated, to third parties. Third parties may be liable for interfering with contractual performance, for instance through the tort of inducing breach of contract. Furthermore, a proliferation of idiosyncratic contractual 'fancies' can in fact impede easy transacting, pricing, and assignment. (Hence the proliferation of groups that seek to standardize contracting for their industry—see eg Lloyd's of London, the Baltic Exchange, the International Swaps and Derivatives Association.) However, these and other problems created by freedom of contract may seem relatively minor, readily resolvable by other means, or regrettable but inevitable, to someone who favours private commercial decision-making about commerce and has an abstract picture of contract as instantiating that ideal.

2. Real Property

Keppell v Bailey is a case study in the industrial revolution's impact on the valleys of Wales.[62] Legislation in the 1790s provided for a canal linking inland industry to a port. Owners of nearby mines and quarries were given the power to build auxiliary railways, and to charge 2.5p per ton per mile for carriage of iron ore and limestone. Three local ironworks decided to build an auxiliary railway

[60] Atiyah 1979, 373.
[61] Merrill & Smith 2000, 259.
[62] See further McFarlane 2013.

linking their businesses to a particular limestone quarry. Together with other investors, the ironwork owners executed an indenture, which provided for a carriage rate of 5p per ton per mile, and they purported to bind their successors and assigns to use the railway at that rate. Subsequently, one of the ironworks was sold—to a purchaser who received notice of the indenture. Nonetheless, in 1833 the new owner began to build a new railway in order to link up with a different source of limestone. The other parties to the indenture sued for an injunction.

Lord Brougham LC first considers, and rejects, the argument that the covenant in the indenture is 'repugnan[t] to the rules respecting perpetuity'.[63] He also considers and rejects the argument that the covenant amounts to an unlawful restraint of trade.[64] However, he accepts that the covenant, by purporting to lock the parties into a higher rate of carriage, is 'wholly contrary to the plain intention of the Legislature' in enacting its industrial scheme, 'and in fraud, if not in defiance of it'.[65] Only then, in extensive *obiter dicta*, does the judge consider whether parties can create idiosyncratic covenants that run with the land, and more generally, create whatever 'fancies' they choose as a matter of real property law. Here is the crucial passage of Lord Brougham's reasoning—the first part of which we have already encountered:

> There can be no harm in allowing the fullest latitude to men in binding themselves and their representatives . . . to answer in damages for breach of their obligations. This tends to no mischief, and is a reasonable liberty to bestow; but great detriment and much confusion of rights would arise if parties were allowed to invent new modes of holding and enjoying real property, and to impress upon their lands and tenements a peculiar character, which should follow them into all hands, however remote. Every close, every messuage, might thus be held in a several fashion; and it would hardly be possible to know what rights the acquisition of any parcel conferred, or what obligations it imposed. The right of way or of common is of a public as well as of a simple nature, and no one who sees the premises can be ignorant of what all the vicinage knows. But if one man may bind his messuage and land to take lime from a particular kiln, another may bind his to take coals from a certain pit, while a third may load his property with further obligations to employ one blacksmith's forge, or the members of one corporate body, in various

[63] *Keppell v Bailey*, 1046.
[64] Ibid, 1046–1047.
[65] Ibid, 1048.

operations upon the premises, besides many other restraints as infinite in variety as the imagination can conceive . . . [66]

Lord Brougham then discusses many real or imagined burdens that might be placed on real property—for example to run a blacksmith's shop, to keep a school, to grind all one's corn in a nearby mill, or even to sing in a chapel of the manor.[67] In essence, the judge is worried about the prospect of England and Wales becoming a sort of crazy-quilt of restricted land usages. (Much as tort lawyers often worry about 'unlimited' or 'indeterminate' liability, Lord Brougham fears an unlimited and indeterminate burdening of real property.)

This reasoning seems to betray two key presuppositions about the functions of property law. Together these constitute essentially the same economic ideology we have already encountered in connection with contract. First, as Henry Smith observes, the reasoning presupposes that *impersonal* transacting with respect to real property should be tolerated or even encouraged.[68] Smith invites us to imagine a small, close-knit community, with effective norms governing the community's resource use. These norms might be elaborate and particularistic. (Eg the fruit of this particular tree can be harvested only at night, after the full moon, by married couples, etc.) Even so the norms might be well specified and fairly knowable by all members of the community (eg as a matter of village lore). If a member of this community sought to purchase land, they could fairly easily discover all the relevant restrictions and indeed might be highly motivated to comply with them out of respect for, or fear of, their fellows. Contrast a large, impersonal society, in which people often interact and share or dispute the use of resources with strangers, who may have come from far away and so have little familiarity with local geography and custom. In these circumstances, a purchaser of land may well be, in Lord Brougham's words, 'ignorant of what all the vicinage knows', and it will 'hardly be possible to know what rights the acquisition of any parcel confer[s], or what obligations it impose[s]'.

Other things being equal, then, a society of regular impersonal land transactions may desire a relatively simple and invariant specification of property norms. Then, everyone in the society can be familiar, at least in the abstract, with the norms and act accordingly. There will be an impulse towards the regularization of real property—to make land a more standardized commodity.[69]

[66] Ibid, 1049.
[67] Ibid, 1050–1051.
[68] Merrill & Smith 2001, 793–797.
[69] Marx 1976, 616.

The concern to enable impersonal transactors to discover restrictions on property could admittedly be met, to some extent, by other means. A sophisticated system of land registration might record all restrictions. However, a common law judge could hardly invent such a system afresh. More pertinently to the decision in *Keppell v Bailey*, the publicity problem could to some extent be met by a rule requiring notice to would-be purchasers and perhaps others who interact with property.[70]

It seems reasonable then to believe that Lord Brougham—the avid political economist—was influenced by a second presupposition about the legal regulation of land use. Namely, that land use should insofar as possible be subject to *individual economic decision-making* by those persons who control the land and who would normally seek to apply it to its most desirable or productive use. The owner of a 'messuage' who operates a metalworks, foundry, farm, or other business, should not have substantive restrictions placed on their operations. They should not be bound to obtain their inputs from, or send their outputs to, other particular locations or 'corporate bodies', perhaps at undesirable rates. Let alone bound to maintain a blacksmith's forge, a school, or a choir. Proprietors should freely decide the uses to which they put their land.[71] (And if an owner chooses to burden their land in some particular way they can always do so for the duration of their holding or lifetime—but not beyond, and not so as to burden third parties directly—by contract.) This concern to facilitate individual economic decision-making also arguably animates the areas of the law Lord Brougham discusses at the outset of his judgment: the rules against perpetuities in property law, and against contractual restraints of trade, which arguably safeguard individual choice in matters of property usage and trade.

In sum, both the general freedom of parties to craft their own enforceable exchanges, and the turning of property into a standardized commodity with relatively few substantive restrictions on use, seem well-designed to serve the needs of a mass or impersonal, privately innovative, society oriented towards commerce and production.

[70] McFarlane 2013, 20; but see Merrill & Smith 2000, 43–45: significant information processing costs would still arise here.

[71] Cf the privileging, by property law theorists from Blackstone to Penner and Smith, of the fee simple absolute and the notion of exclusive control of land and other things.

3. Tort

Can the approach developed so far illuminate tort—which (unlike property) lets forms proliferate, but (unlike contract) contains few truly general principles? I suggest that our economic ideology provides a sort of negative explanation, because it pressures tort law towards neither a more restrictive set of forms nor more expansive generalizations.

Perhaps surprisingly, given Bernard Rudden's frequent comparisons of the different domains of private law, when reflecting on the number of tortious forms he does not mention one obvious feature of tort law. Private individuals do not deliberately create torts in the way that contracting parties invent new 'fancies' through their mutual assent to exchange, and property owners threaten to invent fancies ('as infinite in variety as the imagination may conceive') when choosing how to dispose of their land. A tortfeasor generally has no ambition to create, nor a tort victim to suffer, a novel or idiosyncratic form of wrongdoing. When a tort case comes before a court, it is likely that only one party will seek recognition of the new form, while the other strongly resists. Consequently, there is not the same compulsion to recognize new forms in order to satisfy the wishes of individuals ingeniously attempting to exercise decision-making powers about commerce or resource use.[72] Hence it is unsurprising that tort law does not need to set limits on private ingenuity by imposing a *numerus clausus* principle as in property law.

At the same time, tort law does not face the same expansionary pressure as contract. The desire to aid impersonal economic activity and private decision-making does not tell in favour of generalized tort principles. There is no business case, as it were, for a general form of tort liability, in contrast to the case for general principles of contractual exchange. (Which is not to deny that business interests may have shaped particular aspects of tort law, such as the triumph of negligence or fault-based standards over older forms of strict liability.)[73]

Rudden's perplexity about the common law of tort arises in part because of the contrast he draws with the civil law, and especially French law's very general tort provisions. This suggests another reason the common law persists with a 'pigeonhole system of nominate torts'. The impetus to generalize in France is bound up with the existence of a code—and with what John Merryman calls the 'ideology' of civilian codification.[74] Put roughly, the civilian codifier's

[72] Furthermore, tortious wrongs are generally not seen as economically productive or valuable—contrast commercial exchanges and the use of land.

[73] Horwitz 1977, 97–108.

[74] Merryman 1985, 26–27.

ideology is a certain form of enlightenment rationalism—an ideology epitomized by Newtonian physics, Kantian philosophy, and indeed the Napoleonic Code itself. This ideology puts great faith in our ability to understand and regulate the world through abstract or general principles, including principles of human conduct. It exalts a vision of a grand impersonal order of rules and norms.[75]

Common lawyers are less tempted by this form of rationalism, and indeed often react conservatively against it. Rudden gestures towards this when he suggests that the common law may maintain its 'pigeonhole' tort scheme because of a reverence for tradition, and because of 'the attraction to the common lawyer exerted by the precise and the particular'.[76] One might take a still broader view and link the common law mindset to one often attributed (at least in the past) to the English people generally:

> It is a commonplace that the characteristic virtue of Englishmen is their power of sustained practical activity, and their characteristic vice a reluctance to test that activity by reference to principles. They are incurious as to theory, take fundamentals for granted, and are more interested in the state of the roads than in their place on the map. . . . It leaves the mind free to focus on profitable activities, because it is not distracted by a taste for unprofitable speculations.[77]

As the reference to profitability suggests, one might even link this aspect of the English mindset to a broader bourgeois social ethic which esteems private economic decision-making and activity.

Relatedly, it seems significant that many common lawyers (as well as some French lawyers) view the *Code Civil*'s attempted generalizations as unsuccessful, obscuring a variety of complex and different forms of reasoning by channelling all sorts of diverse inquiries into an analysis of 'causation' and 'fault'. Rudden, though officially agnostic, makes his sympathies clear. He notes Carbonnier's observation that a system of concrete nominate torts might allow for more precision and engagement with social reality, and concludes with Carbonnier's 'verdict on the great mass of twentieth-century caselaw in this field: "an enormous waste of intelligence and time"'.[78]

75 Taylor 2007, 742–743.
76 Rudden 1992, 127.
77 Tawney 1921, 1.
78 Rudden 1992, 107, 129.

IV. Conclusion

Private law (or at least contract, real property, and tort) is a law of forms: a plurality of relationships and other types of transaction and interaction that the law regards as valuable or disvaluable. It is plausible that the legal system in a certain sort of society—roughly speaking, an advanced bourgeois commercial society like ours—might seek to uphold or disavow these forms. We need not pursue any deeper understanding of the law than this. Nor a more unified understanding: we may be satisfied with the view that private law recognizes, among other things, (i) various forms of exchange and other similar transactions of a largely commercial character; (ii) a variety of forms of relationship that bear on the control and use of land; and (iii) numerous interpersonal legal wrongs. The various forms in each domain do of course share significant family resemblances.

Why is each legal domain more or less generous with respect to the number of forms it is willing to recognize? To understand this it helps to look to the common law's ideology: the implicit views of judges about what sort of society we do and should live in. Here we can see the importance of a certain economic ideology, which esteems impersonal private decision-making about commerce and productivity; and the common law's resistance to a certain politico-philosophical ideology, rationalism.

References

Atiyah, P. S. (1986). *Essays on Contract.* Oxford, Clarendon Press.

Atiyah, P. S. (1979). *The Rise and Fall of Freedom of Contract.* Oxford, Clarendon Press.

Blackstone, W. (1765–69, 1979 facsimile edn). *Commentaries on the Laws of England.* Chicago, University of Chicago Press.

Calabresi, G. (1970). *The Costs of Accidents: A Legal and Economic Analysis.* New Haven, Yale University Press.

Dagan, H. (2021). *The Liberal Theory of Property.* Cambridge, Cambridge University Press.

Dagan, H. and M. Heller (2017). *The Choice Theory of Contracts.* Oxford, Oxford University Press.

Goldberg, J. C. P. and B. C. Zipursky (2010a). *Oxford Introductions to U.S. Law: Torts.* Oxford, Oxford University Press.

Goldberg, J. C. P. and B. C. Zipursky (2010b). 'Torts as Wrongs'. *Texas Law Review* 88: 917–981.

Horwitz, M. J. (1977). *The Transformation of American Law, 1780–1860.* Cambridge, Mass, Harvard University Press.

Kessler, F. (1943). 'Contracts of Adhesion—Some Thoughts About Freedom of Contract'. *Columbia Law Review* 43: 629–642.

Lewinsohn, J. (2020). 'Paid on Both Sides: Quid Pro Quo Exchange and the Doctrine of Consideration'. *Yale Law Journal* 129: 690–772.

Llewellyn, K. N. (1931). 'What Price Contract?—An Essay in Perspective'. *Yale Law Journal* 40: 704–751.

MacFarlane, A. (1978). *The Origins of English Individualism.* Oxford, Blackwell.

McFarlane, B. (2013). Keppell v Bailey (1834); Hill v Tupper (1863): The Numerus Clausus and the Common Law. *Landmark Cases in Land Law.* N. Gravells. Oxford, Hart: 1–32.

Marx, K. (1867, 1976 English edn). *Capital: A Critique of Political Economy.* Volume *I.* B. Fowkes, tr. London, Penguin Books.

Merrill, T. W. and H. E. Smith (2000). 'Optimal Standardization in the Law of Property: The Numerus Clausus Principle'. *Yale Law Journal* **110**: 1–70.

Merrill, T. W. and H. E. Smith (2001). 'The Property/Contract Interface'. *Columbia Law Review* 101: 773–852.

Merryman, J. H. (1985). *The Civil Law Tradition.* 2nd edn. Stanford, Stanford University Press.

Murdoch, I. (1970). *The Sovereignty of Good.* London, Routledge.

O'Malley, P. (2003). 'Moral Uncertainties: Contract Law and Distinctions between Speculation, Gambling, and Insurance'. *Risk and Morality.* R. V. Ericson and A. Doyle. Toronto, University of Toronto Press: 231–257.

Oman, N. (2016). *The Dignity of Commerce.* Chicago, University of Chicago Press.

Penner, J. E. (1996). 'The "Bundle of Rights" Picture of Property'. *UCLA Law Review* 43: 711–820.

Penner, J. E. (1997). *The Idea of Property in Law.* Oxford, Oxford University Press.

Pound, R. (1923). *Interpretations of Legal History.* Cambridge, Cambridge University Press.

Rudden, B. (1987). 'Economic Theory v. Property Law: The Numerus Clausus Problem'. *Oxford Essays in Jurisprudence: Third Series.* J. Eekelaar and J. Bell. Oxford, Clarendon Press: 239–263.

Rudden, B. (1992). 'Torticles'. *Tulane European and Civil Law Forum* 6/7: 105–130.

Singer, J. W. (1996). 'No Right to Exclude: Public Accommodations and Private Property'. *Northwestern University Law Review* 90: 1283–1465.

Tawney, R. H. (1921). *The Acquisitive Society.* New York, Harcourt, Brace and Howe.

Taylor, C. (2007). *A Secular Age.* Cambridge, Harvard University Press.

Weinrib, E. J. (1995). *The Idea of Private Law.* Cambridge Mass., Harvard University Press.

Weinrib, E. J. (2003). 'Poverty and Property in Kant's System of Rights'. *Notre Dame Law Review* 78: 795–828.

Williams, B. (1981). Persons, Character and Morality. *Moral Luck: Philosophical Papers 1973–1980.* Cambridge, Cambridge University Press: 1–19.

Williams, B. (1985). *Ethics and the Limits of Philosophy.* London, Fontana Press.

Wittgenstein, L. (1953). *Philosophical Investigations.* GEM Anscombe, trs. Oxford, Blackwell.

6

Restrictive Covenants

Robert Chambers[*]

I. Introduction

Restrictive covenants came to prominence in the famous 1848 case of *Tulk v Moxhay*.[1] Lord Cottenham LC held that a contract to maintain Leicester Square in its current condition was enforceable not just against the owner who made the contract but against a subsequent owner who purchased the square with notice of it. While Leicester Square is now much more famous than the contract that once protected it, the restrictive covenant holds a peculiar fascination for contract, property, and equity lawyers alike.

Contract lawyers regard the restrictive covenant as a remarkable exception to privity of contract in which contractual rights and obligations can be enforced by and against persons who are not parties to the contract. However, the restrictive covenant quickly evolved into a relationship that cannot be explained in terms of contract. While restrictive covenants are still created by consent, they do not require a valid contract.

For property lawyers, the restrictive covenant seems to be a remarkable departure from the principle against inventing new property rights to land, which was stated in *Keppell v Bailey*,[2] just 14 years before *Tulk v Moxhay*. That apparent inconsistency could be avoided so long as restrictive covenants were regarded merely as contracts, but it became necessary to confront it when they came to be recognized as property rights to land. Restrictive covenants provide additional evidence that the common law never adopted the civil law's *numerus clausus*, but always had a restrained willingness to admit new forms of property rights into the fold.

* I am grateful to James Penner for comments on the penultimate draft of this chapter.
[1] *Tulk v Moxhay* (1848) 2 Ph 774, 41 ER 1143, 1 H & Tw 105, 47 ER 1345.
[2] *Keppell v Bailey* (1834) 2 My & K 517, 39 ER 1042.

Robert Chambers, *Restrictive Covenants* In: *The Property-Contract Interface*. Edited by: James Penner, Irina Sakharova, Henry E. Smith, and Zhong Xing Tan, Oxford University Press. © Robert Chambers 2026.
DOI: 10.1093/9780198951995.003.0008

Finally, the restrictive covenant challenges basic conceptions of the nature of equitable property rights. We understand the trust as a relationship in which the trustee is required by equity to use their legal rights and powers in certain ways. This restriction on the trustee's liberty to use their rights and powers as they please can also be enforced against successors in title, unless they are entitled to a defence such as *bona fide* purchase for value without notice or indefeasible title. It is tempting to use the trust as the paradigm for all equitable property rights. However, restrictive covenants can be enforced against persons who are not successors in title but have acquired different estates in the land or perhaps no estate at all. This requires us to accept that equitable property rights function in several different ways.

II. Restrictive Covenants as Contracts

There is no doubt that the restrictive covenant began life as a contract. It was argued in *Tulk v Moxhay* that the covenant did not run with the land and that it would be contrary to *Keppell v Bailey* to allow people to invent new property rights that could bind successors in title. In *Keppell v Bailey*, the owners of three iron works created a company to construct a railroad and then made a contract with that company that they and their heirs, successors, and assigns would obtain all their limestone from one quarry and use the railroad to transport it. After one of the iron works was sold, the railroad company was unable to enforce the contract against the new owners. Lord Brougham LC said:

> Consider the question first upon principle. There are certain known incidents to property and its enjoyment; among others, certain burthens wherewith it may be affected, or rights which may be created and enjoyed over it by parties other than the owner; all which incidents are recognised by the law. . . . But it must not therefore be supposed that incidents of a novel kind can be devised and attached to property at the fancy or caprice of any owner. It is clearly inconvenient both to the science of the law and to the public weal that such a latitude should be given. There can be no harm in allowing the fullest latitude to men in binding themselves and their representatives, that is, their assets real and personal, to answer in damages for breach of their obligations. This tends to no mischief, and is a reasonable liberty to bestow; but great detriment would arise and much confusion of rights if parties were allowed to invent new modes of holding and enjoying real property, and to impress

> upon their lands and tenements a peculiar character, which should follow them into all hands, however remote.[3]

Lord Cottenham LC responded in *Tulk v Moxhay* to say that 'the question is, not whether the covenant runs with the land, but whether a party shall be permitted to use the land in a manner inconsistent with the contract entered into by his vendor, and with notice of which he purchased'.[4] In other words, the restrictive covenant was not an interest in land but merely a contract regarding the use of that land. A court of equity can enforce that contract against the original parties and would not be thwarted if the land was sold to someone who had notice of it. Privity of contract had to give way.

The idea that the restrictive covenant was a contract and not a property right did not last long. Development schemes are proof of that. They arise when a developer divides land into lots with the intention that each lot would be subject to a restrictive covenant for the benefit of every other lot. As lots are sold one by one, it can be difficult to ensure that the web of covenants is properly in place because the purchasers do not contract with each other. Chancery solved the problem by allowing purchasers to enforce covenants made by subsequent purchasers even though they are neither parties to the contract nor assignees of its benefits. As Parker J said in *Elliston v Reacher*:

> . . . all the various sales are by private treaty and at various intervals of time, the circumstances may, at the date of one or more of the sales, be such as to preclude the possibility of any actual contract. For example, a prior purchaser may be dead or incapable of contracting at the time of a subsequent purchase, and in any event it is unlikely that the prior and subsequent purchasers are ever brought into personal relationship, and yet the equity may exist between them.[5]

Some jurisdictions now have statutes that allow restrictive covenants to be created even though the lands benefitted and burdened by the covenant are owned by the same person. For example, Saskatchewan's Land Titles Act 2000 states:

[3] *Keppell v Bailey* (1834) 2 My & K 517 at 535–536, 39 ER 1042 at 1049.
[4] *Tulk v Moxhay* (1848) 2 Ph 774 at 777–778, 41 ER 1143 at 1144.
[5] *Elliston v Reacher* [1908] 2 Ch 374 at 385 (Parker J); affirmed [1908] 2 Ch 665 (CA).

> An owner of land may grant to himself or herself an easement or restrictive covenant for the benefit of land that he or she owns and against other land that he or she owns.[6]

These statutes do not change the fundamental nature of the restrictive covenant, but merely create a more efficient way to get a web of covenants in place: the developer can do it before any lots are sold.

Even without statutory intervention, it is possible for a restrictive covenant to exist when the benefitted and burdened lots are owned by the same person so long as they hold each lot in a different capacity. Normally, the common ownership of the lots causes the restrictive covenant to come to an end,[7] although that has been changed by statute in some jurisdictions.[8] This rule did not defeat the restrictive covenant in *University of East London Higher Education Corp v Barking and Dagenham London Borough Council*,[9] where a local authority owned the benefitted lands for the purpose of providing housing and owned the burdened lands for the purpose of providing education. Lightman J said:

> For restrictive covenants to be extinguished merely because fortuitously the same public body held for different statutory purposes the dominant and servient properties would be calculated to defeat the objects of the restrictive covenants for no good or sufficient reason.[10]

All of this goes to show that an enforceable contract is not required for the creation of a restrictive covenant or for its continued existence. While contracts are not required, it is true that all restrictive covenants are created by consent. Unlike many other property rights, such as constructive trusts, easements by prescription, easements of necessity, or equitable liens, restrictive covenants do not arise by operation of law or the rules of equity. If we adopt Peter Birks's fourfold classification of the sources of rights into the categories of consent, wrongs, unjust enrichment, and others,[11] restrictive covenants belong in the

[6] The Land Titles Act 2000, SS 2000, c L-5.1, s 147. Also see Land Titles Act, RSA 2000, c L-4, s 68; Property Law Act, RSBC 1996, c 377, s 18; Land Titles Act, RSNWT 1988, c 8, s 76; Land Registration Act, SNS 2001, c 6, s 61; Land Titles Act, 2015, SY 2015, c 10, s 113; Real Property Act 1900 (NSW), s 46A; Land Title Act 2000 (NT), s 109; Property Law Act 1974 (Qld), s 50; Transfer of Land Act 1893 (WA), s 136H.

[7] *Texaco Antilles Ltd v Kernochan* [1973] AC 609 at 626 (PC).

[8] Land Titles Act, RSA 2000, c L-4, s 68; Property Law Act, RSBC 1996, c 377, s 18; Land Titles Act, RSNWT 1988, c 8, s 76; Land Registration Act, SNS 2001, c 6, s 61; The Land Titles Act 2000, SS 2000, c L-5.1, s 147; Land Titles Act 2015, SY 2015, c 10, s 113; Land Title Act 2000 (NT), s 110.

[9] *University of East London Higher Education Corp v Barking and Dagenham LBC* [2005] Ch 354.

[10] Ibid, 354 at 374.

[11] Birks 1985, 53; Birks, 2005, 24.

category of consent whether they are created by contract or not. It is true that restrictions on the use of land are commonly created by statute, but we do not normally think of them as restrictive covenants.

III. Restrictive Covenants as Property

Restrictive covenants are now regarded as equitable interests in land. This is well established by cases dating back to the nineteenth century. The cases are too numerous to mention, but one stands out, like *Tulk v Moxhay*, because the subjects are far more interesting and famous than the law. *Rogers v Hosegood*[12] concerned a restrictive covenant created by the Duke of Bedford in 1869 to restrict the use of the land to one dwelling house per lot. The pre-Raphaelite painter Sir John Millais purchased a lot without knowledge of the restriction. The subsequent owners of that lot were able to enforce the covenant. Collins LJ said:

> These authorities establish the proposition that, when the benefit has been once clearly annexed to one piece of land, it passes by assignment of that land, and may be said to run with it, in contemplation as well of equity as of law, without proof of special bargain or representation on the assignment. In such a case it runs, not because the conscience of either party is affected, but because the purchaser has bought something which inhered in or was annexed to the land bought. This is the reason why, in dealing with the burden, the purchaser's conscience is not affected by notice of covenants which were part of the original bargain on the first sale, but were merely personal and collateral, while it is affected by notice of those which touch and concern the land. The covenant must be one that is capable of running with the land before the question of the purchaser's conscience and the equity affecting it can come into discussion.[13]

Restrictive covenants are interests in land because they restrict the use of land in a way that benefits nearby land. Easements (whether positive or negative) are similar: the use and enjoyment of the servient tenement is reduced in order to provide some benefit to the dominant tenement. *Keppell v Bailey* was different. The contract did not concern the use of the land on which the iron

[12] *Rogers v Hosegood* [1900] 2 Ch 388 (CA).
[13] Ibid, 388 at 407 (CA).

works were located, but attempted to bind future owners to a monopoly for the supply and delivery of limestone.

With very few exceptions, property rights to land, whether legal or equitable, concern the use of that land. A profit à prendre allows the rightholder to do something that would otherwise be a trespass by entering the land and taking away some part of its natural produce.[14] It relates directly to the possessor's right to exclude others. A restrictive covenant does not affect the right to possession, but limits the possessor's power to use that space as they please. An easement can do either of these things, depending on whether it is positive or negative. As Schroeder JA said in *Temma Realty Co Ltd v Ress Enterprises Ltd*:

> There is a sharp distinction between an affirmative easement such as a right of way and a negative easement such as a right to light or air. The former is one which entitles the dominant owner to make active use of the servient tenement, or to do some act which, in the absence of the easement, would be a nuisance or a trespass, whereas the latter is a right in the owner of the dominant tenement to restrict the owner of the servient tenement, in respect of the tenement, in the exercise of general and natural rights of property.[15]

A common law mortgage is a grant of a freehold or leasehold estate to the mortgagee to hold as security for payment of a debt, coupled with the power to sell that estate in the event of default. As Harman J said in *Four-Maids Ltd v Dudley Marshall (Properties) Ltd*, the 'mortgagee may go into possession before the ink is dry on the mortgage',[16] because they hold the estate. Mortgages under a land registration system operate differently, but they also include the right to possession or the power to obtain it.[17] These are rights to use the land.

The common law does recognize some interests in land that seem to be unconnected with its use. A rentcharge is different from rent service, which is due from a tenant to their landlord with respect to a leasehold estate (and usually called rent). The landlord entitled to rent service holds a reversionary estate in the land and clearly has an interest in its use. The holder of a rentcharge has no interest other than the receipt of payment. They do have a power to take possession if the rentcharge is in arrears.[18] Perhaps this remedy provides a sufficient connection to the use of the land, but it is tenuous.

[14] *R v Tener* [1985] 1 SCR 533 at 540–542.
[15] [1968] 2 OR 293, 69 DLR (2d) 195 at [28] (CA).
[16] *Four-Maids Ltd v Dudley Marshall (Properties) Ltd* [1957] Ch 317 at 320.
[17] See, eg, *Morguard Mortgage Investments Ltd v Faro Development Corp Ltd* [1975] 1 WWR 737, 50 DLR (3d) 426 at 433 (Alta CA).
[18] Law of Property Act 1925, s 121.

The liability for chancel repair seems to have even less connection to the use of land. It survives in England as an historical anomaly. At one time, the rector was entitled to tithes from the land in their parish, but this carried an associated liability to repair the chancel (the eastern half of the parish church). The right to tithes has gone, but the liability for chancel repair survives and can be enforced against the subsequent owners of former rectory lands.[19]

While there are some interests in land that bear little or no relation to the use of the land, they tend to be regarded as unusual and undesirable exceptions to the norm. The Rentcharges Act 1977 prohibited the creation of most new rentcharges and will extinguish most existing rentcharges by 2037.[20] In 1985, the Law Commission recommended the abolition of liability for chancel repairs,[21] and in 2003, Lord Nichols called it 'one of the more arcane and unsatisfactory areas of property law'.[22]

Keppell v Bailey should not be read as a prohibition on the creation of new types of interests in land at common law or in equity. It prohibits the attachment to land of obligations that are not connected to the use of land and therefore not capable of being interests in land. This also explains *Hill v Tupper*,[23] in which a leasehold covenant purported to give the tenant the exclusive right to put pleasure boats on the Basingstoke Canal and let them out for hire. A right to put boats on a canal can be a perfectly valid easement,[24] but the parties did not have the power to create a new type of monopoly. Monopolies are either granted by the Crown (like franchises) or enabled by acts of Parliament (like copyrights and patents).

In civil law jurisdictions, there is a *numerus clausus* (ie closed number) of different kinds of property rights less than ownership. As Paul Matthews said:

> . . . the principle is that in relation to any particular thing there should be a single person who has all the rights. The fragmentation (or dismemberment) of property into different estates or interests of different values, each belonging to a different person, so characteristic of property law in the common law world (and especially in relation to land) finds no place in this system. It is true that societal necessity forces the civil law to provide for a limited number

[19] *Aston Cantlow and Wilmcote with Billesley Parochial Church Council v Wallbank* [2004] AC 546 at 580–584; Chancel Repairs Act 1932; Turano Taylor 2004; Law Commission 2025.

[20] Rentcharges Act 1977, ss 2, 3.

[21] Law Commission 1985.

[22] *Aston Cantlow and Wilmcote with Billesley Parochial Church Council v Wallbank* [2004] AC 546 at 553.

[23] *Hill v Tupper* (1863) 2 H & C 121, 159 ER 51.

[24] See Gooderson 1956, 25; *Regency Villas Title Ltd v Diamond Resorts (Europe) Ltd* [2019] AC 553 at 575–576; *Five Forks Hunting Club LLC v Nixon Family Partnership*, 2019 Ark App 371 (2019).

> of real rights which are less than ownership. This so-called *numerus clausus* of lesser real rights includes rights such as the hypothec, the usufruct, the servitude and so on. But they are very much exceptions to the general principle. In the singular, they are usually each referred to as *ius in re aliena*: a right in a thing belonging to someone else.[25]

While the common law does control the creation of new property rights, it does not have a *numerus clausus* in this strict sense, aligning with this civil law ethos of undivided ownership. It does not have a principle in favour of undivided ownership, but has always allowed the possession of land to be distributed among many different persons holding different estates in the same land. It recognizes a wide variety of different ways in which people can make use of land possessed by others and continues to add new property rights to that number, which is never closed.

Bernard Rudden helped stimulate interest in the concept among common lawyers in other jurisdictions when he published 'Economic Theory v. Property Law: The *Numerus Clausus* Problem' in 1987.[26] Many writers rely on *Keppell v Bailey* as the central authority for this proposition. Rudden himself wrote:

> For all interests apparently excluded from the *numerus clausus* of real rights, I shall use the compendious, if contemptuous word 'fancy' taken from Lord Brougham LC's judgment in *Keppel* v. *Bailey* (1834).[27]

Rudden was not a fan of the *numerus clausus* principle (as evident from the title of his essay) nor did he say that it was a feature of the common law. He wrote that 'so far as I know . . . the law of all "non-feudal" systems lays down a restricted list of entitlements which it will permit to count as property interests, or "real rights"'.[28] When it came to the common law, he referred to statements in *Keppell v Bailey*, *Hill v Tupper*, and a few other cases 'as the major premiss of a common-law syllogism'.[29] He went on to say:

> In England, though many feudal property interests have died, only one new type, the restrictive covenant, has been admitted. Since the Romans allowed this, the feat can hardly be said to be strikingly creative.[30]

[25] Matthews 2013, 320.
[26] Rudden 1987.
[27] Ibid, 240.
[28] Ibid, 239.
[29] Ibid, 244.
[30] Ibid, 244–245.

There is academic support for the idea that the common law does have a *numerus clausus* of property rights, especially in the United States.[31] However, some authors use the term '*numerus clausus*' to mean something other than a closed number of property rights. For example, Merrill and Smith argued that 'the *numerus clausus* functions in the common law much like a canon of interpretation . . . or like a strong default rule in the interpretation of property rights' and 'is best described as a norm of judicial self-governance'.[32] They see the *numerus clausus* as a principle that limits but does not prevent the creation of new property rights, with the restrictive covenant identified as 'one major judicial innovation'.[33]

Common law systems are indeed slow to admit new forms of property interests in land, but the fact that they do is proof that their number is not closed. There is no *numerus clausus* in the strict sense comparable to the civilian one. The common law of real property today is very different from how it stood a few hundred years ago. It has evolved. Through observation, Charles Darwin was able to prove that animal species did evolve and change and were not part of a static order that god had created.[34] The evolution of the common law of property is also observable.

To take a recent example, in *Bank of Montreal v Dynex Petroleum Ltd*,[35] the Supreme Court of Canada decided that the overriding royalties used in the oil and gas industry can be interests in land. A person with a right to extract oil or gas has a profit à prendre known in the industry as a working interest. An overriding royalty is a right to a share of the production of the working interest. While the working interest is a well-recognized interest in land, the overriding royalty was not. The reason for the distinction was linked to the classification of interests in land as corporeal hereditaments (which are rights to possess land) or incorporeal hereditaments (which are non-possessory interests in land, such as easements, profits à prendre, and rentcharges). People with rights to possession could grant incorporeal hereditaments, but people with incorporeal hereditaments could not create further property rights to their non-possessory interests. The court held that the common law should adapt and a new property right to land was added to the list. Major J said:

[31] Dorfman 2011; Edgeworth 2006; Hansmann and Kraakman 2002; McFarlane 2011; Merrill & Smith 2000; Pratt 2014; Swadling 2000; Swadling 2026; Weir 2015.

[32] Merrill & Smith 2000, 11.

[33] Ibid, 16.

[34] Darwin 1859.

[35] See, eg, *Bank of Montreal v Dynex Petroleum Ltd*, 2002 SCC 7, [2002] 1 SCR 146.

> The oil and gas industry, which developed largely in the second half of the 20th century and continues to evolve, is governed by a combination of statute and common law. The application of common law concepts to a new or developing industry is useful as it provides the participants in the industry and the courts some framework for the legal structure of the industry. It should come as no surprise that some common law concepts, developed in different social, industrial and legal contexts, are inapplicable in the unique context of the industry and its practices.
>
> The appellant could not offer any convincing policy reasons for maintaining the common law prohibition on the creation of an interest in land from an incorporeal hereditament other than fidelity to common law principles. Given the custom in the oil and gas industry and the support found in case law, it is proper and reasonable that the law should acknowledge that an overriding royalty interest can, subject to the intention of the parties, be an interest in land.[36]

It appears that licences to use land are becoming rights in rem in England. In *Manchester Airport plc v Dutton*,[37] the National Trust had granted a licence to the plaintiff to enter its woods in order to lop and fell trees in the flight path to a proposed runway. The plaintiff was not in occupation and yet was able to evict protestors who had set up camps in and around the trees. The case has been heavily criticized,[38] and it has not been accepted in Australia, where Nicholson J said, 'the majority reasoning in *Manchester Airport* finds no support in Australian law and should not be followed here'.[39] However, it has been followed several times by the Court of Appeal in England.[40]

It is fair to criticize *Manchester Airport plc v Dutton* because it violates the fundamental common law principle of relativity of title. A person who obtains possession of land or goods has a right to possession that is enforceable against all others except someone with a better right to possession.[41] The protestors were in possession. The airport never had a right to possession, let alone a

[36] *Bank of Montreal v Dynex Petroleum Ltd*, 2002 SCC 7, [17]–[18], [2002] 1 SCR 146 at 153–154.

[37] *Manchester Airport plc v Dutton* [2000] QB 133 (CA).

[38] Swadling 2000.

[39] *Bropho v Western Australia* [2007] FCA 519 at [474]. Also see *Georgeski v Owners Corporation SP49833* [2004] NSWSC 1096 at [105]; 62 NSWLR 534; *Hinkley v Star City Pty Ltd* [2010] NSWSC 1389, [218].

[40] *Alamo Housing Co-Operative Ltd v Meredith* [2003] EWCA Civ 495; [2003] HLR 62; *Hall v Mayor of London* [2010] EWCA Civ 817; [2011] WLR 504; *Vehicle Control Services Ltd v HMRC* [2013] EWCA Civ 186; [2013] RTR 24.

[41] *Armory v Delamirie* (1722) 1 Str 506, 93 ER 664; *Costello v Derbyshire Constabulary* [2001] EWCA Civ 381, [2001] 1 WLR 1437.

better right. However, it is not fair to criticize the case because of a violation of the *numerus clausus*.[42] If common law judges wish to create new property rights, they have the power to do so.

There is a wide variety of positive easements (like rights of way and rights to take water) and people are free to create new ones so long as they satisfy the broad criteria for a valid easement.[43] As Santow JA said in *Clos Farming Estates v Easton*: 'Novelty alone is insufficient as bar to the recognition of the creation of an easement.'[44] And as Lord St Leonards LC said in *Dyce v Lady James Hay*:

> The category of servitudes and easements must alter and expand with the changes that take place in the circumstances of mankind. The law . . . frequently moulds its practical operation without doing any violence to its original principles.[45]

Negative easements (like a right to the flow of light and air through a window) are treated differently. While positive easements allow for activities on the servient tenement that would otherwise be a trespass or nuisance, negative easements merely prevent the owners of the servient tenement from exercising some liberty that they would otherwise have to use their land as they please. Since easements can arise by prescription in many jurisdictions, if the failure to exercise a liberty for a sufficiently long period of time could give rise to a new kind of negative easement, that 'would put a brake on desirable improvement', as Lord Denning MR said in *Phipps v Pears*.[46]

In *Phipps v Pears*, two houses stood side by side for many years. When one house was demolished, a wall of the other house was exposed to the weather for the first time and suffered significant damage. The plaintiff who suffered the damage sued their neighbour claiming an easement by prescription to be protected by the weather. Lord Denning MR said:

> There is no such easement known to the law as an easement to be protected from the weather. The only way for an owner to protect himself is by getting a covenant from his neighbour that he will not pull down his house or cut down his trees. Such a covenant would be binding on him in contract: and

[42] See Swadling 2000, 354.
[43] *Re Ellenborough Park* [1956] Ch 131 at 163 (CA).
[44] *Clos Farming Estates v Easton* [2002] NSWCA 389 at [41].
[45] *Dyce v Lady James Hay* (1852) 1 Macq 305 at 312–313. Also see *Attorney-General of Southern Nigeria v John Holt & Co (Liverpool) Ltd* [1915] AC 599 at 617 (PC).
[46] *Phipps v Pears* [1965] 1 QB 76 at 83 (CA).

> it would be enforceable on any successor who took with notice of it. But it would not be binding on one who took without notice.[47]

While the creation of new negative easements is severely restricted at common law, people are free to use restrictive covenants for that purpose. This is because restrictive covenants are always created by consent and do not adversely affect *bona fide* purchasers without notice. As Perell J said in *1832732 Ontario Corp v Regina Properties Ltd*:

> The types of easements are not closed, and new examples may be created. However, there are few negative easements, and the law is reluctant to grant new ones. The work of negative easements is, practically speaking, more often performed by equity through its recognition of restrictive covenants.[48]

It is interesting that restrictive covenants must be restrictive. They can be used to create novel ways to prevent people from using land, but cannot impose positive obligations. The law does allow positive obligations to run with the land in various ways. Leasehold covenants bind subsequent landlords and tenants by virtue of privity of estate.[49] As discussed above, subsequent landowners can be made liable to pay rentcharges[50] and for chancel repairs.[51] Equitable property interests can be created by specifically enforceable contracts of sale and also by options to purchase that would create such a contract if exercised.[52] These can be used to compel successors in title to transfer their land.

Most property rights do not impose positive obligations on others. The right to possession imposes a general duty of non-interference on other members of society but does not compel anyone to act. Normally, we need some good reason (like a contract, tort, or statute) in order to make someone liable to pay money or perform services. The restrictive covenant is easier to justify as a property right that can bind others if it merely prevents them from acting.

[47] Ibid, 83–84 (CA).

[48] *1832732 Ontario Corp v Regina Properties Ltd*, 2018 ONSC 7643, [42]. See also *Attorney-General of Southern Nigeria v John Holt & Co (Liverpool) Ltd* [1915] AC 599 at 617 (PC); *Mulvaney v Jackson* [2003] 4 All ER 83, [20]; *Regency Villas Title Ltd v Diamond Resorts (Europe) Ltd* [2017] Ch 516, [51]; varied [2019] AC 553.

[49] See *Amsprop Trading Ltd v Harris Distribution Ltd* [1997] 1 WLR 1025 at 1028–1029 (Ch D).

[50] See, eg, *Orchard Trading Estate Management Ltd v Johnson Security Ltd* [2002] EWCA Civ 406; *McDonald v Bode Estate*, 2018 BCCA 140.

[51] *Aston Cantlow and Wilmcote with Billesley Parochial Church Council v Wallbank* [2004] AC 546 at 580–584.

[52] *London and South Western Railway Co v Gomm* (1882) 20 Ch D 562 at 581; see *Canadian Long Island Petroleums Ltd v Irving Industries Ltd* [1975] 2 SCR 715; *Pritchard v Briggs* [1980] Ch 338 (CA).

In *Rhone v Stephens*,[53] the owner of a house made a covenant to repair the roof that protected an adjoining cottage. That covenant could not be enforced against a subsequent owner of the house. Lord Templeman said:

> For over 100 years it has been clear and accepted law that equity will enforce negative covenants against freehold land but has no power to enforce positive covenants against successors in title of the land. To enforce a positive covenant would be to enforce a personal obligation against a person who has not covenanted. To enforce negative covenants is only to treat the land as subject to a restriction.[54]

Lord Templeman did say that the 'enforcement of a positive covenant lies in contract', while the 'enforcement of a negative covenant lies in property'.[55] This might be taken to mean that there is a dichotomy between contract and property, but that is not correct. They are intersecting and not opposing categories in the law. Contracts are a source of rights and property is a kind of right. Some contracts create property rights and some property rights are created by contracts. Positive covenants can be created and enforced without contracts. Leasehold covenants are the most common proof of that. Conversely, negative covenants, such as non-competition or non-disclosure agreements, can exist outside the law of property. Restrictive covenants regarding the use of land fall squarely within the law of property even though they are often created by contract.

IV. Restrictive Covenants as Equitable Property

When we introduce students to the law of trusts, we explain that the subject matter of a trust is the trustee's rights to things and not the things themselves. The trust exists because the rules of equity compel the trustee to use their legal or equitable rights in certain ways. It is easy to make the mistaken assumption that all equitable property rights function in the same way. I was guilty of that over-generalization in 2001 when I wrote:

[53] *Rhone v Stephens* [1994] 2 AC 310.
[54] Ibid, 321.
[55] Ibid, 318.

> The essential difference between legal and equitable property rights concerns the things to which those rights relate. Legal property rights relate directly to things, such as land, goods, or intangibles. For example, a legal estate is a right to possess a space on the earth. The thing subject to that right is that space. In contrast, equitable property rights operate indirectly as parasites attached to other rights. The thing subject to an equitable estate is not the space on the earth, but another person's right to that space. The subject of a trust is the trustee's right to something and not the thing itself.[56]

There are equitable property rights that do not fit this model, or at least not well. An equitable lease cannot be explained solely on the basis that the landlord is compelled by equity to use their legal fee simple estate for the benefit of the tenant. Both parties have covenants to perform. They have a landlord–tenant relationship that is recognized in equity. For almost every purpose, an equitable tenancy is no different from a legal tenancy.[57]

In *Walsh v Lonsdale*,[58] the defendant agreed to grant a seven-year lease to the plaintiff, who went into possession. The plaintiff argued that the defendant had improperly exercised their right to distress for non-payment of rent because that was a legal remedy, the only legal tenancy was from year to year, and rent was not in arrears under that tenancy. That was rejected by the Court of Appeal. Jessel MR said:

> There is an agreement for a lease under which possession has been given. Now since the *Judicature Act* the possession is held under the agreement. There are not two estates as there were formerly, one estate at common law by reason of the payment of the rent from year to year, and an estate in equity under the agreement. There is only one Court, and the equity rules prevail in it. The tenant holds under an agreement for a lease. He holds, therefore, under the same terms in equity as if a lease had been granted, it being a case in which both parties admit that relief is capable of being given by specific performance. That being so, he cannot complain of the exercise by the landlord of the same rights as the landlord would have had if a lease had been granted. On the other hand, he is protected in the same way as if a lease had been granted . . .[59]

[56] Chambers 2001, 115. See now the 5th edn: Chambers 2024, [11.90]. See also McFarlane & Stevens (2010).
[57] See *Warren v Murray* [1894] 2 QB 648 (CA); *R v Tower Hamlets LBC, ex parte Von Goetz* [1999] QB 1019 (CA).
[58] *Walsh v Lonsdale* (1882) 21 Ch D 9 (CA).
[59] Ibid, 14–15 (CA).

The trusts model of equitable property rights cannot explain the landlord's rights arising from the equitable lease, nor can it explain the tenant's duties. The landlord is not a trustee and the tenant is not a beneficiary.

It is perhaps easier to apply the trusts model to restrictive covenants. When the holder of a fee simple estate promises that they and their heirs, successors, and assigns will not use their estate in certain ways, that restriction can be enforced against their successors in title. We can think of the restrictive covenant as an equitable property right that is attached to their legal estate for the benefit of nearby estates. The difficulty with this analysis is that restrictive covenants can be enforced against people who are not successors in title but have independently acquired an estate in the land. They can also be enforced against people who do not have an estate but are merely in occupation of the land.

In *Re Nisbet & Potts' Contract*,[60] a fee simple estate was conveyed in 1872 subject to a covenant that restricted building on the land. After the owner died, the land was adversely possessed for 13 years so that the possessors became entitled to their fee simple estate free of the earlier estate. The possessors sold their estate in 1890 to Nisbet, who sold it in 1903 to Potts, who then discovered the existence of the restrictive covenant. The court held that the adverse possessors were bound by the covenant and so were the purchasers because they had constructive notice of it.

If the restrictive covenant was attached to the estate conveyed in 1872, then it should have been extinguished when that estate was extinguished by adverse possession. It should not have been enforced against anyone who was not a successor in title to the earlier fee simple estate. The adverse possessors acquired their fee simple estate independently when they took possession of the land.[61] The land was then subject to two different estates until the earlier estate was extinguished by the passage of time.

These arguments were rejected by Farwell J at first instance and by the Court of Appeal. They held that the restrictive covenant was not attached to the fee simple estate and therefore was not extinguished with it. Farwell J said, 'The burden of these restrictive covenants is not incident but paramount to the estate of the dispossessed owner'.[62] As an equitable interest in the land, the restrictive covenant took priority over the adverse possessors' estate and their successors in title. Romer LJ said:

[60] *Re Nisbet & Potts' Contract* [1905] 1 Ch 391 (Farwell J); affirmed [1906] 1 Ch 386 (CA).
[61] See *Fairweather v St Marylebone Property Co Ltd* [1962] UKHL, [1963] 1 AC 510 at 535.
[62] *Re Nisbet & Potts' Contract* [1905] 1 Ch 391 at 399.

> I think the law is that such a covenant, when validly created, binds the land in equity, and can be enforced as against subsequent owners of the land, subject only to the limitation that, being equitable, it cannot be enforced as against a bona fide purchaser of the land—that is to say, of the legal estate—without notice.[63]

In the earlier case of *Mander v Falcke*,[64] the defendant was using a house as a brothel in breach of a restrictive covenant. The Court of Appeal upheld an injunction against him even though it was not proved that he had any legal or equitable interest in the house. Lindley LJ said:

> I do not proceed on the hypothesis that he is *cestui que* trust of the underlease, for that is uncertain. I treat him simply as an occupier managing the business. He may be neither an assignee nor purchaser, but he is in occupation, and that is enough to affect him, he having notice of the covenants in the lease.[65]

These cases suggest that restrictive covenants are not rights to rights, but rights to things. They are not interests in estates, but equitable interests in land. In this way, they are similar to legal interests in land, like profits à prendre and easements. These are all non-possessory interests in land. We tend to think of them as property rights that are linked to estates in land. They are all burdens on the servient tenement, covenants and easements must provide a benefit to a nearby dominant tenement, and normally those tenements must be possessed by different persons. However, these rights can exist independently of estates and even in the absence of any estate. The Crown can grant profits and easements over Crown land without granting an estate.[66]

An interesting but (as far as I know) unanswered question is whether the benefit of a restrictive covenant functions in the same way as its burden. If the dominant tenement was adversely possessed, would the adverse possessors enjoy the benefit of the restrictive covenant that had been granted to the holders of the previous estate that had been destroyed? There does not seem to be any good reason why the servient tenement should be freed of a restriction on its use just because ownership of the dominant tenement was acquired through adverse possession.

[63] *Re Nisbet & Potts' Contract* [1906] 1 Ch 386 at 405 (CA).
[64] *Mander v Falcke* [1891] 2 Ch 554 (CA).
[65] Ibid, 556.
[66] See, eg, *R v Tener* [1985] 1 SCR 533.

In *Rogers v Hosegood*,[67] discussed above, it was argued that the benefit of a restrictive covenant did not pass to Sir John Millais because it was not mentioned in the conveyance to him and he was unaware of its existence. Farwell J said:

> . . . in my opinion it is immaterial: such knowledge has never been held a necessary condition to success in an action on a covenant which runs with the land at law. The plaintiff's right in such an action does not depend upon what he believes himself to have bought, but upon what he has in fact bought, and he has bought the land with the covenants annexed. The defendant is not injured, for he bought the land with knowledge of the covenant, and he can claim no more than the land with that burden upon it.[68]

The transfer of the dominant tenement does no harm to the owners of the servient tenement, regardless of how that transfer occurs. No new burden is placed on them. Just as the restrictive covenant is an equitable interest in the land burdened by that covenant, it is also an equitable right attached to the land that benefits from the covenant. While we might explain restrictive covenants and easements to our students as rights carved out of one estate and grafted onto another, they are better explained as rights and duties attached to parcels of land.

Restrictive covenants are normally granted by persons with estates in land, but they can exist independently of the grantor's estate. They restrict the use of the land and not just the use of the estate. They cannot be explained as rights to rights and are further proof that there is more than one model of equitable property rights. They are also further proof that there is no closed list of property rights to land at common law or in equity.

References

Birks, P. (1985). *An Introduction to the Law of Restitution*. Oxford, Clarendon Press.
Birks, P. (2005). *Unjust Enrichment*. 2nd edn. Oxford, Oxford University Press.
Chambers, R. (2001). *An Introduction to Property Law in Australia*. Sydney, Law Book Co.
Chambers, R. (2024). *An Introduction to Property Law in Australia*. 5th edn. Sydney, Thomson Reuters (Professional) Australia Ltd.
Darwin, C. (1859). *On the Origin of Species by Means of Natural Selection*. London, John Murray.

[67] *Rogers v Hosegood* [1900] 2 Ch 388 (CA).
[68] Ibid, 398.

Dorfman, A. (2011). 'Property and Collective Undertaking: The Principle of *Numerus Clausus*'. *University of Toronto Law Journal* 61: 467–520.
Edgeworth, B. (2006). 'The *Numerus Clausus* Principle in Contemporary Australian Property Law'. *Monash University Law Review* 32: 387–419.
Gooderson, R. N. (1956). 'Easement—Jus Spatiandi'. *Cambridge Law Journal* 14: 24–25.
Hansmann, H. and R. Kraakman (2002). 'Property, Contract, and Verification: The *Numerus Clausus* Problem and the Divisibility of Rights'. *Journal of Legal Studies* 31: S373–S420.
Law Commission (1985). *Liability for Chancel Repairs*. Report 152.
Law Commission (2025). *Chancel Repair Liability and Registration*. Consultation Paper 274.
Matthews, P. (2013). 'The Compatibility of the Trust with the Civil Law Notion of Property'. *The Worlds of the Trust*. L Smith. Cambridge, Cambridge University Press: 313–339.
McFarlane, B. (2011). The *Numerus Clausus* Principle and Covenants Relating to Land. *Modern Studies in Property Law: Volume 6*. S. Bright. Oxford, Hart: 311–331.
McFarlane, B. and R. Stevens (2010) 'The Nature of Equitable Property' Journal of Equity 4: 1–28.
Merrill, T. W. and H. E. Smith (2000). 'Optimal Standardization in the Law of Property: The *Numerus Clausus* Principle'. *Yale Law Journal* 110: 1–70.
Pratt, N. (2014). 'Conservation Covenants: A Proprietary Analysis'. *The Conveyancer and Property Lawyer*: 328–339.
Rudden, B. (1987). Economic Theory v. Property Law: The *Numerus Clausus* Problem. *Oxford Essays in Jurisprudence Third Series*. J. Eekelaar and J. Bell. Oxford, Clarendon Press: 239–263.
Swadling, W. (2000). 'Opening the *Numerus Clausus*'. *Law Quarterly Review* 116: 354–360.
Swadling, W. (2026). 'Are Choses in Action Property?'. *Restrictive Covenants*. W. Swadling, forthcoming.
Turano Taylor, L. (2004). 'Restoring Chancels and Human Rights'. *Cambridge Law Journal* 63: 7–9.
Weir, M. (2015). 'Pushing the Envelope of Proprietary Interests: The Nadir of the *Numerus Clausus* Principle?'. *Melbourne University Law Review* 39: 651–679.

7

Bilateral Broadcasting and the Foundations of Private Law

Zhong Xing Tan

I. Introduction

In their seminal work on the property-contract interface,[1] Merrill and Smith refocus attention on the problem of information costs in shaping the relational architecture of private law, in particular the distinction between in personam and in rem rights entitlements. In so doing they capture something deeply significant in our understanding of private law as a system of rights and duties, and provide a necessary corrective against some of the more outlandish suggestions of law and economics scholars that sometimes appear to take an instrumentalist view of private law entitlements as fully malleable as a function of transaction cost engineering.

This chapter takes inspiration from these insights but offers a different non-consequentialist framework for understanding a foundational problem in private law: the challenge of what I term 'bilateral broadcasting'. As I argue, whether one is concerned with contract, property, or other fields (tort, equity, and so on), there is a sense in which 'bilateral' relationality remains operative, depending on various levels of abstraction in our characterization of persons, relations, conduct, and categories of interests protected. Next, I point out that private law has to distribute among classes of potential right and dutyholders the burden of *communication* and *verification* of various entitlements, in a manner that is not simply about overall welfare, but consistent with interpersonal justice. I explain how these are reflected in certain building blocks of private law, including concepts such as foreseeability, objectivity, good faith, and notice, and I refer to selected case studies on economic torts, three-party undue influence, and the *bona fide* purchaser defence to develop this core

[1] Merrill & Smith 2001.

Zhong Xing Tan, *Bilateral Broadcasting and the Foundations of Private Law* In: *The Property-Contract Interface*.
Edited by: James Penner, Irina Sakharova, Henry E. Smith, and Zhong Xing Tan, Oxford University Press.
 DOI: 10.1093/9780198951995.003.0009

insight. Lastly, I suggest how the morality of broadcasting constitutes something like a 'minimal content' of private law, differing from 'high' theory or full-blooded accounts of fields of private law, while revealing something distinctive across the terrain of private law.

II. The Information Costs Conundrum

As Merrill and Smith argue, the distinction between in personam contract (binding only contractual parties) and in rem property rights (binding the rest of the world) exists as a function of information costs. Characteristically, in personam contracting imposes larger informational burdens on a small number of identified persons, while in rem rights impose a small informational burden on a large and indefinite number of persons. These two modalities allow us to regulate resources in cost-effective ways. In rem rights typically correspond with simple bright-line rules of exclusion, involving standardized packages of negative duties applying automatically to many persons in a large community, in undemanding ways. On the other hand, in personam contract rights can be fine-tuned as part of a flexible governance strategy for delineating specific use rights or interests in certain resources, allowing for more complex structures of positive or negative performance obligations, in situations where there are more intensive informational demands on contracting parties, and fewer external burdens on third parties.

At the same time, Merrill and Smith observe that the in personam/in rem distinction may be seen as a spectrum rather than as hermetically sealed categories. They start with Hohfeld's explication of paucital/in personam and multital/in rem rights: a paucital right is 'a unique right residing in a person (or group of persons) and availing against a single person (or single group of persons); or else it is one of the *few* fundamentally similar, yet separate, rights availing respectively against a few definite persons'.[2] A multital right, on the other hand, is '*one* of a large *class* of *fundamentally similar* yet separate rights, actual and potential, residing in a *single* person (or single group of persons) but availing *respectively* against persons constituting a very large and indefinite class of people'.[3] While Hohfeld attempted to close the gap between the paucital and multital by suggesting that the latter simply represents the aggregate of a large and indefinite number of in personam rights and duties, and are not

[2] Hohfeld 1917, 718 (emphasis in original).
[3] Ibid.

distinguished by supposed thing-relatedness (since jural relations must concern persons), Merrill and Smith reassert the importance of separate and distinct objects (as opposed to abstract rights) in mediating between rightholders and dutybearers, by signalling straightforward duties of abstention that require little information regarding the individuality of parties. Thus 'in rem' connotes neither social relations per se nor a relationship between a person and thing, but relations between persons regarding a certain object. Nonetheless, Merrill and Smith find it useful to take reference from Hohfeld on notions of *numerosity* and *indefiniteness*, which they see are contingent variables marking the spectrum from in personam to in rem: pure in personam/paucital rights are singular and definite, pure in rem/multital rights are numerous and indefinite, and in between are compound-paucital rights (concerning numerous but definite dutyholders) and quasi-multital rights (concerning singular but indefinite dutyholders). By fleshing out this spectrum, Merrill and Smith are able to identify different types and intensities of informational demands.

III. Bilateral Broadcasting

1. Bilateralism Revisited

Compare a different view of relationality, one that acknowledges how private law is often seen as involving 'bilateral', 'bipolar', or 'correlative' entitlements and obligations, as famously described by Weinrib:

> The most striking feature of private law is that it directly connects two particular parties through the phenomenon of liability . . . In singling out these two parties and bringing them together this way, private law looks neither to the litigants individually nor to the interests of the community as a whole, but to a bipolar relationship of liability.[4]

Private law obligations are indeed about what we owe each other. The challenge is in defining the relevant *level of generality* at which we conduct this 'bilateral' inquiry, and how we might toggle between inquiries at different levels of abstraction for various purposes. As I will explain, bipolar relationality typically encompasses some *ex-ante* aspect where the relevant classes of parties, interests, and prohibited or mandated action or conduct are described

[4] Weinrib 2012, 1–2.

in a fairly general and conceptual way, and where the relevant descriptors are necessarily indefinite to some degree. At the same time, room is made for *ex-post* context-specific application of these components through a process of concretization. This suggests something like a multitiered approach to examining relationality. Rights (and duties) can be understood as loosely relational, having an initial if non-conclusive directive force (as when we speak of the right to privacy or a right to bodily integrity), yet they can also be expressed in more specific ways, referring to particular enjoined acts and interests harmed or infringed. As these observations apply across contractual and proprietary entitlements, grasping this perspective is essential to reframing the in personam/in rem divide, while retaining Merrill and Smith's core insights as to the relevance of information costs.

As Webb explains:

> [R]ights can be stated in different terms and at different levels of generality. My right not to be assaulted means that, if I am standing in front of you, I have a right that you not punch me, poke me or stamp on my toes; if I am crossing the road you are driving down, I have a right that you not run me over . . . These context-specific rights and the directions they give to the duty bearer speak to particular individuals at particular points in time, but not to others. My right that you not falsely imprison me is mirrored by rights I have against people generally and so operates, in this sense, in rem. Yet, where you are solely responsible for me being locked in my office, of all those who could secure my release, you alone are duty-bound to do so . . .'[5]

At the levels of norm articulation and application, private law routinely encounters this issue of abstraction in characterization. A contractual duty of Y to protect X's family against threats of a certain infectious disease can include a duty to address the specific threat of a certain disease-carrying pest, though the initial framing of the duty entertains a zone of indeterminacy in that it does not enumerate the specific actions to be taken by Y, and leaves open what exactly Y has to do until one can foresee or contemplate the risk of such pests arising, which depends on contingent facts about the world.[6] And there is yet an even higher level of generality at which we might contemplate the contractual obligation: as between all classes of promisors and promisees invoking the power-conferring institution of contract law. My contractual right to a good or service

[5] Webb 2018, 260–261.
[6] Newman 2022, 277–279.

is a 'context-specific instantiation of my general right that others perform their contracts with me', and in this formulation, 'this right operates *in rem*'.[7] We all have general—and in this sense in rem—rights and duties as potential promisors and promisees, yet these necessarily bottom out in specific arrangements with particular content applying to identified parties.

The same is true of non-contractual rights. At one level, tort law as an institution of civil recourse contemplates the generic rights and duties of all classes of victims and wrongdoers, underpinned by general justifications of remedying injuries, ensuring accountability for unjustified incursions, and promoting equal access to justice.[8] Yet particular torts can vary in terms of the level of specificity in the syntax of duties. For a given object (tangible or intangible) in which the rightholder has some recognized interest, whether land, chattel, physical person, reputation, and so on, we can enjoin some specified activity by a defendant directed towards an identified object (touching a rightholder's physical body), or enjoin a specific action and consequential effect on an interest (a competitor using a trademark in a way that creates a likelihood of confusion among consumers, so as to take advantage of a business' goodwill), or leave the activity itself unspecified and the consequential effect more indirectly stated (foreseeably causing harm to person or property).[9]

Recognizing various levels of abstraction in depicting the relational character of private law is important for a number of reasons. First, it presents a somewhat different challenge to the in personam/in rem divide than the one presented by Merrill and Smith: '[W]hen understood as a distinction between rights good against a single person or determinate group and those good against people generally, individual rights can often be allocated to either class depending on the terms in which we choose to state them.'[10] Once we factor in levels of abstraction, there is no linear movement from in personam contract to in rem property based on numerosity or indefiniteness. At higher levels of generality, both contractual and property-based duties are *indefinite* to some degree, in that descriptors of the relevant parties, interests, objects, and enjoined or mandated actions leave room for contextual specification. Whether such general contractual or non-contractual duties actually apply to one or many definite persons, namely, the issue of *numerosity*, as well as the range of specific actions to be taken by such persons (eg what acts or precautions

[7] Webb 2018, 261.
[8] Goldberg and Zipursky 2020.
[9] Newman 2022, 286.
[10] Webb 2018, 268.

constitute due care), depends contingently on the state of the world (driving in full traffic versus on an empty road).

Second, we need to appreciate the place of both the general depiction of relationality, typically undertaken *ex ante*, as well as contextual and *ex post* specifications of relational content. Hohfeld, of course, has often been understood to take the position that 'only perfectly individualised or "atomic" relationships are proper legal relations'.[11] This is not least because of his view that an in-rem claim-right is necessarily correlative to one of many fundamentally similar in personam duties owed by many different individuals. Under this so-called 'rights multiplication' model, the owner of Blackacre has as many claim-rights in rem as there are existing persons in the world, that others (minus themselves) should not enter Blackacre.[12] This view in turn has elicited Penner's well-known critique that the Hohfeldian model presupposes that 'to comply with one's duties, one must know the identity of each right-holder and each item of property he particularly owns',[13] when such a duty is arguably not owner-specific. If we insist on such granularity, there is no longer a single persistent property right, but 'innumerable discrete duties . . . constantly winking into and out of existence as the state of the world changes'.[14]

The short answer is that both the general and granular levels of analysis are relevant for epistemic and informational reasons. If one key purpose of private law is to provide practically reasonable normative guidance to its addressees on their personal rights and duties, it needs to articulate and communicate certain basic obligations in a way that does not require the acquisition of too much information before the relevant duty can be processed and complied with. The cognitive focal point of a general non-trespassory duty is typically some tangible thing or intangible yet identifiable object whose characteristics allow the straightforward inference that someone is exercising ownership or control over it, without the dutyholder needing to know the actual identity of the rightholder or further information as to the particular state of the object, or conversely, the rightholder having to know who the dutybearers are. Our cognitive experience of general rights and duties thus takes the form of bilateral normativity, but as between generic classes of rightholders and dutybearers, such as employers and employees, injurers and foreseeable victims, neighbours, and so forth.

[11] Eleftheriadis 1996, 45.
[12] Sreenivasan 2024, 9.
[13] Penner 2020, 97.
[14] Newman 2022, 279.

But this does not mean that the *ex-post* context-specific perspective is unimportant. The general duty is not in reality a single joint or shared duty amongst all members of the class. It is a placeholder for independent duties that specific persons in fact come under and may be guilty of breaching, thus giving rise to the bipolar character of private law disputes. Acknowledging this does not require one to buy into an information-intensive characterization of in personam Hohfeldian relations. A recognition of separate and distinct duties is compatible with descriptions being incomplete or ambiguous, at least at the *ex-ante*, conduct-guiding level. The fact that I don't know the identities of a group of persons standing below my apartment is consistent with my owing duties to each of them not to throw killer litter in a way that might cause them foreseeable risks of death or personal injury.[15] Again, to take duties of care as an example, the general duty question focuses on broad classes of claimants and defendants and categories of interests protected, giving guidance to actors who 'have limited capacity for information and calculation, and use simplifying methods to manage their lives'.[16] But there is also further space for the 'factual duty' question,[17] which focuses on what an individual defendant owes an individual claimant, dovetailing with remoteness or proximate-cause inquiries. Here we tailor relationality to particular claimants and defendants, taking into account actors' capacity to foresee and avoid consequences of action, specific circumstances of interaction, types of hazards, and risks of harm, and the kinds of damage that might be suffered, and it is at this level that we say 'negligence is a relation between particular individuals'.[18] So we necessarily toggle between two levels of relationality: the general and specific, *ex ante* and *ex post*, where conduct-guiding rules are articulated and where they are applied.

2. The Burdens of Broadcasting: Communicating and Verifying Putative Entitlements

So we must be attentive to the level of generality at which we depict rights and duties in private law. But a further architectural issue arises in this regard. It is said that the 'fundamental tasks' of any legal system are to 'identify duties of restraint such that the costs of compliance borne by each individual are exceeded by the benefits expected from the universal compliance of others', and to 'define

[15] Sreenivasan 2024, 12.
[16] Howarth 2006, 456.
[17] Nolan 2013, 573.
[18] Goodhart 1930, 452.

and communicate those duties in a way that is cognitively manageable, so that the costs of recognizing them do not tip the balance against compliance'.[19]

Every time the perimeter of protection of an entitlement is pushed in a farther direction, extending the classes of persons responsible for 'keeping off' or otherwise giving effect to such an entitlement, there must be substantively good reasons for doing so, and the need for protection must be effectively broadcast to each additional class of dutybearers in a way that is epistemically acceptable from an information costs perspective. This is a calculus that informs what one might term the pregnability of privity or partitioning rules in private law, which are essentially concerned with managing informational burdens.[20]

Of course, we can say that the obligation to provide proper guidance on rights and duties is ultimately placed on the state as lawgiver. I have elsewhere pointed out that Fuller's well-known notion of the internal morality of law—requiring the lawgiver to create legal norms in compliance with the desiderata of generality, publicity, non-retroactivity, clarity, avoidance of contradiction and impossibility, relative constancy over time, and congruence between announced rules and actual administration—can be understood as what Rex owes his subjects in the course of promulgating and maintaining a system of laws.[21] But the lawgiver has then to further distribute, or delegate, the burdens of broadcasting bilaterally as among classes of potential claimants and defendants in a manner that they cannot reasonably reject. These burdens include the responsibility for communicating protected interests, on the one hand, and the responsibility for verifying the existence of such entitlements, on the other. What then constitutes a fair allocation of responsibility?

Part of the solution has been glimpsed at by commentators who observe something like a negligence or fault-based analysis present even in trespass-type doctrines of strict liability concerned with fairly straightforward norms of exclusion. Sterk, for instance, points out that property law has developed 'surrogates' for negligence rules in situations where it is costly or difficult to determine the boundaries of property entitlements, such that a potential user or taker's conduct is assessed by reference to her reasonable (even if unsuccessful) efforts to ascertain such boundaries.[22] Sterk's examples include first-in-time (or race) recording acts for land ownership in many American states that have been supplemented with notice requirements for the protection of bona fide

[19] Newman 2022, 284.
[20] Gergen 2020, 484.
[21] Tan 2023.
[22] Sterk 2012, 2133.

purchasers, such that a subsequent purchaser cannot prevail over a prior purchaser simply by filing first, but must also demonstrate that they had neither actual nor constructive knowledge of the prior claim. If a deed is properly recorded, a prior purchaser has discharged their burden of broadcasting and the subsequent purchaser is fixed with constructive notice of the deed. On the other hand, a 'wild deed' that is not properly recorded or adequately described may not be sufficient to discharge the prior purchaser's duty of communication, and the subsequent purchaser who bought the property in reliance on a reasonable title search is protected. Even if the prior purchaser fails to record, they may be protected where other existing indicia outside the record could have put the subsequent purchaser on actual or constructive notice of the interest (eg possession of premises at the relevant time).[23]

A similar idea is expressed by Dorfman and Jacob, who discuss the simple case of trespass to land, but highlight that the existence of authorization or non-authorization for entry is often the responsibility of the landowner to communicate. Dutyholders are then obligated to 'draw reasonable inferences with respect to the right-holder's point of view'[24] concerning licences to enter and use-authorisation. Given that dutyholders cannot be expected to be mindreaders, they rely on proxies like language ('no entry'); gestures (a nod); context (residential home versus store); custom, convention, and culture (American or Bedouin society); or other sources of intersubjective meaning, in order to infer the subjective state of the owner's mind. The dutyholder bears no liability as long as they act reasonably in relation to this 'second-best means of decoding what is truly going on in the owner's mind'.[25] These examples hone in on the informational challenges of communicating and verifying protected interests. While Dorfman and Jacob suggest that the burden lies with the owner in communicating authorization to what would otherwise be a trespass, the allocation of responsibility goes both ways, as between classes of claimants and defendants, hence we may speak of it as bilateral broadcasting.

Moreover, from a functionalist angle, one can conceptualize the problem as a form constrained cost-benefit analysis, as Hansmann and Kraakman have done in their work on verification rules in property.[26] Hansmann and Kraakman focus on the informational issues that arise when rights in assets are intended to run with the asset, and are sought to be enforced against transferees of the asset. Their solution is one of broadcasting in the form of 'regulation of

[23] Ibid, 2141–2143.
[24] Dorfman & Jacob 2015, 64.
[25] Ibid, 65.
[26] Hansmann & Kraakman 2002.

the types and degree of notice required to establish different types of property rights'.[27] This is so that a third party who might otherwise presume the consolidation of rights in a single owner is adequately alerted to the fact that there is in fact an existing partitioning between two initial rightholders. The choice of verification regime involves a mix of user, non-user, and system costs. Hansmann and Kraakman illustrate what they see as an overall efficiency calculus with respect to an artist's right to integrity, which can be broadcast in different ways. We might think of giving the artist a mandatory and unwaivable right of control over the alteration and destruction of their work to protect its artistic value, though this might appear paternalistic and involve the costs of educating the public as to the existence of such rights. Short of this solution, we might allow an artist's right of integrity to be created and verified by labelling (analogous to a copyright sign). That would allow an artist to broadcast their rights of control to subsequent purchasers if so desired, in a way cheaper to implement and verify than a series of contractual commitments stipulating restrictions upon resale, but still involving some costs of public education (as to the effect of the label). One can also publicize rights of integrity through a registry, which would involve costs of establishment and maintenance but provide low cost and reliable verification. Hansmann and Kraakman postulate that where rights are of value and more widely used, broadcasting regimes that make it less costly for users, though more burdensome for non-users (those who do not wish to be governed by the right) and the legal system, are likely to be more efficient.

Let me put the insights of the above commentators in a way that is consistent with the logic of interpersonal justice in private law. With respect to the two-way burdens of communication (by claimants) and verification (by defendants), I agree that something like the logic of due care is operational with respect to responsibility for determining the very existence of entitlements. The negligence principle embodies the notion that we can require all reasonable precautions be taken to reduce the risks of harm, at a reasonable cost, to those adversely affected by such risks. In this regard, a claimant who can undertake a lesser burden by clearly communicating through objective indicators their rights with respect to person or property, would be obligated to do so. In such circumstances, not requiring such a 'precaution' of broadcasting would be to place even greater burdens on a defendant who would not be able to divine the claimant's true state of mind, and hence be liable beyond

[27] Ibid, 374.

the scope of their capacity for verification. Conversely, if it is within the scope of the defendant's capacity to verify the boundaries of entitlements (having actual knowledge or being put on inquiry by certain indicators), and they can take a fairly non-burdensome step to corroborate this and avoid an unauthorized taking or using, even in circumstances where the claimant does not take all the relevant steps to broadcast her entitlements, it is appropriate to fix the defendant with liability for boundary-crossing. Insofar as we can imagine ourselves as potential rightholders as well as dutybearers (in respect of our person, chattels, or land), we reciprocally benefit from such a system of bilateral signalling and verification. Colloquially, one might speak of this as some form of 'cheapest cost avoider' reasoning, in the sense that if the 'acquisition and dissemination of information about competing property claims [is not] costless', the relevant 'burdens should be placed on the holder of the property interest who can handle them most cheaply'.[28] In standard law and economics, however, the cheapest cost avoider notion has become associated with models of efficient deterrence that are purely instrumental, not tied in any meaningful way to deontological precepts of responsibility and wrongdoing, and practically inoperable due to a lack of relevant empirical information. Accordingly, we might put the point more generally as the search for the class of persons that can best bear the burdens of communication or verification. The balance between communication and verification duties may be struck in different ways in different contexts, as we will see, but the aim is to reduce the collective burdens of bilateral broadcasting in a manner acceptable to all who operate within the system of private law entitlements.

IV. Bilateral Broadcasting: Doctrinal Concepts

1. Foreseeability

Consider foreseeability, alluded to earlier when speaking of how we tailor general rights and duties to specific circumstances across different points in time. Foreseeability is primarily a defendant-sided concept concerned with the capacity for verifying the potential existence of entitlements. Foreseeability is 'a crucial moral cog for responsibility' because it is suggestive of a defendant's

[28] Baird & Jackson 1983, 188–189.

capacity to appreciate the causal possibilities and consequences of contemplated action—the kinds of hazards that may result in harm to person property.[29] As Perry explains, the possession of the capacity to foresee and ability and opportunity to avoid a harmful outcome which the actor causally contributes to, is a 'plateau' or baseline of responsibility that allows outcomes of choices to be acknowledged as attributable to one's agency.[30]

But foreseeability-related doctrines sometimes encompass aspects of both claimant-sided broadcasting and defendant-sided verification, as demonstrated by the well-known *Hadley v Baxendale*[31] rule governing remoteness in contract damages. The first 'imputed knowledge' limb deals with losses arising according to the usual course of things or flowing naturally from a breach of contract under ordinary circumstances. The second limb, on the other hand, deals with 'actual knowledge', involving the actual communication by the claimant to the defendant of special circumstances under which the contract was made, outside the usual course of things.[32] Each promisee typically best knows their own position, and so would bear the burden of communicating the relevant facts that might have a bearing on the type(s) of losses that could eventually arise within the reasonable contemplation of the parties. In the same way that persons rely on context, convention, and other objective proxies, parties might depend on shared general knowledge of what constitutes 'normal' business operations and what kinds of disruptions and losses might ordinarily occur upon breach, *a fortiori* if they share the same market or industry.[33] Such knowledge may come within the promisor's capacity for information-gathering, hence imputed to them. However, the position of the promisor might be that the relevant circumstances are beyond their capacity for verification unless specially brought home to them by the promisee, who thus has the burden of specially communicating additional information. The defendant-common carrier in *Hadley* appreciated that it was carrying a broken shaft from the claimant's mill, but not that any delay would cause the mill to be at a standstill for five more days with consequential losses of profit, unless the relevant circumstances (eg absence of a spare shaft and continued operations entirely hinging on the defendant) were specially communicated.

29 Owen 2009, 1277–1278, 1281–1286.
30 Perry 2001, 91–92.
31 (1854) 9 Exch 341.
32 *Victoria Laundry (Windsor) Ltd v Newman Industries Ltd* [1949] 2 KB 528 (CA) 539.
33 *Balfour Beatty Construction (Scotland) Ltd v Scottish Power plc* (1994) 71 BLR 20 (HL).

2. Objectivity

Consider next the objective standard of care, focusing on the position of a 'prudent and reasonable' person[34] placed in the shoes of the defendant at the time of breach, such as that of a reasonable motorist or medical professional, not necessarily a 'paragon of circumspection',[35] but with no allowance being made for personal shortcomings.[36] Hence, the fact that a defendant is an inexperienced driver is no reason to hold them to a standard lower than that of a reasonable driver of ordinary experience;[37] and similarly, an inexperienced professional (such as a novice doctor) is held to the standard of the post they hold within their unit or area of specialization.[38] A defendant may hold themselves out to a certain limited standard (such as jeweller offering ear-piercing services holding themselves out to the medical standards of reasonable jeweller and not that of a surgeon);[39] and conversely, one may hold oneself out to reach a certain standard, regardless of whether one actually possesses the ability or qualifications to meet it.[40]

The objective standard is also concerned with broadcasting, but in this respect it is the defendant's capacity for care that is being broadcast to the claimant. Commentators have long since argued against excessive individuation of an unrealistically variable standard of care; Holmes famously opined on the 'impossibility of nicely measuring a man's powers and limitations'.[41] This is not simply because such determinations would increase litigation expenses and likely involve judicial error and uncertainty. More fundamentally, it is about the demandingness of epistemic burdens. In most of our tort-like interactions with strangers, there is no plausible means (time, opportunity, resources) for a potential victim of injury to verify the defendant's true capacity for care. While a certain standard of reasonable precaution may be genuinely outside the defendant's subjective domain of competence, there may be little to put the claimant on notice of this, especially in situations where there are no prior interactions.

As between the defendant and claimant, who then should bear the responsibility for broadcasting or verification? Defendants arguably should take

[34] *Blyth v Birmingham Waterworks Co* (1856) 156 ER 1047, 1049.
[35] *AC Billings & Sons Ltd v Riden* [1958] AC 240 (HL), 255 (Lord Reid).
[36] See, eg, *Vaughan v Menlove* (1837) 3 Bing NC 468.
[37] *Nettleship v Weston* [1971] 2 QB 691 (CA).
[38] See *Wilsher v Essex Area Health Authority* [1988] AC 1074 (HL).
[39] *Phillips v William Whiteley Ltd* [1938] 1 All ER 566.
[40] *The Lady Gwendolen* [1965] P 294, 350.
[41] Holmes 1881, 108.

responsibility for how they convey themselves to others, in that they are generally in a better position to do so than claimants who lack the means of verification. An inexperienced motorist who may in fact lack the ability to drive on a busy highway nonetheless makes an implicit communication that they can do so; an inexperienced surgeon who enters the operating theatre signals an expected level of competence, whatever the true case may be. Even if a defendant lacks a certain subjective capacity and may not be fully in control of the level of competence they are signalling to others, we might reasonably accept that the burdens should remain with defendants, lest all tort victims are left fundamentally uncertain and insecure as against the conduct of others. We can agree that preserving the tightest possible connection to subjective capacity would place undue burdens of verification on claimants. The objective standard substantially reduces these burdens of verification, as we can safely ignore any concealed idiosyncrasies and shortcomings. This rationale is also fully consistent with higher standards where defendants more actively hold themselves out to meet the requirements of certain roles or professions, insofar as this information is voluntarily broadcast to persons in the positions of potential claimants. On the other hand, the so-called partial subjectivization of standards for children undertaking the risks of child activities is also sensible. Children in such contexts broadcast to each other (and their caregivers) that they have a more limited capacity for care than adults, and should only be held to the standard of care applicable to someone their age. On the other hand, if a child engages in adult activities (taking a car on the road) the child is imposing heightened non-reciprocal risks on other road users who may not have the means to access this information and protect themselves accordingly, and so is rightly held to a higher standard of care.

3. Good Faith and Notice

Notions of good faith and notice are also linked with a defendant's capacity for verification. I am not concerned with a thicker notion of good faith associated with exploiting a position of dominance or power. My present concern is a thinner conception of good faith understood as acting without notice, and evident in familiar articulations of the principle that the 'person who takes in good faith and for value without notice should get good title',[42] or the idea that

[42] *Bishopgate Motor Finance Corporation Ltd v Transport Brakers Ltd* [1949] 1 KB 322 (CA) 336–337.

equitable rights are good against all persons except a bona fide purchaser of a legal estate for value without notice.

One classic example is the doctrine of unilateral mistake as to terms in contract law,[43] which operates where one party is mistaken and the other party knows, or ought reasonably to know, of such a mistake. A contracting party is best positioned to communicate its preferences: 'the intent of man cannot be tried, for the Devil himself knows not the intent of a man'.[44] If A makes a subjective, self-induced mistake as to the terms of the contract, without any means for B to verify this, the contract is not invalidated, as B can only rely on external manifestations of meaning, and not any undisclosed intentions or beliefs.[45] The broadcasting failure is A's and they should take the risk of their mistake. If, however, there are objective sources of shared meaning allowing B to draw reasonable inferences as to the existence of a mistake and to what A must have meant, it then comes within B's responsibility to verify this, rather than proceeding to 'snatch up' a deal too good to be true. Where the buyer must have realized or did know, based on customs of trade and prior dealing, that the seller means to sell hare skins at a price fixed 'per piece' when they say, 'per pound', the contract can be set aside.[46]

Even in areas where statutory regulation has phased out notice as a controlling concept, such as the Land Registration Act (LRA) 2002, the underlying principles of bilateral communication and verification still factor into consideration. It is pointed out that 'notice is reintroduced into our land registration system to some extent by the LRA 2002 provisions about overriding interests', in particular the important class of interests of persons in actual occupation under Schedule 3 para 2.[47] While registration constitutes the relevant act of publicity by the landowner, it would be unreasonably burdensome for all encumbrancers to register their rights, some of which are created more informally by persons who do not appreciate the need for registration. Of course, if an unregistered interest-holder has the opportunity to communicate their interest, but fails to disclose this in response to an inquiry made before the registered disposition, in circumstances where they could reasonably have been expected to do so,[48] they bear the consequences for not taking an easier means to signal their interests. Where the interest-holder is relying on actual

[43] *Smith v Hughes* (1871) LR 6 QB 597.
[44] Anon (1478) YB 17 Edw 4, Pasch Fo 1, pl 2 (Brian CJ).
[45] See Endicott 2000.
[46] *Hartog v Colin & Shields* [1939] 3 All ER 566.
[47] Clarke 2020, 629.
[48] Schedule 3 para 2(b) of the LRA 2002.

occupation to broadcast their entitlements, some physical presence must be required,[49] as well as some degree of permanence and continuity (as opposed to fleeting presence or acts preparatory to occupation),[50] though temporary absence with evidence of presence on land is acceptable,[51] and the court will have to determine if the relevant actions show a continuing intention to occupy.[52] The occupation must be obvious on a reasonably careful inspection of the land at the time of disposition.[53] In addition, if the transferee had actual knowledge of the occupier's interest, even if the occupation is not obvious, the unregistered interest will override.[54] Accordingly, if the transferee can rely on fairly clear and obvious proxies to infer actual occupation, they have the responsibility to do so. And if they acquire actual knowledge, they will have verified the existence of the interest. The statutory regime thus contains its own calibration of communication and verification responsibilities, as between unregistered interest-holders and transferees.

V. Bilateral Broadcasting: Case Studies

1. Torts Protecting Contractual Interests

Consider how a contractual obligation is given tortious protection. In *OBG v Allan*,[55] the majority of Lord Hoffman, Lord Walker, and Lord Brown deemed it a step too far to extend strict liability in conversion beyond chattels to choses in action. The minority, Lord Nicholls and Baroness Hale, were in favour of extending liability for conversion to intangible contractual rights, in a case where invalidly appointed administrative receivers had innocently taken control of the claimant's business, terminated contracts, and settled claims. The minority view sounds attractive at first glance. Conversion requires a claimant with a superior possessory right in an asset, a deprivation by the defendant of the claimant's full benefit of that right, and an assumption by the defendant of the possessory rights of the claimant.[56] But why exclude assets in the form of intangible contractual rights? For some, there are 'no convincing reasons,

49 *Williams v Glyn's Bank v Boland* [1981] AC 487, 504–505.
50 *Abbey National Building Society v Cann* [1991] 1 AC 56.
51 *Link Lending Ltd v Bustard* [2010] EWCA Civ 424.
52 *Thompson v Foy* [2009] EWHC 1076 (Ch), [27].
53 Schedule 3 para 2(c)(i) of the LRA 2002.
54 Schedule 3 para 2(c)(ii) of the LRA 2002.
55 *OBG v Allan* [2007] UKHL 21, [2008] 1 AC 1.
56 Green & Randall 2009, 75–78.

either conceptual or policy, for excluding many forms of intangible personal property from the ambit of the legal protection afforded to tangible property'.[57]

This limitation, however, makes more sense from the perspective of bilateral broadcasting. Recall that liability in conversion is strict:

> At common law one's duty to one's neighbour who is the owner . . . of any goods is to refrain from doing any voluntary act in relation to his goods which is a usurpation of his proprietary or possessory rights in them . . . it matters not that the doer of the act of usurpation did not know, and could not by the exercise of any reasonable care have known of his neighbour's interest in the goods. This duty is absolute; he acts at his peril.[58]

This imposition of strict liability only makes sense if there is a clear and easily verifiable signal that others should 'keep off' interfering with an asset. In general, it is difficult for a third party to verify whether they are interfering in X's contract with Y, by dealing with Y in a certain way. Hence, in order to broadcast the existence of a contractual obligation, we usually need to locate the obligation in a separate and distinct object, the possession of which sends a 'keep off' signal to others. Thus, while conversion is not available for intangible contractual obligations, it can be applicable where there is a document embodying or recording a debt or obligation, a simple example being a negotiable instrument physically embodying a payment obligation, with the transfer of the chattel necessitating the transfer of the payment obligation. In this situation it makes sense to resort to the law of conversion when the instrument is taken unlawfully.

In other circumstances concerning purely intangible contractual rights, tortious protection is available via the doctrine of inducing breach of contract, tracing back to *Lumley v Gye*[59] where the defendant was liable for inducing a well-known opera singer to break her contract with the claimant theatre in order to obtain her services. This involves inducement in the sense of persuasion leading to a breach, coupled with subjective knowledge of an existing contract and its breach (including a conscious decision not to inquire), and intention to procure the breach as a means to an end, or an end in itself.[60]

[57] Ibid, 139.
[58] *Marfani & Co Ltd v Midland Bank Ltd* [1968] 1 WLR 956, 971 (Diplock LJ).
[59] *Lumley v Gye* (1853) 2 E & B 216, (1853) 118 ER 749.
[60] *OBG* [8], [39]–[44], [172]–[173], [191]–[192], [264], [302]–[303], [319].

These tighter *mens rea* requirements are critical to managing informational burdens. As Gergen puts it: '[r]ules that require subjective culpability impose relatively small information costs on an actor because liability requires that an actor know that she is committing a wrong.'[61] The responsibility for 'keeping off' another's contractual right is engaged only where the defendant has verified the existence of the contract and the fact that breach will be procured by their action. As explained by Lord Hoffman in *OBG*: 'It is not enough that you know that you are procuring an act which, as a matter of law or construction of the contract, is a breach. You must actually realise that it will have this effect. Nor does it matter that you ought reasonably to have done so.'[62] Moreover, in order to 'keep off' the contract, what the defendant needs to know is the existence of the contractual obligation, hence liability does not require knowledge of all the precise terms or details of the contract.[63] The focus on subjective knowledge attenuates the burdens of verification, exempting from liability situations where a defendant has an honest doubt as to whether a contract exists, and even where a defendant illogically believes that no breach will occur. Some space is left for subjective reckless indifference where the circumstances have put the defendant on inquiry but they consciously choose not to act or deliberately turn a blind eye,[64] since the defendant can take a non-burdensome step in this regard, but there is no general duty to actively inquire about contracts with others.[65]

Moreover, the defendant's liability is only triggered if they possess the requisite intention to procure a breach. A defendant who refuses to honour a contract to sing with a recording company, inevitably leading to the latter's breach of contract with the claimant who provided technical and musical services, would not be liable if the claimant's contract rights were not intentionally attacked.[66] This intention requirement thus acts as an additional limit on knowledge, directed only to those who adopt as a part of a plan the act of inducement as an end or as a means to some end. Liability for interfering with abstract and intangible contractual rights obtains only where they come squarely within the defendant's capacity for verification.

[61] Gergen 2020, 491.
[62] *OBG* [39].
[63] *Emerald Construction Co Ltd v Lowthian* [1966] 1 WLR 691, 700.
[64] OBG [41].
[65] *Leitch & Co v Leydon* [1931] AC 90.
[66] *OBG* [43] (Lord Hoffmann), rejecting the majority decision in *Millar v Bassey* [1994] EMLR 44.

2. Three-Party Undue Influence

Another well-known example is the law on non-commercial guarantees. A bank usually has no foolproof means of verifying whether a guarantee given to it by Y for the purposes of X's business (to which the bank has extended credit) was procured by X's undue influence over Y (or some other vitiating factor such duress or misrepresentation). But certain circumstances may be present to put the bank on inquiry as to the circumstances in which Y agreed to stand as surety.

While the factual scenario here evidently takes place in quite different circumstances from an economic tort or ostensible ownership-type conflict, there is a shared underlying logic. As was observed by Lord Browne-Wilkinson in *Barclays Bank plc v O'Brien*:

> The doctrine of notice lies at the heart of equity. Given that there are two innocent parties, each enjoying rights, the earlier right prevails against the later right if the acquirer of the later right knows of the earlier right (actual notice) or would have discovered it had he taken proper steps (constructive notice). In particular, if the party asserting that he takes free of the earlier rights of another knows of certain facts which put him on inquiry as to the possible existence of the rights of that other and he fails to make such inquiry or take such other steps as are reasonable to verify whether such earlier right does or does not exist, he will have constructive notice of the earlier right and take subject to it.[67]

The wife's entitlement is her equity to set aside the guarantee, the possibility of which must minimally be broadcast to the bank, before the law may impose certain responsibilities upon the latter, not exceeding its capacity for verification or compliance.

In *Royal Bank of Scotland v Etridge (No 2)*,[68] it was held that a bank may be 'put on inquiry' (an update on the terminology of 'constructive notice') in circumstances where the relationship between X and Y is non-commercial, the standard case being where a wife offers to stand as surety for her husband's business debts without deriving any direct benefit. While recognizing that lenders could not be expected to probe into emotional or sexual relationships, the House of Lords held that the above circumstances were objective

[67] [1994] 1 AC 180, 195–196.
[68] [2002] 2 AC 773.

indicators sufficient to signal the possibility of undue influence, going beyond the narrower test for notice in *Barclays Bank* that relied on a manifestly disadvantageous transaction and substantial risk that the husband had committed a legal or equitable wrong.[69] These indicators suggest that the bank then has responsibility in relation to the guarantee. The law thus calibrates the bank's own duty of further verification, which involves taking reasonable and fairly non-burdensome steps to satisfy itself that the guarantor understands the nature and effect of the transaction, such as informing the guarantor that it requires a solicitor's confirmation, providing necessary financial information to the solicitors, and obtaining the relevant confirmation that the guarantor has been duly advised as to the effect of the guarantee and the seriousness of the risk involved for their financial position. The allocation of contractual risks hence depends on the division of responsibility as to two-way communication and verification between the parties.

3. Triangular Conflicts, Equity's Darling, and the Bona Fide Purchaser Defence

Lastly, take another classic triangular conflict, where B obtains property from A and makes an unauthorized transfer to C. A regulative principle that invariably favours first owner A gives short shrift to the fact that transferee C may have provided value constituting an 'equivalent, offsetting type of loss that the second-in-time competing party might suffer',[70] and may in many cases impose upon C an unduly onerous burden of verification, since 'generally purchasers of assets or rights in assets are unable to take any meaningful precautionary measures to verify whether a prior conflicting claimant exists'.[71] Indeed, where A consents to or volitionally places the asset in question with intermediary B, they take some risk that they are 'misleading' parties in the position of C by not clearly broadcasting their interest in the asset. On C's end, however, it might be said that 'whenever the purchaser acts with actual knowledge or presumed suspicion of the existence of a prior conflicting claim, the purchaser is the party best located to prevent the conflict by avoiding the transaction'.[72]

Turning to doctrine, recall that the 'equity's darling' defence operates as follows: where C receives property (eg trust property) from B (as trustee) in

[69] Ibid, 803–804.
[70] Menachem 1991, 120.
[71] Ibid, 117.
[72] Ibid, 116.

which A (as beneficiary) has a prior equitable proprietary interest, A's equitable interest will be extinguished,[73] insofar as C has given value for the legal estate, and acts in good faith, without actual or constructive notice of A's equitable interest and that the transfer was in breach of trust.[74] Constructive knowledge is understood in the sense of knowledge that would have come to C if they had made all inquiries that would have been made by a reasonable person in C's position, particularly where facts known to C are indicative of transactional impropriety and the need to seek a further explanation.[75] It is observed that the 'innocent purchaser who never benefitted from the trust arrangement is more deserving of protection than the beneficiary who enjoyed the various freedoms arising from the equitable nature of her right (eg freedom from the restrictions of *numerus clausus* and registration requirements)'.[76] The non-public arrangement of the trust, while advantageous to beneficiaries, means that third parties would find it generally difficult and in some cases beyond their capacity to discover the division of legal and equitable interests, where not effectively broadcast to them. On the other hand, a third party with actual knowledge can simply avoid entering the purchase and engendering a conflict of proprietary interests with the loss placed on the equitable owner. And a third party with constructive knowledge can take relatively less costly steps to inquire into the nature of the deal, and similarly avoid a more burdensome loss to the equitable owner. Hence, if certain facts known to a bank, such as the manner through which debt repayments were made to it by a (fraudulent) art dealer using a web of entities and raising the risk of fraud or money laundering, were to give a reasonable banker cause to question the propriety of the transaction and take further investigation, the bank cannot claim the bona fide purchaser defence against the claimant-owner of the art, as its responsibility for verification has been engaged.[77]

[73] *Boscawen v Bajwa* [1996] 1 WLR 328, 334; see also *Akers v Samba Financial Group* [2017] UKSC 6; [2017] AC 424.

[74] See *Byers v Saudi National Bank* [2023] UKSC 51 at [20] (Lord Hodge).

[75] See *Crédit Agricole Corporation and Investment Bank v Papadimitriou* [2015] UKPC 13, [2015] 1 WLR 4265, [20].

[76] Nair & Samet 2020, 285.

[77] *Crédit Agricole Corporation and Investment Bank v Papadimitriou* [2015] UKPC 13, [2015] 1 WLR 4265.

VI. The Morality of Broadcasting and the Minimum Content of Private Law

As I have argued, private law has developed various rules and concepts for dealing with the informational demands of broadcasting and verifying entitlements, and in a somewhat rough-and-ready way distributing or calibrating the relevant burdens to those who are best able to bear them. But what is normatively significant about bilateral broadcasting, and how does it differ from other accounts we find in private law theory?

While foundational, the question addressed herein is of a different order from that of high theory. My goal is not to address how and why contract or property law is justified, as a matter of will, labour, personhood, human flourishing, distributive justice, and so forth. Neither am I making a 'convergence'-type argument that Merrill and Smith have importantly made regarding property's morality, which is that the 'core of property depends on robust and automatic prelegal intuitions that it is wrong to violate property rights, especially by stealing, crossing boundaries, and interfering with possession',[78] and that this simple yet robust morality of 'no taking' is consistent with a 'range of consequentialist, deontological, and eudaimonistic theories that take seriously basic problems of implementation such as information and complexity'.[79] I also resist the inference, *pace* Dorfman and Jacob, that the recognition of some due diligence component in communicating authorization to entry naturally leads to a 'conception of social responsibility that is *inherent* in property',[80] such as a more protective standard of care owed by landowners to entrants and some trespassers.

Rather, to (loosely) appropriate a Hartian phrase, bilateral broadcasting involves the *minimum moral content* of private law. I am not concerned here with the issue of human self-preservation or survival, but with the essential building blocks of any system of private law. In this regard, I would posit that the recognition of the capacity and responsibility for communication and verification is usually a threshold for the imposition of obligations in private law. For sure, the need for bilateral broadcasting is a check against plasticity and bundle-of-rights views that may lean more indiscriminately towards widening circles of privity. But bilateral broadcasting does not always support 'exclusion'

[78] Merrill & Smith 2007, 1894.
[79] Smith 2009, 967.
[80] Dorfman & Jacob 2015, 88 (emphasis in original).

over 'governance'-type entitlements, or vice versa, for that matter. It is not directly for or against proprietary rights, or the expansion of private law liability. As we have seen, bilateral broadcasting constraints may explain why we should not extend liability for conversion to intangible contractual rights, while allowing for the tort of inducing breach of contract. Yet notice-based doctrines can be interpreted in a fertile way, such that a bank may take some responsibility for verifying the position of a wife who potentially signs a guarantee under undue influence, where reasonable steps can be taken to reduce the risk of this happening.

While minimal, the morality of broadcasting comes distinctively with the territory of private law. The morality of bilateral broadcasting is *sui generis* in this sense. The pure moral philosopher can speak of what we owe to distant strangers, taking into account the extent of interdependence and the reverberating effect of economic activities on other communities of persons. The political philosopher likewise can speak of global and international justice, and what more privileged peoples or countries owe to the less privileged in terms of duties of humanitarian intervention, poverty aid, climate change, and the like. But the private lawyer necessarily deals with the implementation and operation of legal rules governing basic (as well as more complex) interactions in society. As Charles Fried once wrote:

> It is the peculiar task of law to complete this structure of ideals and values, to bring it down to earth; to complete it so that it is seated firmly and concretely and shelters real human beings against the storms of passion and conflict. That last twenty feet may not be the most glamorous part of the building—it is the part where the plumbing and utilities are housed. But it is an indispensable part.[81]

The morality of bilateral broadcasting lies in the last twenty feet connecting high theory to practical implementation. Informational demands, effective communication and publicity, verification, notice and good faith, and priority conflicts, are not the 'sexiest' topics for philosophers. But to ignore these issues is to miss something of essence in the relational character of private law.

[81] Fried 1981, 57.

References

Baird, D.G. and Jackson, T.H. (1983). 'Possession and Ownership: An Examination of the Scope of Article 9'. *Stanford Law Review* 35: 175, 188–189.

Clarke, A. (2020) *Principles of Property Law.* Cambridge, Cambridge University Press.

Dorfman, A. and Jacob, A. (2015). 'The Fault of Trespass'. *University of Toronto Law Journal* 65: 48.

Eleftheriadis, P. (1996). 'The Analysis of Property Rights'. *Oxford Journal of Legal Studies* 16: 31.

Endicott, T. (2000). 'Objectivity, Subjectivity, and Incomplete Agreements'. *Oxford Essays in Jurisprudence.* J Horder. Oxford, Oxford University Press.

Fried, C. (1981). 'The Artificial Reason of the Law or: What Lawyers Know'. *Texas Law Review* 60: 35.

Gergen, M. (2020). 'Privity'. *The Oxford Handbook of the New Private Law.* A. S. Gold, J. C. P Goldberg, D. B Kelly, E. Sherwin, and H. E. Smith.

Goldberg, J. C. P and B. C. Zipursky (2020). *Recognizing Wrongs.*

Goodhart, A. L. (1930). 'The Unforeseeable Consequences of a Negligent Act'. *Yale Law Journal* 39: 449.

Green, S. and J. Randall (2009). *The Tort of Conversion.*

Hansmann, H. and R. Kraakman (2002). 'Property, Contract and Verification: The *Numerus Clausus* Problem and the Divisibility of Rights'. *Journal of Legal Studies* 31: 373.

Hohfeld, W. N. (1917). 'Fundamental Legal Conceptions as Applied in Judicial Reasoning'. *Yale Law Journal* 26: 710–770.

Holmes, O. W. (1881). *The Common Law.*

Howarth, D. (2006) 'Many Duties of Care—Or A Duty of Care? Notes from the Underground'. *Oxford Journal of Legal Studies* 26: 449.

Menachem, M. (1991) '"The Eternal Triangles of Law": Toward a Theory of Priorities in Conflicts Involving Remote Parties'. *Michigan Law Review* 90: 95.

Merrill, T. W. and H. E. Smith (2001). 'The Property/Contract Interface'. *Columbia Law Review* 101: 773.

Merrill, T. W. and H. E. Smith (2001). 'What Happened to Property in Law and Economics?'. *Yale Law Journal* 111: 357.

Merrill, T. W. and H. E. Smith (2007). 'The Morality of Property'. *William & Mary Law Review* 48: 1849.

Nair, A. and I. Samet, (2020). 'What Can "Equity's Darling" Tell Us about Equity?'. *Philosophical Foundations of the Law of Equity.* D. Klimchuk, I. Samet, and H. E. Smith.

Newman, C. M. (2022). 'Hohfeld and the Theory of *In Rem* Rights: An Attempted Mediation'. *The Legacy of Wesley Hohfeld: Edited Major Works, Select Personal Papers, and Original Commentaries.* S. Balganesh, T. Sichelman, and H. E. Smith

Nolan, D. (2013). 'Deconstructing the duty of care'. *Law Quarterly Review* 129: 559.

Owen, D. (2009). 'Figuring Foreseeability'. *Wake Forest Law Review* 44: 1277–1278, 1281–1286.

Penner, J. E. (2020). *Property Rights: A Re-Examination.*

Perry, S. R. (2001). 'Responsibility for Outcomes, Risk, and the Law of Torts'. *Philosophy and the Law of Torts.* G. J. Postema.

Smith, H. E. (2009). 'Mind the Gap: The Indirect Relation between Ends and Means in American Property Law'. *Cornell Law Review* 94: 959.

Sreenivasan, G. (2024). 'Rights In Rem and the Multital Menagerie'. *Singapore Journal of Legal Studies* 361.

Sterk, S. E. (2012). 'Strict Liability and Negligence in Property Theory'. *University of Pennsylvania Law Review* 160: 2129.

Tan, Z. X. (2023). 'Rethinking Relational Architecture: Interpersonal Justice Beyond Private Law'. *University of Toronto Law Journal* 73: 293–347.

Webb, C. (2018). 'Three Concepts of Rights, Two of Property'. *Oxford Journal of Legal Studies* 38: 246.

Weinrib, E. J. (2012). *The Idea of Private Law.*

8

Toward a Legal Analysis of Externalities

Richard R. W. Brooks

Economics has gained the title of queen of the social sciences by choosing *solved* political problems as its domain. –Abba Lerner

I. Introduction

A 'social cost' is a not particularly difficult concept to grasp. It is the total cost to society of anything and, as economists tell us, everything has a cost.[1] To speak of a social cost, however, is to recognize its two constitutive components: *private cost*, borne by individuals undertaking some action,[2] and *external cost*, which is the cost of that action borne by the rest of society. It is the constitution of 'external cost' and the associated concept of 'externality' that has proven so difficult to comprehend. Since introducing the concept in the late nineteenth and early twentieth centuries, economists have devoted unyielding attention to it.[3] Still, 'externality' remains 'an ambiguous concept',[4] or perhaps more precisely 'a residual concept',[5] as Lagueux puts it, 'defined negatively by the absence of one or another of the traits that are associated with markets'.[6] Alternatively, conditions giving rise to its presence are what economists sometimes use to capture the meaning of 'externality'; as Dahlman

[1] See, eg, Friedman 1975.

[2] This cost may also be described as 'internal' but more often the term 'private' is used. The 'action' in question should be broadly construed to include an act, a forbearance or inaction, a speech act including silence, or a trans*action* taken or avoided.

[3] Most notable, see Coase 1960. See also Knight 1924 and of course Pigou 1920 to whom Coase and Knight were responding and who in turn was building on the concept earlier discussed by Sidgwick 1887 and Marshall 1890.

[4] Demsetz 1967, 348.

[5] Lagueux 2010.

[6] Ibid.

Richard R. W. Brooks, *Toward a Legal Analysis of Externalities* In: *The Property-Contract Interface*. Edited by: James Penner, Irina Sakharova, Henry E. Smith, and Zhong Xing Tan, Oxford University Press.
DOI: 10.1093/9780198951995.003.0010

observes, 'we say that when an externality is present there is a divergence between private and social cost'.[7] These vague notions of absence and presence less reflect evasiveness by economists so much as the elusiveness of what they seek to grasp.

An 'externality' is a term of art among economists, who have sweepingly identified it with 'malevolence and benevolence'.[8] It's a tell. Said when there is really nothing to say, economically speaking, because the analytical tools on which the discipline relies have no grounding in the presence of externalities. To secure some footing from which they can use and apply their tools, economists typically turn to law, in particular property rights, to resolve problems involving externalities. But externalities are not *per se* defined by an absence of property rights, nor is the presence of property rights sufficient to avoid or correct them.[9] So what exactly is an externality? 'An externality is frequently defined to occur whenever a decision variable of one economic agent enters into the utility function (or production function) of some other agent'.[10] Such an understanding would imply that '[e]very cost and benefit associated with social interdependencies is a potential externality'.[11]

To prevent the concept from swallowing up every social interaction, and thereby losing all meaning, there must be some established criteria for the evaluation of conduct, allowing us to exclude some actions or aspects of the behaviours of others that would otherwise be deemed an externality.[12] Here then is the 'deep problem in the interpretation of externalities', as Kenneth Arrow observed. Which 'aspects of others' behavior do we consider as affecting a utility function?'[13] Writing more than a half century ago, when law and society placed greater prohibitions on what 'students of criminal law call

[7] Dahlman 1979, 141.

[8] See Laffont 1987. 'Externalities may be positive or negative and are quite diverse. Major examples include pollution activities (air pollution, water pollution, noise pollution ...), malevolence and benevolence, positive interaction of production activities.' Ibid.

[9] 'Creating a missing competitive market means first creating and allocating property rights; but while such an initial allocation is necessary, it does not in and by itself ensure competitive exchange.' Berta & Bertrand 2014, 336.

[10] Heller & Starrett 1976, 9–10. Heller and Starrett immediately follow this observation by noting 'that this is not a very useful definition, at least until the institutional framework is given', and then they go on to provide their preferred definition of an externality as 'a situation in which the private economy lacks sufficient incentives to create a potential market in some good and the nonexistence of this market results in losses in Pareto efficiency'. Ibid, 10.

[11] Demsetz 1967, 348.

[12] Note that efficiency, the economist's preferred criterion for conduct, will not suffice for the reasons, among others, that disfavour act utilitarianism.

[13] Arrow 1970, 16. 'If we take a hard-boiled revealed preference attitude, then if an individual expends resources in supporting legislation regulating another's behavior, it must be assumed that that behavior affects his utility.' Ibid.

"crimes without victims", such as homosexuality or drug-taking', Arrow inquired whether objecting distant third parties (ie those with 'no direct relation [to] parties' engaged in these so-called crimes) bear any socially cognizable external costs from the conduct of others. 'Do we have to extend the concept of externality to all matters that an individual cares about?'[14]

There is the problem—*the externality problem*: finding that elusive ever-eroding line that limits the concept of an externality from extending to all conceivable harms (and benefits) that persons experience as a consequence of the imagined beliefs and conduct of others.[15] In almost all cases there is no natural or obvious place to draw that line. As Hegel observed, 'no boundary is present *in itself* between what is harmful and what is harmless (even with regard to crime) . . . or between what should be prohibited . . . and what should be exempted from prohibitions'.[16] How might conventional economic approaches inform this problem? Competent economic analyses may reveal whether an action is efficient, or whether strategies comprised of actions constitute equilibria,[17] but these analyses cannot determine whether an action *in itself* is an externality, as opposed to merely having an external effect on others, which describes, of course, all social interdependencies. Our socially interdependent lives afford extraordinary benefits as well as great costs. Allocation of these costs and benefits—who in the end must bear them—is not simply an economic problem of social cost but rather a more fundamental problem of social conflict.

[14] Ibid. 'Or, in the spirit of John Stuart Mill, is there a second-order value judgment which excludes some of these preferences from the formation of social policy as being illegitimate infringements of individual freedom?' Ibid.

[15] Although this terminology has been used before, I am unaware of any analyses that deploy it in the manner ascribed in this chapter. For instance, in a thoughtful article Carl Dahlman (Dahlman 1979) invokes the term 'the problem of externality' (indeed he uses it as the title of the article) but his usage throughout the article reveals its intended meaning is closer to 'the problem of social costs', conventionally understood. In his article Dahlman points to politics and ideology as commonly unacknowledged forces behind beliefs about which institutions (eg contractual bargaining, market competition, or government intervention) are seen as best able to address 'problems associated with externalities'. In contrast to the argument of this chapter, Dahlman's appeal to normative evaluation is directed at the purported solutions to the problem, but not to the determination or identification of the problem itself. Accordingly, 'the concept of externalities', to Dahlman, is not based on any content but on a normative determination of the need for government action. Ibid, at 143. Given this diagnosis, he calls for a comparative institutionalist approach to problems of social costs—a call later taken up by Farrell (1987) and Papandreou (1994) among others.

[16] Hegel 1820, §242.

[17] Actions which are permitted and prohibited are taken for granted in most economic models. '[T]he existence of norms that prevent individuals from taking certain actions . . . is also implicitly assumed in any market model. Thus, the standard general equilibrium model is not solely a price-based model but rather is a price-and-norms-based model.' Richter & Rubinstein 2020, 2.

II. Social Conflict and the Problem of Externality

It is sometimes suggested, often implicitly, that all conceivable external effects are indeed externalities, unless or until they are cured through bargaining or some market mediation. What remains then, the uncured external effects, are the residuum of externalities to which economic social welfare (efficiency) analysis properly concerns itself. By bringing these residual externalities within the domain of the market, or taxing them, or providing subsidies for them, or making them subject to contractual exchange, or reducing the transaction costs around bargaining over them, or improving information or institutions for their exchange, or by pursuing various combinations of these strategies, we are led to appreciate that economic analyses offer various solutions to the problem of social cost. In other words, by reducing the problem to an economic transaction (ie making it a 'thing' that may be marketed, taxed, bargained over, or otherwise exchanged), competing welfare and comparative institutional analyses offer a variety of ways 'to deal with the "things" whose marginal costs and prices are to be brought into equality'.[18]

Such are the conventional economic responses to the problem of social costs and benefits. These responses, however, do not offer a solution to the underlying problem of externality so much as assume them away. Abba Lerner stressed this point in his discussion of consumer sovereignty,[19] observing that such an apparent 'solution is essentially the transformation of the *conflict* from a political *problem* to an economic *transaction*. An economic transaction is a solved political problem'.[20] Lerner's point applies with force to the problem of externality. An externality is fundamentally a problem of social conflict, not one of social costs. The problem of social cost is the failure of full marginal costs and benefits (including all cognizable external effects) 'to be brought into equality'.[21] But not all external effects count or even are cognizable in this economic equilibration. Identifying which effects count and which ones don't is a prior problem of social conflict and standing.

When a thing goes from merely exhibiting an external effect to being seen as an externality (ie a thing that someone has standing to complain about and perhaps even do something more than complain about, such as undertaking

[18] Lerner 1972, 259.

[19] 'The basic idea of consumer sovereignty is really very simple: arrange for everybody to have what he prefers whenever this does not involve any extra sacrifice for anybody else.' Ibid, 258.

[20] Ibid, 259. Although 'every "thing" is a set of rights', observes Lerner, '[e]ach set of rights begins as a conflict about what somebody is doing or wants to do which affects others. . . . With or without a fight, there is a settlement or compromise in which the rights are defined.' Ibid.

[21] Ibid.

self-help) it becomes a political problem—one involving matters of policy and calling for the weighing of interests. It is a problem antecedent to the efficiency concerns of social costs and benefits, and more critical too. An externality, unlike a mere external effect, is a threat to social order. Correctly seen, an externality is a problem of legal, political, and social conflict. We may usefully view these conflicts and their resolutions in terms of jural entitlements that provide or deny standing to make claims and seek redress from legal, political, and social authorities.[22] From this view there is, undoubtedly, a line separating mere external effects from externalities, but the line is neither fixed nor discernible from formalist economic arguments. Conventional economic models cannot distinguish external effects from externalities because the arguments of those models attend only to physical relations, that is, 'relation[s] perceivable by the senses, between two physical objects',[23] whereas externalities, unlike mere external effects, are normative relations.

An externality is a normative relation regarding contestable legal, political, and social entitlements. There is a tendency among economists to assume an absence, or better, an inadequacy of legal entitlements in the context of what they call an 'externality', and in consequence they then propose to establish 'property rights', variably understood, as a necessary condition to address inefficiencies arising from unequilibrated social costs and benefits at the margin. In this approach economists tend to elide (i) the essential juridical nature of externalities and (ii) the moral and political implications of recognizing (and not recognizing) certain external effects as externalities. That is not to say their approach is characterized by a true absence of law or politics, as others have noted.[24] Rather, in their approach these matters of contestation are settled from the start. To paraphrase Lerner, an externality is a solved political problem. How then are we to assess the problem before its resolution?

Law itself is a solved political problem. It results from and reflects all sorts of moral and political compromises. Taking a legal analytical approach to the problem of externality, what may be called 'a legal analysis of externalities', can shed light on these often-implicit settlements from which conventional economic analyses of the problem of social cost depart. I have elsewhere referred

[22] As John Commons wrote of Hohfeld's framework in law and economics: 'his is practically an analysis of the way in which the common practices of *any* going concern control the individual members of that concern and hold them to the conduct necessary to *preserve the existence of the concern*.' Commons 1925, 375.

[23] Corbin 1919, 164.

[24] 'It is thus doubtful whether the term "externality" has any meaningful interpretation, except as an indicator of the political beliefs and value judgments of the person who uses (or avoids using) the term.' Dahlman 1979, 156.

to this general approach as 'legal analysis of economics' (a counterpart and companion to economic analysis of law) which looks to identify subtle or often unstated premises and presuppositions of law in economic arguments, concepts, and models.[25] I am hardly the first to see or suggest such an approach. In a 1925 article, entitled 'Law and Economics', John Commons saw the potential of this 'reverse action' whereby careful legal analysis can inform and ground economics.[26] 'I take it this is', said Commons, 'the grand contribution which the science of law gives to the science of economics'.[27]

A more recent 'legal analysis of economics' was undertaken by Thomas Merrill and Henry Smith in an article related to and published the same year as 'The Property/Contract Interface'.[28] In their analysis, Merrill and Smith unpack the implications of Coase's wholesale adoption of the realists' conception of property as a 'bundle of rights' in his demonstration of costless bargaining as a solution to the problem of social cost. That judicial opinions now commonly invoke the terminology of 'bundle of rights' reflects the success of the legal realists' conceptualization of property, but it is not the only conception (or even the primary one) that judges espouse when resolving property disputes in the everyday world of conflict, friction, and non-zero transaction costs. Legal analyses building on alternative and quite plausible conceptions of property (not simply as a bundle of finely separable entitlements) can shed light on competing economic solutions to the problem of social cost.[29] A legal analytical approach may also illuminate the prior problem of externality.

A legal analysis of the problem antecedent to those of social costs and benefits, that is, the externality problem, can clarify what's implicit or taken for granted in standard economic approaches to externalities. Consider, for example, Harold Demsetz's expansive departing notion that '[n]o harmful or

[25] See, eg, Brooks 2025.

[26] After noting that 'the science of economics . . . is a science of the fundamental concepts on which the science of law is also grounded', Commons then observed: 'But there is a reverse action wherein the science of economics is being grounded, in recent times, on concepts derived from the common law.' Commons 1925, 374.

[27] Ibid, 376.

[28] See Merrill & Smith 2001. While the 'The Property/Contract Interface' laid the groundwork for their analysis of the interface between in rem property rights and in personam contract rights, in this follow-up article Merrill and Smith applied their insights to Ronald Coase's 'Problem of Social Cost', revealing a vanishingly thin conception of property adopted by Coase and later scholars of law and economics. See also Lee & Smith 2012, 145–155.

[29] See, eg, note 90 below and accompanying text (discussing Common's conception of property. See also Lee and Smith, who concede that 'in a world of zero transaction costs, setting up basic entitlements with fine-grained *in personam* contract-style rights could be done costlessly', yet in the real world of actual conflict, as Coase himself stressed, 'transaction costs are positive, and [consequently] . . . as the numbers become very large, positive transaction costs make such bargains increasingly inefficient, and ultimately impossible in practice. The structure of property itself then can be explained as a response to these implications of positive transaction costs.' Merrill & Smith 2001 152–153.

beneficial effect is external to the world'—which he immediately qualifies by adding, '[s]ome person or persons always suffer or enjoy these effects'.[30] So from the start the pains and pleasures experienced by animals appear to be excluded unless registered by some person or persons. Moreover, not all persons who suffer or enjoy external effects are themselves subjects of externalities. Jenny Wahl illustrated this point in her historical treatment of externalities in the US Southern slave economy, where externalities felt by enslaved persons matter only insofar as they affect 'free society'.[31] James Buchanan and Craig Stubblebine, in their well-known article entitled 'Externality', observe that the subjects of externalities are 'presumed to be [] member[s] of the same social group'.[32] Implicit in this observation lies even more variation. Namely, as legal and social boundaries vary—expanding or contracting the membership and status of persons (legal or natural) who count—so too do the subjects of externalities.

Activities that constitute externalities also exhibit great variation in the literature. Buchanan and Stubblebine 'define an activity here as any distinguishable human action that may be measured, such as eating bread, drinking milk, spewing smoke into the air, dumping litter on the highways, giving to the poor, etc'.[33] Yet it is the effect of these activities that create the varieties of externalities. What about a felt disgust at the sight of someone eating or drinking? Traditionalists would restrict externalities to physical effects, but it is hard to maintain that line.[34] What if physical illness follows from the sight of someone eating (the most disgusting thing you can imagine)? What about '[t]he effect of my bad breath on another',[35] or pure envy, which generates 'positional externalities' without any physical manifestations? As already noted, some theorists include malice itself,[36] while others reject the suggestion that any malicious

[30] Demsetz 1967, 348.
[31] Although a number of cases cited by Wahl indicate that courts gave direct weight to the harms suffered by enslaved persons, in Wahl's analysis these persons were essentially excluded as subjects of externalities. Wahl 1997, 2.
[32] Buchanan & Stubblebine 1962, 372.
[33] Ibid.
[34] Complaining about the 'arbitrary extensions of its original meaning', Mishan earlier wrote, '[i]f the cutting edge of this powerful analytic tool is to be restored, an attempt must be made to chip away much of the accumulating accretions of meaning that have attached themselves to this term over time'. Mishan 1965, 5.
[35] Hausman 1992, 95–113.
[36] 'I mean by malice', as Holmes wrote, 'a malevolent motive for action, without reference to any hope of a remoter benefit to oneself to be accomplished by the intended harm to another', Holmes 1894, 2. Buchanan and Stubblebine place 'desire' at the core of their definition of whether an external effect is a potentially relevant externality: 'An externality is defined as potentially relevant when the activity, to the extent that it is actually performed, generates any *desire* on the part of the externally benefited (damaged) party (A) to modify the behaviour of the party empowered to take action (B) through trade, persuasion, compromise, agreement, convention, collective action, etc.' Buchanan & Stubblebine 1962, 373–374 (emphasis added).

intent or other deliberate motive can constitute externalities.[37] By unpacking these various, often implicit and competing, claims regarding the activities and subjects of externalities, legal analyses of the models and methods employed by economists may offer insight into how they come to see what constitutes social costs and benefits—or, in other words, how *they* 'solve' the problem of externality.

A legal analysis of externalities may also be informed by how courts and other legal institutions themselves address problems of externalities. Attending to doctrine and legal practice can shed light on whether and how law recognizes and gives standing for redress of external costs and benefits. A fruitful study might depart from the laws concerning nuisance (harms) and unjust enrichment (benefits), but the scope of inquiry may usefully extend to almost all areas of law within given jurisdictions and particular periods (jurisdictional and temporal variations are to be expected). That is, by closely looking at law and how lawmakers, broadly understood, deal with problems of legally cognizable external harms and benefits we may better glimpse the shifting boundaries that define externalities in practice. A sketch of the law of externalities is briefly presented in the concluding pages of this chapter. A brief discussion, however, first follows on the taxonomy, origins, and ongoing evolution of external effects and externalities.

III. Taxonomy of External Effects and Externalities

Each year thousands of articles, books, and other manuscripts adopt the language of externalities to advance some purported solution to a social problem or describe its insoluble nature.[38] An externality is always a problem. Even when it is beneficial (ie positive) there is never enough of it. To say the term is like calling out an ominous spirit that you know is there though you can't make out its exact form. In the vast literature on the topic, externalities are

[37] For example, Mishan, among others, observe 'the essential feature of the concept of an external effect is that the effect produced is not a deliberate creation but an unintended or incidental by-product of some otherwise legitimate activity'. Mishan 1971, 2.

[38] Boundreaux & Meiners found that in law review articles alone there was 'an average of almost a thousand articles per year that mention externalities. Economics journals are similarly rife with discussion of externality issues.' Boundreaux & Meiners 2019. While far from complete, a serviceable partial list of critical and insightful contributions to the literature includes Pigou 1920; Knight 1924; Viner 1932; Ellis & Fellner 1943; Meade 1952; Scitovsky 1954; Bator 1958; Coase 1960; Buchanan & Stubblebine 1962; Turvey 1963; Demsetz 1964; Castle 1965; Ayres & Kneese 1969; Kapp 1969; Arrow 1970; Mishan 1971; Starrett 1972; Heller & Starrett 1976; Polinsky 1979; Schweizer 1988; Papandreou 1994; Lagueux 2010; Berta & Bertrand 2014; and Boundreaux, Frischmann, & Marciano 2014.

rarely defined so much as the conditions for their existence are described. A commonly stated necessary condition for the existence of an externality is the failure of its internalization because the costs of doing so exceed the benefits.[39] Should that strike you as vacuous or tautological then you are not alone.[40] Fortunately, there are other criteria that have been suggested, but they too aren't fully persuasive.

For instance, a common way of describing the necessary condition for the existence of an externality is the presence of transaction costs—'in the theory of externalities, transaction costs are the root of all evil'.[41] However, the presence of transaction costs, properly understood, does not imply the existence of externalities, nor does the absence of transaction costs imply the elimination of externalities.[42] Something else or something more is required for both the existence and elimination of externalities. In addition to zero transaction costs, argued Ronald Coase, known and enforceable property rights are necessary elements of the bargaining that he proposed would eliminate externalities.[43] That is, if property rights are established and well known, then in a zero transaction cost world (ie where parties can costlessly bargain and enforce their agreements) contracting will resolve the problem of negative externalities (or social costs).[44]

Kenneth Arrow similarly assumed the necessity of property rights in offering a competitive market solution to the problem of social cost. Economists have long supposed a 'close relationship between property rights and externalities', as Harold Demsetz revealingly observed:

> Harming a competitor by producing superior products may be permitted, while shooting him may not. A man may be permitted to benefit himself by

[39] 'One condition is necessary to make costs and benefits externalities. The cost of a transaction in the rights between the parties (internalization) must exceed the gains from internalization.' Demsetz 1967, 348.

[40] 'Thus if one assumes rationality, no transaction costs, and *no legal impediment* to bargaining, all misallocations of resources would be fully cured in the market by bargains. Far from surprising, this statement is tautological, at least if one accepts any of the various definitions of misallocation.' Calabresi 1968 (emphasis added).

[41] Dahlman 1979, 142.

[42] '[N]o kind of known transaction costs can possibly generate anything looking like a Pareto-relevant externality. Once the logical implications of bargaining under transaction costs are fully accepted, it is seen that all existing side effects are internalized one way or the other.' Ibid, 150.

[43] Coase 1960.

[44] There are numerous qualifications to this argument, which will not be rehearsed here. One point that should be noted, however, is that property rights are not obviously needed in the Coasean framework, as a number of commentators have observed. For instance, Brian Lee and Henry Smith have written: 'In the zero transaction cost world, the nature and scope of property rights might seem not to matter: any deficiency in the allocation of those rights can be made up for by contracting (or by any other hypothetically costless institutional mechanism).' Lee & Smith 2012, 147.

> shooting an intruder but be prohibited from selling below a price floor. It is clear, then, that property rights specify how persons may be benefited and harmed, and, therefore, who must pay whom to modify the actions taken by persons.[45]

Notice the leap from *permissions* and *prohibitions* to *property rights* and then to *payments.* To be sure, the presence of property rights resolve most matters of permissions and prohibitions, excluding them (according to some theorists) from being characterized as externalities. But an absence of property rights does not imply an absence of law concerning externalities, or an inability of a society to respond to the threats posed by the problem of externality.[46] Additional uncertainty is caused by the competing terms used to describe externalities.[47] Thirty years ago Papandreou helpfully organized many of these labels according to their distinctive theoretical features,[48] yet as the literature continues to grow more usages and novel taxonomies are introduced.[49] Rather than attempting to catalogue the current jargon for this sempiternal concept, it may be more useful to go back to the beginning—when the notion of external effects (or 'economies') was first introduced by economists—to appreciate how legal analysis can help us understand the externality problem.

IV. Origins of External Effects and Externalities

The concept of an 'externality' derived from the economically uncontroversial idea of economies of scale—that is, cost savings resulting from greater levels of production either within a firm or more broadly the industry in which a firm operates. Scale and specialization were, of course, central themes in Adam Smith's discussion of the division of labour, promoting productive efficiency

[45] Demsetz 1967.

[46] In fairness to these thoughtful contributors to the law and economics literature on externalities, while their approaches to addressing externality problems prioritize property rights, they and others do concede other possibilities, although usually without much elaboration. An important exception in this regard, but not the only one, is Guido Calabresi who, individually and in co-authored work, has written extensively on the role of law and politics in the determination of externalities. See, eg, Calabresi 2016 and Calabresi & Melamed 1972, 1112.

[47] These include 'diseconomies', 'disservices', 'external costs', 'external economies', 'external effects', 'indirect effects', 'missing markets', 'non-convexities', 'social costs', 'social effects', 'spillovers', 'unintended side effects', 'unwanted side effects' (presumably only for negative externalities), 'unpriced effects', 'unpriced factors', and 'unpriced interdependencies', among other labels.

[48] Papandreou 1994.

[49] See, eg, Paniagua and Rayamajhee 2024. See also Bertrand, 2023, describing certain 'transformations' and 'presuppositions' in the concept of an externality as it expands into new fields.

through the elimination of waste in terms of energy, time, and materials.[50] It is, however, Alfred Marshall, the nineteenth-century English economist, who is generally credited with the founding exposition on externalities:

> We may divide the economies arising from an increase in the scale of production of any kind of goods, into two classes—firstly, those dependent on the general development of the industry; and secondly, those dependent on the resources of individual houses of business engaged in it, on their organization and the efficiency of their management. We may call the former external economies, and the latter internal economies.[51]

In Marshall's exposition, the term 'internal economies' simply means economies of scale (or reductions in costs) that result from a firm expanding its own productive activities. When a firm appreciates cost reductions from the activities of other firms in its industry Marshall called that phenomenon 'external economies' (of scale). Simple enough. Yet, a century and a half later, the reflective welfare economist Tibor Scitovsky would observe that the 'concept of external economies is one of the most elusive in economic literature'.[52]

It's true, the varied usages in the literature on external economies can be difficult to grasp, but one aspect of the concept remains as simple as it was in Marshall's initial account. We are concerned here with activities and effects within firms and industries. External economies are externalities strictly within the 'sphere of production', as Peter Bohm usefully put it.[53] It is the first and principal limitation on the scope of externalities in the economics literature. Within this restricted scope of concerns the responses (or solutions) have a distinct valence and normative resonance. For example, industrial waste and non-remunerative by-products are to be avoided for the benefit of the firms and industries that produce them (productive efficiency), not for the advantages (or avoided disadvantages) of parties outside of the sphere of production who might inadvertently or involuntarily consume the waste (allocative

[50] Smith 1776.
[51] Marshall 1890, Bk iv, Ch 9.
[52] Scitovsky 1954, 143.
[53] Bohm 2008. See also, eg, Broadberry & Marrison 2002. In an important contribution to the literature, Meade described a distinction between external economies within a given industry and economies that cut across industries, 'where what is done in one industry reacts upon the conditions of production in the other industry in some way other than through the possible effect upon the prices of the product or of the factors in that other industry', leading to external (dis)economies. Meade 1952, 56. 'As an illustrative example,' Bohm offers 'the case where a dam constructed by a hydroelectric power plant eliminates flooding of farmers' crop fields—external economy—or reduces the catches of fishermen downstream—external diseconomies; a producer's pollution which increases the costs of, *inter alia*, other producers is perhaps the most important case of externalities.' Bohm 2008.

efficiency).[54] Moreover, the relationships and going-concerns that matter are the firms and industries that define the relevant sphere of production.

While Marshall concentrated on the external benefits between firms and within industries, it was his student, Arthur Pigou, who breached the sphere of production, leaving a wedge wide enough for armies of economists to pour through—largely ill-equipped to apply their tools and training to what they would encounter—in the moral, political, and social spheres. Pigou picked up where Marshall (and Henry Sidgwick) left off, at least briefly, with uncompensated external benefits in business settings, such as lighthouses providing their *services* to passing commercial vessels from which they found it difficult, if not impossible, to collect payment.[55] But he soon cast his gaze beyond strictly commercial concerns, for example, to pedestrians and other passersby who benefit from 'lamps erected at the doors of private houses, for these necessarily throw light also on the streets'.[56] In economics, as well as in law, the provision and prevention of light (artificial and natural) are often seen as sources of externalities.[57]

Pigou also brought a new emphasis to external costs, which he sometimes referred to as *disservices*, including 'the running of motor cars that wear out the surface of the roads', 'the production and sale of intoxicants' along with the predictable disservices that often follow, and the now prototypical negative externality, air pollution, specifically—'smoke from factory chimneys':

> for this smoke in large towns inflicts a heavy uncharged loss on the community, in injury to buildings and vegetables, expenses for washing clothes and cleaning rooms, expenses for the provision of extra artificial light, and in many other ways.

[54] Marshall's discussion of the elimination of industrial waste focuses on the advantages it affords to the firms which reduce or make use of its waste by-products (realizing economies) rather than the harm avoided by others due to the reduced or eliminated waste (diseconomies), emphasizing then-recent advances in 'the utilizing of what had been a waste product'. Marshall 1890, 279. Marshall noted it was more the returns to skill and managerial planning from economies of scale, rather than invention, that drove the elimination of firm and industrial waste. Ibid.

[55] 'Sidgwick observes, 'it may easily happen that the benefits of a well-placed lighthouse must be largely enjoyed by ships on which no toll could be conveniently levied'. Pigou 1920, 160 (citing Sidgwick 1887).

[56] Pigou 1920.

[57] There is a long history of economics discourse on the use of lighthouses as the quintessential positive externality and a robust debate, beginning with Coase in 1974, on whether public support or strictly private provision could (or did sustain) these enterprises. See Coase 1974; Van Zandt 1993; Bertrand 2006; Barnett & Block 2007. In his 1960 article, 'The Problem of Social Cost,' Coase does not discuss lighthouses, but does offer sunbathers losing their light as an example of an externality: 'A recent case in Florida concerned a building which cast a shadow on the cabana, swimming pool and sunbathing areas of a neighbouring hotel.' Coase 1960, 8 (citing *Fontainebleu Hotel Corp v Forty-Five Twenty-Five, Inc.* 114 So 2d 357 (1959)).

Through these and a number of other examples Pigou illustrated external effects or, as he put it, 'divergences between social and private net products',[58] that were beyond the sphere of production and transactions not subject to contract or market mediation. For instance, he suggested that

> the crowning illustration of this [divergence] is afforded by the work done by women in factories, particularly during the periods immediately preceding and succeeding confinement; for there can be no doubt that this work often carries with it, besides the earnings of the women themselves, grave injury to the health of their children.[59]

Before concluding this section there is a final point that's worth noting, as others have previously observed.[60] Namely, Pigou did in fact consider contracting as a strategy to correct divergences he observed, but this strategy appeared infeasible to him in the absence of privity between the relevant parties:

> It is plain that divergences between [private] and social net product of the kinds we have so far been considering cannot, like divergences due to tenancy laws, be mitigated by a modification of the contractual relation between any two contracting parties, because the divergence arises out of a service or disservice rendered to persons other than the contracting parties.[61]

With the contractual solution seemingly unavailing, he then suggested that 'the State, if it so chooses, to remove the divergence', may be able to do so using 'bounties and taxes'.[62] From there the idea of Pigouvian subsidies and taxes would soon be launched into the literature, often without much of the nuance and subtlety with which it was originally offered.

V. Ongoing Evolution of External Effects and Externalities

Almost immediately following Pigou's expansive treatment of externalities, and ever since, economists have sought to either exclude some considerations

[58] Elsewhere, Pigou adds 'values' and 'marginal' when characterizing the divergences between the social and private net product: 'divergences between the values of marginal social and marginal private net product'; 'divergences between the values of social and private net product' (Pigou 1920, 114).
[59] Ibid, 162.
[60] See, eg, Simpson 1996; Hovenkamp 2009; Spash 2021.
[61] Pigou 1920, 168.
[62] Ibid.

from their scope of concern or expand the set of solutions beyond the 'extraordinary restraints' (taxes) and 'extraordinary encouragements' (subsidies) suggested by Pigou. The first exclusion resulted from an 'early controversy associated with the names of Pigou, [Frank] Knight, [Jacob] Viner, and [Joan] Robinson',[63] who eventually agreed that direct economic activities among or between parties which increase or decrease market prices, and in consequence affect third parties, that is, a *pecuniary externality*, is not a source of concern, but a feature of normal market processes.[64] Economists have largely maintained this early consensus on excluding pecuniary externalities from the domain of academic and policy concern.

Considerably less agreement is found among economists regarding the nature and status of other categories of externalities, such as *technological externalities* resulting from production, *positional externalities* driven by consumption, *network externalities* realized through expanding interconnected usage, and *mental externalities* emanating from affective states that give rise to repugnance and the like, or from more cognitive and moral considerations. Not just across these categories (and others not listed) but also within each category, it's not hard to find disagreement over what counts as an externality. Take, for example, what Richard Epstein calls a 'hard' externality—that is, resulting when one or more persons undertake permitted actions that cause physical harm to innocent third parties or their property—in contrast to 'soft' or purely 'symbolic' external effects: 'Hard externalities count[;] Soft externalities should always be ignored.'[65] Yet, while Epstein adopts a negative liberty (do no physical harm) approach in defining external physical harms that count, economists and legal scholars like Louis Kaplow and Steven Shavell point out that failing to rescue or help someone in need also contributes to their physical harm, above and beyond any 'symbolic' external effects.[66]

None of this is meant to suggest that, among economists, purely symbolic or more broadly non-physical harms and benefits fall outside the class of

[63] Mishan 1971, 4.

[64] As Mishan notes, it was Jacob Viner who introduced the term 'pecuniary' external effect in his 1931 article clarifying the controversy, although as for the terminology, Mishan himself felt it was unnecessary and potentially confusing.

[65] Hard or durable externalities on this account includes not only actual and threatened 'physical injury to person or property' but also 'economic harm' from exercising monopoly power. Epstein 1995, 2323 and 2325. See also Epstein 1997.

[66] Writing on how moral sentiments may be enlisted to reduce actions or inaction that cause external harms, Kaplow and Shavell suggest, for instance, that efforts (or simply failing) to rescue or help someone in need may count as externalities—positive in the case of virtue signalling and negative if failing to assist others is evaluated as a kind of acting. Kaplow & Shavell 2007, 497 and 497, fn 4 and 6. That's a pretty big net, and probably not one they intended to cast so widely. Still, they and others may resist the more restrictive views adopted by some economists.

actionable external effects or externalities. In recent years, mental and moral externalities have received increased attention among economists, as behavioural and experimental economics open up venues for their measurement and manipulation. To be sure, repugnance, merit goods, and other related notions are not new to economic thinkers (see, eg, Calabresi, Musgrave, and Roth),[67] but new methodological drivers are inviting more economists to engage with these forms of externalities. At the same time, philosophers[68] and social theorists in commodification studies[69] and allied fields contest the general economic exclusion of moral externalities as well as, interestingly, the long-held exclusion of pecuniary externalities.[70] What does a lawyer or legal analyst have to offer?

VI. Juridical Character of the Externality Problem

Ordinary economies of scale (ie 'internal economies') involve one party only; the effect of increasing scale is internal to the party undertaking the action. Where one party's action has an effect on a second party's productive or consumptive capacity, then 'external economies' (when the effect is positive) and 'diseconomies' (when the effect is negative) come into being. These effects—whether internal or external and whether positive or negative—simply describe physical relations.[71] Yet, unlike economies of scale and external economies, it is my aim to propose here that an 'externality' describes a normative relation between persons.[72] What kind of normative relation is an externality?

An external effect is a thing, whether physical or incorporeal. An externality is a relation between persons, like a property relation—not simply a relationship of a person to a thing or between two things. Moreover, and again like property, an externality has the quality of a *jural* relation, although one more elusive than property. What sort of jural relation describes this elusive concept? To determine the jural relations between any two persons, say *A* and *B*, Arthur Corbin proposed that we begin the inquiry by asking three basic questions:

[67] Musgrave 1959; Roth 2007; Calabresi 2014; Calabresi 2016; Calabresi & Melamed 1972.
[68] Satz 2010; Sandel 2012.
[69] See Bertrand 2023.
[70] Endörfer 2022; Wilkinson 2022; Kogelmann & Carroll 2024.
[71] 'This would include relations of space, time, weight, color, density, and the like.' Corbin 1919, 164.
[72] Papandreou has already described the importance of recognizing the institutional aspects apart from the physical aspects of the economic environment. Papandreou 2000, 2.

(1) What *may A* (or *B*) do, without societal penalty assessed for the benefit of the other?
(2) What *must A* (or *B*) do, under threat of societal penalty assessed for the benefit of the other?
(3) What *can A* (or *B*) do, so as to change the existing legal relations of the other?[73]

Answers to the first question are referred to as *privileges*, to the second *duties*, and the third *powers*, which concern legal and normative powers and not 'mere *physical* power'.[74] To this list a fourth question may be added: (4) What *can A* (or *B*) *get away with* doing (ie *immunities*) without change to their existing legal relations?

Answers to what someone *may*, *must*, or *can do*, or *can get away with doing* in any given society provide clarity and content to the jural entitlements (and their correlatives) of members of that society. These answers, however, do not directly address what distinguishes externalities from mere external effects. What does it mean to say that an externality is a jural relation? Here, again, Corbin offers useful guidance while speaking in terms of strictly legal relations. 'A statement that a legal relation exists between *A* and *B* is a *prediction* as to what society, acting through its courts or executive agents, will do or not do for one and against the other.'[75] With the idea that a legal relation is a prediction of what society will or will not do or tolerate, we may now draw (perhaps sketch) a line between external effects, on the one hand, and externalities, on the other. To say that some activity constitutes an externality is to recognize it as a problem to which a society *may* or *ought* predictably respond.

A societal response is predictably (not certainly) called for, not because of some abstract (or actual) efficiency concerns or social costs, but because when an external effect is contestable—politically, socially, or legally—it gives rise to an externality problem. In other words, externalities are unsolved 'political problems', that is, unsettled conflicts of interests in a context of social interdependence.[76] Imagine, for example, a society wherein some activity, *x*, is strictly prohibited and perfectly enforced. Here there would be no externality from this activity because no one is allowed to *x* and the society perfectly

[73] Corbin 1919, 165.
[74] Ibid.
[75] Ibid, 164. 'If A invades B's house, we are able to predict that the police will eject A, that a court will give judgment for damages, and that the sheriff will levy execution.' Ibid.
[76] Of course, inefficiency itself may be a threat to the continuity of the society, but in that case the efficiency concern is indirect. The direct concern is the continuity of the society's existence or its essential order.

enforces this rule. Now, suppose that enforcement becomes imperfect, but the law concerning x remains well settled (ie x is strictly prohibited or else is allowable, but only with the permission of all affected parties). Absent perfect enforcement there may be external effects if A engages in x (ie $x > 0$) without permission, but so long as the law remains well settled these external effects are not considered to be externalities.

A car taken without permission is a theft, not an externality; a car parked on another's property without permission is a trespass, not an externality; a broken contractual promise to deliver a car where there was no release, excuse, or justification for non-delivery is a breach, not an externality; a fender-bender caused by one's carelessness is a tort, not an externality; a car stereo loudly blasting music late at night in a residential neighbourhood is a nuisance, not an externality; and so on. In all these cases, action taken in the absence of permission or payment is not an externality, but rather is a wrong.[77] These are all settled matters of law. You don't have to put up with people taking your property or parking themselves or their possession on your land, although you may have to settle for damages in tort cases and in most cases when contracts are breached. And you may have to put up with a noisy neighbour, but not at unreasonably late hours. These are well-settled matters of rights, privileges, powers, and immunities (and their correlatives) in our society.[78]

Talk of externalities arises where matters are less well settled, in contexts where it is unclear whether or how a society should or will respond to the external harms or benefits caused by the otherwise privileged activity. To be sure, all privileged activities, including exercises of basic rights, are seldom, if ever, settled once and for all. Yet, in every society some entitlements are more settled than others at any given moment. Strong privileges, let's call them that, are tolerated even when they generate negative external effects. Such privileges are rarely viewed in terms of externalities. Weak privileges, in contrast, are subject to greater contestation when they generate negative external effects. It is a question of standing. That is, whenever an external effect, whether negative or positive, plausibly gives someone standing to demand redress (legally, politically, or socially) the effect comes within the scope of externalities.

[77] One might contend that these examples show the law imperfectly internalizing externalities due to less-than-perfect enforcement. But all law is subject to under-enforcement. Under-enforcement is orthogonal to the externality problem. As Heller and Starrett note, the problem of enforcing property rights in 'externality-producing' situations is different at most in degree rather than in kind from other contexts. Heller & Starrett 1976, 12.

[78] Likewise, everyone knows that some harms (and some benefits received at the expense of others) are simply not legally cognizable injuries (or expenses). See Weeks 1879. Yet, while this doctrine of *damnum absque injuria* ('damage without injury') is a fixture of all societies, what falls within the category legally (and socially or politically) non-cognizable harm may be contestable and less well settled.

Standing, of course, doesn't imply that redress or remedy will necessarily follow, but that's not the point. Invoking the notion of standing here is not meant to resolve an externality problem so much as to identify it. Indeed, resolution occludes the externality problem, transforming 'the *conflict* from a political *problem* to an economic *transaction*',[79] as Lerner put it, or in other words, converting it into a problem of social costs. An externality is a problem of social conflict, not social costs. One may address problems of social costs through Pigouvian taxes or Coasean bargaining or other mechanisms meant to equilibrate marginal costs and benefits. No formula or economic calculation, however, can address the problem of externality, which is a question of how to distinguish it from a mere external effect. For legal and economic scholars of a more formalist bent this poses a hindrance because 'the moment you leave the path of merely logical deduction you lose the illusion of certainty which makes legal reasoning seem like mathematics'.[80] Nonetheless, a law and economics approach may yet provide insight into the externality problem.

Acknowledging and allowing for unsettled conflicts of interests are essential and necessary aspects of any actual analysis of the externality problem. 'Those interests are fields of battle.'[81] And while formalists won't go forward unless armed with rigid mechanical notions of property rights and related doctrines (so as to render externalities amenable to conventional economic analyses), a more integrative law and economics approach may clarify the problem of externality itself. 'In place of these mechanical and coercive doctrines', as Commons observed, a more nuanced analysis may, for instance, see 'the concept of property as a complex set of acquired rights, of imposed duties, and of permitted liberties and exposures, derived from a great variety of customs'—an observation echoed by Lerner,[82]— 'and further, that these fundamental social relations of rights, duties, liberties and exposures, are grounded, *not on the state*, but in the daily habits, practices and customs of the people'.[83] That is, a law and economics analysis of externalities may be undertaken without assuming that the state has, or even can, solve the political problem that underlies them.

[79] Lerner 1972, 259.
[80] Holmes 1894, 7. 'But the certainty is only an illusion, nevertheless.' Ibid.
[81] Ibid.
[82] 'There can be no greater misunderstanding of the origin of market economies' wrote Lerner, than the failure to appreciate that '[t]housands of habits of behavior and of enforced laws had to be developed over millennia to establish the nature and the minutiae of property rights before we could have buying and selling'. Lerner 1972, 259.
[83] Commons 1925, 376 (emphasis added).

VII. Conclusion

An externality is commonly defined as the effect of one party's actions on the welfare or activities of other individuals, beyond what is mediated by markets or contracts. Since individuals must bear the external effects (absent compensation or consent) of another party's actions, economists have come to see externalities as a problem of social costs. There is, however, a 'deep problem in the interpretation of externalities',[84] as it has no limiting principle. 'Every cost and benefit associated with social interdependencies is a potential externality.'[85] An alternative interpretation of the externality problem is offered in this chapter. Properly understood, the externality problem is less a matter of social costs than one of social conflict. As such, externalities are best appreciated and analysed as normative relations where those who would bear the costs of external effects have standing—legally, politically, or socially—to demand redress.

References

Arrow, K. (1970). 'Political and Economic Evaluation of Social Effects and Externalities'. *The Analysis of Public Output*, Julius Margolis. Cambridge, National Bureau of Economic Research: 1–30.

Ayres, R. U. and A. V. Kneese (1969). 'Production, Consumption and Externalities'. *American Economic Review* 59(3): 282–297.

Barnett, W. and W. Block (2007). 'Coase and Van Zandt on Lighthouses'. *Public Finance Review* 35: 710–733.

Bator, F. M. (1958). 'The Anatomy of Market Failure'. *Quarterly Journal of Economics* 72(3): 351–379.

Berta, N. and E. Bertrand (2014). 'Market Internalization of Externalities: What is Failing?' *Journal of the History of Economic Thought* 36(3): 331–357.

Bertrand, E. (2023). 'Contemporary Anti-Commodification Arguments—Market Failures'. *The Routledge Handbook of Commodification.* E. Bertrand and V. Panitch. London, Routledge: 52–71.

Bertrand, E. (2006). 'The Coasean Analysis of Lighthouse Financing: Myths and Realities'. *Cambridge Journal of Economics* 30: 389.

Bohm, P. (2008). 'External Economies'. *The New Palgrave Dictionary of Economics.* S. N. Durlauf and L. E. Blume. London, Palgrave Macmillan.

Boundreaux, D. J. and R. Meiners (2019). 'Externality: Origins and Classifications', *Natural Resources Journal* 59: 1.

Boundreaux, D. J., B. M. Frischmann, and A. Marciano (2014). 'Understanding the Problem of Social Cost'. *Journal of Institutional Economics* 11(2): 329–352.

Broadberry, S. and A. Marrison (2002). 'External Economies of Scale in the Lancashire Cotton Industry, 1900–1950'. *Economic History Review* 55: 51.

[84] Arrow 1970, 16.
[85] Demsetz 1967, 348.

Brooks, R. R. W. (2025). 'Economics and Contract Law'. *Research Handbook on the Philosophy of Contract Law*. M. Chen-Wishart and P. Saprai. Northampton, Edward Elgar Publishing: 56–71.
Buchanan, J. M. and W. C. Stubblebine (1962). 'Externality'. *Economica*, New Series 29(116): 371–384.
Calabresi, G. (1968). 'Transaction Costs, Resource Allocation, and Liability Rules: A Comment'. *Journal of Law and Economics* 11: 67.
Calabresi, G. (2016). *The Future of Law and Economics: Essays in Reform and Recollection*. New Haven, Yale University Press.
Calabresi, G. (2014). 'Of Tastes and Values'. *American Law and Economics Review* 16: 313.
Calabresi, G. and A. D. Melamed (1972). 'Property Rules, Liability Rules, and Inalienability: One View of the Cathedral'. *Harvard Law Review* 85: 1089–1128.
Castle, E. N. (1965). 'The Market Mechanism, Externalities, and Land Economics'. *Journal of Farm Economics* 47(3): 542–556.
Coase, R. H. (1960). 'The Problem of Social Cost'. *Journal of Law and Economics* 3: 1–44.
Coase, R. H. (1974). 'The Lighthouse in Economics'. *Journal of Law and Economics* 17: 357.
Commons, J. R (1925). 'Law and Economics'. *Yale Law Journal* 34: 371–382.
Corbin, A. L. (1919). 'Legal Analysis and Terminology'. *Yale Law Journal* 29: 163–173.
Dahlman, C. J. (1979). 'The Problem of Externality'. *Journal of Law and Economics* 22(1): 141–162.
Demsetz, H. (1964). 'The Exchange and Enforcement of Property Rights'. *Journal of Law and Economics* 7: 11–26.
Demsetz, H. (1967). 'Toward a Theory of Property Rights'. *American Economic Review Papers and Proceedings* 57(2): 347–359.
Ellis, H. S. and W. Fellner (1943). 'External Economies and Diseconomies'. *American Economic Review* 33(3): 493–511.
Endörfer, R. (2022). 'Should Market Harms be an Exception to the Harm Principle?' *Economics and Philosophy* 38: 221.
Epstein, R. A. (1995). 'Surrogacy: The Case for Full Contractual Enforcement'. *Virginia Law Review* 81: 2305.
Epstein, R. A. (1997). 'Externalities Everywhere: Morals and the Police Power'. *Harvard Journal of Law and Public Policy* 21: 61.
Farrell, J. (1987). 'Information and the Coase Theorem'. *Journal of Economic Perspectives* 1: 113–129.
Friedman, M. (1975). 'There's No Such Thing As a Free Lunch: Essays on Public Policy'. Chicago, Illinois, Open Court Publishing Company.
Hausman, D. M. (1992) 'When Jack and Jill Make a Deal'. *Social Philosophy and Policy* 9(1): 95–113.
Hegel, G. W. F. (1991). 'Elements of the Philosophy of Right'. *Part Three: Ethical Life, Section 2: Civil Society, Part C. The Police and the Corporation*. A. W. Wood and H. B. Nisbet. Cambridge, Cambridge University Press (Original work published 1820): 261.
Heller, W. P. and D. A. Starrett (1976). On the Nature of Externalities. *Theory and Measurement of Economic Externalities*. S. A. Y. Lin. New York, Academic Press: 9–27.
Holmes, O. W. Jr (1894). 'Privilege, Malice and Intent'. *Harvard Law Review* 8: 1.
Hovenkamp, H. (2009). 'The Coase Theorem and Arthur Cecil Pigou'. *Arizona Law Review* 51: 634.
Kaplow, L. and S. Shavell (2007). 'Moral Rules, the Moral Sentiments, and Behavior: Toward a Theory of an Optimal Moral System'. *Journal of Political Economy* 115: 494.
Kapp, K. W. (1969). 'On the Nature and Significance of Social Costs'. *Kyklos* 22(2): 334–347.

Knight, F. H. (1924). 'Some Fallacies in the Interpretation of Social Cost'. *Quarterly Journal of Economics* 38(4): 582–606.

Kogelmann, B. and J. Carroll (2024). 'The Moral Status of Pecuniary Externalities.' *Journal of Business Ethics* 195: 121–132.

Laffont, J. J. (2008). Externalities. *The New Palgrave Dictionary of Economics*. S. N. Durlauf and L. E. Blume (2nd ed.). New York, Palgrave Macmillan.

Lagueux, M. (2010). 'The Residual Character of Externalities'. *European Journal of the History of Economic Thought* 17(4): 957–973.

Lee, B. A. and H. E. Smith (2012). 'The Nature of Coasean Property'. *International Review of Economics* 59: 145–155.

Lerner, Abba P. (1972). 'The Economics and Politics of Consumer Sovereignty'. *American Economic Review* 62(1/2): 258–266.

Marshall, A. (1920). *Principles of Economics: An Introductory Volume*, 8th ed. London, Macmillan and Co.

Meade, J. E. (1952). 'External Economies and Diseconomies in a Competitive Situation'. *Economic Journal* 62(245): 54–67.

Merrill, T. W and H. E Smith (2001). 'What Happened to Property in Law and Economics?'. *Yale Law Journal* 111(2): 357–398.

Mishan, E. J. (1965). 'Reflections on Recent Developments in the Concept of External Effects'. *The Canadian Journal of Economics and Political Science/Revue canadienne d'Economique et de Science politique* 31(1): 3–34.

Mishan, E. J. (1971). 'The Postwar Literature on Externalities: An Interpretative Essay'. *Journal of Economic Literature* 9: 1.

Musgrave, R. A. (1959). *The Theory of Public Finance: A Study in Public Economy*. New York, McGraw-Hill.

Papandreou, A. A. (1994). *Externality and Institutions*. Oxford, Oxford University Press.

Papandreou, A. (2000). Externality, Convexity and Institutions (Nota di Lavoro No. 48.2000). Fondazione Eni Enrico Mattei (FEEM). https://hdl.handle.net/10419/155102.

Paniagua, P. and V. Rayamajhee, (2024). 'On the Nature and Structure of Externalities'. *Public Choice* 201: 387–408.

Pigou, A. C. (1920). *Economics of Welfare*. London, Macmillan.

Polinsky, A. M. (1979). 'Controlling Externalities and Protecting Entitlements: Property Right, Liability Rule, and Tax-subsidy Approaches'. *Journal of Legal Studies* 8(1): 1–48.

Roth, A. E. (2007). 'Repugnance as a Constraint on Markets'. *Journal of Economic Perspectives* 21: 37.

Richter, M. and A. Rubinstein (2020). 'The Permissible and the Forbidden'. *Journal of Economic Theory* 188: 1–20.

Satz, D. (2010). *Why Some Things Should Not Be For Sale: The Moral Limits of Markets*. Oxford, Oxford University Press.

Sandel, M. (2012). *What Money Can't Buy: The Moral Limits of Markets*. New York, Farrar, Straus and Giroux.

Schweizer, U. (1988). 'Externalities and the Coase Theorem: Hypothesis or Result?' *Journal of Institutional and Theoretical Economics* 144(2): 245–266.

Scitovsky, T. (1954). 'Two Concepts of External Economies'. *Journal of Political Economy* 62 (2): 143–151.

Sidgwick, H. (1887, 2011 reprint). *Principles of Political Economy*. Cambridge, Cambridge University Press.

Simpson, A. W. B (1996). 'Coase v. Pigou Reexamined'. *Journal of Legal Studies* 25: 53.

Smith, A. (1776). *An Inquiry into the Nature and Causes of the Wealth of Nations*. London, W. Strahan and T. Cadell.

Spash, C. L. (2021). 'The History of Pollution "Externalities" in Economic Thought'. Social-Ecological Research in Economics (SRE) Discussion Paper 01/2021, Institute for Multi-Level Governance & Development Department of Socio-Economics, Vienna University of Economics and Business.

Starrett, D. A. (1972). 'Fundamental Nonconvexities in the Theory of Externalities'. *Journal of Economic Theory* 4(2): 180–199.

Turvey, R. (1963). 'On Divergences between Social Cost and Private Cost'. *Economica* 30(119): 309–313.

Viner, J. (1932). 'Cost Curves and Supply Curves'. *Journal of Economics* 3: 23–46.

Wahl, J. B. (1997). 'Legal Constraints on Slave Masters: The Problem of Social Cost'. *American Journal of Legal History* 41(1): 1–24.

Weeks, E. P. (1879). *The Doctrine of Damnum Absque Injuria Considered in Its Relation to the Law of Torts*. San Francisco, S. Whitney & Co.

Wilkinson, H. (2022). 'Market Harms and Market Benefits'. *Philosophy and Public Affairs* 50: 202.

Van Zandt, D. E. (1993). 'The Lessons of the Lighthouse: "Government" or "Private" Provision of Goods'. *Journal of Legal Studies* 22: 47.

III.

INSTITUTIONS ALONG THE PROPERTY-CONTRACT INTERFACE

9

Bailment and the 'Three Body Problem'

*Katy Barnett**

I. Introduction

The 'three body problem' in physics refers to the fact that if three bodies orbit each other in space, there is no general equation that will always provide the answer to the trajectory of the three bodies. The position of the three bodies can only be shown by mathematical estimation. By contrast, when two bodies orbit each other in space, there is a general equation that will indicate their trajectory.

Often, bailment cases also involve 'three bodies': the bailor, the bailee, and a third party. And, as this chapter will discuss, there is no general equation which can solve the problem of the three bodies, particularly given the complexity of bailment generally, and the uncertainty as to whether it stems from property, contract, or is *sui generis*. General equations have been suggested to solve the 'two body' problem of bailment,[1] but uncertainty remains even as to the basis of the relationship between bailor and bailee.

The liability of third parties for damage to a car subject to a bailment was so uncertain that in *Armstead v Royal & Sun Alliance Insurance Company Ltd*,[2] a claim for £1,560 made it all the way to the United Kingdom's apex court. There were three bodies involved in this case (bailor, bailee, and tortfeasor) but lurking behind them were two insurers. It was, of course, the insurers who pursued the case, in search of certainty as to liability.

Bailment creates difficulties precisely because it exists on the property-contract interface, and because it is not immediately evident who has ultimate title to the thing which is the subject of the bailment. In what follows, I will

* Thank you to Harold Luntz (may his memory be a blessing), Timothy Chan, Henry Smith, and James Penner for their very helpful comments on various drafts of this chapter. I am also grateful to the organizers and participants of the Property-Contract Interface Workshop, Faculty of Law, National University of Singapore, 16–18 December 2024 for their helpful comments and papers.

[1] Merrill & Smith 2001; Bell 1998; Palmer 2009; Newman 2015.

[2] [2024] UKSC 6, [2025] AC 205 ('*Armstead*').

Katy Barnett, *Bailment and the 'Three Body Problem'* In: *The Property-Contract Interface*. Edited by: James Penner, Irina Sakharova, Henry E. Smith, and Zhong Xing Tan, Oxford University Press. © Katy Barnett 2026.
DOI: 10.1093/9780198951995.003.0012

analyse the *Armstead* case using Merrill and Smith's division between paucital rights (rights in personam), compound-paucital rights, quasi-multital rights, and multital rights (rights in rem), suggested in their 2001 article.[3] They attempt to rationalize how courts may deal with the different possibilities thrown up by legal doctrines situated on the property-contract interface, including bailment.

In this instance, while the lower courts treated the dispute in *Armstead* as a compound-multital dispute, and denied liability for the contractual loss accordingly, the Supreme Court decided that the claimant was to be treated no differently from any other owner of property where damage to property resulted in liability under a contract.

It might seem at first blush as though the court took a view which emphasized the proprietary, possessory nature of the interest of Ms Armstead, and drew an apparent bright-line rule: that possession by a bailee is enough by itself to entitle a claimant to damages,[4] and those damages may include losses consequential on physical damage to the claimant's property, including those arising from a third-party contract.[5] However, a closer look shows that the court was distinctly aware that the dispute involved both compound-paucital rights and quasi-multital rights. These concerns were dealt with by imposing a remoteness rule—damages would be available only for losses that were reasonably foreseeable.

It seems from *Armstead* that, where the tort concerned is negligence, the remoteness rule must be qualified or perhaps it does not apply strictly at all, because the concern of the court is to evaluate and balance liability according to what is reasonably foreseeable. Although *Armstead* was a case of negligence, the remoteness rules applied in this case incorporated policy considerations of a kind most commonly associated with contract, perhaps because this is the fairest way to limit liability for pure economic loss in a bailment situation which raises compound-paucital rights.

II. The *Armstead* Case

The claimant, Ms Armstead, was involved in an accident as a result of a negligent driver, and her car had to be repaired. She was obliged to hire a car from

[3] Merrill & Smith 2001.
[4] *The Winkfield* [1902] P 42.
[5] *Armstead* [2024] UKSC 6, [2025] AC 205 [31].

a company named Helphire, but her insurer indemnified her for this cost. Clause 16 of the hire contract provided that if the hire car became unavailable to Helphire for any reason, Ms Armstead was liable to pay Helphire, the bailor, the daily rental rate for the car for that time, up to a certain number of days.

Ms Armstead, as bailee, was in possession of the hire car, but it was Helphire, as bailor and owner, who had the right to have the hire car returned. Ms Armstead's rights as bailee arose under the hire contract with Helphire. So too did her liability for the hire costs pursuant to cl 16.

Unfortunately for Ms Armstead, while she was in possession of the hire car the defendant third party, Mr Galewski, drove his van negligently and ran into the hire car, rendering it undrivable. Ms Armstead was not at fault. Ms Armstead was liable to pay for the hire of the car even if, whilst she was in possession of it, it was unusable because of damage caused by herself or a third party, or through any other mechanical failure. Mr Galewski's insurer was Royal & Sun Alliance Insurance Company Ltd (RSA) (standing in the shoes of the third-party wrongdoer). Although the action was brought in Ms Armstead's name, the true claimant was her insurer, also standing in her shoes. Ms Armstead's insurer sought to recover two amounts from RSA: first, the cost of repair of the rental car and second, Ms Armstead's liability under cl 16 of her hire contract with Helphire.

At first instance, the County Court judge refused to hold the third-party wrongdoer liable on the basis that Ms Armstead had no proprietary interest in the hire car. On the first appeal,[6] the Recorder held that the hire fee imposed under the contract was not equivalent to damages for loss of use of the car,[7] and that the amount was not a reasonable pre-estimate of Helphire's loss of use. Consequently, Ms Armstead's liability under the hire contract was not reasonably foreseeable. On the second appeal,[8] the Court of Appeal dismissed the appeal on five bases. First, the hire contract (and therefore the liability pursuant to cl 16) was an 'internal arrangement' between the bailor and the bailee, and therefore compensation for that liability was not recoverable from a third party. Second, it was said that the liability under cl 16 was not a true and independent agreement. Third, it was said that cl 16 was not a genuine and reasonable attempt to assess loss. Fourth, it was said that the liability pursuant to cl 16 represented an 'irrevocable pure economic loss' because it arose from an

[6] *Armstead v Royal & Sun Alliance Insurance Company Ltd* [2022] Lloyd's Rep IR 574.

[7] Following *Beechwood Birmingham Ltd v Hoyer Group UK Ltd* [2010] EWCA Civ 647, [2011] QB 357.

[8] *Armstead v Royal & Sun Alliance Insurance Company Ltd* [2022] EWCA Civ 497, [2022] RTR 23.

'internal arrangement' and consequently it was not recoverable. Fifth, it was said that the loss was therefore not reasonably foreseeable.

The Supreme Court allowed a third appeal and said that Ms Armstead (really her insurer) could recover damages from the tortfeasor (really his insurer) representing Ms Armstead's liability to Helphire for the hire fee, pursuant to the hire contract. It seems extraordinary that such a question should be so uncertain as to require the matter to go right up to the Supreme Court, but it is indicative of the uncertainty surrounding the 'three body problem' which besets bailment cases.

III. Why Was the *Armstead* Case so Difficult for the Courts?

The difficulty courts faced in this case relates to the uncertainty regarding the property-contract interface. Merrill and Smith have argued that bailment gives rise to relationships which they describe as 'compound-paucital',[9] in Hohfeldian terms. In other words, the identities of the parties are definite, but there are numerous parties on one side of the relationship. In the instance of a hire car business, one party is clearly the hire company (in this case, Helphire) but there may be many, many identifiable hirers of Helphire's cars, for limited periods of time.

The courts at each level had no difficulty in holding the negligent driver liable for the repair costs to the hire car. On the other hand, the lower courts held that the bailee could not recover her liability to the bailor for rental fees for the period when the car was unavailable from the third-party wrongdoer. This was because it arose out of a private agreement between the bailee and the bailor, and the third-party wrongdoer would have no notion of its terms. The Recorder and the Court of Appeal focused on whether the terms of the contract were such as to be foreseeable and reasonable in the circumstances. The Court of Appeal was particularly focused on the fact that the third-party wrongdoer was not a party to the contract and should therefore not be bound by its terms.

Merrill and Smith have noted that these kinds of issues are typical of a 'compound-paucital' relationship. They say:

> The singular entity on one side of the transaction has a large amount at stake, equal to the individual benefit from each transaction times the total number

[9] Merrill & Smith 2001, 804–817.

> of parties on the other side. But each member of the class of definite but numerous parties on the other side has only his or her individual transaction at stake, which is certainly small in absolute value relative to the amount that the singular entity has at stake. This asymmetry may create opportunities for the singular entity to exploit its superior information about the terms and conditions of the obligation to the detriment of the class.[10]

The lower courts focused on the risk that the bailor (the hire company) could impose detrimental terms on the numerous bailees (the hirers of cars) precisely because of the information asymmetry between the parties. The hirers of cars had voluntarily accepted those terms, but the third-party wrongdoer had not, and the courts were unprepared to make the third-party wrongdoer liable for the costs arising from the hire contract as a result. Indeed, the Supreme Court explicitly acknowledged that this was the concern of the lower courts in its judgment:

> Both the Recorder and the Court of Appeal were troubled by the idea that the amount which the defendant is liable to pay as damages in this case should be determined by the terms of the contract between the hire company and its customer. They clearly had in mind the commercial reality that the contract terms are drafted by the hire company and that the liability imposed on the hirer by clause 16 (or any similar clause) is primarily a means by which the hire company, suing in the name of the hirer, can recover damages from the defendant's liability insurers for its loss of use of the vehicle. They were understandably concerned that the hire company should not be able, simply by stipulating an amount of money in a contract to which the defendant is not a party and over which it has no control, to recover an amount which exceeds a fair or reasonable estimate of loss actually suffered.[11]

The dispute could also be viewed as 'quasi-multital' in Merrill and Smith's terms. In other words, the identity of one of the affected parties is indefinite. While the bailor (Helphire) and the bailee (Ms Armstead) are both known and the terms of the agreement between them are knowable, the identity of the third-party wrongdoer is indefinite, and only becomes known when the wrong occurs. Merrill and Smith say, 'because the identity of [the third party] is indefinite, it is difficult to foresee exactly what issues will arise and what

[10] Ibid, 804–805.
[11] *Armstead* [2024] UKSC 6, [2025] AC 205 [29] (Lord Leggatt and Lord Burrows for the court).

contingencies must be protected against'.[12] They argue that in these situations, the law tends to take two different strategies: the 'notice strategy' (which facilitates the provision of information to third parties) or the 'protection strategy' (which favours the uninformed party to reduce their need for information gathering).[13]

In *Armstead* itself, at first blush it appears that the court decided to go down the 'multital' route and adopt a bright-line rule, treating it as a 'two body' problem between possessor and negligent third party. However, closer inspection indicates that the court was distinctly aware of both the 'compound-paucital' and 'quasi-multital' issues raised by bailment, and that they attempted to deal with these issues by applying a more contractual-style remoteness rule to reflect the concern about imposing an unfair burden on a third party. This flows from the concern about information costs which arises in cases of negligent damage to property more generally.

IV. The Nature of the Property Right in *Armstead*

The Supreme Court described bailment as follows:

> A relationship of bailment arises where a person voluntarily, whether gratuitously or under a contract, takes temporary possession of property from another with that person's consent.[14]

Therefore, to establish bailment in England and Wales, several elements must be made out. First, the bailee must be in temporary possession of the chattel, 'temporary' signifying the fact that the bailee will at some point have an obligation to restore possession to the bailor. Second, the bailee must voluntarily assume possession of the chattel. Third, the bailee must be aware of the bailor. Fourth, the bailor must consent to the bailee's assumption of possession.[15] This takes bailment further away from a contractual or consensual analysis, and more towards a property-based analysis. Reflecting this, the court

[12] Merrill and Smith 2001, 805.
[13] Ibid.
[14] [2024] UKSC 6, [2025] AC 205 [22] (citations omitted). Interestingly, this definition does not seem to cover bailees who are finders.
[15] Cf Bell 1998, 469–70, who argues that the Privy Council case, *The Pioneer Container* [1994] AC 324, did not require consent.

also expressly endorsed *The Winkfield*, finding that possession by a bailee is enough by itself to entitle a claimant to damages,[16] a multital analysis.

Merrill and Smith have argued that multital rights tend to give rise to 'exclusion rules' which restrict access to a particular resource.[17] Because in rem rights may make a large and indefinite class liable for interference with those rights, it is necessary to have highly standardized bright-line rules about what is and what is not permissible. This creates certainty for third parties who deal with property.

This chimes with Crawford's 'exclusion model' of property rights and possession, in which he argues that the right to exclude, not the right to possess, is at the core of property rights.[18] In his view, possession is simply a fact which leads to the creation of property rights. He suggests that there is an asymmetrical but simple explanation for property rights over tangible things.[19] The holder of a property right has a certain liberty to use property in a myriad of ways, and there is a duty upon others not to physically interfere with that property, enforced by proprietary torts such as trespass, conversion, and detinue,[20] but also, relevantly for present purposes, negligence. The important point is that the owner has certain *liberties* in relation to the property that others do not. It follows from this that the notions of 'possessory title' or 'possessory rights' simply operate as a hint that title in this case might be relative: the right in question may not be the oldest right and there may be others who hold other rights in the thing.

Possession of a chattel plays an *expressive* function beyond simply controlling the thing itself.[21] Hence, Crawford says:

> The significance of the physical element of possession lies instead in its expressive function. Certain acts qualify as 'possession' because, whether they amount to actual control, they send the recognised signal by which someone communicates his intention to claim a stake in some thing . . . [T]his account does not argue that physical control is irrelevant. Rather, it argues that its relevance is confined to the clarity of the signal that such acts send to the relevant audience.[22]

16 [1902] P 42.
17 Merrill & Smith 2001, 791–797.
18 Crawford 2020, 25–29. A similar analysis is provided in Smith 2003, 1115–1125.
19 Crawford 2020, 24–26.
20 Ibid 29–37.
21 Hegel 1821; Rose 1985; Rose 1994; Rose 2015; Crawford 2020, ch 3.
22 Crawford 2020, 63.

The social signal sent by Ms Armstead's possession and use of the car on the road was that she had a claim and a stake in the car. This is precisely why bailment leads to the 'three body problem'. As Merrill and Smith have explained:

> . . . the institution of bailment creates a pervasive problem of ostensible ownership. Ordinarily, possession of chattels signifies ownership. If one drives around in a certain car, or has a certain painting hanging in one's house, third parties will justifiably assume that one owns the car or the painting. Bailees have possession of chattels but do not have ownership rights. Thus the institution of bailment creates a serious danger of confusion on the part of third parties.[23]

The risk with bailment is that the wrongdoer may be unable to point to the fact that another party has a better right (the *jus tertii* defence).[24] This can be illustrated by *The Winkfield*, a case where a ship called the *Mexican* was carrying the mail to recipients, when another ship called the *Winkfield* collided with the *Mexican*. The *Mexican* sank, resulting in the loss of much of the mail. The plaintiff, the Postmaster General, was the bailee of the mail. He sued the defendant owners of the *Winkfield* for damages for the value of the letters and packages lost, even though he was, by statute and contract, not liable to the owners of the mail aboard the *Mexican* (some of whom would presumably never know what had been lost). The Court of Appeal found that the defendant was liable to the plaintiff, notwithstanding the lack of liability to the ultimate owners of the letters and packages. Collins MR said:

> Therefore it is not open to the defendant, being a wrongdoer, to inquire into the nature or limitation of the possessor's right, and unless it is competent for him to do so the question of his relation to, or liability towards, the true owner cannot come into the discussion at all; and, therefore, as between those two parties full damages have to be paid without any further inquiry.[25]

Traditionally, the *jus tertii* defence means that even if the claimant has only a limited right of possession to the goods, damages for conversion (or detinue,[26]

[23] Merrill & Smith 2001, 812.
[24] See *The Winkfield* [1902] P 42, 55; *Wilson v Lombank Ltd* [1963] 1 All ER 740; Chambers 2024, [6.50].
[25] [1902] P 42, 55.
[26] In the United Kingdom, the tort of detinue has been abolished. See the Torts Interference with Goods Act 1977 (UK), s 2(1).

in jurisdictions where it remains) are not reduced. So, for example, even if a bailment is due to end shortly, if goods are converted, the bailee can sue for the full value of the converted goods, and damages are not reduced to reflect the finite nature of the claimant's interest. In England and Wales, the *jus tertii* has been amended by s 8(1) of the Torts Interference with Goods Act 1977 (UK), which provides:

> The defendant in an action for wrongful interference shall be entitled to show, in accordance with rules of court, that a third party has a better right than the plaintiff as respects all or any part of the interest claimed by the plaintiff, or in right of which he sues, and any rule of law (sometimes called *jus tertii*) to the contrary is abolished.

Consequently, this particular aspect of *The Winkfield* might not be decided the same way under modern English law.

As Chambers has noted, the *jus tertii* is difficult to explain. There are three relevant explanations.[27] First, if the bailor has only a right to future possession, they are not entitled to sue for damages for conversion,[28] and accordingly, it is necessary to allow the bailee to sue for damages to ensure that the tortfeasor does not avoid responsibility. Chambers has observed that the bailee can recover the full value of the goods even when the interference with goods has caused permanent damage for which the bailor can sue. Second, and consequently, another reason is that bailees might be liable to bailors for damage to goods or their inability to return the goods. However, bailees can sue for the full value even when it is proven that the bailee is not liable to the bailor for the goods. Third, as outlined earlier by Collins MR, it might be thought that a wrongdoer should not be able to point to the absence of liability to a third party to avoid the consequences of their wrongful act. However, as Chambers has also observed, the rule can operate harshly, particularly where interference with goods has been committed innocently and in good faith, because they will be fully liable regardless. It has been argued, therefore, that the only explanation is that the claimant's right to possession is measured by valuing the right,[29] generally by looking at the diminution in value based on the market for the good in question, but that it does not have to reflect any necessary diminution in the bailee's economic situation. In the *Winkfield*, for example, the

[27] Chambers 2024, [6.50].
[28] Cf however, American Law Institute (1965) § 243 which provides that a convertor will be liable to a person entitled to future possession.
[29] Stevens 2007, 59–92; Stevens 2009, 171.

bailor was not economically worse off as a result of losing the packages and letters, because it was not liable to the owners.

In any case, the *jus tertii* was not an issue in this case, perhaps because the wrong consisted of negligent damage to goods, rather than a usurpation of the owner's title or right to possession. If a multital approach was taken, there would be no question as to the van driver's liability, nor any question of whether the burden was fair (as in the *jus tertii* cases). Smith has suggested that an exclusionary rule (namely a rule that people can be excluded from interfering with particular property) does not apply in the case of nuisance.[30] For similar reasons to nuisance, the exclusionary rule does not apply in negligence, but focuses more on governance (namely a rule about what actions can be taken).[31] In both instances, courts evaluate and balance liability according to what is reasonably foreseeable, assessing a fair balance of liability from both an interpersonal justice perspective and a community welfare perspective. By contrast, proprietary torts tend to be ones of strict liability.

It is suggested that the ability to adjust liability is a significant reason why the court was prepared to treat Ms Armstead's liability as recoverable. It is true that, on the face of it, there was no way of knowing about Helphire's interest in the car, or of Ms Armstead's liability to Helphire. However, this is not an issue which is exclusive to bailment, and courts have made defendants liable for such losses previously outside bailment, even though the liability might be unknowable. Hence, the Supreme Court said, 'There is no reason in principle why recoverable loss should not include a contractual liability to a third party provided that the liability is consequential on physical damage to the claimant's property.'[32] In fact, the concern was not to make bailment special in this regard, but to bring it under the general principle. Hence, they said:

> *The Winkfield* did not decide that, where the bailee suffers loss arising from a contractual liability to the bailor, such loss cannot be recovered from the wrongdoer. Indeed, the premise of the decision is that such a liability does give rise to a recoverable loss - the issue in the case being whether the bailee could still recover in the absence of such a liability. Nor did The *Winkfield* (or any other case cited to us) decide that the bailor and bailee are treated as having one set of rights when it comes to claiming damages. To the contrary, *The Winkfield* and other authorities recognise that the bailor and the bailee

[30] Smith 2004.
[31] Smith 2011.
[32] *Armstead* [2024] UKSC 6, [2025] AC 205, [31].

> may each be entitled to sue for the loss of or damage to the property. The only restriction is that there cannot be double recovery. Thus, a wrongdoer who has already paid compensation to the bailee for the value (or diminution in value) of the property has an answer to such a claim by the bailor... Likewise, the wrongdoer has a defence to such a claim by the bailee where the bailor has sued first and recovered compensation...[33]

V. Cases Involving Liability for Damage to Chattels and Loss Arising from Contracts with Third Parties

Liability for damage to chattels and loss arising from contracts with third parties raises issues which go beyond bailment. Generally, as the Supreme Court notes, there is a broader concern in cases which involve damage to property to ensure that the uninformed third party is not subjected to unexpected and burdensome liabilities. The fear with 'pure economic loss' is that, as Cardozo CJ noted long ago, it may impose liability 'in an indeterminate amount for an indeterminate time to an indeterminate class'.[34] Courts do not want to make the information costs too high.

The issue of pure economic loss flowing from negligent damage to property has been surprisingly contentious across common law jurisdictions. The Supreme Court cited *Ehmler v Hall*,[35] a case where the defendant crashed his van into a showroom. The tenant did not have to pay the landlord rent while the showroom was unavailable, and the landlord successfully claimed damages from the defendant, reflecting the lost rental payments as well as the physical damage to the premises. It also cited *Network Rail Infrastructure Ltd v Conarken Group Ltd*,[36] where the claimant, Network Rail Infrastructure (NRI) owned a railway bridge and the defendant crashed into it. NRI had agreements with various train companies promising that the bridge would be available, and was forced to pay the train companies' losses arising from the inability to use the bridge. NRI successfully claimed these amounts from the defendant.

Each of these cases might appear to be a 'two body' case, but in effect, once the recoverability of contractual liability comes into the picture, they are more readily seen as raising a broader 'three body problem', where the property owner may have incurred liability under a contract made with another, and there is a

[33] Ibid, [40].
[34] *Ultramares Corp v Touche* 174 NE 441, 444 (Cardozo CJ).
[35] [1993] 1 EGLR 137.
[36] [2011] EWCA Civ 644, [2012] 1 All ER (Comm) 692.

question of whether the wrongdoer should be liable for the contractual liability flowing from the property damage. The ownership is not uncertain in the same way as in bailment—and there are less likely to be compound-paucital issues—but there is still the risk of an unknowable liability under a contract to which the third party is not a party, if liability is allowed. In this sense, these disputes raise quasi-multital issues.

These cases are not always straightforward. In the Victorian case of *Metrolink Victoria Pty Ltd v Inglis*,[37] the Victorian Court of Appeal was divided upon liability for negligent damage to a tram. Again, behind the parties were the insurers. The defendant, Mr Inglis, collided with a tram owned and operated by Metrolink Victoria Pty Ltd ('Metrolink'). The damaged tram and other trams operated by Metrolink were delayed until the motor vehicle was removed from the tracks, which resulted in the operator incurring 'operational performance penalties' for non-compliance with its timetabling obligations under its operating agreement with the Director of Public Transport. This affected the calculation of the operator's remuneration. As in *Armstead*, the defendant admitted negligence and liability for the cost of repairs to the tram but denied liability for the penalties. At first instance, the magistrate categorized the plaintiff's pecuniary loss as 'the reduction of a financial benefit payable by a third party to the plaintiff or the imposition of a financial penalty upon the plaintiff by a third party' and dismissed that claim on the basis that such losses were not of a kind reasonably foreseeable.

In the majority, Redlich JA (with whom Williams AJA agreed) found that the loss was foreseeable, and that the magistrate had categorized the loss too narrowly. Rather than characterizing the loss as 'pure economic loss', it could be characterized as 'revenue lost as a result of the inability to use the tram'. As financial injury consequent upon property damage, this was reasonably foreseeable.[38] By contrast, Neave JA dissented. Her Honour held that 'pure economic loss' was of a fundamentally different nature to physical damage to a tram, and that remoteness considerations for pure economic loss tend to be stricter.[39] She said:

> The categorisation of the genus of loss suffered by Metrolink as a loss of business income or a loss of revenue is too broad because it would mean that any loss arising as the result of disruption of a contract made with a third party

[37] [2009] VSCA 227, (2009) 25 VR 633.
[38] [2009] VSCA 227, (2009) 25 VR 633 [99]–[103] (Redlich JA with whom Williams AJA agreed).
[39] Ibid, [17] (Neave JA).

> was potentially compensable. A loss suffered as the result of failure to meet performance targets under a contract with the State government is a loss of a different character to the loss of fares caused by a tram becoming inoperative because it is damaged.[40]

Nonetheless, the balance of authority seems to suggest that if a defendant negligently damages property, leading to the claimant being liable under a contract with a third party, this is recoverable, subject to the normal limitations upon damages.

Moving back to the *Armstead* case, it was clear that the Supreme Court wished to develop a principle which cohered with the law regarding liability under a contract with a third party and damage to property. They outlined three principles:

> First, a person owes a duty of care not to cause physical damage to another person's property (such as a car) and, if in breach of that duty, is liable to pay damages to compensate that person for the diminution in value of the property and any other financial loss consequent on the damage. This is subject to the general principles which limit the recovery of damages in tort, including the limitation that loss is not recoverable if it is too remote a consequence of the wrong.
>
> Second, by contrast, someone who negligently causes physical damage to another person's property is not liable to pay compensation to a third party claimant who suffers financial loss as a result of the damage. It is not enough that the claimant had contractual rights which were rendered less valuable by the damage if the property in question was not the claimant's. . . .
>
> Third, to count as the claimant's property for this purpose it is sufficient that the claimant has a right to possession of the property. At common law a person in possession of property has a right to possession of it as against a stranger. Thus, a bailee in possession of property can claim damages from a stranger whose negligence results in the loss of, or physical damage to, the property . . .[41]

However, it was important to the court to ensure that the damages imposed upon the defendant were not unduly harsh.

[40] Ibid, [22] (Neave JA).
[41] *Armstead* [2024] UKSC 6, [2025] AC 205 [19]–[20] (Lord Leggatt and Lord Burrows for the court).

VI. Limitations Upon Liability in *Armstead*: The Principles of Remoteness

In *Armstead*, the court said that a loss is too remote if it is not reasonably foreseeable as at the time of breach, but it is not necessary to foresee the precise manner in which the loss occurred.[42] Moreover, reflecting the general principles above, financial loss resulting from loss of use of a car is reasonably foreseeable, as is the liability of the claimant to pay damages to the hire company.[43] Pivotally, to be reasonably foreseeable in the context of a bailment, the claimant's liability must reflect the loss of use of hire. Consequently, a 'reasonable pre-estimate' of loss of use will be reasonably foreseeable, but an unreasonable pre-estimate will not be.[44] The court enunciates the policy behind this rule:

> One might add that the underlying policy reason for the remoteness rule is to ensure that an excessive burden of liability does not fall on the defendant. A line must be drawn to ensure that the defendant is not held liable for all loss factually caused by the tort, however far removed in time and space. . . . [W]e have noted the danger that in a case of this kind, without an insistence that the contractual liability is a reasonable pre-estimate of the hire company's loss of use, the contractual clause might specify a sum to be paid by the claimant (even if expressed as being for loss of use of the car) that would impose an excessive liability on the defendant. Put another way, without that restriction there is a danger that this sort of contractual arrangement would be open to abuse and would inappropriately burden the defendant with a liability that does not reflect any actual loss.[45]

Consequently, Helphire's fee would be recoverable only if it were a reasonable pre-estimate of the loss of use.[46] The court integrated its analysis into the law regarding penalties and unfair terms, saying that a fee will only be reasonably foreseeable and thus recoverable if it is a genuine contractual liability, that is, a genuine pre-estimate of loss.[47] There was no room for the defendant or its

[42] Ibid, [47](i) citing *Overseas Tankship (UK) Ltd v Morts Dock & Engineering Co Ltd (The Wagon Mound (No 1))* [1961] 1 AC 388 and *Hughes v Lord Advocate* [1963] AC 837.
[43] *Armstead* [2024] UKSC 6, [2025] AC 205, [47](ii).
[44] Ibid, [47](iii).
[45] Ibid, [47](iv).
[46] Ibid, [47](v).
[47] Ibid, [52].

insurer to argue that Ms Armstead (or her insurer) should have challenged the validity of the clause as a penalty or an unfair term.[48]

The court's attempt to limit the recovery of damages in this way reflects the problems posed by the 'compound-paucital' aspects of bailment. In other words, as between the bailor and bailee, the hire company could impose unfair or punitive clauses on hiring parties because of the information asymmetry between the parties. The court was also attempting to deal with the 'quasi-multital' aspects of bailment. In other words, while the bailor and bailee are known to each other, and (at least notionally) voluntarily undertake the duties and liabilities in relation to the property, the third party is not known until the wrong occurs and has not voluntarily undertaken that liability. However, as noted above, this problem is not unique to bailment. It applies to all cases involving physical damage to property where that damage causes the property owner to breach a contract.

Consequently, although the judgment focuses on Ms Armstead's property rights, underlying it are concerns about liability under contract, which reflect the way in which bailment lies on the contract-property interface.[49]

It is interesting to compare *Armstead* with the decision of the High Court of Australia in *Arsalan v Rixon*,[50] where the court rejected 'loss of use' as a measure of the consequential loss and the need to hire a replacement car after a motor vehicle accident. It was said that this was necessary because 'loss of use' did not 'identify the manner or extent of any loss to a plaintiff'.[51] It was also said that 'loss of use' cannot be a correct characterization of the loss, because in shipping cases, substantial damages can be awarded even where a substitute or a spare ship is available, as in *The Mediana*.[52] The High Court therefore described the loss in the following way:

> . . . (i) the physical inconvenience from the plaintiff's inability to use the damaged vehicle during the period of repair and (ii) loss of amenity or enjoyment of the use of the vehicle. Those heads of damage can usually be inferred from the plaintiff's ownership and past usage of the vehicle and, but for the damage, the plaintiff's ability to continue to use the vehicle during the period of repair. Recovery of damages under these heads of damage will usually be necessary to restore the plaintiff to the position they would have been

[48] Ibid, [54].
[49] Georgiou 2024 has stringently criticized this aspect of the judgment.
[50] [2021] HCA 40, (2021) 274 CLR 606, [18].
[51] [2021] HCA 40, [18].
[52] [1900] AC 113, 122.

> in but for the defendant's actions that caused the accident. Once the plaintiff acts to mitigate that loss by hiring a substitute vehicle, the onus of proof will lie upon the defendant to show that the costs incurred in mitigation were unreasonable.[53]

In other words, the High Court said that the true basis of the loss was 'physical inconvenience' and 'loss of amenity or enjoyment of the use of the vehicle'.[54] This seems to involve a multital analysis, where the court looked at the loss as related to the inconvenience and loss of amenity as flowing from the damage to the chattel in question. Mitigation played a fundamental role in measuring the amount of the loss, as the plaintiff's actions in hiring a substitute car during the period their car was unavailable constituted reasonable mitigation, and the onus then lay on the defendant to show that the cost was unreasonable. Perhaps, by bringing in 'use' at the stage of mitigation, it could be argued that the High Court was attempting to ensure that the availability of compensatory damages and the limits upon them remained tethered to the plaintiff's property interest.[55] In any case, it is clear that the contractual nature of the hire agreement only came in via mitigation.

There was no mention of bailment or hire car contracts in the decision. It is not clear from *Arsalan v Rixon* how the liability of Ms Armstead under the hire contract for the replacement car would be treated, or whether the van driver would be liable for such liability. Presumably, under the High Court of Australia's formulation, Ms Armstead again suffered 'physical inconvenience' and 'loss of amenity or enjoyment of the use' of the hire vehicle, when it was damaged. Would her liability under the hire contract reflect that loss? This shows some of the difficulties in the High Court of Australia's formulation in *Arsalan v Rixon*; it is much easier to see how Ms Armstead's 'loss of use' was reflected in the liability for hire fees under the hire contract with Helphire.

Accepting for the moment that a 'loss of use' approach is more appropriate in car hire cases (and that it accommodates the concerns involved in bailment to a greater degree), it is necessary to look at the policy behind the remoteness rules in *Armstead*, and how the Supreme Court accommodates the property-contract interface in the rules it applies.

[53] [2021] HCA 40, [2025] AC 205, [3].

[54] I leave to the side whether the 'loss of amenity' is subjective or objective. It is not clear from the cases relied upon by the High Court which approach will be taken.

[55] I am indebted to Henry Smith for this observation.

VII. The Policy Behind Remoteness in *Armstead*: What Does it Reflect?

I have argued elsewhere that remoteness in private law reflects two concerns of justice. First, it reflects interpersonal fairness concerns (namely, those concerns regarding that claimant and that defendant, or concerns regarding similarly situated claimants and defendants), which tend to reflect corrective justice norms. Second, it reflects community welfare concerns (namely, those concerns focusing not on the claimant and defendant, but on the ramifications of imposing liability for society generally), which tend to reflect distributive justice norms and are anterior to the interpersonal fairness concern.[56]

It is instructive to look at the way in which remoteness operates in this context, as a diagnostic, to better understand the property-contract interface. I have suggested that in contract, remoteness considerations focus on interpersonal justice concerns, including whether the loss was predictable, the extent of the defendant's control over events, and whether the defendant would be subject to an unreasonable burden. The morality of breach is not generally a concern. Nor, in many cases, are community welfare concerns explicitly considered, and they tend not to be determinative even when they are. By contrast, in tort, remoteness principles tend to be shaped, not only by the interpersonal justice concerns mentioned earlier, but also by interpersonal justice concerns about morality and wrongdoing (particularly where the wrong is intentional) and the broader community welfare beyond the individual parties.[57]

As noted earlier, the Supreme Court said that the central question was whether the burden upon the defendant was excessive. Certainly, that is one important concern, but it is not the only policy concern present. Other interpersonal justice concerns include whether the consequence of the breach is predictable—the more predictable it is, the more likely a defendant is to be liable—as well as the defendant's control over their actions. Remoteness in contract will be treated differently from tort because contracts are a result of an agreement between the parties, where the parties (at least notionally) turned their minds to performance of the contract at the time of entering the bargain. As noted earlier, for many torts, there need be no pre-existing relationship, as in the accident in this case. By contrast, the remoteness rules in contract assume that the parties have considered the consequences of a breach and planned accordingly.

[56] Barnett 2014; Barnett 2025.
[57] Barnett 2025.

In this case, the remoteness rules adopted reflect the liminal nature of bailment. The court starts with the basic position of the tort of negligence, namely a loss is too remote if it is not reasonably foreseeable at the time of the breach, but it is not necessary to foresee the precise manner in which the loss occurred. However, the concerns then listed reflect *contractual* concerns about unfair burdens, the predictability of the loss, and the third-party defendant's lack of control and lack of ability to assume the risk of the liability. This is an effort to deal with the compound-paucital aspect and quasi-multital aspects of bailment: namely that the bailor can impose unfair terms and that the third party has no choice and no knowledge of the liability to which they might be exposed. Consequently, the court considers it important for recovery that the amount be a 'reasonable pre-estimate' of the loss, although they are not unduly prescriptive about the manner in which this achieved.[58] They found that there was no reason to suppose that cl 16 did not represent a genuine pre-estimate of loss,[59] but that even if it was not, Ms Armstead would still be able to recover any reasonably foreseeable loss in that regard.[60]

VIII. Conclusion

I have not been able to solve the 'three body problem' and give a general equation which will solve the liability of bailor, bailee, and third parties. Nor do I think it would be possible to establish such an equation as the law currently stands.

I have managed to use Merrill and Smith's rubric for understanding the property-contract interface to unpick the issues in this particular case. It might seem as though the court took a view which emphasized the proprietary, possessory nature of the interest of Ms Armstead, and drew an apparent bright-line rule: that possession by a bailee is enough by itself to entitle a claimant to damages.[61] However, once the court drew the case into the broader stable of cases dealing with losses consequential on physical damage to the claimant's property, including those arising from a third-party contract, quasi-multital issues were raised.[62]

58 *Armstead* [2024] UKSC 6, [2025] AC 205, [54].
59 Ibid, [65].
60 Ibid, [72], citing *Cory v Thames Ironworks and Shipbuilding Co Ltd* (1868) LR 3 QB 181.
61 [1902] P 42.
62 *Armstead* [2024] UKSC 6, [2025] AC 205, [31].

A closer inspection shows that the Supreme Court in *Armstead* was aware of the compound-paucital issues raised by contracts of hire (namely that the bailor could impose unfair fees on the bailee by reason of information asymmetry). This issue is particularly likely to arise in bailments and contracts of hire.

It was also aware of the quasi-multital issues, namely that while the bailor and bailee might be known, the third-party wrongdoer cannot be known until the accident occurs and cannot know what the terms of the contract for rental are. Courts are concerned that in any instance (whether involving a bailment or not) third-party wrongdoers might be subjected to unfair damages which were not knowable in advance. Remoteness rules are used as a 'protection strategy', so that third parties are not required to inquire to discover unexpected liabilities, but they will be liable for expected liabilities.

The remoteness considerations the court took into account in *Armstead* were highly reminiscent of those that apply in contract law, and perhaps on a par with those principles. This shows that the approach that the court took was sensitive to the quasi-multital aspects of this situation. A strict exclusionary approach was qualified by other concerns, particularly interpersonal justice concerns about the predictability of damage and the burden upon the defendant. Therefore, the compound-paucital aspects of bailment, and the potential unfairness which might arise if a hirer was forced to enter into an unreasonable contract, were ameliorated by the requirement that the recoverable damages reflect a reasonable pre-estimate of loss on the part of the bailor.

Hidden in plain sight are questions of distributive justice and community welfare: ultimately the parties paying for the loss in any event are the insurers of Ms Armstead and the van driver who collided with her. The court did not think that this fundamentally changed the principles, but the decision certainly involved a determination of the fair distribution of burdens and benefits, as indicated by the fact that the insurers chose to pursue the case to the highest court.

References

American Law Institute (1965). *Restatement (Second) of Torts.*

Barnett, K. (2014). 'Equitable Compensation and Remoteness: Not So Remote From the Common Law After All'. *University of Western Australia Law Review* 38(1): 48–79.

Barnett, K. (2025). 'The Policy Behind Contract Damages: Beyond Voluntary Assumption of a Risk or Gap Filling'. *Politics, Policy and Private Law Volume 2.* A. Goymour and J. O'Sullivan. Oxford, Hart: 49–69.

Bell, A. (1998). 'The Place of Bailment in the Modern Law of Obligations'. *Interest in Goods.* N. Palmer and E. McKendrick. 2nd edn, London, Lloyd's Legal Press: 461–489.
Chambers, R. (2024). *An Introduction to Property Law in Australia.* 5th edn. Pyrmont, NSW, Thomson Reuters.
Crawford, M. J. R. (2020). *An Expressive Theory of Possession.* Oxford, Hart.
Georgiou, A. (2024). 'Property Damage, Remoteness and Consequential Contractual Liabilities'. *Lloyd's Maritime and Commercial Law Quarterly* 386–391.
Hegel, G. W. F. (1821, 1942). *Philosophy of Right ['Grundlinien der Philosophie des Rechts'].* T. M. Knox, tr. Oxford, Clarendon Press.
Merrill, T. W. and H. E. Smith (2001). 'The Property/Contract Interface'. *Columbia Law Review* 101: 773–852.
Newman, C. M. (2015). 'Bailment and the Property/Contract Interface'. *George Mason Legal Studies Research Paper No LS* 15–12, ssrn.com/abstract = 2654988.
Palmer, N. (2009). *Palmer on Bailment.* 3rd edn. London, Sweet & Maxwell/Lexis Nexis.
Rose, C. M. (1985). 'Possession as the Origin of Property'. *University of Chicago Law Review* 52(1): 73–88.
Rose, C. M. (1994). *Property and Persuasion: Essays on the History, Theory and Rhetoric of Ownership.* Boulder, Colorado, Westview Press.
Rose, C. M. (2015). 'The Law is Nine-Tenths Possession: An Adage Turned on its Head'. *Law and Economics of Possession.* Y. C. Chang. Cambridge, Cambridge University Press: 40–64.
Smith, H. E. (2003) 'The Language of Property'. *Stanford Law Review* 55: 1105–1191.
Smith, H. E. (2004). 'Exclusion and Property Rules in the Law of Nuisance'. *Virginia Law Review* 90(4): 965–1049.
Smith, H. E. (2011). 'Modularity and Morality in the Law of Torts'. *Journal of Tort Law* 4(2): 1–32.
Stevens, R. (2007). *Torts and Rights.* Oxford, Oxford University Press.
Stevens, R. (2009). 'Damages and the Right to Performance: A Golden Victory or Not?' *Exploring Contract Law.* J. Neyers, R. Bronagh, and S. Pitel. Oxford, Hart: 171–198.

10

The Property/Contract Interface

Hybrid Leases

Thomas W. Merrill

I. Introduction

Leases are an extremely important institution of property—probably second only to ownership as the legal form in which assets are most frequently held. Residential property is more commonly leased than owned in most countries. Leases are universally used for organizing the space in shopping centres and office complexes with multiple occupants. Leasing is widely used in expanding and contracting the acreage available for agricultural operations. And personal property leasing, of everything from cars to construction equipment to aircraft, is exploding throughout the world.[1]

Leases clearly reside in the contested terrain between property and contract. We see this clearly from a comparative law perspective. In civil law countries, leases are regarded as a type of contract. In common law countries, leases are generally regarded as a form of property. There has been some convergence, with civil law systems adopting elements said to 'reify' lease contracts, and common law systems increasingly drawing upon contract doctrine in determining the appropriate remedies for breaches of lease obligations. But the convergence is far from complete.[2]

When Henry and I published the 'Property/Contract Interface',[3] it came on the heels of our article on the *numerus clausus*.[4] The former article posited a sharp dichotomy between paradigmatic property rights, such as a full ownership of land and personal property, and paradigmatic contract rights. The

[1] Merrill 2020, 2–7.
[2] Chang and Merrill 2025.
[3] Merrill & Smith 2001.
[4] Merrill & Smith 2000.

Thomas W. Merrill, *The Property/Contract Interface* In: *The Property-Contract Interface*. Edited by: James Penner, Irina Sakharova, Henry E. Smith, and Zhong Xing Tan, Oxford University Press.
DOI: 10.1093/9780198951995.003.0013

former impose in rem duties of noninterference on 'all the world'; the latter create in personam obligations binding only the parties to the contract. Hence, property creates a large-numbers information cost problem not present in the case of contracts. This in turn, we argued, explains why property rights come in standardized forms not present (as a matter of law) with respect to contract rights.

The central objective of the Interface article was to try to explain areas of property law that fall in between the strong standardization characteristic of conventional property and the individuation permitted in the realm of contract. One of the areas we considered was leasing. Leases include a mix of property-like and contract-like features. With respect to third parties who trespass on leased land or convert leased property, leases function like property, imposing strict duties of non-interference on strangers. But with respect to the parties to the lease, leases impose obligations that are purely in personam, such as the obligation of the lessee to pay rent to the lessor. To this extent, leases appear to conform to the basic thesis of the *numerus clausus* article, although the nature of the legal obligations toggles between the external (property) and internal (contract) perspectives within the institution.

The puzzle we sought to explain in the Interface article was why certain property institutions contain features of partial standardization, such as a menu of limited options with respect to certain issues. The gist of the explanation was that these institutions encounter situations involving large numbers of third parties or third parties whose identities are indefinite *ex ante*. In these situations, we argued, the law gravitates towards a fixed menu of options in order to reduce the information costs associated with such uncertainties. Lease law contains two such pockets of fixed options. One is the limited number of permissible forms of leases: the term of years, the periodic lease, and the lease at will. The other is the limited number of permissible ways in which lessees may be transferred to a third party: assignments and subleases. In both contexts, courts will construe the intentions of the parties as fitting within one of the permitted options, following the rule of construction that characterizes the way the *numerus clausus* principle is enforced in common law systems more generally.[5] The 2001 article explained that these are contexts in which there is an informational externality intermediate between that posed by duties imposed on all the world or its absence in a purely in personam context. The limitation of

[5] In civil law systems, the limited number of permissible forms is often reflected in a rule of positive law embodied in the code. In common law systems, there is no such legislated rule, but courts will construe the intentions of the parties as adopting one of the permissible forms, rather than reflecting some novel type of arrangement (Chang & Smith 2019, 797–798).

leases to three forms is important to the potentially infinite number of possible purchasers of the lessor's reversion, who would like to have precise information about the expected duration of existing leases. The limitation on transfers by lessees to assignments and subleases provides important information to the lessor, who is not a party to these transactions, about what sorts of rights and obligations will exist going forward between the lessor and the transferee, whose identity is initially unknown.

The discussion of leases in the 2001 article was limited to a handful of issues designed to illustrate the more general thesis about intermediate standardization in some property institutions. The article did not purport to provide a general characterization of the relationship between property and contract concepts in the law of leasing. This chapter provides an overview of the efforts of the forthcoming *Restatement (Fourth) of Property* to present a more fully integrated conception of leasing as a hybrid institution composed of both property and contract elements.

II. Some History

If we consider the history of the common law, we discover that concepts of property and contract have long competed for primacy in the legal understanding of leases. When leases first emerged in the twelfth century in England, they were evidently regarded as purely contractual.[6] The only remedy available to a lessee was an action in covenant against the lessor. This was inconvenient, especially if the lessee was ousted by a third party. So in the thirteenth century Chancery devised a new writ, called *ejectione firmae*, that allowed a lessee to sue anyone interfering with the lessee's possession. This proved to be very popular, and eventually evolved into the action for ejectment, available to freeholders as well as leaseholders. From that point on, leases were effectively regarded as a type of non-freehold property, since lessees were legally protected against interference by all the world. The solicitude for lessees was quickly counterbalanced by added protection for lessors. The Statute of Marlbridge in 1267 made lessees liable for waste if they damaged the lessor's reversion.[7] This was reinforced by the Statute of Gloucester of 1278, which subjected lessees to treble damages if they committed waste.[8]

[6] Simpson 1986, 74–77.
[7] 52 Hen 3.
[8] 6 Edw 1.

A further evolution towards the property characterization occurred when Henry VIII confiscated large numbers of lands held by monasteries and convents. Many of these properties had been leased, and the lessees balked at paying rent to their new lessor. Parliament stepped in, enacting a statute that provided that 'grantees of reversion and patentees of the king' would have an action against recalcitrant lessees.[9] Thus, leases came to be regarded as an interest running to successors in interest, another attribute of property.

Notwithstanding these developments establishing leases as a form of property, disputes between lessors and lessees over issues like unpaid rent continued to be adjudicated under the writ of covenant, and later debt.[10] In such cases, leases were regarded as bundles of independent promises running between the parties to a lease. Thus, a breach by one party gave rise to an action for damages by the other. But the breach, without regard to its severity, did not excuse the counterparty from performing its promises. The only exception was a breach by the lessor of the covenant of quiet enjoyment, which excused the lessee from the obligation to pay rent as long as the lessor interfered with the lessee's possession.[11] But the general conception of remedial rights, grounded in the fifteenth-century law of covenant, persisted until well into the twentieth century. Thus, with regard to the relations between lessor and lessee, leases operated under a model of contract, rather than property.

Flash forwards to the 1960s and 70s in the United States. This was a period of creative lawyering and significant reform of aspects of private law. For example, products liability emerged at this time as a distinct tort action having aspects of strict liability. One of the targets of the reformers was the law of leasing, especially as it applied to low-income residential tenancies.[12] Partisans of the reform movement attacked the idea that a lease is a conveyance of property. This was said to be a holdover from a bygone era when leases were primarily agricultural. The remedy, it was proclaimed, was to discard the idea of the lease as a form of property, and embrace the civil law conception of the lease as purely contractual. The influential opinion in *Javins v First National Realty Corp*,[13] which gave recognition to the idea of an implied warranty of habitability in residential leases, explicitly endorsed this perspective. Caveat

[9] 32 Henry VIII ch 34 (1540).
[10] See, eg, *Paradine v Jane*, 82 Eng Rep 897 (KB 1647).
[11] See, eg, *Smith v McEnany*, 48 NE 791 (Mass 1897) (Holmes J).
[12] Rabin 1984.
[13] 428 F 2d 1075 (DC Cir 1970).

lessee was condemned as a relic of feudalism, and courts were exhorted to regard residential leases as a type of bilateral services contract, with the lessor supplying heat, water, electricity, and security from the elements, in return for periodic payments of rent.

The idea that leases should be regarded as a species of contract spread, giving rise, for example, to decisions in many jurisdictions imposing a duty on residential landlords to mitigate the tenant's damages when a tenant abandoned or repudiated a lease before its termination.[14] The American Law Institute (ALI), as part of the *Restatement (Second) of Property*, published two volumes on landlord and tenant law in 1977. This effort partially embraced some of the reforms said to be inspired by the contract conception of leases, but stopped short in other respects.

III. The *Restatement (Fourth) of Property*

When the ALI launched the *Restatement (Fourth) of Property*, headed by Henry Smith as Reporter, a central aspiration was to produce a more complete restatement of property than had been provided by the first three property restatements (Merrill 2023). In order to make a more comprehensive treatment possible, Smith has been joined by a committee of Associate Reporters, including the author. Lease law is obviously part of the enterprise, and is a topic on which the author has been assigned to work.

The effort to restate the law of leases anew has been greatly assisted by the fact that the ground was thoroughly ploughed by the 1977 volumes. Of course, the older work requires updating. More seriously, the 1977 effort did not provide a coherent conception of the relationship between property and contract principles in the law of leasing. Indeed, it did not offer any kind of definition of a lease at all. So the first task of the new *Restatement* was to clarify the architecture of leasing as a legal institution.

As it has emerged, the basic conceptual scheme is relatively straightforward. At its core, a lease entails the conveyance of property. But the creation of a lease, and the remedies for enforcing it, are governed by principles of contract. This is congruent with the history of the common law. As we have seen, the common law has long regarded leases as a conveyance of property, and

[14] Eg *Sommer v Kridel*, 378 A 2d 767, 773 (NJ 1977).

has given the leasehold in rem effect characteristic of property rights. But the common law has also understood that leases are created by a contract between lessor and lessee, and that when one party or the other has committed a breach of the lease, the remedies are those that the law has recognized for a breach of contract more generally.

In effect, the new *Restatement* adopts a substance versus procedure distinction in describing the division between property and contract in lease law. This is not fundamentally different from what we see in a sale of personal property or land. The object of the transaction—the thing being sold—is understood to be property, and as such enjoys the protections the law provides for property more generally. But the transfer of the thing is made possible by a contract. Whether the thing is successfully transferred or not depends on whether the parties have entered into a legally binding contract. And if there is a breach of this contract, the law of contracts generally steps in to define the remedial rights of the parties to the transaction. So one can say that a sale of personal property or land, no less than a lease of personal property or land, is a hybrid phenomenon that exists along the property-contract interface.

To be sure, a lease is a more complex transaction than a simple sale of property. For one thing, the rights to the property that is the subject of a lease are split over time. One party, the lessee, has the rights to the property for a delimited period of time (the term), and the other party, the lessor, has the rights to the property after this period of time ends (the reversion). For another thing, payment for the transfer of the property is rarely given in a lump sum, as is conventional in a sale. Rather, the payment is nearly always made in the form of periodic installments called rent. Sales of personal property and land may be accompanied by warranties of various types, although this is not required. Leases—perhaps because of the division of rights over time—are always accompanied by warranty-like obligations, such as the lessor's promise not to interfere with the lessee's possession during the term (the covenant of quiet enjoyment) and the lessee's promise to return the property to the lessor at the end of the lease in the same condition (the duty not to commit waste).

IV. The Definition of a Lease

A critical step in the *Fourth Restatement*'s effort to integrate the property and contract elements of leasing is the adoption of a general definition of a lease. That definition presents a lease as having both a core of property elements but also as being created by and enforced by contract. To borrow a title from a recent law review article (on a different subject), a lease is 'contract wrapped property'.[15]

The property core includes three elements: the transfer of the right to possession of the thing from the lessor to the lessee; the transfer of a broad right to use the thing consistent with what an owner would be able to do with such a thing; and the right of the lessor to have the thing returned at the end of the term in the same condition as at the beginning of the term, ordinary wear and tear excepted. The contract dimension supplies two further elements. A lease is created by a binding contract, which means it must be supported by consideration and must comply with the other formalities necessary to make an enforceable contract, such as the statute of frauds. Finally, breaches of lease obligations by either party give rise to the remedies generally available for a breach of a bilateral contract.

As stated more succinctly in the new *Restatement*:

> § 1.1 Definition of a Lease
> A lease is a transfer of the rights of possession and use of an asset for a time less than the asset's expected useful life in return for consideration.[16]

The three property elements are captured by the transfer of the right of possession and the right of use of an asset, both implicitly going to the lessee, and by the stipulation that the transfer must be for a time less than the expected useful life of the asset, which means the lessor will always have a reversion. The contract elements are embedded in the requirement that the transfer must be supported by consideration, a necessary condition for creating a binding contract. Compliance with the statute of frauds and the contract-based remedies for breaches of a lease obligation are covered in separate chapters and are not directly alluded to in the definition.

Before examining the five elements in more detail, it is worth pausing to consider what it means for a restatement of property to offer a 'definition' of a lease. As should be obvious, a restatement of the law has no authority to dictate legal rules. Such authority belongs to the courts and the legislature. In the United States, at least with respect to property law, that means the highest courts and the legislatures of the fifty states. What authority a restatement has is roughly the same as the authority of one state's supreme court to influence the judges

[15] D'Onfro 2024.
[16] *Restatement (Fourth) of Property*, Vol IV, Div 3, § 1.1 (Tentative Draft No 5, April 2024) (boldface type omitted).

of another state. If the opinions of the rendering court reflect a conscientious effort to remain faithful to settled propositions of law, and give persuasive reasons for modifications in that law, they have a chance of being followed in another judicial system. If the opinions are merely the product of the idiosyncratic views of the judges of the rendering court, they will very likely be ignored. The history of the various iterations of the *Restatement of Property* largely reflects this pattern (Merrill 2023).

The new *Restatement*'s definition of a lease was adopted in an attempt faithfully to reflect existing practice. The transfer of possession for the term of the lease has been a theme of the common law for centuries, as reflected in the non-disclaimable covenant of quiet enjoyment protecting the lessee's possession from interference by the lessor. The requirement that the lessee gives consideration, usually in the form of rent, is consistent with nearly universal practice, and is required in any event to treat leases as a binding contract enforced by standard contract remedies. The Reporters' Notes to the section in which the definition appears recite that two other elements were largely drawn from recent efforts by the Uniform Law Commissioners (UCC) to distinguish leases from security interests, and by the Financial Accounting Standards Board (FASB) to distinguish leases from other types of off-balance-sheet risks.[17] The UCC effort is responsible for emphasizing that a lease lasts for a time less than the expected useful life of an asset, which is consistent with the universal understanding that the lessor retains a reversion after the end of the term. And the Accounting Board effort is responsible for the emphasis on the conveyance of a broad right to control the use of the leased asset, which again is consistent with general practice and understanding.

The new *Restatement*'s adoption of an explicit definition of a lease serves several interrelated functions. One is to distinguish leases from other legal institutions, such as licences, bailments, security interests, servitudes, and sales. The idea is that if a particular transaction does not conform to the definition, it should be regarded as something else, like a licence, an easement, a security interest, or a sale. Another function is to provide an organizing principle for the twelve chapters of the new *Restatement*. Thus, the new *Restatement* starts with general principles that govern the formation of a lease, then turns to the lessee's right of possession, then covers the lessee's right of use, then considers the lessee's duties to give consideration and to preserve the lessor's reversion, and concludes with the rights of the parties to transfer their respective interests to third parties. A third function is to highlight the respects in which leases

[17] Ibid. Reporters' Notes, 8–9.

reflect property elements, and the ways in which leases are treated like contracts. Care is taken throughout to distinguish mandatory rules that correspond to the elements derived from property law (the right to possession, the right to use, and the duty to preserve the reversion); the mandatory rules associated with contract (the duty to give consideration, to comply with the statute of frauds, and the domain of different remedies); and to distinguish mandatory rules from default rules, which generally operate in a purely contractual fashion.[18]

V. The Lessee's Right to Possession

The lessee's core property right is the right to possession of the asset during the term of the lease. This is reflected in the longstanding covenant of quiet enjoyment, which is implied in every lease, as well as in the rules of tort law that give lessees standing to sue third parties for interferences with the leased property.

There is older case law that says a lease begins only when the lessee takes *actual possession* of the leased property; before then, the lessee had only an *interesse termini,* which was regarded as a kind of contract right. The distinction has largely disappeared, at least in US law. And it makes no sense once a lease is understood as conveying a *right to possession.* A right to possess can commence today even though actual possession will begin sometime in the future. Often this is what happens: the parties enter into a lease today and the lessee moves in next week. Today, it is possible to have a contract to enter into a lease and a lease that is to commence in the future.[19] A contract to make a lease does not convey a right to possess but only a promise to enter into a lease. Once a lease is formally executed, it will convey a right to possession, which may or may not mean actual possession.

The right to possession distinguishes a lease from a licence. A lease conveys a right to possession, which means the lessee has the right to exclude others during the term of the lease. A licence may put the licensee in de facto possession, but it does not convey any right to exclude others. Or if it does, it confers such a right only because of the terms of the licence agreement, it does not

[18] Property concepts also play a large role in determining the consequences of a transfer of leased property. Upon an assignment of either the lessor's reversion or the lessee's leasehold, the provisions of the original lease carry over to the transferee as a matter of 'privity of estate'. This includes all provisions that do not vary with regard to the personal identity of the lessor and lessee, and clearly reflects the view that a lease is a form of property. *Restatement (Fourth) of Property*, Vol IV, Div 3, §§ 11.4, 12.4 cmt b (Council Draft No 11, Dec 2024).

[19] *Restatement (Fourth) of Property*, Vol IV, Div 3, § 2.6 cmt a (Tentative Draft No 5, April 2024).

follow automatically from the nature of the interest created. The distinction is important in a variety of contexts. In the real property world, it differentiates a hotel guest, who has no inherent right to exclude others, and was traditionally regarded as a lodger. In contrast, someone who has exclusive access to a storage locker, and who therefore has a right to exclude others, is regarded as a lessee.[20] In the personal property context, the right to possession differentiates someone who rents a car from Hertz, whose rights are determined by contract, from someone who leases a car from Ford, who has a right to possession during the term of the lease and has rights against third parties similar to an owner.

The right to possession also helps clarify the respective rights of the parties when the property that is the subject of the lease disappears, as when it is taken by the government under the power of eminent domain or is destroyed by fire or hurricane. Many older authorities, reflecting the independent covenants model of leases, held that when the property is taken by eminent domain the lessee must continue to pay rent to the lessor, but has a claim for just compensation from the government for the monetary value of the lease. The better view, adopted by the new *Restatement*, is that the taking of the property eliminates the right to possession, and therefore automatically terminates the lease.[21] The lessee is necessarily excused from further obligations to the lessor, including the obligation to pay rent. But unless the value of the lease has increased above the rent reserved, the lessee has no claim for just compensation from the condemning authority: if the rent reserved is equal to fair market value of the lease, the cancellation of the liability to pay rent means the lessee has no compensable right.[22] A somewhat similar analysis applies to destruction by fire or flood.

VI. The Lessee's Right to Use

The transfer to the lessee of the right to use the property in the manner an owner would use the property is not usually emphasized as a defining element of a lease. But it is implicit in the practice of leasing, as confirmed by the FASB's definition of a lease as conferring 'the right to control the use of' an identified asset.

[20] See ibid, § 1.2 illus 1 (Tentative Draft No 5, April 2024).
[21] Ibid, § 5.5(a) cmt a (Tentative Draft No 5, April 2024).
[22] Ibid, § 5.6(b)(1) cmt d.

The transfer of the right to use the property serves a valuable function in distinguishing leases from other kinds of property. In the personal property context, it differentiates a lease from a bailment. Bailments entail the transfer of possession from the bailor to the bailee, but typically the transfer of possession in this context is made for one specifically defined purpose, such as repair, cleaning, storage, or transportation of the thing.

Likewise, the transfer of a right of general use distinguishes a lease from an easement or servitude. Easements and servitudes convey the right to use property for a specific use, such as crossing the property of another or hanging an advertising sign on the side of a building.[23] A lease, in contrast, confers on the lessee a right to engage in a general range of uses consistent with the discretion conferred on an owner of the asset.

Finally, the transfer of the right to use also helps sort out who has the right to do what when property is subject to a mortgage or similar security interest. A mortgage, whether of the lessor's reversion or the lessee's leasehold, does not entail a transfer of the right to use the property. The security interest is only an inchoate right to take possession of the asset in the event of a default and sell it to satisfy the debt. Only when the asset is sold, either to a third party or to the mortgagee itself, is the right to use transferred to the purchaser at the sale.

One of the more difficult issues to rationalize in terms of the framework of the new *Restatement* is the implied warranty of habitability (IWH) in residential leases. The issue is not difficult in terms of the basic norms governing restatements. Today, the IWH is required in all American jurisdictions.[24] Nor is it difficult as a matter of policy. In this regard, it is helpful to compare the purchase of real property (including residential property) where *caveat emptor* mostly still applies, and a lease of residential property. Purchasers of real property have enough at stake in such a transaction to investigate the quality of the land and structures before signing a sales contract, including paying for a professional inspection. With respect to leases of residential property, which are generally short term (two years or less), it does not pay to hire a professional to inspect the property before signing a lease. Nor would it make much sense to adopt a warranty of habitability as a default rule, since lessors would probably override the warranty in standard form leases, and again, there is not enough at stake in a short-term residential lease to justify hiring a lawyer to review and

[23] See *Baseball Publishing Co v Bruton*, 18 NE 2d 362 (Mass 1938).

[24] Restatement (Fourth) of Property, Vol IV, Div 3, § 6.1, Reporters' Notes, 133–135 (Tentative Draft No 5, April 2024).

renegotiate the lease before signing it. So a mandatory IWH makes sense as a kind of consumer protection law.

The difficulty comes in rationalizing the adoption of a mandatory IWH as a matter of common law, consistent with the property and contract elements of a lease emphasized by the new *Restatement*'s definition. The solution adopted by the Reporters is based on the understanding that a lease conveys the right to use the property. The *Restatement* posits that when the intended use of the property is for residential purposes, this presupposes that the property will be fit for human habitation.[25] This sounds nice, but in reality what it means is that in residential leases there is a non-disclaimable warranty that the property is fit for its intended purpose. This is in tension with lease law more generally, which does not require that leased property be fit for its intended purpose. In the end, the justification for the departure is social policy. Residential leases are different, because of the concern for human health and safety, and the short term of residential leases makes it impractical to think that *caveat lessee* will provide an adequate measure of protection for these interests.[26]

Another difficult issue is presented by the doctrine of constructive eviction, which applies to residential and commercial leases alike. As previously noted, all leases include a covenant of quiet enjoyment, which means the lessor cannot interfere with the lessee's right to possession during the term of the lease. The lessee's obligation to pay rent was historically regarded as being dependent on the lessor's compliance with this covenant. The doctrine of constructive eviction is based on the idea that if the lessor allows the condition of the property to deteriorate to the point where the lessee is compelled to vacate, then the lessor has 'constructively' evicted the lessee and the lessee is relieved of any further obligation to pay rent. The doctrine traditionally required the lessee to abandon the premises in order to invoke the doctrine. This presented the lessee with a cruel choice, since if the court rejected the claim, the lessee would be liable for unpaid rent and would have given up any value left in retaining possession of the property.

The 1977 *Restatement* sought to revise the doctrine of constructive eviction by grounding it in a violation of the right of use rather than a fictional violation of the right to possess. Thus, the 1977 volumes posited that if the lessor

[25] Ibid, § 6.1(a) (Tentative Draft No 5, April 2024).

[26] This is not to say that the IWH has improved the welfare of low-income residential lessees. Any mandatory warranty of quality will increase both the costs of supplying the product and the demand for the product, causing prices to rise. Even if many low-income lessees would be willing to pay the higher rents, the IWH is not enforced with enough frequency to affect the quality of low-income housing (Summers 2020; Super 2011).

'interferes with a permissible use of the leased property by the tenant' the lessor is in breach of the lease, and the lessee can invoke appropriate remedies including damages.[27] The revision had the virtue of being more honest—the problem was interference with use, not possession—and more equitable to lessees. Under the revised doctrine, the lessee could litigate first and elect to terminate further performance or sue for damages if successful, rather than having to vacate first and then endure the risks of litigation afterwards.

Unfortunately, in the forty-five years since this reformulation was advanced, no court has adopted it. Courts have continued to invoke the doctrine of constructive eviction, however fictitious, and when they do, they have generally required the lessee to vacate in order to raise the claim. This poses a dilemma for the new *Restatement*. The 1977 revision seems to be a salutary idea. And there is undoubtedly a presumption in favour of one restatement adhering to the views of the previous restatement. But it is difficult to claim that the 1977 revision has the support of even a minority of courts. A glimmer of hope is provided by the fact that at least one state supreme court has repudiated the idea that the lessee must vacate before invoking constructive eviction.[28] And a handful of courts appear to have adopted the view that the covenant of quiet enjoyment protects the lessee's right to use and enjoyment—however contrary this may be to the historical understanding of the meaning of 'quiet enjoyment'. On the basis of these glimmers, the new *Restatement* follows the 1977 version in characterizing what was formerly called constructive eviction in terms of a significant interference with permissible use.[29]

This reframing does not create a general warranty of fitness for intended purpose. The concept is not that the lessee must be able to achieve success in the particular use it has chosen for the property. As is implicit in the law of constructive eviction, the idea is that the lessor may not take some action or fail to fulfil some obligation that deprives the lessee of the ability to pursue any permissible use of the property. Thus, if the lessor permits a serious leak in the roof to persist, the property can be said to be unusable for any purpose. The parties remain free to specify in the lease what uses are permissible, and to negotiate specific warranties of quality if they so desire. As long as the lessor does not significantly interfere with any permissible use, the lessee remains responsible for appropriate management of the property, much in the way an owner would be.

[27] *Restatement (Second) of Property: Landlord and Tenant* § 6.1 (1977).
[28] *Echo Consulting Services, Inc v North Conway Bank*, 669 A2d 227 (NH 1995).
[29] *Restatement (Fourth) of Property*, Vol IV, Div 3, § 7.2 (Tentative Draft No 5, April 2024).

VII. The Importance of a Reversion

The requirement that a lease be for a time less than the expected useful life of the asset means that a lease must be followed by a reversion in the lessor. This is consistent with practice: every lease has a reversion. A ground lease for ninety-nine years has a reversion, since land is assumed to have a perpetual existence. And the land will be there, for the lessor's heirs to resume possession of it, when the ninety-nine years are up. A document that purports to create a perpetual lease should be construed to be something else, presumably a sale.

The cases and treatises do not explain why every lease has a reversion. There are a number of functional reasons for this.[30] One is that the reversion reduces the cost of holding an asset, because the lessee acquires less than the full economic value of the asset. That is why the monthly payments for the lease of a new car for three years are less than the monthly payments for purchasing the same car with a three-year loan. Another is that the reversion reduces the risk of holding an asset, because the risk is shared between the lessee and the lessor. A third is that the lessor's reversion, in conjunction with the expectation of receiving periodic payments of rent, gives the lessor a strong interest in overseeing the asset and assuring that it is properly maintained and managed. This engagement with the asset makes the lessor an appropriate party to serve as the manager of a complex of assets, like a shopping centre, an office building, or a high-rise apartment building.

Given the functional importance of the reversion, it would seem that the law of leasing would insist that the lessee return the asset at the end of the lease in the same condition as when the lease commenced, ordinary wear and tear excepted. In other words, that lease law would strictly enforce the doctrine of waste. In fact, however, the doctrine of waste has been understood since it was first adopted in the thirteenth century to be a default rule subject to modification by the parties. The default is frequently modified in many ways, such as specifying which party is responsible for making repairs or requiring that notice be given to the lessor when the lessee is contemplating making modifications to the property. Still, the basic proposition—return the property unchanged—provides the baseline against which these specific lease provisions are drafted. Unless modified by more specific obligations, the commission of waste by the lessee is a material breach of the duties imposed on the lessee by law.

[30] Merrill 2020, 12–39.

The doctrine of waste applies both to leases followed by reversions and to life estates followed by future interests. In the lease context, it is often possible to give the lessee more flexibility in making changes than in the context of life estates. Specifically, as the new *Restatement* affirms, the lessee should not be charged with waste if the lessee can remove any materials or machinery ('annexations') to the property before the end of the lease without material damage to the property. Lessees should often be able to do this, whereas life estate holders, who will be dead when their interest expires, commonly would not be able to take advantage of such a dispensation. The new *Restatement* makes clear that these kinds of corrective actions by the lessee should not be considered waste if taken before the expiration of the lease.[31]

VIII. The Formation of a Binding Contract

Although contract law is associated with individualization and default rules, contract law also includes mandatory rules. As in the case of the mandatory rules associated with property, these rules are necessary in order to determine whether one has a contract or something else, and what sort of remedies are available when a contract is breached. One of these requirements is that a lease must be supported by consideration. Another is that the statute of frauds requires that leases of a certain duration must be in writing and signed by the party to be bound. In most states, this means any lease for a term longer than one year.

The new *Restatement* makes clear that a lease must be supported by consideration. This is consistent with practice. Leases are commercial instruments. They are not bestowed as gifts. Nor does one see leases used for family wealth transmission, either in a will or a family trust. Moreover, since lease law borrows many features from contract law, including the remedies prescribed by contract law, it would seem that leases must satisfy the minimal requirements for the formation of a binding contract.

The proposition that a lease requires consideration helps solve a small doctrinal puzzle: whether it is possible to make a lease that does not require the payment of rent. Courts have long stated that every lease includes an implied covenant to pay rent, and if a lease does not include a stated rent, courts will imply a reasonable rent.[32] But is it possible to make a lease that provides for no

[31] See *Restatement (Fourth) of Property*, Vol 1, Div 3, Ch 1, Topic 4, §§ 1.24, 1.25 (Tentative Draft No 4, April 2023); ibid, § 9.3(b) (Tentative Draft No 6, April 2025).

[32] See ibid, Vol 4, Div III, Ch 9, § 9.2 cmt b (Tentative Draft No 6, April 2025).

payment of rent? Legal sources, especially in England, disagree about this.[33] The new *Restatement* makes clear that, whether or not rent is always required, consideration is required in every case. Otherwise the contractual aspects of the hybrid institution would fail. This appears to be consistent with the reported cases. In the tiny number of leases in which rent is not required, the lessee gives consideration in some other form, such as providing valuable services to the lessor.

IX. Contract-Based Remedies

The explicit adoption of contract law as the foundation for remedies for breaches of lease obligations helps clear up a number of other doctrinal puzzles. This is especially clear with respect to the remedies available to both lessees and lessor for a breach by the other. The general strategy of the new *Restatement*, taken from the *Restatement (Second) of Contracts*, is to distinguish between material breaches and nonmaterial breaches.[34] Material breaches give rise to stronger remedies, most prominently, 'termination of further performance' under the lease by the party suffering a breach. Non-material breaches are remedied by damages. Damages include the possibility of a set-off against monies otherwise owed under the contract, which in the lease context is referred to as an abatement of rent.

As to what constitutes a material breach, the new *Restatement* provides that any breach of one of the mandatory duties established by the property dimension of leases is material. Thus, a lessor's violation of the lessee's right to possession or right to use the property will generally give rise to a right on the part of the lessee to terminate further performance (vacate the premises and stop paying rent) or possibly to sue for specific performance, and in addition to sue for damages for any residual harm incurred. Similarly, the lessee's violation of the lessor's right to receive consideration (typically rent) or to have the property returned at the end of the lease without waste will give rise to a right on the part of the lessor to terminate further performance (institute eviction proceedings terminating the lessee's right to possession) or to obtain an injunction in the case of waste, and in addition to sue for damages for any loss of the original

[33] Compare *Street v Mountford* [1985] AC 809 (stating that rent is a requirement) with the Law of Property Act 1925, 205(1) (xxvii) (defining a term of years as not requiring rent) and *Ashburn Anstalt v Arnold* [1988] 2 WLR 706 (rent not an essential requirement).

[34] See *Restatement (Second) of Contracts* § 237 cmt a (1981).

benefit of the bargain. Other breaches of lease obligations can also be material, if they are shown to have been a significant inducement to the other party to enter into the lease. Determining whether this condition is met will generally require further investigation into context. A covenant by the lessor not to compete or not to allow other lessees to compete with the business of the lessee might qualify.[35] Or a covenant to allow the lessee to construct a building on the leased premises might qualify. Non-material breaches give rise to a claim for damages or abatement of rent. A breach of a promise to maintain the property (by either party) might be an example.[36]

The 1977 *Restatement* moved part way towards embracing contractual remedies. In particular, it recognized that in many circumstances serious breaches can be remedied by a right of the counterparty to 'terminate' the lease, whether or not the lease contains a clause authorizing forfeiture of the lease for such violations. But when it spoke of right to 'terminate', the Second *Restatement* would sometimes also provide that the party suffering the breach could sue for damages. This created an obvious puzzle. If the lease has been terminated, what is the basis for suing for damages? The new *Restatement* avoids this conundrum by adopting the more felicitous expression of the Restatement (Second) of Contracts, to the effect that a breach of a material obligation authorizes the aggrieved party to 'terminate further performance' under the lease.[37] Thus, for example, if the lessee fails to pay the rent, the lessor can terminate further performance, that is, is no longer required to provide possession and use to the lessee, but can still sue the lessee for non-payment of rent that has accrued up to the time when the lessor declares it has terminated further performance—and for any loss of the benefit of the bargain that remains after the lessor has terminated further performance.

The 1977 *Restatement* rejected the idea that the lessor has a duty to mitigate damages when the lessee abandons the property or repudiates the lease. The duty to mitigate damages is a well-established feature of the law of contract remedies. This is grounded in considerations of social welfare. If one party to a contract cannot perform its obligations, it makes no sense to allow the other party to do nothing and permit damages to accumulate. Far better for

[35] See *Medico-Dental Bldg Co v Horton and Converse*, 132 P 2d 457 (Cal 1942).

[36] Following the case law and statutes adopting the IWH, the new *Restatement* takes the position that a breach of the IWH is material, and thus gives rise to rights on the part of the lessee to terminate further performance (vacate and stop paying rent) or to sue for specific performance. Interestingly, however, empirical studies indicate that the remedy sought in nearly every case is an abatement in rent (Summers 2020).

[37] See, eg, *Restatement (Fourth) of Property*, Vol 1, Div 3, Ch 8, § 8.1 (Tentative Draft No 4, April 2023).

the promisee to find a substitute party to perform the promise, and then sue the breaching promisor for any lost benefit of the original bargain. The same reasoning applies when a lessee abandons or repudiates a lease. Better for the lessor to advertise for a substitute lessee, and then sue for any lost benefit of the bargain under the original lease. The 1977 *Restatement* resisted this argument, on the implausible ground that imposing a duty to mitigate might encourage vandalism.[38] Allowing the property to stand empty while pursuing damages from the abandoning tenant would seem to be more likely to invite vandalism. The new *Restatement* makes the duty to mitigate mandatory with respect to residential leases.[39] It recognizes that in the context of commercial and agricultural leases the lessee may at times be the 'cheaper mitigator', for example by finding a substitute lessee.[40] So outside the residential context, the duty to mitigate is an implied obligation, but can be modified by a lease provision expressly requiring the lessee to assign the lease or enter into a sublease.

Another example: a majority of courts evidently take the position that a promise by the lessor to repay a security deposit at the end of the lease, if the lessee is not in default in any respect, is merely an unsecured debt of the lessor. Thus, if the lessor declares bankruptcy, the security deposit is unlikely to be returned, because the lessee will be only a general creditor standing in line with other general creditors of the lessor. The new Restatement seeks to undo this line of authority, based on an analysis of Article 9 of the Uniform Commercial Code, which indicates that a security deposit is a security interest in the nature of a pledge of assets, and thus should have priority over general creditors.[41] The new Restatement also takes issue with the cases holding that a security deposit does not run with the land if the lessor sells the reversion to a third party. This is obviously unfair and makes no sense. The lessee's promise to pay rent and not to commit waste both run to successors of the lessor.[42] The security deposit is designed to assure that these obligations are performed. So the promise to repay the security deposit should likewise run to successors when its function in seeing that these obligations have been performed has been fulfilled.[43]

38 *Restatement (Second) of Property: Landlord and Tenant* § 12.1 cmt i (1977).
39 *Restatement (Fourth) of Property*, Vol 1, Div 3, Ch 10, §10.3(c) (Tentative Draft No 6, April 2025).
40 Ibid, cmt f.
41 Henning & Freyermuth 2013.
42 See *Restatement (Fourth) of Property*, Vol 1, Div 3, Ch 11 (Council Draft No 11, Dec 2024).
43 Ibid, § 10.3 cmt J (Tentative Draft No 6, April 2025).

X. Mandatory and Default Rules

The new Restatement takes full advantage of the distinction in contract law between mandatory rules and default rules. Leases necessarily contain certain mandatory duties, as we have seen, which serve to define an agreement as a lease. But over a large range of questions, the parties are free to establish their respective obligations as they see fit. With respect to some of these issues, such as whether the lessee can keep pets, it is difficult, if not impossible, to identify a 'majoritarian' preference, and thus the Restatement is silent on the issue. With respect to other issues, it is plausible to state a majoritarian preference, at least with respect to residential leases, if not other types of leases. With respect to these sorts of issues, the new Restatement often specifies that the majoritarian preference is a default rule, but is subject to override by appropriate language in the lease.

A good example concerns the obligations to repair and provide routine maintenance. With respect to residential leases, the new Restatement says that the lessor has a default obligation to repair, and the lessee has a default obligation to provide routine maintenance.[44] For other types of leases, no default rule is specified, since it is difficult to imagine what the majoritarian rule would be. The allocation of responsibilities here is routinely specified in the lease or emerges by implication from the conduct of the parties.

Another example concerns who has the burden of removing a squatter or holdover tenant who is present on the property when the term of the lessee begins. Under the so-called English rule, the lessor has the burden of removing the squatter or holdover. Under what has been called the American rule, the lessee has this burden (American states are actually divided on the subject). Selection of the proper rule in this context is difficult, because in many circumstances (eg residential leases in an apartment complex) the lessor is clearly the 'cheaper evictor'. But in other circumstances (eg a lease of agricultural land by an absentee lessor) the lessee may be the cheaper evictor. The new Restatement again resolves the issue by making the lessor responsible to clear the premises of illegal occupants at the beginning of the lease, because this probably makes the most sense in most contexts. But it is stated as a default rule, because there will be exceptions, and therefore the parties should be allowed to contract around the rule by appropriate lease agreement.[45]

[44] Ibid, § 6.3 (Tentative Draft No 5, April 2024).
[45] Ibid, § 5.4 (Tentative Draft No 5, April 2024).

XI. Conclusion

The great popularity of leases as a mode of holding assets is attributable in significant part to the flexibility of leases in dividing and allocating responsibility among different parties over the use of assets. In this respect, leases can be viewed as an example of relational contracting, in which parties specify their respective roles with respect to specific assets in light of their particular circumstances, and their shared understanding is sustained based on norms of reciprocity. From this perspective, leases are very much a form of contract. But leases also impose duties on strangers to the property, and serve more broadly to allocate control over specific assets, and from this perspective they very much fall within the family of doctrines we associate with property. They are thus the quintessential hybrid institution: part property, part contract. Rather than dogmatically insisting leases must be one or the other, the Restatement (Fourth) of Property attempts to describe how and why the integration works—and why it evidently works well enough that leasing continues to proliferate as a form of holding valuable resources.

References

Chang, Y. and T. W. Merrill (2025). 'The Nature of Leasing'. *Cornell International Law Journal* 58: 1–35.

Chang, Y. and H. E. Smith (2019). 'Convergence and Divergence in Systems of Property Law: Theoretical and Empirical Analysis'. *Southern California Law Review* 92: 785–808.

D'Onfro, D. (2024). 'Contract-Wrapped Property'. *Harvard Law Review* 137: 1058–1136.

Henning, W. H. and R. W. Freyermuth (2013). 'Article 9 and the Characterization and Treatment of Tenant Security Deposits'. *University of Arkansas Little Rock Law Review* 35: 999–1030.

Merrill, T. W. and H. E. Smith (2000). 'Optimal Standardization in the Law of Property: The *Numerus Clausus* Principle'. *Yale Law Journal* 110: 1–70.

Merrill, T. W. and H. E. Smith (2001). 'The Property/Contract Interface'. *Columbia Law Review* 101: 773–852.

Merrill, T. W. (2020). 'The Economics of Leasing'. *Journal of Legal Analysis* 12: 221–272.

Merrill, T. W. (2023). 'The Restatement of Property: The Curse of Incompleteness'. *The American Law Institute: A Centennial History*. A. S. Gold and R. W. Gordon. Oxford, Oxford University Press: 203–218.

Rabin, E. H. (1984). 'The Revolution in Residential Landlord-Tenant Law: Causes and Consequences'. *Cornell Law Review* 69: 517–584.

Simpson, A. W. B. (1986). *A History of the Land Law*. Oxford, Oxford University Press.

Summers, N. (2020). 'The Limits of Good Law: A Study of Housing Court Outcomes'. *University of Chicago Law Review* 87: 145–221.

Super, D. A. (2011). 'The Rise and Fall of the Implied Warranty of Habitability'. *California Law Review* 90: 389–463.

11

The Nature of the Interest of an Object of Trust or Power

Lusina Ho[*]

I. Introduction

Scholars have long debated the nature of equitable interests under a trust. Two decades ago, Thomas Merrill and Henry Smith broke new ground by showing how information costs illuminate the in rem features of trust law.[1] The authors place interests under trusts in the intermediate zone between in rem and in personam rights.[2]

Taking a different path, Ben McFarlane and Robert Stevens analyse these interests as persistent rights against the trustee's rights—a distinct category in itself.[3] They argue that the term 'beneficial ownership' is misleading, as it suggests that beneficiaries have direct rights to trust property that bind third parties. More recently, McFarlane has clarified that the trustee's right, which is subject to duty, can be a power, or can include powers over the trust property.[4]

Whilst the aforementioned scholars have shed valuable light on how the obligational relationship between the trustee and beneficiary affects third parties, their accounts attempt to reduce the complex legal advantages in a trust into a single right. These accounts invite yet further refinement to address three crucial features of the interests of objects of a trust or power.[5]

* This chapter benefitted greatly from comments received at the Property-Contract Interface Workshop, particularly those of Katy Barnett, and from research assistance by Nick Hsu. Special thanks to Timothy Chan and William Swadling for their incredibly helpful comments on an earlier draft of the chapter.

1 See Merrill & Smith 2001, 777–778, 843–849.

2 Ibid; Smith 2023, 328 (also using the term the 'twilight zone').

3 McFarlane & Stevens 2010.

4 McFarlane 2026, citing Eldrige 2024 and Penner 2014. See also Zaccaria 2019.

5 By 'objects of a trust or power', I mean the beneficiaries of a trust or objects of a power of appointment which has been granted to the trustee or a party not subject to fiduciary duties in the exercise of the power.

Lusina Ho, *The Nature of the Interest of an Object of Trust or Power* In: *The Property-Contract Interface*. Edited by: James Penner, Irina Sakharova, Henry E. Smith, and Zhong Xing Tan, Oxford University Press. © Lusina Ho 2026.
DOI: 10.1093/9780198951995.003.0014

First, these interests are not only limited to the regulation of the trustee's exercise of powers over the trust rights, but also include the trustee's purely personal obligations towards the beneficiaries. Second, even parties who have no individual right to direct the trustee to convey the trust asset to them, such as objects of powers and discretionary trusts, trustees, and the Attorney General, have the power to seek judicial relief to enforce the proper administration of the trust.[6] Third, whilst interests under a trust bind third parties who have assisted a breach or received the trust rights, the liability imposed on them is fundamentally different from that of a trustee.

To fully capture these features, I propose a different conceptual model: that the interests of trust and power objects are best understood as a bespoke bundle of in personam rights or powers that can bind third parties with an affected conscience. This bundle operates on two levels: first, it governs both the trustee's exercise of powers over the trust rights and their personal obligations owed to trust and power objects; second, it regulates third-party involvement in the trust relationship, including receipt of misapplied trust rights and assistance in a breach of trust.

At the first level, against the trustee, this bundle comprises: bespoke rights tailored to the nature of each object's potential distribution as defined by the trust deed; identical but separate powers that the objects have to enforce the trust's due administration; and rights and powers regarding the trustee's purely personal obligations. At the second level, against third parties, each object has an identical but separate power to invoke the court's jurisdiction, thus giving this power the 'hallmark of [a] right in rem'.[7] This in rem appearance is, however, deceptive. Unlike liability under erga omnes rights, which is universal for everyone bound, the liability of these third parties is distinct from that of the original trustee and arises only when their conscience is affected. Their liability arises either by receiving through a chain of successive transfers or assisting in a breach of trust. Crucially, such liability is grounded in the interference with the trust relationship itself, rather than with the trustee's right.

My argument unfolds in two parts. First, I sketch the claim-rights and powers held by objects and office-holders under a trust. With these legal advantages enumerated, I consider the traditional in rem/in personam model and the recent rights-against-rights thesis before proposing a third one.

[6] McFarlane 2026, xx. Cf Smith 2017, 22–24; Penner 2022, paras 4.31–4.33, 4.51–4.55, 4.60–4.76.
[7] *Akers v Samba Financial Group* (*Akers*) [2017] UKSC 6, [2017] AC 424, [82] (Lord Sumption).

II. The Interests of Trust and Power Objects

As McFarlane aptly observed, interests under a trust defy the simplistic paradigm in which A holds rights on a bare trust for B, and B brings a proprietary or knowing receipt claim against C.[8] These interests vary significantly depending on the trust terms, including the extent of any discretion over who receives benefits and in what quantum. Some objects may have rights to receive specific trust benefits, while others may have merely a possibility of receiving them. Further, the objects not only hold these interests against the trustee and third parties, but have the power to invoke the court's jurisdiction to give directions, order relief, or even execute the trust.

1. Rights/Powers against the Trustee

This part of the chapter begins by examining the objects' distinct packages of rights with respect to trust distribution. It then analyses the enforcement powers held by all objects, trustees, and the Attorney General with respect to the due administration of the trust and the rights held by some objects regarding the observance of purely personal fiduciary obligations. Because the trust allows bespoke arrangements regarding the use and distribution of rights, it gives rise to a wide spectrum of interests. Any attempt to make sense of that spectrum must begin with the core categories of trust arrangements.

A. Trusts versus powers

At the most fundamental level, a distinction can be drawn between the *duty* in a trust to distribute trust assets to beneficiaries and the *power* given to a donee to select one or more objects to receive trust assets. This basic framework becomes more nuanced when duty and power are combined.[9] For instance, in a fixed trust, the trustee has the duty to distribute the trust assets but no discretion (or power) to determine who benefits from the trust. In contrast, a discretionary trust imposes a duty to distribute the trust assets, yet grants the trustee a power to select which member(s) of a designated class will receive a share and in what proportion. A further layer of discretion is introduced in a non-exhaustive discretionary trust, where the trustee is given a power to accumulate income rather than distribute it. In such cases, the accumulated income

[8] McFarlane 2026.
[9] *Harvey v Van Hoorn* [2023] Ch 500 (*Harvey*), [12]–[15].

may be distributed to the income beneficiaries at a later time, or at the latest, upon the trust's vesting date.

In powers of appointment, the donee has the power but not the duty to select who is to receive the trust assets. Powers of appointment can be classified based on the identity of the donee.[10] When a power is vested in a trustee or a fiduciary protector *ex offcio*, it is a fiduciary power and its exercise is governed by the duty to act in good faith in the best interests of the objects and those in default, not for the personal benefit of the donee.[11] This contrasts with a personal power held by a non-fiduciary, which is not subject to such a duty. Because a power is discretionary, its non-exercise does not constitute a breach of duty, and so the objects have no right to compel its exercise or seek a remedy for such a failure to act. The assets will simply devolve to takers in default, whose interest, as trust objects, can itself be structured in various ways, such as an absolute interest, a trust, or a further power of appointment. In this situation we have two distinct classes of potential recipients: the objects of the power, whose interests are contingent upon the donee's discretion, and the takers in default, whose interests as beneficiaries at the outset are defeasible by the exercise of the power to appoint among the objects.[12]

B. Divergent rights/powers regarding trust distribution

Having established the fundamental distinction between trusts and powers and identified their major sub-categories, we now proceed to examine the interests in each category.

Among trust beneficiaries, three categories hold the right to demand the transfer of all or their share of the trust fund from the trustee, with this right being exercisable either individually or collectively depending on the beneficiary's status. First, the single beneficiary of a bare trust is absolutely and indefeasibly entitled to the trust property, as a bare trustee either has no active duty beyond that to convey the trust property to the beneficiary (or anyone directed by them), or has agreed to do whatever the settlor instructs.[13]

Second, a fixed trust beneficiary has an interest in an ascertainable part of the trust property; this interest generally carries the right to demand the trustee to convey the beneficiary's share of the trust fund consistent with the trust terms.[14] The trustee has no discretion over benefit distribution but rather

[10] Powers of appointment may also be classified according to how broadly or narrowly the class of objects is defined, into general, special, or hybrid powers.
[11] Ho 2026, xx.
[12] *Lambert v Thwaites* (1866) LR 2 Eq 151, 155; *Re Clark* [1923] 2 Ch 407, 419.
[13] Tucker, Le Poidevin, and Brightwell 2020, §§ 1-028, 1-037; Matthews 2005, 267.
[14] Dal Pont 2023, § 20.20.

a duty to distribute. When fixed trust beneficiaries have a present entitlement, they have a fixed interest that constitutes an interest in possession[15] under the trust, and that interest is assignable.[16]

Third, in jurisdictions that recognize the rule in *Saunders v Vautier*, if all beneficiaries of a discretionary trust are ascertained, of full age and capacity, and acting together, they have the right to terminate the trust and demand the transfer of the trust fund to them, even though individually each has merely a hope of receiving distribution.[17] This rule is justified on the basis that they are beneficially entitled to the trust property collectively because the trustee must distribute among any one or more of them; as such, they could supersede the settlor's intention by acting as one.[18] However, this collective right remains largely theoretical, as it can be avoided by careful drafting and is, in any event, subject to the trustee's indemnities.

In contrast, objects of fiduciary powers of appointment do not have the right to receive a distribution, whether individually or collectively, for the fundamental reason that the donee is under no duty to appoint the trust assets to any or all from the class of objects. Even though a fiduciary power requires the donee to exercise their power in the best interests of the objects, it does not compel the appointment itself. In this respect, the position of an individual object of fiduciary power is broadly similar to that of an individual beneficiary under a discretionary trust. Both groups do not hold any substantive right to demand for the transfer of the trust right. Instead, they have procedural rights pertaining to the exercise of discretion: to be considered as potential recipients of benefit and to have trustees consider exercising their discretion from time to time (including to enquire about and ascertain, in broad terms, the size and composition of the class of objects and to understand the relevant considerations for the exercise of discretion).[19] Where the two groups differ, is that

[15] An interest in possession is a present and immediate right to enjoy the benefits of an asset, which means the right to receive the income generated by that asset.

[16] Matthews et al. 2022, art 5.1(2), 67; *Schmidt v Rosewood Trust Ltd* (*Schmidt*) [2003] UKPC 26, [2003] 2 AC 709, [40], [51], [54], [66].

[17] (*Saunders*) (1841) Cr & Ph 240; 41 ER 482, *Re Smith* [1928] Ch 915; *Re Nelson (Note)* [1928] Ch 920 (reported as a note to *Re Smith*) (exhaustive discretionary trust with a closed class of beneficiaries); *Re Beckett's Settlement* [1940] Ch 279, 285; *Harvey*, [16]. For an excellent account of the historical origin of the rule, see Lupoi & Graziadei 2025.

[18] Lewin (1837), 489; *Re Smith*, 918–919 (Romer J). Cf Morris 2026.

[19] *Re Gulbenkian's Settlement Trust (No 1)* (*Re Gulbenkian*) [1970] AC 508, 518; *Re Hay's Settlement Trusts* (*Re Hay's*) [1982] 1 WLR 202, 209; *Re Gestetner* [1953] Ch 672, 687–688; *Gartside v IRC* [1968] AC 553, 606, 617–619; *McPhail v Doulton* [1971] AC 424, 449; *Harvey*, [15]. See Thomas 2012, §§ 10.06–10.22. The trustees must also act within the scope of the power, give adequate deliberation, and exercise the power for proper purpose: *Grand View Private Trust Co Ltd v Wong* [2022] UKPC 47, [2023] WTLR 149; *Dawson-Damer v Grampian Trust Co Ltd* [2025] UKPC 32, [2025] 1 WLR 3530.

beneficiaries of discretionary trusts have an additional right: that trustees exercise their conferred discretion.[20]

From these aforementioned rights flow several enforcement powers with respect to the distribution of trust assets, namely, powers to compel trustees to exercise their discretion in the case of a discretionary trust and to require the consideration of an exercise of discretion in the case of a fiduciary power;[21] contest a failure to consider the claimant when exercising discretion; challenge improper exercises of discretion (such as taking into account irrelevant considerations, overlooking relevant considerations, acting for improper purposes, acting capriciously, or exceeding the scope of powers); challenge distributions made outside the specified class of objects; and seek the removal of trustees who fail either to consider the claimant or to exercise their discretion.[22] Crucially, none of these powers confers upon objects of trusts and powers any right to call for the transfer of the trust rights to them.

Objects of non-fiduciary powers of appointment occupy an even weaker position, as the donees of such powers owe them no duty to consider whether to exercise their power or to consider them as potential recipients.[23] The donees have a duty not to exceed the limit of these powers or exercise them for an improper purpose, so an appointment outside the designated class of objects is ultra vires and thus invalid for exceeding this scope.[24] In *Re Gulbenkian's Settlement Trust (No 1)*, Lord Upjohn suggested that those entitled to trust rights in default of appointment have standing to challenge any excessive exercise of a power, as such appointments would unlawfully diminish or defeat their interests.[25] By the same logic, objects of non-fiduciary powers should also have standing to challenge an appointment as ultra vires. Although they have no right to be appointed, they still have a right against the trustee: namely, that the trustee not act contrary to the trust terms, thereby excluding them from a potential distribution; an invalid exercise of the power unlawfully prejudices their prospect of future distribution.

[20] Thomas 2012, § 10.21.

[21] *Gartside v LRC* [1986] AC 553, 617G.

[22] *Re Manisty's Settlement Trusts* (*Re Manisty's*) [1974] Ch 17, 25; *Mettoy Pension Trustees Ltd v Evans* (*Evans*) [1990] 1 WLR 1587, 1614; *Harvey*, [22]. Note the traditional position that objects of fiduciary powers have standing only to seek the removal of trustees who fail to give due consideration to an exercise of their fiduciary powers, not to seek any other kind of relief, although this approach is unlikely to survive *Schmidt*.

[23] Matthews et al. 2022, art 1.69(b).

[24] *Re Wright* [1920] 1 Ch 108, 117; Matthews et al. 2022, art 1.85.

[25] *Re Gulbenkian*, 524H–525B.

C. Identical but separate powers to enforce proper trust administration

In addition to rights/powers regarding their individual distribution, trust and power objects also need standing to enforce the due administration of the trust. At its heart, due administration requires the trustee to use the powers that come with their trust rights in accordance with the terms of the trust. Although the trustee holds the trust right, and with it, powers to use, manage, destroy, and transfer the right, they do not hold it for their own benefit. Their use of these powers is constrained by the limits set by the trust terms.[26]

The powers to enforce these constraints include powers to seek court orders to:

1. require trustees to render an account[27] and provide 'trust documents'[28] (as an essential step to allow parties to monitor and enforce trustees' performance of the trust);
2. compel trustees to administer the trust property in accordance with the trust's terms; and
3. require trustees to reconstitute the trust fund if it has been dissipated or depleted through a breach of trust.

These enforcement powers are foundational because they protect the trust fund, which is the trust's most essential component. Since the very purpose of a trust is to dedicate resources to the settlors' goals, its viability depends on the fund's integrity. This is why a trust will not fail for want of a trustee, but it will for lack of funds.

Until *Schmidt v Rosewood Trust Ltd*, at least in relation to beneficiaries' right to inspect trust documents, courts have adopted the flawed reasoning that their right stemmed from their proprietary interest in the trust property.[29] This view treated the documents as trust property, and the beneficiaries as merely exercising their right to view property that already 'belonged' to them.

In line with this 'proprietary' approach is the view that trust objects who have individual rights to call for the transfer of the trust property, however minute or remote, have standing to enforce the due administration of a trust.[30]

[26] Hudson 2023.

[27] Beneficiaries not only have the power to seek a court order to compel the trustee to produce the trust account, but also the right to demand it from the trustee directly: *White v Lady Lincoln* (1803) 8 Ves Jun 363; *Pearse v Green* (1819) 1 Jac & W 135.

[28] For the circular definition of 'trust documents', see *Re Londonderry's Settlement* (*Re Londonderry*) [1965] Ch 918, [1965] 2 WLR 229.

[29] *O'Rourke v Darbishire* [1920] AC 581; *Re Londonderry*. See Smith 2017, 22.

[30] Tucker, Le Poidevin, and Brightwell 2020, § 41-072; *Bartlett v Bartlett* (1845) 4 Hare 631; *Clowes v Hilliard* (1876) 4 Ch D 413, 415.

Their enforcement powers are treated as incidents of their right to receive a distribution. The proprietary view was recently adopted by the UK Supreme Court in relation to claims for knowing receipt.[31]

On this approach, the standing of discretionary trust beneficiaries, who have only a possibility of receiving a distribution upon a favourable exercise of trustee discretion, is justified on the basis that they are beneficially entitled to the trust property collectively.[32] However, the proprietary reasoning struggles to justify the standing of objects of fiduciary powers to enforce proper trust administration, as they cannot be said to be collectively entitled to the trust property.[33]

This struggle is due to the failure of the proprietary approach in distinguishing between an object's standing to receive a distribution from the trust fund and their standing to enforce proper trust administration. Properly interpreted, the beneficiary principle established in *Morice v Bishop of Durham* is concerned with this latter point of accountability.[34] The court's reasoning was not about defining 'beneficial ownership', but about establishing the necessary nexus for invoking judicial supervision, that there must be someone who can bring the trustee before a court. Whilst demonstration of an individual or collective right to trust distribution is a relevant factor, if not a sufficient ground, for granting standing to enforce proper trust administration, it should not be a prerequisite. To hold otherwise would create an enforcement vacuum for modern discretionary trusts, which involve objects of fiduciary powers and a removable residuary beneficiary (typically a charity) who may not be aware of the existence of the trust.

These practical concerns may have driven the pivotal shift in *Schmidt v Rosewood Trust Ltd* to extend standing to seek the disclosure of trust information to all objects of discretionary trusts and powers.[35] In this decision, Lord Walker held that standing flows not from any 'proprietary' right but from the court's inherent supervisory jurisdiction over trusts. His Lordship rejected any 'bright dividing line' based on the nature of the claimant's beneficial entitlements while emphasizing that the courts always retain the discretion to

[31] *Byers v Saudi National Bank* (*Byers*) [2023] UKSC 51, [2024] 2 WLR 237 (*Byers*).

[32] *Joel v Mills* (1857) 4 K & J 458, 473–476; *Cosser v Radford* (1863) 1 De G J & S 585.

[33] Smith 2017, 20–23; Penner 2015, 486, 495–496; *Re Manisty's*, 25–26; *Re Hay*, 209; *Evans*, 1614. Cf *Curwen v Vanbrack Pty Ltd* [2009] VSCA 284, [2009] 26 VR 335; *Randall v Lubrano*, published as an annexure to *McDonnald v Ellis* (2007) 72 NSWLR 605, 621, discussed in Hudson 2021, 24.

[34] *Morice v Bishop of Durham* (1804) 9 Ves 399, 404–405; 32 ER 656, 658.

[35] *Schmidt*, [51].

grant relief after considering a number of factors, including the strength of the claimant's interest.[36]

Lord Walker was right in emphasizing that standing in trust law is not confined to the common law paradigm of bipartite enforcement of rights.[37] Objects of fiduciary powers have standing to seek an order for disclosure against the trustee even though they only have a potential right to distribution. Since judicial relief for trusts is discretionary, the court would consider the likelihood of actual benefit in determining whether to order the disclosure.[38] Crucially, the court's role is not limited to adjudicating disputes between trust parties. It has supervisory jurisdiction to give directions, authorize emergency acts of administration, and even approve variations to trust terms, often without the institution of a suit.[39]

Schmidt has since been extended beyond information rights to the full range of reliefs mentioned earlier.[40] As Masters Matthews observed in *Lewis v Tamplin*:

> The whole direction of travel is in equating the position of the discretionary object to that of the fixed interest beneficiary, and not the other way round.[41]

In the recent decision of *Harvey v Van Hoorn*, Master Matthews reinforced this point by clarifying that objects of a fiduciary power have a bundle of rights to enforce the due administration of trust even though they do not have a vested right, present or future, to possession or enjoyment of any part of the trust assets.[42] The judicial observations in *Lewis* and *Harvey* suggest that despite the differences in their rights in respect of trust distribution, all objects of a trust or power have identical but separate powers to seek the court's jurisdiction to

[36] Ibid; *BNP Paribas Jersey Trust Corp Ltd v Crociani* [2018] JCA 136A, [26]–[50] (relief refused because of the remoteness of the claimant).

[37] Liau 2023, 96. Liau acknowledges that trust law departs from this foundational position. See Hudson & Mitchell 2026.

[38] *Schmidt*, [51]. For an excellent theoretical account of the discretionary nature of equitable rights generally, see Katz 2024.

[39] See Ho & Nolan 2020.

[40] *Lewis v Tamplin* [2018] EWHC 777 (Ch), [2018] WTLR 215 (*Lewis*) [39]; *Orb ARL v Ruhan* [2015] EWHC 262 (Comm), [110]; *Serious Fraud Office v Litigation Capital Ltd* [2021] EWHC 1272 (Comm) (*Serious Fraud Office*), [205]. For a similar position in Australia, see *RnD Funding Pty Ltd v Roncane* [2023] FCAFC 28; *Elliot v Secretary, Department of Education, Employment & Workplace Relations* (2008) 249 ALR 182, 193, [39]; *Cong v Shen* [2019] NWSC 1675, [83]. For the traditional restrictive approach, see *Re Manisty's*, 25–26; *Re Hay's*, 209; *Evans*, 1614: only those entitled in default can sue.

[41] *Lewis v Tamplin*, [41]; *Harvey*, [23].

[42] Liau 2023, 96. Liau acknowledges that trust law departs from this foundational position. See Hudson & Mitchell 2026.

enforce the due administration of the trust and when necessary to order a reconstitution of the trust fund.[43]

It bears noting that Master Matthews grounds the standing of objects of a trust or power in their interest (or potential right) to receive a distribution, even though they do not hold any existing right to receive one. This is a significant improvement from Lord Walker's discretionary approach in *Schmidt*, which obscures this rationale by emphasizing that disclosure is a matter of the court's inherent jurisdiction, with the likelihood of an object's distribution being only one factor for the court's consideration. Lord Walker's approach also fails to resolve several puzzles about standing in trust law.

First, it fails to clarify whether discretionary objects act in a representative capacity for those with rights to receive a distribution, similar to when one party has power to enforce another's right against a dutybearer.[44] Second, analysing these objects as aiding the court's supervisory jurisdiction rather than enforcing their rights fails to explain why are they not subject to a duty to act in the interest of the trust in conducting the litigation.[45] Third, and finally, if standing is truly anchored on a claimant's facilitation of judicial supervision of trustees rather than the claimant's interest in distributions, it becomes difficult to justify well-established rules that deny standing in respect of the part of the trust property to which a claimant has no actual or potential right.[46] A remainderman with a vested interest in the capital, for instance, has no standing to sue for a loss of income that would benefit only the life tenant if recovered. Further, whilst a single beneficiary may insist on bringing a claim even though other beneficiaries who have a claim to the same part of the trust fund have no intention to do so, the court may still refuse the claim if this beneficiary's financial interest is unaffected by the refusal. In *Dance v Goldingham*, where the court restrained an unauthorized sale at the behest of a beneficiary with only a minor stake, crucially, it also indicated that the injunction would have been refused if the other beneficiaries had offered to make good the claimant's loss.[47]

An analysis that resolves the foregoing puzzles more satisfactorily would recognize that the standing of trust and power objects arises from their interest in trust distribution. Although they do not need a right to a distribution to

[43] *Schmidt*, [51]; *Harvey*, [23].

[44] *Shovlin*; *Carson v Sloane* (1884) 13 LR Ir 139, 147; Seymour 1999, 570–571; Hafeez-Baig & English 2021, §5.12.

[45] *Dance v Goldingham* (1873) LR 8 Ch App 902, 912: it is irrelevant to the court that the claim is brought for some collateral object other than to enforce the claimant's equities before the court.

[46] Tucker, Le Poidevin, and Brightwell 2020, § 41-076; *Harbin v Masterman (No 2)* [1896] 1 Ch 351.

[47] *Dance v Goldingham*, 912.

establish standing, they have a right against the trustee, namely, that the trustee not act contrary to the trust terms in a way that would exclude them from a potential distribution. Put another way, they have a right to proper process and purpose in trust administration, which would secure the trust fund from which they might benefit.[48]

This analysis explains why recovered sums are paid not to claimants personally but to the trustee for ongoing trust administration, and why trust objects have standing only to sue in respect of the part of the trust property in which they have a right, as their standing flows from their right to secure that part of the trust property for due administration.[49] They share a common interest with other objects of the same part but do not represent them, and thus they may litigate, at their own expense, even if others are content with the trustee's actions.

Ultimately, the threshold requirement for standing lies in the settlor's intention to benefit the claimant through a direct distribution made under the trust's terms. A discretionary object can sue because the trust deed identifies them as a potential recipient of the settlor's bounty. This distinguishes them from parties who derive incidental benefits, who are denied standing because they are not the intended objects of the trust. Accordingly, in *Shaw v Lawless*, standing was denied to the headmaster of a school that would have merely received fees from a scholarship trust.[50]

The same idea provides a clear framework for interpreting s 115 of the UK Charities Act, which permits 'any person interested in the charity' to bring actions to ensure its due administration.[51] Such a stipulation would not extend standing to those deriving incidental benefits from trust performance, such as the lessees of land owned by a charity pursuing their own commercial interests through the litigation.[52] Likewise, in a private express trust, the principle would exclude a beneficiary's family members, even if they share in a benefit such as living in a house provided by the trust to the beneficiary. By contrast, trustees and the Attorney General have standing to enforce proper trust

[48] An apt analogy might be children awaiting gifts from Santa's sack. Although the children have no right to receive a particular gift, they have a right not to be wrongfully excluded from the possibility of obtaining a gift. Just as destroying presents in the sack would wrongfully exclude them from potential gifts, the unauthorized disposal of trust assets removes property that should have been available for distribution.

[49] *Maguire v Makaronis* [1997] HCA 23; 188 CLR 449, [63]; *Commissioner of Stamp Duty (Queensland) v Hugh Duncan Livingston* [1965] AC 694, 714A–C (in relation to estates).

[50] (1838) 5 Cl & Fin 129.

[51] For a comprehensive study of s 115, see Jing 2022.

[52] *Haslemere Estates Ltd v Baker* (1982) 1 WLR 1109; *Bradshaw v University College of Wales* [1988] 1 WLR 190 (no standing for the executor of the settlor of a charitable trust).

administration based on their official duties, not on a right to a distribution—a right they do not have.[53] Trustees are given (fiduciary) powers to enforce their duties against those (including themselves) who interfere with the performance of those duties, while the Attorney General acts for the state to protect the public interest in charities and the integrity of the trust as a social institution.[54] In both cases, the power to sue is a tool to perform their duties, not to secure a personal benefit.

D. Trustee's personal obligations

The economic significance of a trust distribution makes it tempting to view the interests of trust and power objects as purely relating to the trustee's exercise of powers, especially the power of disposal, over the trust rights. This perspective overlooks the objects' equally vital interests in regulating trustees' conduct within the fiduciary relationship itself rather than how they deal with trust property. For instance, when trustees use personal funds to purchase a trust object's equitable interest, they must comply with the fair-dealing rule even though they are not exercising powers over the trust property.[55] Such a purchase is voidable unless the trustee first provides full disclosure of all material facts to enable the beneficiary to give fully informed consent.[56] The vice this rule addresses is the trustee's personal act of taking advantage of information obtained from managing the trust property; it does not involve spending or using any trust property.[57]

Similarly, trustees must account for any personal gains obtained through their position even when those gains involve no conflict with their power over trust rights.[58] On this view, a trustee who acts on confidential knowledge that the trust's planned investment in Company A will indirectly boost the share price of Company B is liable to account for any gains obtained from purchasing

[53] Note that trustees' standing is not limited to bringing proceedings against former trustees, but extends to those against beneficiaries and third parties: *Young v Murphy* [1996] 1 VR 27, 281–283 (action against a former trustee for an account and equitable compensation); *Shovlin (as sole surviving trustee of the SPH Trust) v Site Civils and Surfacing Ltd* (*Shovlin*) [2024] EWCA Civ 585 (action against a former trustee and an third party to recover misapplied trust property); *Pulvers v Chan* [2007] EWHC 2406 (Ch) (action against a third party for knowing receipt).

[54] Smith 2023, 294, 348. I have benefitted from discussions with Charles Mitchell and Lionel Smith on these points.

[55] Tucker, Le Poidevin, and Brightwell 2020, §§ 46-091–46-096; Matthews et al. 2022, art 58.45–58.49; Conaglen 2006, 373–384.

[56] *Dougan v Macpherson* [1902] AC 197.

[57] *Luff v Lord* (1864) 10 Jur (NS) 1248 (where the transaction was upheld because the beneficiary initiated it with knowledge of factors affecting the value of his equitable interest, and the trustee was a reluctant purchaser).

[58] *Regal (Hastings) Ltd v Gulliver* [1967] 2 AC 134n, 144, 149, 153, 154, and 158; *Boardman v Phipps* [1967] 2 AC 46; *Rukhadze v Recovery Partners GP Ltd* [2025] UKSC 10, [2026] AC 209.

Company B's shares, even if the trust only has the intention or means to invest in Company A.[59] Further, a trustee must not disclose confidential information about the trust and power objects without authorization; such a duty is aimed at upholding the integrity of the fiduciary relationship itself, rather than protecting the trust right.

2. Powers against Third Parties

It is a long-standing principle that beneficiaries of both fixed and discretionary trusts have the power to seek the court's intervention to:[60]

1. trace and recover misapplied trust property from third-party recipients for ongoing trust administration; and
2. order personal remedies against third parties who have dishonestly assisted a breach of trust, knowingly received trust property, or dealt inconsistently with it.

The recent extension of these enforcement powers to objects of fiduciary powers is pivotal.[61] The power of these objects to bring claims against third parties cannot be grounded in the violation of a proprietary right, for the simple reason that they have none.[62]

It also bears noting that third-party recipients are not subject to the full range of trustees' duties, liabilities, and power restrictions. For example, successors-in-title are not bound by a trustee's duties to invest or distribute the trust fund. Instead, they are only subject to the limitation on their power to dispose of trust rights in a manner inconsistent with the terms of the trust and that they may be ordered by the court to reconvey misapplied trust rights for ongoing trust administration in accordance with the trust terms.

Moreover, equity tailors a third party's liability according to the circumstances of their title acquisition, as summarized below.

1. Bona fide purchasers and their transferees (including those with knowledge) are free from any liability to be ordered to reconvey the trust

[59] This scenario is based on a modification of the facts of *Boardman v Phipps*; see also Glister 2017, 177–178.

[60] *Joel v Mills* (1857) 4 K & J 458, 473–476; *Cosser v Radford* (1863) 1 De G J & S 585.

[61] *Schmidt*; *Lewis*; *Harvey*, [22].

[62] Cf *Byers*.

property to the trustee. Bona fide purchasers extinguish trust and power objects' rights not merely for the purchasers themselves but also their successors-in-title.[63]

2. Recipients with knowledge have a liability to be ordered to reconvey the trust property or pay its current market value.[64]
3. By contrast, trustees who regain trust rights from a bona fide purchaser remain bound by all of their original duties, as these duties were their initial undertaking, which they never discharged.[65]
4. With respect to innocent recipients who gave no value, their liability to be ordered to reconvey trust property is conditional upon the acquisition of notice. Before they acquire notice, they are free to dispose of the property without being liable for innocently substituting or dissipating it.[66] However, unlike bona fide purchasers for value, their non-liability (or, in this context, immunity) is only temporary. Once they receive notice, they are liable to be ordered to reconvey the retained trust property or its substitute even if their innocent investments are of a higher value than that of the original trust property.

III. The Nature of the Interests of Objects of a Trust or Power

Having enumerated the bundle of rights and powers under a trust, we are in a position to analyse the nature of these interests. For over a century, legal scholarship has struggled to classify them within 'the dichotomy of rights in personam and in rem'.[67] This long-standing challenge has, to a great extent, been addressed by McFarlane and Stevens's illuminating rights-against-rights thesis.[68] They conceptualize interests under trusts and powers not as rights against persons nor in relation to a thing directly, but as rights against the trustee's rights to the trust property, which persist and bind subsequent recipients.

[63] *Gervys v Cooke* (1522) YB 14 Henry VIII fol 4, pl 5, reported in (2002) 119 Selden Society 108, 115 per Fitzherbert J, 116 per Broke J. See Fox 2018; Bacon 1642.

[64] See *Re Rothko* 43 NY 2d 305; 372 NE 2d 291 (1977), in which knowing recipients who sold the estate at a lower price were ordered to restore its (higher) market value at the time of trial.

[65] *Bovey v Smith* (1682) 1 Vern 144; 23 ER 377; *Kennedy v Daly* (1803) 1 Sch & Lef 355, 379; *Byers*, [24].

[66] *Independent Trustee Services Ltd v GP Noble Trustees Ltd* [2012] EWCA Civ 195, [2013] Ch 91 [76].

[67] For details of the respective advocates of the in rem and in personam characterization, see Foster 2023, 128–137.

[68] McFarlane & Stevens 2010. See also Smith 2008, 381, who argues that the interests of trust and power objects are obligations that can affect third persons, and Webb 2011.

Whilst all these conceptualizations are partially correct, McFarlane and Stevens offer a foundational breakthrough by correctly locating the objects' interest as not being in the trust property itself, but in the trustee's powers over it.[69] As such, the objects' interests are derivative of the trustee's powers and correlative to the limits on these powers. However, their approach—along with the others—remains reductive. It attempts to define the objects' interest as a single concept, thereby failing to capture the complex bundle of rights and powers held by them.

1. In Rem/In Personam

In his *Lectures on Jurisprudence*, John Austin emphasized that the in rem/in personam dichotomy turns on a right's scope of application.[70] In personam rights correlate to 'duties which are incumbent *exclusively* on persons specifically determinate', whereas in rem rights bind 'persons generally' without identifying the specific dutybearers.[71] It bears noting that the distinction between determinate and indeterminate rights rests not on the number of dutybearers. In rem rights are indeterminate because the criterion for identifying a dutybearer does not entail any particular number of people. In rem rights bind individuals based on their default status in society—a person is included in the class of dutybearers simply by being in the jurisdiction. Thus, any conclusion about the number of dutybearers requires extraneous evidence about the number of inhabitants in that jurisdiction at the relevant time. By contrast, with in personam rights like those in contracts, the content of the contract defines the person who is bound and thus entails the number of dutybearers per instance of the right. The total number of dutybearers corresponds directly to the number of instances of the right.

Therefore, a right to a chattel is indeterminate because the same right is held respectively against an indefinite class, even if only ten people inhabit the jurisdiction. Conversely, a franchisor's contractual right is determinate because it is held against a definite network of franchisees, no matter how large. This distinction reveals the error of classifying a trust or power object's interest as an (equitable) in rem right based on the reasoning that because the object's

[69] Their analysis highlights the error in *Shell UK Ltd v Total UK Ltd* [2010] EWCA Civ 180; [2011] 1 QB 86, where the court allowed a beneficiary to sue a third-party tortfeasor directly for damaging trust property.

[70] Austin 1885, 369–371.

[71] Ibid, 363–364; Cook 1915, 42; Hohfeld 1917, 718–720; Stone 1917.

interest binds the whole world minus the bona fide purchaser for value and their successor in title, it is merely a weaker version of a common law in rem right.[72]

Further, by focusing the in rem/in personam distinction on the compass (or scope) of the right, Austin's analysis fails to stress that a right in rem is always one of a collection of identical yet separate rights, where each identical claim, typically for non-interference, is held individually against every person in the world.[73] Bearing the identical nature of in rem rights in mind, powers to impose liability on dishonest assistants and recipients are not in rem, as liability is restricted to determinate individuals identified by their personal fault, and their remedial obligations differ markedly from the trustee's. Whilst jointly and severally liable with the trustee for loss, assistants are required to account only for profits they personally made.[74] Similarly, recipients are not subject to the full range of trustees' duties. I propose that these enforcement powers are properly classified as in personam because they avail against a determinate group. Further, they are paucital (enforceable against a defined group) rather than unital (binding only a single individual) in personam powers.[75]

2. A Third, *Sui Generis* Category?

In contrast, McFarlane and Stevens prefer to classify interests in a trust or power as a distinct third category, namely rights against the trustee's own rights over the trust property, on the ground that this model better reflects how an object's interest constrains the trustee's exercise of powers, and thus dismantles the fallacy that it is a right held directly against the trust property itself. However, by focusing on the structure rather than the content of these interests, their model trades completeness for elegance, making it under-inclusive for not capturing the full scope of an object's interests. Two aspects of their thesis warrant closer analysis: the nature of a 'right against a right' and its quality of persistence.

[72] *Akers*, [82] (Lord Sumption); criticized in Agnew & McFarlane 2019. It is telling that Austin himself, without full explanation, treated the purchaser's right in a vendor–purchaser constructive trust as an equitable 'jus in rem or ownership': Austin 1885, 377.
[73] Hohfeld 1917, 718; but see the trenchant criticisms of this view in Penner 2020, chs 5 and 6.
[74] *Ultraframe (UK) Ltd v Fielding* [2005] EWHC 1638 (Ch), [2006] FSR 17 [1600]; *Stevens v Hotel Portfolio II UK Ltd* [2025] UKSC 28, [2025] 3 WLR 293.
[75] Hohfeld 1917, 718.

A. Rights against rights

Whilst the rights-against-rights model correctly captures a fundamental truth about the structure of an object's interest, it does not adequately define either of the 'rights' it invokes.

First, consider the right of the trust and power objects. The label 'right' is a crude over-simplification for a complex and non-homogeneous bundle of legal advantages that differ significantly between beneficiaries under a fixed trust and objects of a power. A more precise and comprehensive analysis reveals that trust and power objects hold a bundle of distinct rights and powers against the trustee as well as identical but separate powers to enforce the trust's proper administration.[76] Crucially, not all of these rights and powers are held against the trustee's or successor's right over the trust property. They also include, for example, powers to sue dishonest assistants, who need not have obtained the trust right. Second, even a modified rights/powers-against-rights/liabilities model remains bilateral and thus incomplete for a trust. Such a framework omits the court's critical supervisory jurisdiction to hear applications, give directions, issue orders, and even execute the trust when necessary. Such applications need not involve the institution of a suit between two parties. A comprehensive picture of interests under a trust must therefore include the power of relevant parties, including the objects and office-holders such as the trustee and the Attorney-General, to invoke the court's discretionary oversight to ensure the trust's proper administration.[77]

Third, the model struggles to accommodate charitable trusts, which, by their nature, often lack any rightholder. This point was well articulated by Harman LJ in *Attorney General v Cocke*, a case concerning charitable trusts to display an art collection for the benefit of the public. His Lordship observed the 'nonsense of alleging that there is any beneficiary in any meaningful sense' in such trusts, emphasizing that 'No "right" properly so-called ever vests in any member of the public individually'.[78] Indeed, even the Attorney General does not hold a right, but rather a power to seek judicial relief in the performance of the Crown's *parens patriae* function.[79]

Finally, the model is vague about the actual content of the object's right. Since a right can only correlate to a duty, not to another right, the phrase 'right

[76] For details of these rights and powers, see the text to notes 26–58; 61–67 above.

[77] See Katz 2024 for the role of courts in the equity jurisdiction and refinements of the right-against-rights thesis in McFarlane 2026.

[78] [1988] Ch 414, 419, 420. I am grateful to William Swadling for drawing this decision to my attention.

[79] See Penner 2022, paras 18.1–18.4, for the argument that the special rules for charitable trusts derive from their public law nature.

against a right' is a punchy misnomer. It actually describes the object's right to compel the trustee's performance of duties or observance of limits in exercising the powers associated with their trust right. Herein lies the model's critical ambiguity, as it only notes that the trustee 'is under a duty to hold a specific claim-right or power, in a particular way' for the object, without specifying the content of that duty.[80] If such a duty is confined to managing or disposing of the trust right, the model does not account for crucial obligations that govern the parties' fiduciary relationship. These personal obligations include the fair-dealing rule, the no-profit rule, and the duty to keep the objects' private information confidential,[81] all of which regulate the trustee's use of trust information, not the management or disposal of the trust right itself. If the model intends to encompass these personal obligations, the objects' rights are not against the trustee's rights *to the trust assets.*

To fully capture interests under a trust, I propose understanding them as in personam rights and powers held by objects and office-holders that both constrain trustees' conduct within the fiduciary relationship and restrict how they and subsequent recipients exercise powers over trust rights.

B. Persistence?

A key challenge in understanding the nature of interests under a trust or a power lies in explaining trust and power objects' ability to bypass trustees and seek recovery directly from third parties. These include dishonest assistants and recipients who acquire misapplied trust rights with knowledge or as volunteers.

Although McFarlane and Stevens do not address accessory liability, they argue that their rights-against-rights thesis explains how equitable interests persist against recipients without operating as in rem rights. Their reasoning is that unlike conversion, recipients do not interfere with trustees' trust rights, and so it is not the trustees who bring the claim against recipients.[82] Rather, recipients acquire rights that '*derive[] from*' trustees' trust rights (or 'exercise of powers'), and because these trust rights are initially held on trust for the objects, the objects' '*pre-existing*' right under the trust also prima facie binds recipients.[83] For them, the fact that even innocent recipients are bound proves that the object's pre-existing right is one that persists beyond the trustee's unauthorized disposition, and it is not merely an in personam right binding

[80] McFarlane & Stevens 2010, 2.
[81] For details of these rules, see the text to notes 56–60.
[82] McFarlane 2026.
[83] McFarlane & Stevens 2010, 5 (emphasis added).

only the trustee; if the object only has an in personam right, it would require the third party to have acted unconscionably to generate a new right against them.[84]

As a descriptor, 'persistence' effectively conveys the idea that interests in trusts and powers are not extinguished by a trustee's unauthorized transfer. Yet it creates the false impression of conintuity that the initial interest simply carries over to bind the third party. The authors might have reinforced this impression by emphasizing that a recipient's liability stems from deriving title from the trustee's rights.

However, just because recipients derive rights through the trustee's unauthorized disposition, it does not follow that they are also bound by the objects' rights. Assignment generally transfers only the benefits of rights, not their burdens. Implicit in the assertion that recipients, who derive rights through trustees, are prima facie bound is the assumption that trustees' duties somehow remain 'stapled' to the transferred rights so as to bind recipients. This assumption is questionable. Not all recipients who derive their rights from the trustee's trust rights are bound. Notably, the recipients of authorized transfers, bona fide purchasers without notice of misapplied trust property and the subsequent recipients of property from such purchasers, even with knowledge of the breach of trust, are not so bound.[85] Innocent volunteers are not liable for dissipating trust property before they acquire notice. These examples show that the idea of persistent rights prima facie binding all successors is too sweeping.[86] Moreover, the idea does not explain why recipients who are liable are nonetheless spared from certain trustee duties, such as the fiduciary duty of loyalty. A fuller account of how and why equity imposes liability on recipients may lie elsewhere.

For this purpose, metaphors that depict interests under trusts or powers as stapled or 'engrafted onto . . . the legal estate' are problematic.[87] Whilst such imagery correctly locates the object of the beneficiaries' interest in the trust right rather than the underlying trust property, it explains neither how that interest jumps across to the traceable substitutes, nor why it does so against some recipients but not others.

In reality, the trust simply imposes obligations on the trustee and limits their powers over the trust right. When an unauthorized disposition occurs, the equitable interest does not travel down the chain of substitution to bind recipients. Instead, a recipient's liability is generated anew at each link in the chain,

[84] Ibid, cf McFarlane 2026.
[85] *Byers*, [19], [39].
[86] McFarlane and Stevens 2010, 1, 3, 4, 7.
[87] *DKLR Holding Co (No 2) Pty Ltd v Commissioner of Stamp Duties* [1980] 1 NSWLR 510, 519.

based on that recipient's own conduct vis-à-vis the objects and on the application of priority rules designed to balance competing policies. Each subsequent unauthorized disposition therefore triggers a fresh iteration of liability.

Within this iterative process, the chain of substitution performs an evidential role in supplying the factual inputs that the balancing exercise requires, such as whether the right held by the recipient is transactionally linked to the trust right, whether the trust relationship is no longer protected due to the intervention of a bona fide purchaser for value without notice, and whether the recipient provided value or took with notice. In short, the chain carries the facts on which each new iteration of liability is separately constructed. The new liability is modelled on the obligations of express trustees, specifically mirroring the duty of a bare trustee, who likewise has no active duties to perform, to reconvey the trust right for ongoing trust administration. This iterative process has three key stages.

First, the trustee must have transferred the trust property contrary to the restrictions on their power of disposal. These restrictions may be found in the terms of the trust or arise from the fiduciary requirement to exercise disposal powers in good faith in the interest of trust objects. Violation of these restrictions renders the disposition voidable or impugnable at the option of trust objects.

Second, the law does not indiscriminately bind every recipient of misapplied trust rights but determines their liability on a party-by-party basis, taking into account priority rules and the circumstances of their acquisition of title. For instance, registered owners and bona fide purchasers for value override trust law's protection of beneficiaries, and this immunity extends even to a recipient who takes from them with knowledge. By contrast, innocent volunteers who still retain the trust right are bound to restore it, reflecting the law's preference for static security of title.[88]

Third, the final element, which is often overlooked, is that third-party recipients are not subject to the full range of trustees' duties. Equity models the recipients' remedy by analogy to bare trustees who have no active duty to perform, holding these recipients liable to be ordered by the court to reconvey misapplied trust rights for ongoing trust administration. Knowing recipients are additionally liable to reconstitute the trust fund because, as McFarlane persuasively explains, they obtain or retain the trust right knowing it was acquired through an unauthorized disposition.[89]

[88] See, eg, s 29 of the Land Registration Act (UK); *Byers*, [19]; Demorgue 1916, 428–429; Ho & Mitchell 2026, 297–299.

[89] McFarlane 2026; Ho & Mitchell 2026.

IV. Conclusion

David Foster notes that the English conception of the trust has evolved over the centuries—from being viewed as confidence reposed in the trustee personally (and in a select few deemed 'privy' to the estate) to an interest attached to the trust property.[90] His research covers the period in which fixed trusts were standard. However, the advent of discretionary and massively discretionary trusts in response to higher taxation in recent decades has upended this picture. Whilst revisionists such as McFarlane and Stevens have moved away from proprietary discourse, traditionalists such as Lord Briggs and Lord Burrows continue to adopt it.[91]

Both views have merit, yet both overlook a key point: interests in a trust or power are not homogeneous. Recognizing this diversity allows us to frame these interests as a bundle of personal rights and powers that, under the court's supervision, regulates two distinct spheres: internally, the trustee's exercise of powers associated with the trust right and performance of obligations towards the objects; and externally, the actions of third parties who would undermine the trust relationship. Further, these third parties are bound not by an initial 'persistent' right that travels down the chain of substitution of the trust right, but by a fresh iteration of liability arising at each link in that chain.

References

Agnew, S. and B. McFarlane (2019). 'The Paradox of the Equitable Proprietary Claim'. *Modern Studies in Property Law, Vol 10*. S. Agnew and B. McFarlane. Oxford, Bloomsbury Publishing: 303–319.

Austin, J. (1885). *Lectures on Jurisprudence*. R. Campbell, 5th edn. London, John Murray.

Bacon, F. (1642). *The Learned Reading of Sir Bacon upon the Statute of Uses*. London, Matthew Walbancke and Leonard Chapman.

Cook, W. W. (1915). 'The Powers of Courts of Equity. I. "In Rem" and "In Personam"'. *Columbia Law Review* 15: 37–54.

Conaglen, M. (2006). 'A Re-Appraisal of the Fiduciary Self-Dealing and Fair-Dealing Rules'. *Cambridge Law Journal* 65(2): 366–396.

Dal Pont, G. E. (2023). *Equit and Trusts in Australia*. 8th edn. Pyrmont, NSW, Lawbook Co.

Demogue, D. (1916). 'Security'. *Modern French Legal Philosophy*. A. Fouillée et al. Boston, Boston Book Co: 418–445.

Eldrige, E. (2024). 'Rights That'. *Oxford Journal of Legal Studies* 44: 808–831.

[90] Foster 2023; *Federal Commissioner of Taxation v Carter* (2022) 274 CLR 309, [41], per Edelman J referring to the beneficial interest as 'annexed to', 'engrafted', or 'impressed upon' the trust property.

[91] *Byers*.

Foster, D. (2023). 'Historical Conceptions of the Express Trusts, c 1600–1900'. *Philosophical Foundations of the Law of Express Trusts.* Simone Degeling, Jessica Hudson, and Irit Samet. Oxford, Oxford University Press: 110–138.

Fox, D. (2018). 'Purchase for Value Without Notice'. *Defences in Equity.* P. Davies, S. Douglas, and J. Goudkamp. Oxford, Hart Publishing: 53–80.

Glister, J. (2017). 'Accounts of Profits and Third Parties'. *Equitable Compensation and Account of Profits.* S. Degeling and J. Varuhas. Oxford, Hart Publishing: 175–196.

Hafeez-Baig, M. and English, J. (2021). *The Law of Tracing.* Sydney, Federation Press.

Ho, L. and Nolan, R. (2020). 'The Performance Interest in the Law of Trusts'. *Law Quarterly Review* 136: 402–426.

Ho, L. (2026) 'An Anatomy of Good Faith'. *Theoretical Inquiries in Law* 27.

Ho, L. and Mitchell, C. (2026). 'Knowing Receipt, Equitable Proprietary Rights, and Duties of Due Administration'. *Modern Law Review* 89: 278–303.

Hohfeld, W. (1917). 'Fundamental Legal Conceptions as Applied in Judicial Reasoning'. *Yale Law Journal* 26: 710–770.

Hudson, J. (2021). 'Mere and Other Discretionary Objects in Australia'. *Asia-Pacific Trusts Law, Vol 1: Theory and Practice in Context.* Y. K. Liew and M. Harding. Oxford, Hart Publishing: 19–38.

Hudson, J. (2023). 'Equity's Gloss on Authority'. *Equity Today: 150 Years after the Judicature Reforms.* B. McFarlane and S. Elliott. Oxford, Hart Publishing: 27–48.

Hudson, J. and Mitchell, C. (2026). 'Standing in Trusts Law, the Beneficiary Principle and the Juridical Nature of Trustee Duties' *Law Quarterly Review* 142: 211–235.

Jing, H. (2022). 'Enforcing Charitable Trusts: A Study on the English Necessary Interest Rule'. *Legal Studies* 42: 228–245.

Katz, L. (2024). 'Rights Without Standing'. *Methodology in Private Law Theory: Between New and Private Law and Rechtsdogmatik.* T. Kuntz and P. Miller. Oxford, Oxford University Press: 327–343.

Liau, T. (2023). *Standing in Private Law.* Oxford, Oxford University Press.

Lewin, T. (1837). *A Practical Treatise of the Law of Trusts and Trustees.* London, A. Maxwell.

Lupoi, M. and M. Graziadei (2025). 'The Historical Context of *Saunders v Vautier*'. *The Edinburgh Law Review* 29(1): 31–66.

Matthews, P. (2005). 'All about Bare Trusts: Part 1'. *Private Client Business* 5: 266–273.

Matthews, P. et al. (2022). *Underhill and Hayton: Law Relating to Trusts and Trustees.* 20th edn. London: LexisNexis Butterworths.

McFarlane, B. and Stevens, R. (2010). 'The Nature of Equitable Property'. *Journal of Equity* **4**: 1–28.

McFarlane, B. (2026). 'Understanding Equitable Property: More Complex than ABC?' *Current Legal Problems* 79.

Merrill, T. and H. E. Smith (2001). 'The Property/Contract Interface'. *Columbia Law Review* 101: 773–852.

Morris, A. (2026). 'Rights of Objects of Powers'. *Oxford Handbook of Comparative Trusts Law.* M. Bennett et al. Oxford, Oxford University Press.

Penner, J. (2014). 'The (True) Nature of a Beneficiary's Equitable Proprietary Interest under a Trust'. *Canadian Journal of Law and Jurisprudence* 27: 473–500.

Penner, J. (2020). *Property Rights: A Re-Examination.* Oxford, Oxford University Press.

Penner, J. (2022). *The Law of Trusts.* Oxford, Oxford University Press.

Seymore, J. (1999). 'Representative Procedures and the Future of Multi-Party Actions'. *Modern Law Review* 62: 564–584.

Smith, H. E. (2023). 'Equitable Meta-Law: The Spectrum of Property'. *150 Years after the Judicial Reforms*. B. McFarlane and S. Elliott. Oxford, Hart Publishing: 319–337.
Smith, L. (2008). 'Trust and Patrimony'. *Revue Générale de droit* 38: 381–403.
Smith, L. (2017). 'Massively Discretionary Trusts'. *Current Legal Problems*. 70: 17–54.
Smith, L. (2023). *The Law of Loyalty*. Oxford, Oxford University Press.
Stone, H. (1917). 'The Nature of the Rights of the "*Cestui Que Trust*"'. *Columbia Law Review* 17: 467–501.
Thomas, G. (2012). *Thomas on Powers*. 2nd edn. Oxford, Oxford University Press.
Tucker, L., Le Poidevin, N., and Brightwell, J. (2020). *Lewin on Trusts*. 20th edn. London, Sweet and Maxwell.
Webb, C. (2011). 'The Double Lives of Property'. *Jurisprudence* 2(1): 205–216.
Zaccaria, E. C. (2019). 'The Nature of the Beneficiary's Right Under a Trust: Proprietary Right, Purely Personal Right or Right Against a Right?' *Law Quarterly Review* 135: 460–483.

12

Intermediate Rights—Bridging the Theory/Doctrine Divide

Lee Pey Woan and Zhang Wei

I. Introduction

The floating charge has long been a hallmark of English law. It emerged as a flexible legal innovation in the nineteenth century, offering businesses a way to secure loans against fluctuating assets while maintaining operational freedom. Using Merrill and Smith's information costs framework, this chapter explores the floating charge as an intermediate legal construct that combines property and contractual features. The floating charge offers a fascinating context for examining the interplay of property and contract as it is a classic instance of property creation by contractual agreements. This dynamic generates an inherent tension because contracting parties are prone to asserting their autonomy to inject greater flexibility into property rights that are traditionally governed by mandatory or immutable rules.[1]

Indeed, as we shall see, the history of the floating charge is replete with attempts by lenders to strengthen their protection against risk by crafting contractual arrangements aimed at circumventing statutory rules on property allocations. These efforts have sparked ongoing debates and controversies, making the floating charge a fertile ground for examining the effects of contractual activities on property rights.

In this chapter, we draw on Merrill and Smith's insights to understand the dynamics affecting the development of the floating charge, with particular focus on the role of information costs and its relevance for potential reform. We observe that the historical development of the floating charge usefully illustrates Merrill and Smith's prediction of lower standardization in the intermediate

[1] This tension is not, of course, limited to the context of security rights but would arise whenever contracts are the 'initiating legal act' that gives content to property: Akkermans 2017, 100.

Lee Pey Woan and Zhang Wei, *Intermediate Rights—Bridging the Theory/Doctrine Divide* In: *The Property-Contract Interface*. Edited by: James Penner, Irina Sakharova, Henry E. Smith, and Zhong Xing Tan, Oxford University Press.
 DOI: 10.1093/9780198951995.003.0015

zone. This is likely explained by the emphasis placed on private ordering. However, intense contractual activities to reorder property rights tend to have destabilizing effects on property, resulting in uncertainty that amplifies information and other costs. Heightened uncertainty not only raises transactional and verification costs but also undermines the modularity that underpins the property system. The jurisprudence in this area also raises the critical question of the extent to which property rights should be delimited by private ordering. We argue that such freedom is curtailed not only by the architectural form of property law but also by distributional concerns. However, fundamental reordering of property structures is, as Merrill and Smith suggest, better effected by the legislature than the courts.

II. Information Costs Theory and the Property-Contract Interface

The question whether property rights constitute a distinctive legal phenomenon has long fascinated scholars. Among law and economics theorists, Merrill and Smith are the most prominent and influential in restoring the vision of property as a legally significant conception that is distinct from other private law obligations. In their account, the institution of property is structurally distinguished from that of contracts. Property rights are subject to the *numerus clausus* principle, which restricts the types of property rights recognized at law to a fixed number of forms. Contractual rights, by contrast, may be as 'whimsical or fanciful' as the parties desire subject only to constraints of public policy.[2] Merrill and Smith justify this unique structure of property—the standardization of forms—on the ground that it reduces third-party information costs. Property rights impose information costs on third parties because they are in rem (good against the world) in nature. By restricting the permissible number of property forms, the *numerus clausus* principle minimizes the third-party measurement costs that would otherwise constitute significant externalities if there were no limits on idiosyncratic property forms.

In Merrill and Smith's schema, property rights are also exclusionary.[3] This 'exclusion strategy' is integral to the institution of property as it serves the important function of allocating control over a resource to a designated owner to prevent access by non-owners except with the owner's consent.[4] Exclusion is

[2] Merrill & Smith 2000, 3.
[3] Merrill & Smith 2001, 792–797.
[4] Merrill & Smith 2020, 141.

uniquely suited for regulating in rem rights because it relies on simple, bright-lined rules ('keep off, don't take'[5]) that minimize the information burden on third parties. Consequently, in rem rights can be enforced against a large number of dutyholders whilst keeping information costs relatively low. In contrast, in personam (including contractual) rights are characterized by the governance strategy, which regulates resources through detailed specifications about permitted uses and users. As this approach is more complex and information-intensive, it is better suited for smaller groups of dutyholders.[6] The regulation of resources will often involve a combination of exclusion and governance strategies[7] but the exclusion strategy is at the 'core'[8] of property's architecture by reason of its substantial cost advantages.

However, the traditional dichotomy of property and contract as, respectively, in rem and in personam rights do not fully capture the complexity of modern legal institutions. Merrill and Smith propose, instead, that legal institutions can be understood as existing along a spectrum, with in rem and in personam rights as the two endpoints. Between these extremes lie intermediate rights, which combine elements of property and contract.[9] Compared to pure in rem rights, intermediate rights generally involve lower information costs because they typically affect fewer or identifiable groups of persons. Consequently, the legal rules governing intermediate rights tend to be less standardized and more flexible. In such cases, the law often may adopt one of two strategies: the notice strategy to promote information disclosure, or the protective strategy, which safeguards the less-informed party by reducing their need to gather information.[10]

The learned authors identified four legal institutions—bailment, landlord and tenant, security interests, and trusts—as intermediate cases that exist along the property-contract interface. These institutions exemplify intermediate situations, which are hybrid or mixed cases that exhibit more 'contract-like' characteristics in some situations and more 'property-like' characteristics in others.[11] Merrill and Smith sought to demonstrate that the legal doctrines governing these situations align well with the specific information needs of the respective contexts, vindicating the explanatory force of the information costs thesis.

[5] Ibid, 142.
[6] Smith 2002, S455.
[7] Merrill & Smith 2020, 143–144.
[8] Smith 2012, 1705.
[9] Merrill & Smith 2001, 777.
[10] Ibid, 805.
[11] Ibid, 777.

While standardization reduces measurement costs for third parties, it also leaves less flexibility for parties to fulfil their intention in transactions. This downside of standardization is referred to as frustration costs. However, standardization does not always block transaction parties' intentions completely. As Merrill and Smith aptly observed, standardization often creates an effect of price discrimination. Those who value their transaction objectives substantially can incur extra planning and implementing costs to achieve their ends in a more circuitous way.[12] The transaction purpose may not be fully realized even after such planning, in which case there can still be a certain amount of residual frustration. Therefore, frustration costs encompass the sum of costs suffered by two types of actors. First, there are those who abandon their objectives altogether, losing the full value of the transaction. Second, there are those who attempt to circumvent standardization through special designing, incurring costs in both the design and implementation of the circumvention, as well as the residual loss of transaction value, if any, due to incomplete circumvention. Where a particular transaction objective is shared by more parties, the overall frustration cost due to standardization also becomes more pronounced.

Merrill and Smith identify security interests as a clear instance of intermediate rights, combining elements of both in rem and in personam rights.[13] Drawing on Hohfeld's taxonomy, they explain[14] in personam (paucital) rights as one-to-one jural relations involving a single person and one or more identified parties. These are situations where the parties are limited and identifiable. In contrast, in rem (multital) rights are one-to-many jural relations between a single person and a large and indefinite class of dutybearers. In rem rights are therefore characterized by both numerosity and indefiniteness.[15]

Intermediate rights occupy the conceptual middle ground between in rem and in personam rights. They may take the form of compound paucital rights, where the duty bearers are numerous but identifiable, or the quasi-multital form, where the number of dutybearers is limited but their identities are indefinite.[16] For example, a business offering services to a large number of customers under standard-form contracts generates compound paucital rights, as the customers are both numerous and specifically identified. Conversely, a right to assign a contractual benefit would be an instance of a quasi-multital

[12] Merrill & Smith 2000, 35.
[13] Merrill & Smith 2001, 834.
[14] Ibid, 780–789.
[15] Ibid, 784. Cf. Penner who points out that neither numerosity nor indefiniteness sufficiently defines in rem rights: see Penner 2020, 89–90. See also Kocourek 1920, arguing (at 335) that a right is in rem if it's 'essential investitive facts do not serve directly to identify the person who owes the incident duty'.
[16] Merrill & Smith 2001, 785.

right as the identity of the possible assignees is indefinite and their number is likely to be small. Merrill and Smith posit that intermediate rights impose lower informational burdens than in rem rights because of their narrower scope or greater identifiability. However, they expect increased standardization as the numbers or indefiniteness of third parties increases.[17]

Secured lending may generate intermediate relations that are compound paucital or quasi-multital in nature. Compound paucital relations are commonly observed in the context of consumer financing, where lenders provide secured loans to a large number of consumers on standard terms. Although each loan and security agreement is in personam in character since the contracting parties are finite and known to each other, such agreements in aggregate may become more property-like when a large number of borrowers owe duties to a single lender on standard terms. Information asymmetry arises in such cases as individual consumers will typically have little incentive—or ability—to scrutinize the terms of the transactions.[18] To address this information imbalance, the law intervenes through consumer protection legislation. Such legislation exemplifies the protective strategy, which 'inject standardized duties into contractual relations designed to protect informationally disadvantaged parties'.[19]

Beyond consumer financing, much of secured lending involves quasi-multital relations. In this context, the emphasis shifts to the information needs of third parties—such as subsequent lenders and assignees. Here, the uncertainty surrounding the identities of third-party transferees and the broader range of potential problems makes the protection strategy inappropriate.[20] Instead, the notice strategy is often adopted to address the information needs of disadvantaged parties. It operates through 'strong defaults'[21] that shift the burden of disclosure to the party best positioned to produce the information cost effectively, and who otherwise lack the incentive to disclose for self-interested or strategic concerns.[22] Compelling disclosure ensures that parties with incomplete information can access relevant details about encumbrances on assets.

In both compound paucital or quasi-multital situations, the principle of a bona fide purchase for value without notice allows third parties to acquire

[17] Ibid, 807.
[18] Ibid, 806.
[19] Ibid, 838.
[20] Ibid, 808.
[21] Ibid, 840.
[22] Ibid, 805.

assets free of encumbrances. Within Merrill and Smith's framework, this common law principle is an instance of the protective strategy.[23] It imposes on true owners a strict liability to notify potential purchasers of any encumbrances on the assets, thereby safeguarding the interests of bona fide purchasers who lack knowledge of such claims.

The information cost theory advanced by Merrill and Smith is certainly insightful. It rightly draws attention to the communication function of law and to the varying information burdens associated with different legal structures. However, commentators[24] (including Merrill and Smith[25]) have cautioned against overstating the extent to which idiosyncratic property rights may give rise to externalization of information costs. On the one hand, under our current private property system, the public generally operates under a default assumption that they have no entitlement to use or interfere with property owned by others. This baseline expectation significantly reduces the information needed to avoid infringing upon others' rights. One need not understand the precise contours or content of another's property entitlements: the mere (passive) awareness that one lacks a right of access or use—which is true by default—is usually sufficient. Therefore, the creation of fancy rights over one's own property does not, in and of itself, generate new information costs for third parties seeking to avoid wrongful interference.

On the other hand, since our legal system has general rules of protecting bona fide purchasers of property, information cost externalization may not be an issue even for the other market participants who will deal in or with the same type of property on which fancy rights are created. If the information of property rights over this type of property is not disseminated through a centralized system, such as real estate registration, but rather by holders of such rights individually, then only those who have indeed created fancy rights need to inform their counterparties of such rights, resulting in the counterparties having to process the same information. In other words, using Merrill and Smith's original example, when I do not have a fancy right on my watch, my dealing of the watch does not involve costs of transmitting the information of such a right even when others might have created this type of right on their watches. Only if a centralized information disclosure system is established, will 'the other market participants' in Merrill and Smith's words,[26] have to incur cost verifying the existence of any fancy property rights over the potential

[23] Ibid, 840.
[24] Hansmann & Kraakman 2002, S381; Stern 2017, 1209.
[25] Merrill & Smith 2007, 1853–1854; Smith 2012, 1703.
[26] Merrill & Smith 2000, 28.

subject matter of their dealings to avoid being attributed constructive knowledge that can defeat the bone fide purchaser protection rule. In this case, however, the real cause of information cost externalization does not seem to be non-standardization of property rights, but, instead, the decision to establish a centralized information disclosure system for certain types of property.

Moreover, an economic account of property rights focused on the transacting parties, including the information cost externalization theory, may overstate the importance of the private parties in formulating the property right scheme, paying insufficient attention to the role of the state in this process. In addition to the facilitation of private ordering, property law is a fundamentally public institution that establishes the legal framework within which ownership is defined, allocated, and regulated. It is through this framework that the state sets the conditions for ownership and mediates competing claims over the use and control of valuable resources.[27] As we shall see,[28] Merrill and Smith do not deny the public functions of property law but their theoretical architecture is constructed largely on the paradigm of private law.

III. The Floating Charge and *Numerus Clausus*

A key insight of Merrill and Smith's thesis is that the *numerus clausus* principle is explainable as the law's attempt to achieve the optimal standardization of property forms, by striking a balance between the legitimate and diverse use of property and the minimization of information costs for third parties.[29] Broadly understood, the *numerus clausus* principle stipulates that property can only be held in a limited number of legally recognized forms. Transacting parties are not free to create idiosyncratic property rights. The principle is well established in civilian jurisdictions, although its precise form and content varies across jurisdictions.[30]

In contrast to civilian jurisdictions, the status of *numerus clausus* in English law is less clear. Some scholars consider the concept to be inherently embedded in English law, even if the term is not explicitly articulated in its jurisprudence.

[27] Davidson 2008, 1602.

[28] See text to notes 94–98. Some aspects of the state's regulatory functions are also explainable by information costs. For example, the use of title records (by registration or recordation) may lead to reduced information costs: see Arruñada 2003, 416–420. However, Smith argues that title recording is better seen as supplementing (rather than substituting) the need for standardization in property to reduce information costs: see Smith 2011, 165–167.

[29] Merrill & Smith 2000, 69.

[30] For a helpful discussion of the principle's operation in European jurisdictions, see von Bar (2023), 70–92.

For instance, Swadling asserts that '[there] is, in English law, as with all developed legal systems, a *numerus clausus* (closed number) of property rights'.[31] Supporting this view are the provisions of the Law of Property Act 1925 that restrict the types of estates that may subsist in relation to land.[32] Similarly, Merrill and Smith argue that the principle operates in English law as 'a norm of judicial self-governance'.[33] Judges typically decide whether a set of facts constitute property rights by reference to a closed list of recognized property forms.

However, this view of English property law is not universally shared. Sparkes, for example, contends that the civilian notion of *numerus clausus* does not aptly describe English law except at a high level of abstraction.[34] While English property law is constrained by a general principle of certainty,[35] its preferred technique is to carve out an 'enclosed space' rather than enumerate a closed list.[36] The absence of a single definition of a property right makes the notion of *numerus clausus* illusory.[37] Legal estates are fixed and limited at common law but novel property interests may be formed through the 'gradual accretion' of cases in equity.[38] *Tulk v Moxhay*,[39] the landmark case that upheld the restrictive covenant as an equity binding on successors in title, is evidence that equity is not past the age of childbearing.[40] Equity therefore enables English property law to maintain 'the balance between stasis and innovation'.[41] From a civilian perspective, however, *numerus clausus* in English law is diluted by equity's capacity for innovation in so far as that weakens the rigidity of the content (as opposed to type) of property rules.[42]

[31] Swadling 2013, 175. Swadling cites three authorities: *Hill v Tupper* (1863) 2 H&C 121, 159 ER 51 (an exclusive right to put pleasure boats in a canal is not a property right); *Keppel v Bailey* (1834) 2 My & K 517, 39 ER 1042 (a lessee's promise for himself and successors in title to purchase all supplies of limestone from a specific quarry is not a property right that binds a successor); and *King v David Allen (Billposting)* [1916] 2 AC 54 (an exclusive right to affix bills, posters, and advertisements on the flank wall of a picture house was not a property right binding on the lessee of the property).

[32] See, eg, ss 1 and 4 of the Law of Property Act 1925. See also McFarlane 2011.

[33] Merrill & Smith 2000, 11.

[34] Sparkes 2012, 771.

[35] Ibid, 774.

[36] 'Property is kept in a discrete area protected by an enclosure and prevented from spreading out into the surrounding hordes of obligations': ibid, 790. Cf. Smith, who argues that *numerus clausus* is an important *starting point*, but that this does not preclude other forms of standardization: see Smith 2011, 150. On this view, the 'enclosed space' subsists alongside the 'closed list'.

[37] Sparkes 2012, 788.

[38] Ibid, 774–775.

[39] (1848) 2 Ph 774, 41 ER 1143.

[40] For a contrary view, see Swadling 2013, 182. Sparkes's argument finds support in the view that the *numerus clausus* principle does not constrain the content of equitable property rights, which is instead determined by distinct conceptual criteria: see McFarlane 2011, 320.

[41] Sparkes 2012, 775. In a similar vein, Smith characterizes equity as a type of 'meta-law'—a 'law about law' that 'presupposes law and supplements it, sometimes overriding it, and occasionally modifying it, especially over time': Smith 2023, 320.

[42] See, eg, Von Bar 2023, who observes at 87 that 'the common law . . . mitigates its strict *Typenzwang* with a relatively weak form of *Typenfixierung*'.

Although the possibility of taking security over a company's 'undertaking' was first suggested by the Companies Clauses Consolidation Act 1845,[43] the floating charge in its modern incarnation is largely born of judicial innovation.[44] In a seminal article,[45] Pennington identified two key judicial developments in the nineteenth century that paved the way for the judicial acceptance of the floating charge in its current form. The first was the recognition that a charge could extend to after-acquired property, enabling the chargee's equitable interest to vest in such property automatically upon its acquisition by the chargor. The second was the clarification that a floating charge over a company's circulating assets would not paralyse the company's operations whilst it remained a going concern but would do so only upon a subsequent cystallization event.

The floating charge is traditionally seen as a response to the nineteenth-century industrial and commercial expansion, providing businesses with access to loan capital while satisfying lenders' need for security.[46] It allowed lenders to secure a broad class of assets without restricting borrowers' ability to deal with the assets in the normal course of business. However, Getzler disputes this view, arguing that there is no evidence of capital shortage or excess circulating assets at the time.[47] Instead, he attributes the rise of the floating charge to institutional lenders' preference for short-term liquidity. By securing liquid assets like receivables, floating charges offered lenders readily realizable security that made them an attractive option. It is this liquidity advantage, Getzler contends, that was a key factor in the widespread adoption of the floating charge.

Whether its invention was driven by the needs of lenders or borrowers, more pertinent for present purposes is the fact that the floating charge had originated from contractual arrangements between parties. Its eventual judicial recognition was a result of its increasing acceptance and use in the credit market[48] because of the perceived economic advantages of allowing for floating securities.[49] The nineteenth-century courts validated this market innovation as they recognized 'the value of allowing parties freedom to modify their allocations of proprietary rights'.[50] To the extent that the floating charge constituted a

[43] Pennington 1960, 638.
[44] *Re Spectrum Plus* [2005] 2 AC 680, [97].
[45] Pennington 1960. See also *Agnew v Commissioner of Inland Revenue* [2001] 2 AC 710, [5]–[8].
[46] See, eg, *Re Spectrum Plus Ltd* [2005] 2 AC 680, [95].
[47] Getzler 2006.
[48] See eg. Nolan 2004, who traced the evolution of the floating charge through legal precedents adopted by contracting parties over time.
[49] Goode 1996, 193–194.
[50] Armour 2004, 29.

new species of security, however, it was a departure from the principle of *numerus clausus*. The willingness of the Chancery courts to embrace a new form of security instrument, albeit through a gradual development over time, demonstrated that equity was not bound by *numerus clausus* in developing new property rights. This flexibility in property creation also aligns with Merrill and Smith's observation of reduced standardization in the context of intermediate rights.[51]

By deferring to private ordering, these early authorities had framed the issues primarily as those concerning the allocation of in personam rights. This would imply, according to Merrill and Smith, that the burden of information gathering rests predominantly on transacting parties, with minimal impact on external parties in terms of information costs.[52] However, the emphasis on contractual freedom obscured the reality that a floating security created *property* rights capable of adversely affecting third parties. Where such externalities were acknowledged, early cases appeared to place the onus on third parties, such as unsecured creditors, to ascertain whether a company's assets were encumbered.[53]

Over time, sentiment shifted with growing appreciation of the unfair effects of floating charges on unsecured creditors.[54] A series of legislative reforms were introduced, which included subjecting the floating charge to preferential claims,[55] requiring the perfection of the security by registration,[56] providing for the avoidance of a floating charge created close to the commencement of winding up proceedings,[57] and more recently, mandating that a company that has commenced insolvency proceedings set aside a 'prescribed part' of its charged assets for unsecured creditors in priority to the floating chargee.[58] These legislative responses were consistent with the notice and protective

[51] Merrill & Smith 2001, 804. See also note 40.

[52] Merrill & Smith 2001, 799–800.

[53] See, eg, *Re General South America Company* (1876) 2 Ch D 337 at 341–343, where the court reasoned that general creditors should have known the company was free to charge its assets and should have made inquiries because the company was limited in liability; cited by Armour 2004, 32. This reflected the view, which lasted until the nineteenth century, that secret liens could bind third parties as title was established on the basis of possession: see Arruñada 2003, 406. A registration regime would compel the disclosure of such interests but whether priority should be fixed by reference to the third party's actual knowledge of the prior interest is a distinct issue: see Baird and Jackson 1984, 314–318.

[54] A 'great scandal' per Lord Macaghten in *Salomon v A Salomon & Co Ltd* [1897] 1 AC 22 at 53; an 'injustice' per Buckley J in *In re London Pressed Hinge Company, Ltd; Campbell v London Pressed Hinge Co, Ltd* [1905] 1 Ch 576 at 583. See also Armour 2004, 32.

[55] The Preferential Payment in Bankruptcy Amendment Act 1897, s 2. Now consolidated in the Insolvency Act 1986, ss 40 and 175; Companies Act 2006, s 754.

[56] Companies Act 1900, s 14; now Companies Act 2006, s 860.

[57] Companies Act 1907, s 13; now see Insolvency Act 1986, s 245.

[58] Insolvency Act 1986, s 176A, as amended by Enterprise Act 2002.

strategies that Merrill and Smith predicted are likely to be deployed in the zone of intermediate rights. We are mindful, of course, that classic economic theories posit that external parties, such as unsecured creditors, would not usually be affected by additional information costs arising from a borrower's grant of security because they can adjust the terms of their credit in view of the potential risks associated with floating charges.[59] However, it seems likely that the protective reforms were more focused on non-adjusting creditors such as employees.[60] In this case, the protection strategy under Merrill and Smith's analytical framework appears appropriate since the non-adjusting creditors, while they may be numerous in number, generally fall into identifiable categories.

In summary, this section has shown that the historical development of the floating charge aligns closely with Merrill and Smith's predictions. During the nineteenth century, the Chancery Courts' recognition of contractual formulations of the floating charge reflected a broader acceptance of new property rights in the intermediate zone where contractual autonomy is prioritized. However, where the property rights impact a large group of parties subject to externalized costs, legislative intervention became necessary to address informational asymmetry and safeguard vulnerable parties from exploitation. In the case of the floating charge, unsecured creditors represent the most at-risk group, prompting the introduction of both protective and notice-based legislation.

IV. Information Costs and Legal (Un)Certainty

A hallmark of the English law of security is its flexibility.[61] This flexibility affords transacting parties significant autonomy in structuring their security arrangements to meet specific commercial needs. With the help of skilled draftsmen, parties can shape and define security interests into existence, as exemplified by the development of the floating charge. However, such flexibility is also inherently inconsistent with the bright-line rules that are typically associated with property rights, as a result of which a greater degree of instability is observed with respect to how 'property' interests are conceptualized and applied in this context. This instability is perhaps best observed in the caselaw surrounding the distinction between fixed and floating charges.[62]

[59] Schwartz 1981.
[60] Bebchuk & Fried 1996.
[61] Beale, Bridge, Gullifer, & Lomnicka 2018, 1.13.
[62] See Gullifer & Payne 2006, 66.

They illustrate the ongoing tension arising from the market's desire for contractual freedom and the need for legal certainty, a tension that falls on the courts to resolve.

For much of its history, the jurisprudence on floating charges was bedevilled by attempts to 'upgrade'[63] securities over circulating assets to that of a fixed charge. Where they succeed, chargees enjoy 'the best of both worlds':[64] they acquire a fixed security with priority over preferential and other creditors in the event of insolvency without impeding the chargor's freedom to deal with the charged assets when it is a going concern. This strategy reached its high watermark in *Siebe Gorman & Co Ltd v Barclays Bank Ltd*.[65] The chargor in this case purported to create a 'first fixed charge' over (inter alia) its present and future book debts in favour of the chargee bank. The arrangement required the chargor to pay the proceeds of the book debts into a bank account held with the chargee and prohibited charging or assigning the book debts without the bank's prior consent. However, the chargor could freely draw funds from the account and use them in the ordinary course of business.[66] Slade J found on these facts that the charge in question was a fixed security.[67] In reaching this conclusion, he laid particular stress on the parties' intention, evidenced by their labelling of the security as a 'fixed charge'.

In the next twenty-five years, 'fixed' charges of the *Siebe Gorman* mold became prevalent.[68] However, fissures had also emerged as subsequent decisions retreated from the decision, culminating finally in its overruling in *In re Spectrum Plus Ltd*.[69] The charging provisions in *Spectrum Plus* were very similar to those of *Siebe Gorman* but the House of Lords was unanimous in characterizing the security as a floating charge. The decision made clear that the critical feature of the floating charge was the chargor's freedom to deal with the charged assets until a further event occurred to terminate that liberty.[70] *Siebe Gorman* was a classic instance of such liberty, so the court in that case was wrong to characterize the security as a fixed charge.

Spectrum Plus was a momentous decision that overturned twenty-five years of banking practice. It made clear that the characterization of a security was a matter of law, not merely the product of the parties' declared intention or

[63] *In re Spectrum Plus* [2005] 2 AC 680, [135].
[64] *Agnew v Commissioner of Inland Revenue* [2001] 2 AC 710, [27].
[65] [1979] 2 Lloyd's Law Reports 142.
[66] Ibid, 142, 158.
[67] Ibid, 159.
[68] *In re Spectrum Plus Ltd* [2004] 2 WLR 783, [97].
[69] [2005] 2 AC 680.
[70] *In re Spectrum Plus Ltd* [2005] 2 AC 680, [111] and [138]–[139].

chosen label.[71] This was a significant clarification as it underscored the role of judicial characterization as a vital constraint on the freedom of parties to define and delineate property rights.[72] The decision was also important for identifying the concept of control as the key criterion for distinguishing between fixed and floating charges, clarifying that a chargee must exert sufficient legal control over the charged assets to qualify as a fixed chargee.

Despite the doctrinal coherence restored by *Spectrum Plus*, the fixed/floating distinction has remained elusive. Other than unambiguous instances of absolute prohibitions against dealings, the level of control required over charged assets to constitute a fixed charge remains uncertain. For example, does a chargee exercise sufficient control if it is required not to unreasonably withhold consent to the release of charged assets?[73] Or if withdrawals of charged assets could only be withdrawn with a chargee's consent, but such consent is routinely granted?[74] What about a purported fixed charge that permits the chargor to freely substitute the charged assets provided their value is maintained?[75] If a charge is executed over income-generating assets, must the fixed chargee have control over both the asset and the generated revenue? In the light of such uncertainty, leading textbooks have leant on the side of caution to venture the view that 'only total prohibition of all dealings and withdrawals without permission is enough to create a fixed charge'.[76] However, the High Court rejected such a categorical approach in *Re Avanti Communications Ltd*.[77] Instead, the court adopted a more nuanced approach, taking into account the circumstances of the case and factors identified in caselaw—such as the chargor's licence to deal with the assets and whether the charged assets were circulating or fluctuating assets—to determine whether a charge should be classified as floating or fixed. On this view, the test of 'control' is not reducible to a bright-line rule; rather, it accommodates limited and conditional use of the charged assets by the chargor. Accordingly, property interest inherent in a floating charge is not governed by a rigid exclusionary rule, but rather by a blend of exclusion and governance strategies. This explains the conceptual

[71] Ibid, [80] and [141].

[72] The process of characterization 'raises the question as to whether parties should be allowed to create whatever interests or types of contract they want, even if this has the effect of defeating the policy aims of the relevant statute': see Gullifer & Payne 2006, 65.

[73] Beale, Bridge, Gullifer, & Lomnicka 2018, 6.115.

[74] Ibid, 6.116.

[75] Beale, Bridge, Gullifer & Lomnicka 2018 argues at 6.129 that 'a general power to substitute, limited just by the criteria that the value of the security remains the same, is not consistent with that level of control [required for a fixed charge]'. Cf. *Re Avanti Communications* [2023] 2 BCLC 355, [108]–[121].

[76] Goode & Gullifer 2023, 4-23. See also Beale, Bridge, Gullifer, & Lomnicka 2018, 6.110.

[77] [2003] 2 BCLC 355, [108]–[120].

fuzziness of the fixed–floating divide and, as will be argued, undermines the efficacy of the floating charges as a security device.

The uncertain fixed/floating boundary is not the only contentious aspect of the floating charge but it is arguably the most criticized feature because it has important consequences not only for the parties inter se but also for third parties pre- and post-insolvency.[78] *Spectrum Plus* is itself a striking illustration: the amount disputed in the case was a mere £16,136 but the dispute was litigated all the way to the House of Lords because its resolution could potentially affect several hundred liquidations.[79] Equally, the distinction is important pre-insolvency as it is often critical for lenders to know *ex ante* whether a loan is secured by a fixed or floating charge to determine the relevant terms.[80] Given its importance, it is unsurprising that the absence of a clear distinction has spawned costly and complex litigation as parties seek to exploit the legal uncertainty to establish priority,[81] and has increased the burden and expense for those structuring secured loans.

In practice, the clarification in *Spectrum Plus* has not altered lenders' preference for fixed securities. However, borrowers are unlikely to grant fixed charges over circulating assets as that would entail surrendering significant control to lenders, potentially crippling their businesses. Consequently, lenders have increasingly turned to debt factoring as an alternative.[82] This involves the assignment of receivables to lenders, which allows them to claim the receivables as assignees in the event of the borrowers' insolvency. Unlike charges, however, assignments are not registrable securities and do not require public disclosure. Debt factoring, therefore, provides lenders with an effective and secretive alternative to fixed charges for securing their position. As Walton astutely points out, however, this revives an historical problem that the legislature has always sought to prevent—'the ability of a debtor to use a secret device to secure for itself all, or a large proportion, of a debtor's assets'.[83]

While the floating charge is undeniably a stroke of genius that has had a profound impact on banking practices over the last two centuries, it has become unwieldy and ineffective over time, due in large part to unsatisfactory attempts at balancing the interests of secured and unsecured creditors through

[78] See the comprehensive discussion in Gullifer & Payne 2006.
[79] *In re Spectrum Plus Ltd* [2005] 2 AC 680, [76].
[80] Goode & Gullifer 2023, 4 10.
[81] Goode 2006, 21; Gullifer & Payne 2006, 55.
[82] Walton 2015, 4. Armour 2006 had predicted (at 203) this shift to asset-based financing. See also Akintola 2015, who observed that floating charges were still in use but more for the purposes of appointing administrators than for realization of security.
[83] Walton 2015, 6.

the fixed/floating distinction. Leading commentators such as Goode have long advocated reform, condemning the security as an 'anachronism'[84] that has outlived its usefulness by reason of complexity and confusion that cannot be resolved by piecemeal judicial lawmaking.[85] In contrast, jurisdictions such as the US, Canada, Australia, and New Zealand have demonstrated that it is possible to preserve the benefits of floating security without fragmenting security interests into disparate categories governed by different rules. Just after the turn of the millenium, the Law Commission proposed eliminating the fixed/floating distinction by introducing a broad concept of security interests that enjoys a fixed status whilst allowing the chargor to continue to deal with circulating assets.[86] Unfortunately, the proposal was eventually abandoned, apparently due to confusion as to its scope and effects, as well as uncertainty regarding its implications in insolvency.[87]

The law relating to the floating charge may indeed be ripe for reform but our greater concern in recounting the travails of this once-brilliant invention is to better understand the intense interaction between contractual freedom and property rules in this context from the lens of efficiency. We offer four observations.

First, the uncertainty surrounding the elusive fixed/floating distinction underscores the systemic costs of unclear property rules. As Merrill and Smith observed, bright-line rules reduce information costs for third parties. The common law's failure to articulate with clarity the distinction between fixed and floating charges increases information costs not only for the immediate parties and creditors, but also third parties who must rely on these classifications to structure transactions or resolve competing claims in insolvency. In addition to the information costs of deal planning and transacting, legal ambiguity also generates enforcement costs when attempts to enforce the securities are contested. This highlights a broader issue: that ill-defined property rights can significantly impair private parties' ability to achieve business purposes in an efficient manner.[88] Against that backdrop, information costs serve as a useful diagnostic tool of legal (un)certainty.

[84] Goode 1996, 201. See also Goode, 2006 and Worthington 2006.

[85] Goode & Gullifer 2023, 4-62.

[86] *Company Security Interests: A Consultative Report* (Law Com No 176), available at https://lawcom.gov.uk/project/company-security-interests/.

[87] *Company Security Interests* (Law Com No 296, Cm 6654), 3.158–3.175, available at https://lawcom.gov.uk/project/company-security-interests/. The Secured Transactions Law Reform Project has similarly called for the abolition of the fixed/floating distinction, to be replaced by a single concept of consensual security interest: see Secured Transactions Law Reform Project: Policy Paper, April 2016, available at https://securedtransactionslawreformproject.org/wp-content/uploads/2016/05/str-general-policy-paper-april-2016.pdf.

[88] Coase 1960.

Second, while Merrill and Smith suggest that intermediate rights involve lower informational needs due to their compound paucital or quasi-multital nature, we argue that numerosity and indefiniteness are not necessarily the primary determinants of informational needs or their legal corresponding strategies. *What is more important is the fact that parties are attempting to create property rights.* Once the proprietary quality is potentially engaged, the range of third parties who may be affected by the rule expands. This is because property rights are usually protected by injunctive reliefs, or essentially, the so-called property rules under the well-known Calabresi-Melamed framework.[89] Once a right is classified as a property right, the rightholder's consent will be essential for its transfer or alienation. This intensifies the interactions between private parties and amplifies the complexity of transactions involving such rights. Consequently, the greater the flexibility afforded to contracting parties to customize property rights, the higher the information needs for transacting these rights effectively.

Third, the instability of the fixed/floating divide also casts doubt on the information efficiency of intermediate rights through the attenuation of modularity. For Merrill,[90] and especially Smith,[91] modularity is a defining feature of property: it partitions complex entitlements into bounded modules or clusters, each presenting a simplified external interface that enables low-cost interaction with other legal actors. This structure allows property law to manage complexity efficiently. In the context of intermediate rights, however, modularity may not always be a salient or even coherent feature. To the extent that intermediate rights are highly customizable, the boundary between a module's internal configuration and its external legal interface becomes blurred. The floating charge exemplifies this ambiguity: can it be regarded as a standalone module when its scope and effects are dynamic and contingent? The lack of a stable modular boundary undermines the clarity and predictability that property law typically provides through exclusion strategies, reinforcing the view that intermediate rights may not deliver the systemic informational efficiencies associated with fully modular property forms.

Finally, we have seen that the attempts to create fixed securities over circulating assets—and the ensuing controversy over the fixed/floating distinction—were primarily driven by lenders' attempts to avoid the protective rules legislated to promote equity with respect to those informationally

[89] Calabresi & Melamed 1972.
[90] Merrill 2012.
[91] Smith 2012.

disadvantaged.[92] These efforts constitute, in Merrill and Smith's framework, frustration costs that comprise the expense of structuring around the floating charge regime and residual loss (if any) if the alternative arrangement fails to fully achieve the lenders' objectives. However, what may not be so readily quantifiable are third party costs arising from ringfencing borrowers' assets for the benefit of 'secured' lenders via the alternative route of title-based financing. This is because English law has a restrictive definition of security interests that excludes title-based financing–such as assignments and factoring—as secured transactions.[93] Consequently, lenders 'secured' by title-financing are not obliged to register or otherwise give notice of the asset-based lending, leaving certain informational gaps unaddressed. In other words, title-based financing, in spite of its proprietary quality, escapes the legal framework set for property rights to address information cost externalization. If such externalized information costs are assessed to be significant, then the solution may lie in streamlining the legal frameworks governing apparatuses that serve similar economic functions. The current state of the law is unsatisfactory because its regulation of these legal structures through disparate rules encourages regulatory arbitrage and undermines coherence in the legal treatment of secured transactions.

V. Beyond Information Costs

Property as conceptualized by Merrill and Smith is a form of legal architecture that is structurally and analytically distinct from contracts. Within this architecture, information costs play a central explanatory role: they account for the limited menu of property forms (the *numerus clausus*), the use of standardized exclusionary in rem rules, and the modularity of legal entitlements. Yet, as the authors emphasize, information cost minimization is not the sole or exhaustive objective of property law.[94] Instead, they acknowledge that property law serves a plurality of ends, not all of which can be reduced to cost-benefit analysis.[95] Departing from the more narrowly utilitarian assumptions of mainstream law and economics, Merrill and Smith posit that the institution of property is underpinned by the 'simple and robust everyday moral intuition [that]

[92] As Armour explained, 'subjecting voluntary transactions to redistributive liabilities gives parties to those transactions a powerful incentive to structure their affairs differently': see Armour 2006, 196.

[93] In contrast, Article 9 of the Uniform Commercial Code defines security interests more broadly to include arrangements where the title to the collateral resides in the creditor.

[94] Merrill & Smith 2020, 137.

[95] Ibid, 134.

provide crucial support for the core of property – the right to exclude from a thing, good against the world'.[96] While non-core areas of property may demand more pragmatic balancing informed by expert knowledge, this basic moral structure remains essential to their theory.[97] Implicit in this approach is the acceptance that property law necessarily performs distributive functions. However, they refrain from endorsing any particular theory of distributive justice, maintaining that legislative change, rather than judicial innovation, is the preferred agent of change.[98]

In relation to floating charges, we have seen that the issues of characterization were fundamentally driven by distributive concerns. Judicial and legislative efforts to delineate the conditions under which a charge over circulating assets may attain 'fixed' status are not purely formalistic; rather, they involve normative judgements about the permissible limits of private ordering in reallocating firm assets.[99] When such arrangements are perceived to unfairly prejudice unsecured creditors—by enabling secured lenders to extract excessive value on insolvency—courts and lawmakers have intervened to correct the resulting inequities.

From its inception, courts have expressed unease with the idea that a creditor could privately secure a right to sweep up all the company's trading assets upon insolvency. As noted,[100] this concern led to the imposition of a general registration requirement to provide adequate notice to unsecured creditors. Subsequently, the 'prescribed part'—a portion carved out of the secured credit to be paid to unsecured creditors in priority to the floating chargee—was introduced. In addition, employees were elevated as preference creditors in respect of unpaid wages and other related employment benefits. This priority has traditionally been justified on the ground that workmen 'should have a right to be paid out of assets to which they have contributed value'.[101] Another argument is that statutory priority for employees serves as a form of insurance, protecting them against the risks of investing in firm-specific human capital.[102]

Taken together, these measures reflect a broader policy objective: to curtail the excesses of private ordering in order to prevent the unfair concentration of value in the hands of large, adjusting creditors—typically secured lenders—at the expense of non-adjusting creditors, such as employees and public tax

[96] Merrill and Smith 2007, 1890–1891.
[97] Ibid, 1891.
[98] Merrill & Smith 2000, 58–68.
[99] See note 72.
[100] See note 56.
[101] Armour 2006, 196.
[102] Ibid, 220.

authorities.[103] These unsecured claimants are often unable to protect their interests *ex ante* by reason of information asymmetry or the employer's dominant market power. From an economic perspective, the harm they suffer constitutes a form of negative externality that is unlikely to be redressed without judicial or legislative interventions.

Apart from considerations of fairness among creditors, the development of the floating charge has also been influenced by broader distributional concerns. For example, the Enterprise Act 2002 abolished the floating charge holder's right to appoint an administrative receiver, substituting it with a more streamlined administrative procedure. The new approach requires the office-holder to take account of the interests of a wider group of creditors rather than focusing on those of the debenture holder.[104] This reform was part of a larger movement to promote corporate rescues at the initial stages of financial distress.[105] At an even more general level, the reform of securities law may also implicate considerations such as the competitiveness of English law in attracting loan capital from other jurisdictions.[106]

These examples illustrate that distributional and policy considerations—both at the granular level of specific creditor classes and at the broader level of systemic design—can operate as meaningful constraints on party autonomy in defining the form and content of security interests.

VI. Conclusion

In this chapter, we explored the interaction of contract and property using the floating charge as a focal case study. The floating charge offers an intriguing example of property creation through private ordering and the challenges that it poses for legal certainty, fairness, and economic efficiency. Drawing on Merrill and Smith's framework, we note that hybrid rights in the intermediate zone do generate significant information costs and legal uncertainties, in large part because of the destabilizing effects of contractual efforts to reorder property rights. These adverse implications will often necessitate legislative and judicial interventions to protect against the externalization of information and other

[103] Bebchuk & Fried 1996.

[104] Armour 2004, 48. Although a subsequent study suggests no evidence of improved outcomes for administrative proceedings as a result of this shift from a 'dispersed creditor' model of governance to that of a 'controlled creditor' model: see Armour, Hsu, & Walter 2008.

[105] Goode & Gullifer 2023, 4-08.

[106] See Paterson 2016.

costs to third parties—especially those who are unable to secure their position *ex ante* due to information asymmetries or inferior bargaining positions. Freedom of contract will also have to be constrained to achieve distributional outcomes which align with societal values and policy objectives, with legislative reform being the preferred mechanism for fundamental changes in property structures.

References

Akintola, K. (2015). 'What is Left of the Floating Charge? An Empirical Outlook'. *Journal of International Banking and Finance Law* 7: 404–406.

Akkermans, B. (2017). 'The Numerus Clausus of Property Rights'. *Comparative Property: Global Perspectives.* M. Graziadel and L. Smith. Cheltenham, Edward Elgar: 100–120.

Armour, J. (2004). 'The Chequered History of the Floating Charge'. *Griffith Law Review* 13: 25–56.

Armour, J. (2006) 'Should we Redistribute in Insolvency?' *Company Charges: Spectrum and Beyond.* J. Getzler and J. Payne. Oxford, Oxford University Press: 189–225.

Armour, J., A. Hsu, and A. Walters (2008). 'Corporate Insolvency in the United Kingdom: The Impact of the Enterprise Act 2002'. *European Company and Financial Law Review* 5: 148–171.

Arruñada, B. (2003). 'Property Enforcement as Organized Consent'. *Journal of Law, Economics and Organization* 19: 401–444.

Baird, D. and T. Jackson. (1984). 'Information, Uncertainty, and the Transfer of Property'. *Journal of Legal Studies* 13: 299.

Beale, H., M. Bridge, L. Gullifer, and E. Lomnicka (2018). The Law of Security and Title-Based Financing. 3rd edn. Oxford, Oxford University Press.

Bebchuk, L. A. and J. M. Fried (1996). 'The Uneasy Case for the Priority of Secured Claims in Bankruptcy'. *Yale Law Journal* 105: 857–934.

Coase, R. H. (1960). 'The Problem of Social Cost'. *Journal of Law and Economics* 3: 1–44.

Guido Calabresi and A. Douglas Melamed (1972). 'Property Rules, Liability Rules and Inalienability: One View of the Cathedral'. Harvard Law Review 85: 1089–1128.

Davidson, N. M. (2008). 'Standardization and Pluralism in Property Law'. *Vanderbilt Law Review* 61: 1597–1663.

Getzler, J. (2006). 'The Role of Security over Future and Circulating Capital: Evidence from the British Economy circa 1850–1920'. *Company Charges: Spectrum and Beyond.* J. Getzler and J. Payne. Oxford. Oxford University Press: 227–251.

Goode, R. (1996). 'The Exodus of the Floating Charge'. *Corporate and Commercial Law: Modern Developments.* D. Feldman and F. Meisel. London, Lloyd's of London Press Ltd: 193–203.

Goode, R. (2006). 'The Case for Abolition of the Floating Charge'. *Company Charges: Spectrum and Beyond.* J. Getzler and J. Payne. Oxford, Oxford University Press: 11–23.

Good, R. and L. Gullifer (2023). Goode and Gullifer on Legal Problems of Credit and Security. 7th edn. London, Sweet and Maxwell.

Gullifer, L. and J. Payne (2006). 'The Characterization of Fixed and Floating Charges'. *Company Charges: Spectrum and Beyond.* J. Getzler and J. Payne. Oxford, Oxford University Press: 51–104.

Hansmann, H. and R. Kraakman (2002). 'Property, Contract, and Verification: The Numerus Clausus Problem and the Divisibility of Rights'. *Journal of Legal Studies* 31: S373–S420.

Kocourek, A. (1920). 'Rights in Rem'. *University of Pennsylvania Law Review* 68: 322–336.

McFarlane, B. (2011). 'The Numerus Clausus Principle and Covenants Relating to Land'. *Modern Studies in Property Law—Volume 6.* S. Bright. Oxford, Hart: 311–331.

Merrill, T. (2012). 'Property as Modularity'. *Harvard Law Review* 125: 151–163.

Merrill, T. and Smith, H.E. (2000). 'Optimization in the Law of Property: The *Numerus Clausus* Principle'. *The Yale Law Journal* 110: 1–70.

Merrill, T. and Smith, H. E. (2001). 'The Property/Contract Interface'. *Columbia Law Review* 101:773–852.

Merrill, T. and Smith, H.E. (2007). 'The Morality of Property.' *William and Mary Law Review* **48**: 1849–1896.

Merrill, T. and Smith, H. (2020). 'The Architecture of Property'. *Research Handbook on Private Law Theory.* H. Dagan and B. C. Zipursky. Cheltenham, Edward Elgar: 134–154.

Nolan, R. C. (2004). 'Property in a Fund'. *Law Quarterly Review* 120: 108–136.

Paterson, S. (2016). 'The Insolvency Consequences of the Abolition of the Fixed/Floating Charge Distinction'. *Secured Transactions Law Reform Project.*

Pennington, R. (1960). 'The Genesis of the Floating Charge'. *The Modern Law Review* 23: 630–646.

Penner, J. E. (2020). Property Rights: A Re-Examination. Oxford, Oxford University Press.

Schwartz, A. (1981). 'Security Interests and Bankruptcy Priorities: A Review of Current Theories.' *Journal of Legal Studies* 10: 1–37

Smith. H. E. (2002), 'Exclusion Versus Governance: Two Strategies for Delineating Property Rights' *Journal of Legal Studies* 31: S453–S487.

Smith, H. E. (2011). 'Standardization in Property Law'. *Research Handbook on the Economics of Property Law.* K. Ayotte and H. Smith. Cheltenham, Edward Elgar: 148–173.

Smith, H. E. (2012). 'Property as the Law of Things'. *Harvard Law Review* 125: 1691–1726.

Smith, H. E. (2023). 'Equitable Meta-Law: The Spectrum of Property'. *Equity Today: 150 Years after the Judicature Reforms.* B. Macfarlane and S. Elliott. Oxford, Hart: 319–337.

Sparkes, P. (2012). 'Certainty of Property: Numerus Clausus or the Rule with No Name?'. *European Review of Private Law* 3: 768–804.

Stern, J. Y. (2017). 'The Essential Structure of Property Law'. *Michigan Law Review* 115: 1167–1212.

Swadling, W. (2013). 'Property: General Principles'. *English Private Law.* A. Burrows. Oxford, Oxford University Press.

von Bar, C. (2023). Foundations of Property Law: Things as Objects of Property Rights. J. A. Grant, tr. Oxford, Oxford University Press.

Walton, P. (2015) 'Fixed and Floating Charges: the Great British Fund-Off?' *Journal of International Banking and Finance Law* 30: 3–6.

Worthington, S. (2006). 'Floating Charges: The Use and Abuse of Doctrinal Analysis'. *Company Charges: Spectrum and Beyond.* J. Getzler and J. Payne. Oxford. Oxford University Press: 25–49.

IV.
CONTRACT AND CONVEYANCE

13

Property and Contract in the Development of the Sale of Goods

Views of the Victorians

Catharine MacMillan

I. Introduction

This chapter is concerned with the historical interface in the English common law between contract and property in relation to the sale of goods in the nineteenth century. The contract of sale is concerned with both property and contract. English law, unusually in European legal systems, avoids the Roman distinction between contract and conveyance: the contract is the conveyance. This chapter undertakes an exploration of how nineteenth-century jurists formulated concepts of property and contract in relation to the sale of goods. It is argued that these considerations shifted from a focus upon the proprietary nature of the sale of goods to the contractual nature of the sale of goods. This, in turn, shaped the modern law of the sale of goods as it was enacted by the Sale of Goods Act 1893. This enactment, an early form of partial codification in English law, is one largely concerned with the nature of the obligations created in a sale of goods rather than the proprietary effects of the contract of sale. The Act's focus on the nature of obligations created by contractual terms is a departure from the proprietary preoccupations of jurists at the start of the century. The chapter, in examining how and why this occurred, begins with an historical overview of the sale of personal property in the English common law. The foundational work of William Blackstone in relation to sale is explored as a means of understanding the approach of jurists in the first half of the nineteenth century in their treatises on sale. The historical context in which these jurists wrote is then surveyed for an insight into why these changes occurred before exploring the way in which J P Benjamin changed the common law approach to the sale of goods in English law.

Catharine MacMillan, *Property and Contract in the Development of the Sale of Goods* In: *The Property-Contract Interface*. Edited by: James Penner, Irina Sakharova, Henry E. Smith, and Zhong Xing Tan, Oxford University Press.
 DOI: 10.1093/9780198951995.003.0017

II. Property Law and Procedural Remedies

The distinction between real property and personal property in England evolved from the procedural remedies available to claim them.[1] Milsom has observed that in a pre-modern era the question of whether a claim for goods was a matter of contractual obligation or of property was irrelevant.[2] As he explains, though, a distinction gradually grew between the writs used for claims for money (debt) and claims for the goods themselves (detinue).[3] Interests in goods were protected by different actions, notably detinue, trespass, and replevin. While goods might be recovered in an action of detinue or replevin, the recovery of a specific thing (the *res*) could not be guaranteed and the judgment might be satisfied in damages.[4] Personal property was thus afforded a different protection than real property, where actions lay to recover the property itself. In the late eleventh and twelfth centuries, Ibbetson notes, an important shift began across western Europe with regard to the sale of goods from 'the focal plane of property into that of contract, its primary function no longer the conveyance of ownership but the imposition of obligations'.[5] By the early thirteenth century English courts slowly began to recognize the passing of property in executory contracts, a process completed at the end of the fourteenth century.[6] Another significant legal development is that by the mid-fifteenth century most claims were resolved by a jury trial rather than by wager of law.[7] The rules which governed these trials were, however, based upon procedures. Writs determined the course of litigation from beginning to end and, in turn, shaped how lawyers conceived of the law. As Lord Lindley observed, 'with us the tendency was to study remedies and learn principles from procedure, which is less scientific and satisfactory in dealing with new and difficult questions'.[8]

III. Blackstone and the Sale of Goods

The effect of procedural law on formulations of substantive law can be seen in Blackstone's *Commentaries on the Laws of England*.[9] The eighteenth-century

[1] Baker 2019, 404.
[2] Milsom 1981a, 266–267.
[3] Ibid, 262–269; Milsom 1961.
[4] Baker 2019, 404.
[5] Ibbetson 1992, 13.
[6] Ibbetson 1991, 497.
[7] Milsom 1961, 266.
[8] The excerpt is from an unpublished autobiography quoted by Dockray 1986, 103.
[9] Blackstone 2016.

Commentaries provided a starting point and analytical perspective for early nineteenth-century writers on the sale of goods. Blackstone brought no real novelty to his *Commentaries* nor a developed theory of law. The importance of his work lay in expounding 'substantive rules without the procedural framework in which they existed for lawyers',[10] in ordering a disparate mass of materials into a form which explained complex areas of law.[11] Blackstone was innovative in attempting to explain the reasoning and presuppositions behind the legal rules.[12] His *Commentaries* changed the approach of treatise writers generally in the following century.[13] The treatment of contract is thin and unsatisfactory, though, and the contract of sale is considered in his second volume, on the 'Rights of Things'.[14] About a quarter of the volume was concerned with personal property (the rest with real property) but its title is clumsy: Blackstone followed Sir Matthew Hale in his organizational scheme, which was itself derived from the Roman analysis of law into law relating to persons, things, and actions. The better title was the 'Law of Things'.[15] Lobban explains that Blackstone's treatment of contract was impeded by the lack of contemporary contract literature from which he could draw upon.[16] One result was that he tended to treat contract as a form of property rather than as an obligation.[17] The property right was realized by a judicial order for payment according to the agreement: as Lobban notes this reasoning was flawed, for the requirement of the subject to comply with the judicial order was dependent upon a form of social contract which was not explicable in such proprietary treatment.[18] Such a contract-as-property treatment, though, mirrored the organizational structure of the *Commentaries* in the division of rights and wrongs to those rights,[19] although this bifurcation itself lacked a theory to support it and thus left much unexplained.[20]

Blackstone defined personal property as including 'all sorts of things *moveable*, which may attend a man's person wherever he goes; and therefore, being only the objects of the law while they remain within the limits of

[10] Milsom 1981b, 6.
[11] Lobban 2018, 2.
[12] Ibid, 9.
[13] Milsom 1981b, 9.
[14] Blackstone 2016, 260, [384].
[15] Cairns 1984, 344.
[16] Lobban 2018, 10.
[17] Ibid, 19.
[18] Ibid, 20.
[19] Ibid, 19.
[20] Ibid, 11.

its jurisdiction'.[21] In comparison to immoveables (lands, houses, and their profits), personal property was 'not esteemed of so high a nature, nor paid so much regard to by the law'.[22] For these reasons the ancient law books concerned with feudal provisions 'do not therefore often condescend to regulate this species of property'. Blackstone observed that personal property had become important as the subject matter of trade and commerce: 'courts now regard a man's personalty in a light nearly, if not quite, equal to his realty' and 'we have learned to conceive different ideas of it'.[23] The courts of his era had, accordingly, developed rules of dealing with personalty which were not as technical as those applying to realty. These rules, Blackstone observed, were principally drawn 'from reason and convenience' but also from Roman law wherever the rules were well-grounded and applicable to the case in question. He also found a preservation of ancient usages, 'a certain foedal tincture' with regard to branches of personal property.[24]

Property was central to Blackstone's definition of sale: sale 'is a transmutation of property from one man to another, in consideration of some recompense in value'.[25] From this starting point he was principally concerned to examine the nature of the property a man could hold in personalty. He considered that this could arise either in possession (where one had not only the right to enjoy the property but also the actual enjoyment of it) or in action (a bare right without occupation or enjoyment).[26] While he wrote of a new approach to personalty, his consideration of the contract of sale formed a brief element in his examination of the means by which title to personal things could be acquired or lost.[27] Blackstone described a contract as one which 'usually conveys an interest merely in action'.[28] It required an agreement between at least two capable parties, for a consideration ('the reason which moves the party contracting to enter the contract'[29]) of the thing agreed to be done or not done. In relation to personalty, the laws of England provided several forms

[21] Blackstone 2016, 260, [384].
[22] Ibid, 260–261, [385].
[23] Ibid.
[24] Ibid.
[25] Ibid, 302, [446].
[26] Ibid, chapter 25, 'Of Property in Things Personal', 263, [389].
[27] Ibid, chapter 26 'Of Title to Things Personal by Occupancy', 271, [400]. Blackstone identified twelve means of acquisition or loss: (1) by occupancy; (2) by prerogative; (3) by forfeiture; (4) by custom; (5) by succession; (6) by marriage; (7) by judgment; (8) by gift; (9) by contract; (10) by bankruptcy; (11) by testament; and (12) by administration.
[28] Ibid, chapter 30 'Of Title by Gift, Grant, and Contract', 299, [442].
[29] Ibid, 300, [443]–[444].

of contract or agreement which enabled property to pass from one party to another.[30] Sale was the first form he considered and his considerations were entirely taken up with the question of what was necessary to form a valid contract such that property was transferred by the sale and the point at which the property passed, both from a vendor with title and one without. Where the vendor had title, recompense, a *quid pro quo*, was required to make the agreement binding and allowed the vendee to carry the goods away.[31] Without recompense the vendee could not carry the goods away, 'unless the contrary be expressly agreed'.[32]

In certain circumstances, Blackstone observed, property in goods might also be transferred by sale 'though the vendor *hath none at all* in the goods'[33] where the purchaser was unaware that the property was not that of the vendor or that there was any other fraud in the transaction. This exceptional result occurred in fairs or markets *overt* where the sale was good not only between the parties but was also binding 'on all those that have any right or property therein'.[34] Such a result arose to allow a purchaser security in their purchase, without which the commerce would soon end. Where, however, the sale, even in a market *overt*, was of goods which were the property of the king[35] or consisted of a horse,[36] the property was not altered by the contract of sale. Blackstone concluded his discussion of sale with a brief consideration of contractual terms. Borrowing from Justinian's *Digest*, Blackstone wrote that where a vendor sold goods as their own and 'the title proves deficient' English law implied a warranty which allowed the purchaser 'satisfaction from the seller'.[37] He then went on to identify, in a single sentence, the only form of contractual term not concerned with property. English law implied no term as 'to the goodness of the wares'.[38] Unless the vendor 'used any art to disguise them'[39] or misrepresented matters the purchaser was without remedy. Purchasers concerned as to 'goodness' were, thus, left to seek an express warranty to this effect.

[30] Ibid, 301–302, [446]: (1) sale or exchange; (2) bailment; (3) hiring and borrowing; and (4) debt.
[31] Recompense was a partial payment, or any portion of the goods delivered by way of earnest: 303, [448].
[32] Ibid.
[33] Ibid, 304, [449]. Blackstone did not concern himself with relativity of title in his observations.
[34] Ibid.
[35] Ibid.
[36] Ibid, 305, [450]–[451].
[37] Ibid, 306, [452].
[38] Ibid.
[39] Ibid.

IV. The Early Nineteenth-Century Treatises on the Sale of Goods: A Property Approach

The first English treatise on sale was by the barrister George Ross,[40] who followed Blackstone's focus upon property. Ross thought it remarkable that 'whilst there is scarcely a title in our laws which has not been made the subject of a distinct work, the law which regulates the transfer of all the commercial wealth in the country should hitherto have remained unnoticed'.[41] He took Blackstone as his starting point, adopting his definition of sale as a transfer of property from one to another for some price or recompense. The treatise was largely concerned with whether or not the contract had operated to pass property in the goods. An initial consideration of importance in this regard was the validity of the contract of sale under the Statute of Frauds.[42] Contracts for the sale of wares above £10 were only valid if: the buyer accepted (and actually received) part of the goods so sold; or if the buyer gave something in earnest or part payment; or there was a memorandum in writing of the bargain made and signed by the parties or their agents. The treatise thus began by detailing the multitude of cases concerned with the application of the statute because, if the contract was not valid, no property passed. The examination of property was central to the next chapter which detailed the various forms of property a vendor could hold, or did not hold, in goods. Ross considered only briefly, in a short chapter, the subject of warranties.[43] This began by contrasting Roman law, which implied a warranty as to the vendor's title, with English law which did not. Ross departed from Blackstone here because in certain circumstances English law allowed a purchaser to acquire a property in goods from a vendor who had none.[44] It was for a purchaser to seek an express warranty from their vendor as to their property in the goods for 'in such case the maxim is *caveat emptor*'.[45] Most of this brief chapter was given over to express warranties and the consequences attendant upon breach. Ross identified little in the way in

[40] Ross 1811.
[41] Ibid, ix.
[42] (1677) 29 Cha 2, c 3; s 16. Section 7 of the Statute of Frauds Amendment Act 1828 (9 Geo 4, c 14) provided that s 17 of the Statute of Frauds applied to goods to be delivered in the future that were not yet manufactured or not yet fit for delivery.
[43] Ross 1811, 'Chapter the Sixth of Warranties', 281–296.
[44] One such example was a purchase in a market *overt*, to which there were numerous exceptions: ibid, 151–157.
[45] Ibid, 282.

which the law implied any warranties into the contract of sale[46] and his denial of various forms of implied warranty are startling to the modern lawyer.[47] In general, an action on a warranty was only successful where there was an express warranty and this, too, might fail where the warranty was patently false or the falsehood known to the purchaser.[48]

Ross did not live long past the publication of his treatise and a decade later another barrister, George Long, wrote his own treatise to fill the need for a treatise on sale.[49] Long started from Blackstone's definition of sale as a transfer of property from one person to another for a price, with the more specific limitation that it was 'a sum of money paid by the vendee to the vendor'.[50] While Long began with Blackstone's organizational structure as to the nature of property, his work soon descended into a rather haphazard collection of cases grouped under various headings. He began, for example, by considering the capacity of the parties to the sale—an unusual starting point for a subject usually begun with an examination of the validity of the sale. In short, Long's work resembled a digest rather than a treatise; he would have been better to have simply updated Ross's treatise. Contemporaries recognized these deficiencies but noted that it was a popular book 'because the subject is so important a one' and that there was no better book.[51] What it had in common with Ross's treatise was a concern with the property in a contract of sale and the actions by which this could be enforced. The right of an unpaid vendor of stopping goods *in transitu* upon the insolvency of their purchaser is one such example. In a perplexing, but short, chapter Long looked at the contractual nature of warranties. While most of his consideration was of the nature of express warranties that could be given, he did provide a very brief consideration of implied warranties. His treatment of these, though, was marred by a lack of supporting precedent and an often-unacknowledged debt to various portions of Blackstone. Long, for example, wrote that the seller impliedly warranted that the commodity they sold was their own.[52] His treatment of what he identified as implied warranties of merchantable quality and that provisions be wholesome were contradictory, though, and imprecise.

[46] Two such instances were if goods of a different quality were supplied (ibid, 282) or if the whole of the goods sold by sample failed to correspond with the sample (ibid, 284–287).

[47] Ross denied an implied warranty that goods were of merchantable quality (ibid, 287) or that inserting the name of an artist in a catalogue warranted the authorship of the picture (ibid, 284).

[48] Ibid, 284.

[49] Long 1821.

[50] Ibid, 1.

[51] Anon 1839, 473.

[52] Long 1821, 119.

While it might be thought that perhaps the subject of sale simply attracted unfortunate authors in Ross and Long, a perusal of general works on contract in which sale was considered display a similar fixation with the property-ness of sale rather than the contractual terms of the sale. The emphasis upon the proprietary consequences of a contract of sale is seen in two early nineteenth-century treatises on Contract. Comyn[53] was concerned to ascertain what was required to make the contract of sale good in a variety of circumstances in order to ascertain whether an action lay for debt or, possibly, the recovery of an item. Who had property in the goods, and at what point, lay at the heart of his chapter on sale.[54] So, for example, Comyn was concerned with instances of when an unpaid vendor might stop goods *in transitu* where the vendee had become insolvent. Comyn's work is largely a collection of case excerpts; the analysis is unsophisticated and there is little attempt to construct a principled framework for his subject matter. Chitty, in his *A Practical Treatise on the Law of Contracts*,[55] made greater attempts to establish a framework for contract. He dealt with the contract of sale in a section concerned with personal property which also included compositions in lieu of tithes, bailments, wagers, and guaranties. Drawing upon Blackstone's *Commentaries*, and supplemented with judicial decisions, Chitty focused upon the proprietary consequences of sale. He adopted Blackstone's definition of sale and was thereafter concerned to explore when a contract was binding such that there was a 'transmutation of property from one man to another'.[56] His work is directed towards issues such as a sale by a wrongful possessor, the effect of fraud upon ownership, the relative rights of a vendor and vendee in relation to the goods, and the validity of the contract in relation to property under the Statute of Frauds. After these property-based considerations Chitty dealt briefly with warranties attendant in the contract for sale.[57] Following Blackstone, the first of these was the question of an implied warranty of title. Chitty was emphatic that there was no general warranty implied by law in the contract of sale because *caveat emptor* prevailed. He acknowledged, though, that in certain circumstances courts had implied warranties but his treatment of the subject was limited and unsatisfactory.

[53] Comyn 1807, ch VI.

[54] An examination of the sale of contraband, obscene, or libellous goods was also made: ibid, 239–244.

[55] Chitty, 1826.

[56] Ibid, 108.

[57] 133–140.

V. Blackburn's *Treatise on The Effect of the Contract of Sale* (1845) and the Determination of Property in Goods

It was in this intellectual environment that Colin Blackburn wrote his treatise. Published in 1845, *A Treatise on the Effect of the Contract of Sale* was solely concerned 'to discuss how far the property in goods is, by the law of England, affected by an agreement concerning the sale of them'.[58] Although Lord Blackburn is remembered as a nineteenth-century judge of great learning and experience, his beginnings were inauspicious. Called to the bar in 1838 he was rarely briefed. Ballantine described him as a 'profound lawyer' but observed that he was socially reserved and that a 'Scotch accent does not improve a naturally harsh voice, and his demeanour can scarcely be termed graceful, or his manner pleasant'.[59] Even when briefs did come to Blackburn after he wrote his treatise, he became a junior with significant mercantile cases but never the leader.[60] His 'great patron'[61] was Lord Campbell and his later selection of Blackburn as a judge was viewed with surprise and some disdain. Blackburn's early, briefless years were spent in the court rooms of the Queen's Bench and Exchequer Chambers. Here he acquired a great knowledge of the caselaw and reported it in nine volumes. Blackburn's immense grasp of the cases is apparent in his treatise. So, too, is evidence of a much wider reading of civilian legal systems. While it is tempting to see this arising from his Scottish beginnings, his English education—attending Eton and then Trinity College Cambridge—points towards intellectual curiosity. The treatise is a work based on English caselaw and its civilian influences are presented for comparative purposes.

To modern eyes a treatise on sale focused upon property and possession is odd, lacking in those contract considerations which later lawyers view as important. As we have seen, Blackburn's treatise fit within the existing juristic approach to the topic and was regarded by contemporaries as highly accomplished in this endeavour. The treatise closely examined the interaction between contract and property. As Blackburn explained, the significance of determining the property in the goods was both procedural and substantive. At a procedural level it determined the form of action which could be brought and the remedy which might be received. At a substantive level, who held property in the goods determined who bore the risk of loss where goods were damaged and provided the extent of the claim in insolvency. Blackburn began with a

[58] Blackburn 1845, 2.
[59] Ballantine 1883, 297.
[60] Ibid, 401.
[61] Ibid, 400.

chapter on the Statute of Frauds. While the common law required no specific formalities beyond the mutual assent of both parties as to what was agreed upon and consideration for this agreement the Statute of Frauds imposed specific requirements for the sale of any goods, wares, or merchandise worth £10 and above. The centrality of the Statute to English law was that non-compliant contracts were not enforceable and the interest this generated was directed towards the proprietary consequences. What was required to satisfy the provisions of the statute law was thus central to rendering a contract for the sale of goods enforceable. Following his often-minute review of the requirements of the statute and the cases interpreting it, Blackburn turned to what he regarded as the two other points of significance: what contracts amounted to a bargain and sale and what agreements were only executory and what rights were reserved to a vendor following a transfer of the general property to the purchaser before it was delivered into their possession. In examining these points Blackburn dealt with the practical points of a right of stoppage in transit and a vendor's lien. Rights of property and possession are central to both.

Blackburn's treatment of sale is a thoroughly English one. It is based upon caselaw and it is the work of one who is attempting to synthesize and analyse a system of law still largely thought of in terms of actions which can be brought and remedies which can be received. The laws of evidence are also of considerable importance and are thus inter-related with substantive considerations of sale. The analysis of contract is undertaken to determine the proprietary effects of the transaction. In a separate chapter, Blackburn considered in detail how the presumptions of the parties to the contract determined the intention of the right of the property to be transferred at once. This, though, could be varied by the parties themselves. English law had thus moved beyond agreements for ready money, enabling the parties to transfer property in goods upon the purchaser's actual payment of the price and not their engagement to do so. Blackburn observed that the writings of the earlier jurists, based upon a presumption of immediate transfer, had been supplanted by later commercial practices and mercantile intentions.[62] An examination was given to what Blackburn identified as modern rules for determining the intention of the parties as to the passing of property.

The civil law, as Blackburn was at pains to observe in an entire and comparative chapter on the subject, was completely different from English law with regard to the passing of property under a contract of sale. Blackburn chided those English judges and jurists who had inconsistently introduced civilian rules into

[62] Blackburn 1845, 149.

English law. The civil law assumed two principles not recognized by English law: first, that the sale must only be for a fixed monetary price; and second, property cannot be transferred by any agreement unless there was an act of the delivery of possession. 'It seems', Blackburn wrote, 'that this has not always been kept in sight by the English judges.'[63] Nevertheless, he thought it useful to produce extracts in translation from Pothier's *Contrat de Vente* as a means of demonstrating the fundamental principles of the civil law.[64] Blackburn opined that for the civilians a contract of sale without delivery amounted to a binding contract in the same way it did under English law. However, English law also transferred the property in the goods while the civil law had no such effect upon the property. Under the civil law there was a personal right binding only the vendor and not a proprietary right over the goods. In practical terms there might not be much of a difference, Blackburn wrote, because if the vendor was solvent and retained control of the goods he was bound to deliver the goods at the time contractually prescribed. Where, however, the rights of third parties intervened a substantial difference between the two systems emerged.[65] In identifying this difference Blackburn pointed to a problem which has continued to bedevil English law in ways not experienced by modern civilian systems.[66] Where, under English law, a vendor had delivered the goods to another or purported to sell them to another, the rights of the original purchaser to the goods prevailed. Similarly, where a vendor in possession of goods became a bankrupt the assignees in bankruptcy have no property in goods already sold to another and a buyer has their right against the goods. Blackburn disagreed that English law was in some way inferior to the civil law systems, possibly based on a misapprehension of the civil law. The passing of property by the contract was an 'ancient rule such as has existed since English law began'.[67]

Blackburn's treatise was a successful one. It was regularly referred to in court, American[68] and Canadian editions[69] were produced, and two later English editions followed.[70] However, the treatise in its first edition endured

[63] Ibid, 171.
[64] Ibid, 171–187.
[65] Ibid, 187–188.
[66] The arbitrary distinction between a mistake of identity and fraud expounded in *Shogun Finance Limited v Hudson* [2003] UKHL 62 both encapsulates the problem and relates its long and troubled development.
[67] Blackburn 1845, 190.
[68] In 1847, I. G. M'Kinley and J. M. G. Lescure published the work in Harrisburg, PA; later American reprintings also occurred.
[69] Raeburn & Thomas 1910b.
[70] Graham 1885, while the title remained the same the subject matter was greatly enhanced to include matters concerned with the contractual nature of sale; Raeburn & Thomas 1910a; Raeburn & Thomas 1910a was published to incorporate the changes brought by the Sale of Goods Act, 1893.

past the point of its utility. Commercial parties often had concerns about the quality or other aspects of the goods; the property-based approach of a system which also proceeded on the maxim *caveat emptor* did not meet their needs. The next treatise on sale marked a distinct change in the treatment of sale, with an emphasis on the contractual aspects of sale over the proprietary aspects. To understand the reasons behind this change requires a brief digression into the nature of legal history.

VI. English Economic Development and Legal Institutionalism

Legal history is the history of legal change: as a discipline it can be divided into two forms. The first is an 'internal' legal history in which attention is focused on the history of legal doctrines and how they are shaped in relation to each other over time.[71] The second is an 'external' legal history in which the focus is upon the impact of legal agencies on particular institutions and social practice, and vice versa, over time. In this form the historian explores the broader context of law and its effects. The consideration in this chapter has thus far been an internal one. An external perspective, however, provides insight into why the approach of treatise writers on sale changed in the latter half of the nineteenth century. The sale of goods, whether as raw commodities or manufactured products, is a vital element to economies. The treatise writers on sale wrote during a period of immense economic growth in the United Kingdom. Although economic historians differ in their calculation of industrial production, during the period between 1800 and 1830 this grew at an annual rate estimated at a low of 2.70 per cent to a high of 4.4 per cent. From 1830 to 1870 the estimates range from 2.9 to 3.1 per cent annual growth rates.[72] By the middle of the nineteenth century Britain was the workshop of the world. It is beyond the scope of this chapter to examine the many forces which led to this result. One critical factor, though, was the acquisition of scientific and practical knowledge: the understanding of why certain techniques worked and connecting them with formal propositional knowledge of the time. There was a development of technical manuals which worked to improve industrial processes.[73] The treatise writers on sale were producing legal manuals which attempted to

[71] Gordon 1975–76), 11.
[72] Mokyr 1999, 11. See, also, Broadberry et al 2015.
[73] Mokyr 2004, 19–21.

improve legal processes. It is striking that almost all explain this process as a reason for writing their treatises. Chitty wrote of 'the rapid extension of commerce, and the variety and increase of the transactions of mankind'[74] and he confined his contract treatise to 'simple contracts, which are of common occurrence in business, and are consequently of the highest practical utility'.[75] Ross expressly aimed his treatise not only at lawyers but also to educate merchants of the law which regulated their contracts.[76]

In his recent work, Hodgson has sought to explain English economic development on the basis of institutionalism, notably legal institutionalism.[77] Hodgson views as critical the development of legal rules around finance to economic growth: 'the expansion of financial and other markets helped to enhance the conditions for the Industrial Revolution'.[78] One of Hodgson's conclusions is that no one legal factor or institution is a recipe for economic development for 'institutions always depend on and are moulded by complex structures involving other institutions'.[79] Hodgson is not concerned with the law of sale but his institutionalist approach explains why treatises on the subject appeared. They were necessary to the functioning of this area of law. This is particularly true in a common law system. While common law development allowed the fine calibration of rules around infinite particular circumstances the common law requires access to often diffuse law reports and an understanding of the technical legal language within them. Treatises ameliorate the need for law reports and set out rules which enable legal professionals—and merchants—to acquire predictability around trade transactions. These are institutional rules which work to explain economic innovation and development.[80] Writing of the development of rules around sale helps to establish the nature of the rights involved, assists in structuring transactions, and works to predict the resolution of problems.

The need for an ascertainable law of sale was also critical in the functioning of Britain's mercantile empire. The rules surrounding the sale of imported commodities, such as cotton, wool, silk, timber, and tallow critical to manufacturing were significant in facilitating these trades. The same was true of commodities such as tea and sugar which were consumed without manufacturing processes. A significant proportion of imported commodities

[74] Chitty 1826, iii.
[75] Ibid, iv.
[76] Ross 1811, xi.
[77] Hodgson 2023.
[78] Ibid, 157.
[79] Ibid, 225.
[80] Ibid, 16–18.

were re-exported. Imperial trade increased throughout the period in which the treatise writers wrote.[81]

England, alone among European nations, made no concerted attempt to codify its law during this period of rapid economic expansion. English commercial law has been traditionally regarded as the product of the courts, through judicial decisions. Cranston has recently, and convincingly, argued that English commercial law was the product of merchants operating through and with markets, trade associations, and standard form contracts.[82] The driving force in commercial law was private trade associations, which devised a system of rules for market transactions, standard form contracts, and arbitral proceedings. Courts, he argued, tended largely to adapt to these mercantile practices. It is hard, though, to envision these commercial parties acting with a complete absence of legal advice, either obtained directly through works such as the treatises or from legal professionals who, in turn, relied upon treatise writers. In a system of uncodified law, in which this caselaw was formed by reference to procedure rather than principle, the treatise writers responded to a need to create easily accessible institutional rules for trade.

A further factor which worked to stimulate change in the nature of the treatises on sale lies in the extensive changes to the procedures and administration of justice in nineteenth-century England. The procedures of pleading, the process by which English litigants determined their dispute, became ever more cumbersome at the beginning of the nineteenth century; the remainder of the century saw repeated changes to these rules.[83] The most substantial of these changes occurred not long after Blackburn's treatise was published. In 1852, the forms of action were abolished completely[84] and their removal left 'conceptual conundrums'.[85] There has been little consideration of how these procedural changes affected the development of the substantive law. It is argued here that the removal of the forms of action, coupled with changes in evidentiary rules and a reform of the administration of justice resulting in the fused administration of law and equity, created the conditions necessary for jurists to begin thinking about their law in substantive terms, freed from the forms of action. Changed legal procedures created the conditions necessary for principled explanations of law. The process of re-explaining cases decided on procedure by

[81] An overview is provided by Cain 1999 and Zahedieh 2014.
[82] Cranston 2021.
[83] See MacMillan 2010, 71–82 for a detailed discussion of these Commissions and their reforms and some of the impact that this had upon the development of substantive law.
[84] Uniformity of Process Act 1832, 2 & 3 Will IV, c 39; Real Property Limitation Act 1933, 3 & 4 Will IV, c 27, s 36; Common Law Procedure Act 1852, 15 & 16 Vict c 76.
[85] Baker 2019, 76.

means of principle was often messy and as Maitland observed, 'the forms of action we have buried but they still rule us from their graves'.[86]

VII. Benjamin's *Treatise on the Law of Sale of Personal Property* (1868): From Property to Contract

It was within this context, of a need for institutional rules surrounding the sale of goods and a new attitude by jurists to how they articulated these rules, that Judah Benjamin fundamentally changed the way English contract treatises were written. The result of his treatise was to reshape the English law of sale and to cast it in a form familiar to modern lawyers. That this was not his life's ambition is one of history's ironies. Benjamin, like many novice barristers, wrote his treatise[87] to fill his time and to demonstrate his talents. Although a novice barrister, Benjamin was an extremely experienced lawyer when he wrote his treatise on sale. He had extensive experience of commercial law, of commerce, and the customs of merchants. He led an extraordinary life.[88] As a teenager Benjamin made his way to New Orleans, then a busy port with wealth drawn from trading in commodities harvested by enslaved Africans and shipped throughout the world. Benjamin taught himself law, was called to the Louisiana Bar in 1832, and by the 1840s was acknowledged as the preeminent commercial attorney in New Orleans before being admitted to practise before the United States Supreme Court in 1848. In the first fifteen years of his career he argued more appeals in Louisiana than any other lawyer and then repeated this achievement before the United States Supreme Court.[89] He also owned large numbers of slaves who laboured on his sugar plantation outside New Orleans: Benjamin also led innovation in sugar processing. He was a lawyer who had first-hand experience of commodity production. Benjamin's legal knowledge was greater than that of his British contemporaries. Louisiana was, and is, a mixed law jurisdiction. The Louisiana Digest of 1808 was a mixture of French and Spanish law; following the Code of 1825 Louisiana courts continued to consult French, Spanish, and Roman jurists in the application of the Code. Louisiana did not, however, enact the proposed Commercial Code Projet of 1825 and as a result Louisiana commercial law was developed by

[86] Maitland 1948, 2.
[87] Benjamin 1868.
[88] A more detailed consideration of Benjamin's life can be found in MacMillan 2020 and MacMillan 2015.
[89] Pritchett (2000), 73

its judiciary with reference to the commercial law of America. It is clear that Benjamin had a profound knowledge of the English common law in addition to his extensive civilian learning long before he wrote his treatise.[90]

Arriving in Britain in 1865, Benjamin described himself as a political exile. Benjamin had also been a politician. A Louisiana senator in the United States Senate, he left his seat when Louisiana seceded from the Union in 1861 and became a member of the Confederate States of America's cabinet. Fearing execution following the fall of the Confederacy Benjamin fled to England. Here, exceptionally, he became a barrister within a year of his arrival. Briefs came slowly, though, and so Benjamin wrote his treatise on sale. He chose his topic with care. The area was an important one, and Blackburn's treatise was not only confined to the proprietary aspects of sale but it was also outdated and written before the mid-century civil procedure reforms.

Benjamin's treatise was different from all that came before it. The treatise was an avowedly principled exposition of the contract of sale: 'it is not proposed in this treatise to enter into any discussion of questions of procedure'.[91] He began by rejecting Blackstone's definition of the sale of goods because it would include barter, an analogous but not identical transaction.[92] Instead, Benjamin defined sale in the general principles which governed all contracts:

> to constitute a valid sale, there must be a concurrence of the following elements, viz.: (1st), Parties competent to contract; (2nd), mutual assent; (3rd), a thing, the absolute or general property in which is transferred from the seller to the buyer; and (4th), a price in money paid or promised.[93]

Although he did not make the attribution, Benjamin took the definition from the French jurist Robert Joseph Pothier in his *Traité du Contrat de Vente* (1762). The consent, or the will, of the parties to engage in contract was central to Pothier's theory of contract. Benjamin borrowed this will theory and deployed it to provide an analytical framework to structure English contract law on the sale of goods. There was nothing new in this process, for English jurists had from time to time employed discrete elements of Pothier. Benjamin's innovation lay in using Pothier, particularly his will theory, as the central organizing element of his treatise. The borrowing occurred sometimes from Pothier directly and, at other times, through the Louisiana Civil Code.

[90] MacMillan 2020, 219–220.
[91] Benjamin 1868, 564.
[92] Ibid, 1.
[93] Ibid, 1–2.

The structure of Benjamin's treatise resembled that of Pothier's *Traité du Contrat de Vente*; he also drew upon Pothier's *Traité des Obligations* (1761). Will theory allowed Benjamin to develop his topic working chronologically through the life cycle of a contract in a series of five books, further subdivided into chapters. He began in Book I with those elements necessary to form a binding contract at common law. His consideration of the Statue of Frauds fit neatly within this formation although it had nothing to do with will. The next book analysed the effect of the contract in passing property. While the principal consideration was based on English case law, the book concluded with a chapter on the nature and effect of a sale by the civil law. In what amounted to a brief essay he surveyed the development of sale in Roman law before proceeding to consider its state in modern France. Having examined the proprietary aspects of sale, Benjamin returned to the contractual aspects of sale in a book entitled 'Avoidance of the Contract'. This chapter was given over to those elements Pothier identified as preventing consent: mistake, failure of consideration, and fraud. Benjamin included these elements for the same reason—because the vitiating element prevented assent—and also added illegality as English law had long refused to enforce illegal contracts. The next book analysed the performance of the contract of sale. This was undertaken by examining the contractual terms and the duties they imposed upon both vendors and buyers. His discussion of implied warranties as to title and quality were innovative and highly influential. They were based on a careful consideration of English cases and concluded that while *caveat emptor* had originally prevailed, preventing such implied terms, the newer approach was to allow an implied term as to title unless it was clear that the vendor did not intend to transfer title.[94] That this was a satisfactory situation was demonstrated by a discussion of both American and French law, each of which effectively stipulated that a vendor generally warranted that they had title in the good.[95] The final book was given over to a consideration of the effects of a breach of the contract of sale: the treatment firmly situated sale within contract law.

So emphatically did the treatise consider sale as a form of contract, emphasizing obligation over property, that it acted as a model for later writers of contract treatises.[96] Benjamin's treatise was employed by judges within contract cases in ways which changed areas of general contract law. This occurred in relation to the elements necessary to form a contract and also the doctrine of

[94] Ibid, 476.
[95] Ibid, 477–478.
[96] See, eg, Pollock 1876 and Anson 1879.

mistake. Benjamin's treatise is, for example, the driving force behind the (unhappy) creation of a doctrine of mistake in English contract law.[97] While his approach gave sale an intellectual coherence previously lacking it also produced its own problems in English law. It is important to emphasize that Benjamin was not advancing civil law, as such, but the common law organized and analysed on a civilian basis. While Pothier gave him a clear and logical structure, Benjamin raised nuanced, elegant arguments based on English decisions to support the rules he advanced. His emphasis on contract was undertaken both as an ideal intellectual structure for sale, but also because it enabled him to formulate the very rules that merchants, and their legal advisers, required. Approaching the subject as one of contract, based on principled expositions of law deduced from the cases gave the treatise utility as a manual of rules for merchants and their legal advisers. The new emphasis on contractual terms worked to predict resolutions for the practical problems bedevilling mercantile parties who received goods that were unsatisfactory in some way which impaired their utility as trade components.

The treatise is strikingly modern, largely because the contract-based approach to sale came to dominate as a result of Benjamin's work. The treatise met with immediate and unqualified judicial approval. Sir Samuel Martin, it was later said, instructed his clerk 'mind that I never take my seat here again without that book by my side'.[98] One result of this approval was that judges employed the treatise and its reasoning in resolving the disputes before them. A second result was in the sheer longevity and market domination of the treatise itself. Benjamin wrote a second edition in 1873[99] and supervised most of a third edition in 1883.[100] It has continued to the present day in later editions as the leading work on the subject. A third, more profound result was that it was Benjamin's recasting of sale as a matter more of contract than property which was codified as the Sale of Goods Act 1893, a decade after Benjamin's death. *Benjamin on Sale* had had a great impact upon not only on the structure and substance of the codification, but also the very act of codification. The draftsman of the Sale of Goods Act, 1893 was Sir Mackenzie Chalmers.[101] Chalmers was heavily reliant upon Benjamin's treatise in structure, language, and approach. It was Benjamin's recasting of sale as a matter of contract rather

[97] These additions are explored in greater detail in MacMillan 2018.
[98] *The Daily Telegraph*, 10 February 1883, 5.
[99] Benjamin 1873.
[100] Pearson & Boyd 1883.
[101] Chalmers 1886 and Chalmers 1903.

than property which was codified as the Sale of Goods Act 1893, a decade after Benjamin's death.

VIII. Conclusion

The writings of Victorian jurists on the sale of goods shifted from an emphasis on property and the civil procedures which protected it to one based on contract and the terms within it. The changed nature of the jurists' approach completed a process begun in the fifteenth century by firmly placing the sale of goods within the category of contract rather than property. This process provides insight into broader changes in the conceptualization of the English common law upon the basis of principles rather than procedures. It also demonstrates how various civil law ideas became incorporated, with often unfortunate consequences, into the formation of these principles. Finally, this process sheds light on a larger and more fundamental matter, how external economic factors influence legal development. The creation of a contract approach to sale in the nineteenth century was both a response to mercantile demand and also a stimulus for trade.

References

Anon. (1839). 'Critical Notices'. American Jurist and Law Magazine 21: 455–477.

Anson, W. R. (1879). *Principles of the English Law of Contract.* Oxford, Clarendon Press.

Baker, J. (2019). *Introduction to English Legal History.* 5th edn. Oxford, Oxford University Press.

Ballantine, W. (1883). *Some Experiences of a Barrister's Life by Mr Serjeant Ballantine. 8th edn.* London, Spottiswode and Co.

Benjamin, J. P. (1868). *A Treatise on the Law of Sale of Personal Property; with references to the American decisions and to the French Code and Civil Law.* London, Henry Sweet.

Benjamin, J. P. (1873). *A Treatise on the Law of Sale of Personal Property; with references to the American decisions and to the French Code and Civil Law*, 2nd ed. London, Sweet and Maxwell.

Blackburn, C. (1845). *A Treatise on the Effect of the Contract of Sale; on the Legal Rights and Property and Possession in Goods, Wares, and Merchandize.* London, William Benning and Co.

Blackstone, W. (2016). *Commentaries on the Laws of England, Vol 2: Of the Rights of Things* (1765) S. Stern and W. Prest. Oxford, Oxford University Press.

Broadberry, S., B.M.S. Campbell, A. Klein, M. Overton, and B. van Leeuwen. (2015). *British Economic Growth* 1270–1870. Cambridge, Cambridge University Press.

Cairns, J. W. (1984). 'Blackstone, An English Institutist: Legal Literature and the Rise of the Nation State'. *Oxford Journal of Legal History* 4: 318–360.

Cain, P. J. (1999). 'Economics and Empire: The Metropolitan Context'. *The Oxford History of the British Empire, Vol III The Nineteenth Century*. A. Porter. Oxford, Oxford University Press: 31–52.

Chalmers, M. D. (1886). 'An Experiment in Codification'. *Law Quarterly Review* 2: 125–134.

Chalmers, M. D. (1903). 'Codification of Mercantile Law'. *Law Quarterly Review* 19: 10–18.

Chitty, J., Jun. (1826). A Practical Treatise on the Law of Contracts, Not Under Seal; and upon The Usual Defences to Actions thereon. London, S. Sweet.

Comyn, S. (1807). *A Treatise of the Law Relative to Contracts and Agreements Not Under Seal; With Cases and Decisions Thereon in the Action of Assumpsit, vol II*. London, A. Strahan.

Cranston, R. (2021). *Making Commercial Law through Practice* 1830–1970. Cambridge, Cambridge University Press.

Dockray, M. (1986). 'Lord Lindley's Autobiography'. *Journal of Legal History* 7: 102–104.

Gordon, R. W. (1975–76). 'J. Willard Hurst and the Common Law Tradition in American Legal Historiography'. *Law and Society Review* 9: 9–55.

Graham, J. C. (1885). Lord Blackburn, A Treatise on the Effect of the Contract of Sale on the Legal Rights of Property and Possession in Goods, Wares, and Merchandise. 2nd edn. London, Stevens and Sons.

Hodgson, G. M. (2023). *The Wealth of a Nation: Institutional Foundations of English Capitalism*. Princeton, Princeton University Press.

Ibbetson, D. (1991). 'Sale of Goods in the Fourteenth Century'. *Law Quarterly Review* 107: 480–500.

Ibbetson, D. (1992). 'From Property to Contract: The Transformation of Sale in the Middle Ages'. *Journal of Legal History* 13: 1–22.

Lobban, M. (2018). 'Rationalising the Common Law: Blackstone and His Predecessors'. *Blackstone and His Critics*. A. Page and W. Prest. Oxford, Hart: 1–22.

Long, G. (1821) *A Treatise on the Law Relative to Sales of Personal Property*. London, J. & W.T. Clarke.

MacMillan, C. (2010). *Mistakes in Contract Law*. Oxford, Hart.

MacMillan, C. (2015). 'Judah Benjamin: Marginalized Outsider or Admitted Insider?' *Journal of Law and Society* 42: 150–172.

MacMillan, C. (2018). 'Legal Development from a Comparative Perspective: English Contract Law in the Nineteenth Century'. *Global Legal History: A Comparative Law Perspective*. J. C. Tate, J. Reinaldo de Lima Lopes, and A. Botero Bernal. Abingdon and New York, Routledge: 39–52.

MacMillan, C. (2020). 'Trans-Atlantic Connections: The Many Networks and the Enduring Legacy of J.P. Benjamin'. *Networks and Connections in Legal History*. M. Lobban and I. Williams. Cambridge, Cambridge University Press: 210–232.

Maitland, F. W. (1948). *The Forms of Action at Common Law*. Cambridge, Cambridge University Press.

Milsom, S. F. C. (1961). 'Sale of Goods in the Fifteenth Century'. *Law Quarterly Review* 77: 257–284.

Milsom, S. F. C. (1981a). *Historical Foundations of the Common Law*. 2nd edn. London, Butterworths.

Milsom, S. F. C. (1981b). 'The Nature of Blackstone's Achievement'. *Oxford Journal of Legal Studies* 1: 1–12.

Mokyr, J. (1999). 'Editor's Introduction: The New Economic History and the Industrial Revolution'. *The British Industrial Revolution: An Economic Perspective*. 2nd edn. J. Mokyr. Boulder Co, Westview Press: 1–127.

Mokyr, J. (2004). 'Accounting for the Industrial Revolution'. *The Cambridge Economic History of Modern Britain, Vol I: Industrialisation,* 1700–1860. R. Floud and P. Johnson. Cambridge, Cambridge University Press: 1–27.

Pearson, A. B. and H. F. Boyd. (1883). *Benjamin's Treatise on the Law of Sale of Personal Property; with references to the American Decisions and to the French Code and Civil Law.* London, Henry Sweet.

Pollock, F. (1876). *Principles of Contract at Law and in Equity.* London, Stevens and Sons.

Pritchett, C. D. (2000). 'Case Law Reporters in Nineteenth-Century Louisiana. A Law Unto Itself?' *Essays in the New Louisiana Legal History.* W. Billings and M. Fernandez. Baton Rouge, Louisiana State University Press: 58–75.

Raeburn, W. N. and L. C. Thomas (1910a). *Lord Blackburn, A Treatise on the Effect of the Contract of Sale.* 3rd edn. London, Stevens and Sons.

Raeburn, W. N. and L. C. Thomas (1910b). *Lord Blackburn, A Treatise on the Effect of the Contract of Sale,* 3rd edn, with Canadian Notes by the Honorable Mr Justice Russell. Toronto, Canada Law Book Company.

Ross, G. (1811). *A Treatise on the Law of Vendors and Purchasers of Personal Property; Considered chiefly with a View to Mercantile Transactions.* London, R. Bickerstaff.

Zahedieh, N. (2014). 'Overseas Trade and Empire. *The Cambridge Economic History of Modern Britain: Vol I 1700–1870.* 2nd edn. R. Floud, J. Humphries, and P. Johnson. Cambridge, Cambridge University Press: 392–420.

14

Properties of Debt

History and Analysis

Joshua Getzler

I. Introduction

Contracts can have immediate proprietary consequences: for example, at common law a bargain and sale of goods where a price is agreed is capable of moving title once the goods are ascertained, even where possession has not moved and the price has not been tendered.[1] Debt presents a different picture: it is a personal duty binding the debtor to transfer unascertained monetary value to the creditor based on some agreement, and in these terms has no proprietary consequences. Yet debt is set up commonly enough to retire or return a prior loan or debt, sometimes to reciprocate value following an executed transfer of property, and sometimes to carry out a formalized promise to pay on conditions grounding a specific performance order attaching particular property and keeping out rival claimants. Moreover, techniques of debt transfer allow reification of the debt as an assignable value, an instrument of wealth. Debt is clearly embroiled with the institution of property as well as contract, and this chapter seeks to draw out and explain those connections. The study proceeds first by isolating the core incidents of debt, setting out in schematic form some lines of inquiry and analysis. Next comes a denser historical narrative, showing how various legal traditions combined to produce the basics of debt, including development of money instruments and payment mechanisms. We conclude with some reflections on how debt enforcement can locate and partition debtor assets, and generate fresh forms of wealth, further ways in which the personal liabilities of debtorship yield proprietary consequences.

[1] Sale of Goods Act 1979 (UK), ss 17–18. Historically a collateral bailment in favour of the purchaser was implied into a perfected sale to shift title without necessitating a patent conveyance: Milsom 1985, 121–126.

Joshua Getzler, *Properties of Debt* In: *The Property-Contract Interface*. Edited by: James Penner, Irina Sakharova, Henry E. Smith, and Zhong Xing Tan, Oxford University Press. © Joshua Getzler 2026.
DOI: 10.1093/9780198951995.003.0018

II. Fourteen Incidents

Tony Honoré in his famous Ownership paper of 1961 suggested how isolating the typical incidents of a legal institution can assist analysis. He found fourteen incidents of property. The next section is a straight-out homage to and emulation of the Honoréan technique.[2]

1. Debt comprises a duty binding the debtor to pay over a liquid value to a creditor, typically an enumerated money sum.
2. Debt is a duty personal to the debtor, that is, attached to the person of the debtor; at the same time law often makes one person responsible for the debts of another due to conduct or status.
3. There has always been a moral and social quality to personal debt relations going beyond economic and instrumental rationality.
4. The core of debt is contractual, being an agreement to pay a sum set as an entire obligation by the parties.
5. The causes of debt are highly varied and must be identified to work out the contours of the particular debt relationship—paying off a prior loan, paying the price for goods or services, paying rent or hire for the use of assets, meeting a formally covenanted obligation to transfer monetary value, and so on.
6. Contractual debt tends to register as a strict liability, in the sense that the creditor does not have to prove any fault or mind-state pertaining to the debtor, nor assert any proximate loss caused to the creditor as a consequence of non-payment.
7. Debts based on compensation for wrongdoing by contrast may be adjusted to take into account relative fault and proximate causation, and debts for an agreed sum are sometimes converted by the law into damages claims for remedial convenience.
8. A debt does not attach any particular assets of the debtor, without some further legal annex, for example by the operation of a security agreed by the parties or by legal convention, or through the imposition of a receivership or other insolvency regime.
9. There is no necessary temporal dimension to the performance of the payment obligation; debts can theoretically last forever. A due payment date may be specified *ex ante*, or the creditor may have a power to call in a debt without term and thereby fix a payment date *ex post*. Limitation

[2] Cf Honoré 1961, also 1960.

periods historically ran from the inception of an open-ended debt, setting an external term on collection; nowadays time of limitation tends to run from the point of demand.

10. There are many types of obligation to pay fixed sums set by law, for example, judgment debts articulating claims to compensate for wrongs, to make restitution of invalid or unjustified transfers, to level accounts held by fiduciaries, and to pay fines and taxes required by public authority. These various debt forms, all originating in *ex lege* orders, are distinct from the core of contracted debt duties, namely to pay an agreed sum. An order to pay damages for a breach of a contractual debt obligation might be seen as straddling the distinction of agreed sums and judgment debts, but such payment orders are ultimately best classified in the second category, as a species of judgment debt.
11. There is no general right to accrue interest on a contracted debt outside the agreement of the parties, though many other forms of debt, for example, judgment debts do attract court-ordered interest.
12. The personal nature of debt has implications where a debt is incurred on behalf of another, or a debt payment is made on behalf of another, or guaranteed by another. Rules must be formulated to control when the creditor can seek recourse against the debtor, or the debtor's principal, or the debtor's sureties; and conversely, when a debtor or surety laying out money for another can recover the expenditure against the principal. To solve these issues the law must construct rules of authority, vicarious liability, accountability, indemnity, guarantee, and subrogation.
13. Working around the personal nature of debt obligations, the law has developed many forms of effective debt assignment: adjustment of ledger debts to the order of a bank customer; negotiation of commercial claims within mercantile communities, including transfers of commercial paper; equitable assignment by declaration or for value; and legal assignment by novation or statutory attornment. All of these methods are as much accounting measures as transfers of any valuable commodity, and are designed to adjust a dynamic state of obligations between networks of persons trading goods and services and investing capital.
14. The hyper assignability of debt creates losses and systemic fragilities. Parties will now insert anti-assignment clauses in their contracts to maintain the personal principle in debt relations, and to avoid loss of set-off claims and defences. There is also an increased danger of credit bubbles and runs as assignable debts become pyramided and interdependent; this interdependence defeats market estimation of the

expected value of debt. Crypto assets as a novel private system of money and payment compound the problem: it is not clear who controls and guarantees the ledgers recording the state of these debt accounts, and failures in crypto credit can leak into the general payment and banking system.

One could continue listing stipulative definitions covering more of the domains of law where debt operates; but a map covering too much territory starts to resemble the territory itself and becomes useless as a guide.[3] And even with a good guide in hand it is appropriate to concentrate on just a handful of sights on the journey; not every one of my incidents can be explored on this occasion.

III. Personal Liability—Moral and Social Dimensions

The personal nature of debtorship tying the debtor to the creditor was portrayed in ancient legal sources as having a moral basis, not entirely based on the positive virtues of mutual help and fair cooperation, but rather negatively, on shame and exploitation. The Hebrew Bible recommended that the rich should freely lend to the poor to support them in times of dearth, adding an expectation that such debts should be lightly enforced or forgiven; yet entry into debtorship was also portrayed as a sinful weakness on the part of the debtor, linked to dominating and exploitative conduct on the part of the creditor. To be placed into indebtedness was to put oneself into a state of subordination, even in the absence of usurious interest charges owed to the creditor.[4]

In ancient law, there could also be subordinations *within* the class of debtors, with debts extending to bind persons with linked patrimonies, as where a head of a family had authority over and responsibility for the household members. We find this tendency most strongly drawn in Roman law. Husbands might be liable for the debts of wives, fathers for their children, masters for slaves and employees (including noxal liabilities when subordinates misbehaved towards strangers), and so on. The implication was that the head of the family should discipline the members and govern the group to curb liability and avoid indebtedness; the head shared in or was the source of the personal duty to repay debt. One way to structure this responsibility was to accord a fund known as a

[3] Borges 1946.
[4] Cf Exodus 22: 25–27; Deuteronomy 15: 1–11 [KJV 1611]; *Midrash Rabbah* 1977, ii, 378–386; Seabourne 2003, 27–69. The literature on usury and debt is beyond enormous; for suggestive narrative, see Graeber 2014.

peculium to a particular subordinate and so direct creditors to recourse against that fund alone, protecting the family from unlimited liability for the debts of individual members.[5]

The negative moral assessment of debt in ancient law also justified stringent personal enforcement mechanisms levied against the recalcitrant debtor, especially addressing concealment of the means to repay which implied a fraudulent or criminal intent, a kind of theft of means from the creditor. The early Roman self-help tactic of arrest of the person of the debtor to coerce payment or performance merged into the practice of peonage or debt enslavement, in effect bonding the labour of the debtor and allowing the income stream from that labour to be capitalized by onward sale of the person. Such debt peonage is found across many ancient legal systems as a means to recover debt, though there was wide variation in the permitted durations and intensities of bonded labour. For example, classical Jewish law insisted on the continued autonomy and family life of the bonded debtor and enforced his release in the sabbatical (seventh) year, with the backstop of the jubilee (fiftieth) year as a release of all debts whenever contracted, freeing each generation from an oppressive and permanent state of subordination. Certainly the creditor could not transfer the bonded debtor involuntarily to another master. Romans were less forgiving and saw the incompetent debtor as suffering a civic death, going beyond a loss of legal capacity to trade and go to law. At the time of the Twelve Tables the law even seems to countenance *pari passu* division of the body itself of a recalcitrant debtor, with the creditors cutting him up into pieces proportionate to the debts incurred. More likely the hopelessly indebted person simply moved into a permanent state of unfreedom, to be worked or sold at the master's will. Debt could thus turn the person of the debtor into property.

English common law did not countenance enslavement of debtors, but down to the early nineteenth century relied heavily on arrest and imprisonment of debtors as an enforcement mechanism. On the surface this phenomenon is puzzling: although not as permanent as death or enslavement, imprisonment will still nullify or diminish the debtor's free ability to raise money to pay. Imprisonment also used up resources better applied to acquittal of the debt; the incarcerated had to find money to buy food from their gaolers. The true basis of imprisonment of debtors was hostage taking, with the family and friends put to work to raise ransom money to free the debtor, transferring to them the incentive to restore the breadwinner to home, hearth, and gainful employment. If the family circle were dispersed or immiserated and unavailable to pay then

[5] Abatino and Dari-Mattiacci 2020.

incarceration had little point save pleasing a desire for vengeance and deterrence of future debtors. Lord Chancellor St Leonards, Edward Sugden (1781–1875), who came from humble origins and had direct experience of economic insecurity, worked persistently to abolish debtors' prison, seeing that in times of industrialization and urbanization it made little sense to arrest debtors and neutralize their earning capacity with their relatives perhaps out of reach. Charles Dickens (1812–70), whose father was cast into debtors' prison when he was 12, made abolition of imprisonment for debt his cause too, portraying its cruelty and stupidity in *Little Dorrit* (1855–57). Partial abolition of debtors' prison was not attained until 1869, and was retained for fraudulent non-payers and those who flagrantly resisted court orders.[6] By contrast the new United States of America as a frontier society made up of self-improving immigrants largely abandoned the moral stigmas surrounding indebtedness, and banned all imprisonment for debt in 1833, accepting that persons striving to establish themselves in uncertain economic conditions might easily fall into insolvency. This pro-debtor stance passed risk back to their lenders who were expected to assess probabilities of failure and price these into the credit bargain. On some estimates more than half of all free males in nineteenth-century America experienced personal insolvency at some stage of their lives, which helps explain the extreme mobility of labour as persons burdened by debt simply walked away to a new state jurisdiction, generally westward. The federal cross-border insolvency jurisdiction was one legal response to this phenomenon.[7]

Friedrich Nietzsche in *The Genealogy of Morals* perceptively observed that the German phrase *schuld* could mean both a debt owed, and a state of guilt—a rupture of morality.[8] Christian tradition saw debt as tantamount to a sinful condition that was praiseworthy to forgive; charitable gifts to the needy were seen as more ennobling for both sides than lending.[9] Arguably it took the Protestant Reformation to remove the stigma of debt as sin lingering within Christian society, and to see the institution of debtorship as a rational shift of spending power across time and persons, the better to enhance the productive potential of society.[10]

We now turn from the moral history of debt to the legal history.

[6] Markham Lester 1995.
[7] Mann 2009.
[8] Nietzsche 2013, essay 2, ss 1–7.
[9] Matthew 18:27 ff; cf 6:12.
[10] Weber 1985.

IV. The Causes of Debt

1. Classical Roman Law

Historically debt obligations encompassed a duty to convey a fixed or measured or 'liquid' quantum of any fungible good, such as corn, or oil, or metals, precious or not. Return of money to retire a loan was just a sub-class of the idea of a return of fungibles. The return of a liquid debt was seen in the classical law of Gaius (*c* 161 CE) and Justinian (533 CE) as one of the so-called 'real contracts', instituted by a *iusta causa* (just cause) of delivery requiring an exact reciprocation. The relevant contractual sub-category of real contract was known as *mutuum*; being a type of 'repo' contract in modern legal argot, a duty to replace like with like:

> An obligation is contracted by means of the thing itself, as, for example, in the case of a loan in kind (*mutuum*). Now the obligation of loan in kind applies to those things which are estimated by weight, number, or measure, as, for example, wine, oil, corn, coined money, copper, silver, gold, which things we give either by counting, or measuring, or weighing them, in order that they may become the property of those receiving them, and the same things lent are not returned to us, but others of the same nature and quality; and, hence, this is called a *mutuum*, because the thing is so given by me to you that from being mine it becomes yours (*ex meo tuum*). From this contract arises the action termed a *condictio*.[11]

One had to distinguish the *condictio* based on *mutuum* from one based on *emptio* or sale, and distinguish these again from a formalized undertaking to give value known as *stipulatio*. Each had a fundamentally different cause: loan, bargain, promise; though each resulted in debt. The early classical jurist Gaius offers a fascinating discussion of the adjectival law of actions, or the legal methods by which things, *res*, assets both proprietary and obligational, were to be claimed. It was in the law of actions rather than of causes where much of the work of juridical classification and analysis was done. Gaius came down to the view that the return of a loan was a translation through the condiction converting a real claim into a personal form of action. By contrast sales and bonds transferring value upon willed consent or agreement were condictions in the purely personal sphere. These latter actions were to be distinguished from real

[11] Justinian 1987, 14 pr, based on Gaius 1946, 3.90.

actions to secure a specific thing, or its money equivalent as a pecuniary condemnation, perhaps with damages, if there was some bar to real recovery. The Gaian text is worth studying closely:

> It remains to speak of actions. If we ask how many classes of actions there are, the better view is that there are two, real and personal (*in rem* and *in personam*). Those who say that there are four, by including those actions based on wagers (*per sponsiones*) have failed to observe the distinction between species and genus.
>
> A personal action is one which we maintain when we sue someone who is under an obligation to us from contract or delict—that is, when our assertion is that he ought to give, do, or fulfil (*dare, facere, praestare*).
>
> A real action is one in which we assert that a corporeal thing is ours or that a right belongs to us, as for instance a right of use or usufruct, a right of way for man or beast, of aqueduct, or a right to build higher or a right to see out. Conversely, a real action can deny that our opponent has such a right.
>
> Actions being distinguished in this way, it is certain that we cannot claim from another something that belongs to us using the words 'if it appears he ought to give'. For something which is ours cannot be given to us. You will understand that giving something to us is defined to mean giving in such a way as to make it ours and that a thing which is already ours cannot be made more ours. It is clearly from hatred of thieves, to make them liable to more actions, that it has been accepted that, in addition to their liability to fourfold or twofold penal damages, they can also be sued using this form of claim, 'if it appears that they ought to give'. This is in addition to the availability against them of the action in which we assert that a thing is ours.
>
> Real actions are called 'vindications'. Personal actions in which we assert that something ought to be given to, or done for us are called condictions.[12]

To restate the tenor of this analysis: Romans tended to classify actions rather than rights as having an obligational or proprietary dimension. The reason why a contractual debt was enforced by a condiction was because it was an obligation on a particular person to do something (find a payment sum and transfer it) rather than a claim to a particular thing.

Condictio in early procedure did not exactly correlate with a personal duty to pay. It involved a decrying of the debtor in public as a prelude to personal condemnation in the event of non-appearance or non-performance, followed

[12] Gaius 1946, 4.1–4.5; cf Justinian 1987, 4.6.

by enslavement or execution. Later procedure mimicked the less violent self-help procedure of *vindicatio* with a payment into court by *sponsio* of the value of the sought performance. When the type of *condictio* was for a sum certain (*actio certae pecuniae creditae*) then that sum would automatically move to the claimant if successful.[13] Modern legal systems may require sums to be paid into court or bonded as sureties before expensive litigations commence, to ensure at least that the legal professionals get paid, or that a proffered pre-trial settlement is not wastefully scorned; these stakings of wealth to support effective settlement and litigation strategies are a partial echo of the earliest Roman procedures.

Much of this early Roman law as codified in the Twelve Tables showed an obsessive concern with requiring parties actually to turn up when summoned to court. At its most basic level that is the meaning of *condictio*—'with a summons' (*con dictio*) you are called to answer for an obligation before the law. A refusal might result in a declaration of *infamia*, an official labelling that excluded the bearer of the ill repute from accessing the legal system, since one had flouted that very system. Persons labouring under *infamia*, and their households, could be subjected to taunts and violence reducing their dignity (*iniuria*), and perhaps equally important, their contractual word was now worthless and their credit undermined; the infamous might also lose *commercium*, the privilege or power of trading. Other pre-modern legal systems (Viking, Anglo-Saxon and Anglo-Norman) have used a similar tactic of outlawry, which could be the most important available sanction where centralized state enforcement is weak or non-existent.

There were conceptual limits to the Roman actions for a liquid sum. After debate the classical lawyers decided that a bartered exchange (as opposed to a money sale) of non-fungibles could not involve price and was not subject to the debt action of *condictio*, as no monetary transfer had occurred and it was impossible to determine who bore the duties of the seller and who those of the buyer; this was the case even if the parties may have measured the exchange by reference to the putative money price of each object.[14] Classical law nonetheless accepted the adjustment of book debts as a kind of money payment known as *litteris*, that was enforceable if one of the parties denied the adjustment.[15] Moreover a payment where the payor made an error as to the cause requiring payment or mistook the identity of the payee could result in a *condictio* action

[13] Buckland 1963, 682–684.
[14] Justinian 1987 23.2–3.
[15] Ibid, 21.pr.

claiming a debt equivalent to the value of the transferred money. This was acknowledged to be a debt constructed by law, even if the texts spoke of it 'as if" *(quasi)* there were a contract; Gaius notes that it is really an action to 'dissolve' a payment transaction, yielding an oblique counter-payment obligation outside the will of the recipient.[16] There is no sense that the payor can claim back the actual coins; it is not a vindication of the money objects.

2. Common Law

Roman ideas of debt can be seen to reproduce in English common law forms, but using radically different legal language. In 1964 Professor Samuel Stoljar propounded a 'proprietary' theory of restitution for English law, observing that courts from the late seventeenth and eighteenth centuries would often order an *ex lege* money return in cases where property 'without earmark' such as money or fungibles had shifted from one patrimony to another without due cause.[17] Stoljar wove his theory from antique common-law actions of account, bailment, and implied contract ('quasi-contract') and perhaps for reasons of obscure nomenclature his theory found an uncertain reception in the common law world. In a sense Stoljar was reviving the Roman ideas of *condictio* following upon *mutuum*, explaining how liquid debts might arise by transfers or deliveries of fungibles and money independent of contractual agreement. This infusion of Roman principle into common law was continued by Peter Birks with his intensified development of unjust and unjustified enrichment law.[18] The lurking problem with Birksian theory was working through what was meant by 'enrichment' in the absence of an articulate theory of money and debt.[19]

A proprietary theory of debt obligation for the common law can be given more convincing historical support if we move focus to early medieval forms of contract as bargain and promise. Pre-modern common lawyers might have been hard pressed to distinguish a claim to collect a sum certain raised upon an obligation, from a claim to the proceeds or transfer of some property. The blurring of obligational and proprietary categories was found most intensely in the form of action for debt, which by the late thirteenth century was used extensively to recover fixed money sums due under loan, sale, rent, pledge, or bond.[20]

[16] Gaius 1946, 3.91, also Justinian 1987, 14.1.
[17] Stoljar 1964.
[18] Summarized in Birks 2005.
[19] Fox 1996, 2008.
[20] Pollock & Maitland 1895, ii, 208–214.

A like union of obligational and proprietary enforcement may be detected in the early feudal actions of account, replevin, distress, and waste, and also in the later trespassory actions of detinue, trover, conversion, and assumpsit on bargains. Through such personal actions, the law was often concerned to effect the recovery of assets or their value, where title had moved to the obligor subject to some overt or intended reciprocal obligation. The court's judgment might state that the obligor was liable to pay a liquidated sum equivalent to the value of the asset vested with the obligor, whether on an objective measure set by the court or according to the subjective estimate of the parties set by an accompanying agreement.[21] The various narrations or common counts explained why a debt *sur contract* had arisen by the parties' prior conduct. Such claims could be contrasted with debt *sur obligation*, where a covenant deed or bond had been executed stipulating an agreed debt performance. This mirrored the terrain of classical Roman law, deploying *condictiones* to enforce the return of an asset or its value, whether in specie or in some fungible or cash equivalent, in order to satisfy the obligee's settled expectation of return for some original act of transfer to the obligor on terms, contrasting with stipulations enforcing unilateral formal promises independent of exchange.[22]

At the head of the common law tradition, Ranulf de Glanvill (a judicial registrar wielding royal judicial authority akin to a chief justice, writing around 1187-89) overtly drew analogies between the nascent English debt and covenant actions on the one hand, and the Roman real and stipulatory contracts on the other. His text also reproduces many of the features of the *condictio* forms of action in describing the operation of the common law debt procedures.[23] Glanvill also asserted, somewhat surprisingly, a monopoly of Crown common law courts over debt claims, mirroring the real actions and petty assizes asserting a ubiquitous royal jurisdiction over seisin and estates. One surmise is that Glanvill was here tracking the competition between royal and ecclesiastical jurisdiction, in the wake of the quarrel between Henry II and Archbishop Thomas à Becket leading to the latter's assassination. The church courts had been nibbling at royal and secular jurisdiction by imposing spiritual penances on recalcitrant debtors as sinners, and the assertion of a royal monopoly on debt as the lifeblood of commerce helped enhance secular royal

[21] Stoljar 1975, 3-15; Simpson 1975, 9-135. For the overlap of detinue (trespass damages for withholding specific property) and debt (obligation to pay a sum certain of money or a quantum of fungibles), see Milsom 1985, 105–126; Ibbetson 2001, 30–38. Merchants might alternatively plead debt on account to assert complex credit and factoring arrangements: Milsom 1985, 133–144.

[22] Gaius 1946, 4.1–4.9 ff; Justinian 1987, 4.6; Birks 2014, 27-36, 65-155.

[23] Glanvill 1965, 116-132; Ibbetson 2001, 17-21; Hudson 2012, 696-703.

power, just as the possessory assizes led to royal dominance in the feudal property sphere. The result was a claim of the early common law to be the guardian and enforcer of all assets of all subjects, real or personal, overlaying all inferior jurisdictions.

Oliver Wendell Holmes Jr traced an alternative, entirely non-Roman genesis of early English debt, also with a proprietary base but seeing origins in the criminal law. He described the earliest common law debt actions as emerging from procedures to repress felonious takings of property, whereby holders were put on proof in the country to show a rightful descent of their title to goods or land.[24] On accusation of a wrongful taking or withholding, the holder of an asset would make a compurgation—'waging his (or her) law'—in the sense of invoking friendly self-informing witnesses to vouch for the truth of an oath-taking defence asserting a decent origin of the possession, sometimes by gift or finding, more commonly by voluntary transaction. This procedure developed into a contractual action, where a claimant might bring suit or *secta* swearing that a transfer had been conditioned on a reciprocal obligation requiring the defendant to pay a price, so asserting that a debt was owed. In this context, the suit did not address the defendant's title in order to prove or negate a felonious taking, but rather adduced a liability for unperformed payment under a contract. The defendant would then face the jeopardy of finding compurgators to support the denial of, or defence to, liability.[25] If proved or conceded, the debt claim made for an obligation on the person of the defendant to render a transfer of value in cash form, with the pleading showing the circumstances raising the debt *sur contract*, such as a sale or hire of land or goods, a bestowal of personal service, an executed loan, or a surety for the performance or title of another.

Holmes's theory helps explain both a strength and weakness of the action of debt. It won legitimacy by yoking proof of debt to local witnesses prepared to vouch for the truth telling of one or other of the parties; but in its decadence it also allowed the litigation to be swayed by the wealth and deviousness of a party in hiring witnesses prepared to swear his or her cause. It may be that blatant perjurious use of suit was inhibited only by fear of reputational loss. Despite its cumbersome procedures of suit and compurgation, debt provided the key form of contractual action down to the late fourteenth century. The debt action then faded in importance, displaced by actions of covenant, account, and assumpsit, which used formal writing, audit, and jury trial respectively as

[24] Holmes 1882, 251-288.
[25] Simpson 1975, 137-144.

superior modes of proof of payment obligations.[26] A turning point came with *Slade's Case* at the turn of the seventeenth century,[27] which provided that any contractual agreement hitherto sounding in debt could be brought in the alternative as trespass on the case for assumpsit. The court in that case 'commanded judgment to be entered for the plaintiff', covering payment for damage caused by non-performance as assessed by the jury, plus costs, thus in effect constituting the remedy after weighing the causative facts. The implication was that damage or harm to the claimant's fortune caused by contractual misfeasance now lay at the heart of voluntary liabilities; and this displaced the older mode, which saw debt as the expected return on an executed transfer or performance, taking effect as an agreed sum without remoulding for consequential loss, comparative fault, or pre-judgment interest.[28]

Prior to the rise of assumpsit, there was an election between an action for debt, based on compurgation as evidence, and the action on a covenant, a specialty claim involving a formality establishing a strict liability to pay a sum certain if that was what the deed required. By adapting the covenantal duty to pay into a conditional duty alleviated or made defeasible if a contractual performance was rendered, the covenant could be turned into a general law of contract with good security of performance or compensation built into the action. Because the parties were seen to be self-legislating by constitution of their specialty rights outside the general common law process, the courts of common law treated such debts as superior to those arising under the general action of debt or the later trespassory substitute, the assumpsit action. Hence specialty debts had priority over general debts, and were resistant to many of the limitations and defences of the internal common law actions. Covenants theoretically continued as a pathway to debt enforcement into the modern era, but the formality requirements undermined its usage in busy commercial contexts. The idea that parties might strictly contract for the payment of a sum certain subject to conditional defeasance by a valid performance continues on in modern law with the action on the agreed sum, which is not discounted by mitigation or counterfactual assessment of loss.[29]

[26] Palmer 1993, 64-78, 140-213, 328-364; Baker 2019b, 338–368.

[27] *Slade v Morley* (1598–1602) 4 Co Rep 91, 76 ER 1072; Yelv 21, 80 ER 15; Moo KB 433, 467, 72 ER 677; Baker 2019a, 460-479; Simpson 1958; Baker 1971; Ibbetson 1984.

[28] The availability of interest on debts for agreed sums and judgment debts is a complex topic, ably dissected in Lau 2024.

[29] *Cavendish Square Holding BV v Talal El Makdessi* [2016] AC 1172; *Office of Fair Trading v Abbey National plc* [2010] 1 AC 696; *White and Carter (Councils) Ltd v McGregor* [1962] AC 413; Georgiou 2025.

The promise to pay an agreed sum is thus revealed to lie at the core of debt. Peeling away from the procedural history, debt is fundamentally the duty to pay for some exchange value: a price for sale of a good, a rent, hire, toll, or fee for use; a fare or freight for carriage; a wage, commission, retainer, or bonus for labour service; a personal guarantee for security. All these personal contractual debts are agreed sums promised to be paid in a reciprocal relationship. The cause of the debt, and the benefit being procured for the price, may vary widely across these instances, with different legal incidents bearing on each case. But if the creditor's offering is seriously proffered or executed, the debtor then has the simple contractual debt to pay the agreed sum. The special case of the covenanted debt made without the necessity of an exchange can be assimilated to the contractual model as a debt agreed to be paid because of the will to benefit the other side embodied in a formal instrument addressed by obligor to an obligee who does not disavow the benefit.[30]

This category of primary contractual debt may be distinguished from a very wide variety of court orders to pay money, which derive from a spectrum of causes ranging from imposed state controls and sanctions to adjustment or afforcing of voluntary relations. The spectrum includes debts arising from taxes; debts arising from regulatory and criminal penalties and fines; debts to level accounts of agencies, trusts, or estates; debts to be paid out of insolvency procedures and receiverships; debts to reverse unjust enrichments including payments under mistaken or failed transactions; and money orders made generally to compensate losses from wrongs or to react to trespasses (more simply put, damages). All of these debt obligations are formally grounded not in party will, but in public judicial authority reacting to pleading of fact and law in court; each category has an entangled jurisprudence exploring the cause of the debt and its juristic nature. The resulting order is a *judgment debt*, that is, a debt ordered by the courts, to uphold a requirement of public order, or to resolve a judicial matter or cause brought by a private party. Leaving aside the special case of tax debts, such a judgment debt does not exist until the court speaks and makes orders, unlike a contractual loan obligation or duty to pay on a fully or part executed contract. The judgment debt is a step on the path to enforcement of a prior duty. To enforcement we now turn.

[30] *Sharrington v Strotton* (1565) Plowden 298, 75 ER 454.

V. The Consequences of Debt

1. Payment

Debt is acquitted by payment, and this engages a raft of questions as to how the law understands the transfer of monetary value. Handing over instruments of money, coins, or notes, is the obvious meaning of payment, and it is of the nature of money that title to money (ultimate control and disposition of the value embodied in the monetary instrument) passes on delivery. Some Roman texts suggested that delivery or *traditio* of money could be broken down into a directed abandonment, the *traditio incertae personae*, suggesting that there need be no face-to-face encounter of payor and payee.[31]

A key instance of the non-monetary payment of debt, that is, a payment without transfer of monetary instruments, involves the offset of a reciprocal debt or a reduction of an obligation denominated in money's worth, allowing discharge by netting or reduction of an extant counter obligation. Another step is reached when creditor A can instruct debtor B (a deposit-holding bank) to reduce the debt between them by increasing the credit owed by the bank to C, who is simultaneously a creditor of A. The increase of C's credit with B to A's order then retires the A–C debt. This is now probably the most common form of payment: we enlarge and reduce ledger entries recording extant credits of our payors and payees with banks subject to a central clearing system. The system of interlaced book debts managed by banks, involving the constant adjustment of credit value held by individuals against bank deposits, does not change the fundamental legal nature of the payment obligation as a duty to make over a liquid or summed value from debtor to creditor. It does imply that privately held accounting measures replaces state-fiated money as the medium of account, store of value, and means of payment.[32] Attempts to portray banks taking deposits as responsible bailees or fiduciaries for the value left in their charge were repelled by the English courts in the mid-nineteenth century, insisting that the bank was merely a debtor with superadded but restricted account duties including duties to make payments on instruction. Absent any term to the debt, a conventional limitation period was held to apply such that banks could refuse to return deposits after the limitation period had passed; the purely personal nature of the deposit relationship as simple debt could not be shaken. The concept of *depositum irregulare*, requiring a bank to hold

[31] Cf Fox 2008; Daube 1961.
[32] Desan 2014; Fox & Ernst 2016; Gleeson 2018.

sufficient global value to responsibly cover all customer credits, did not take hold.[33] This is an important chapter in the history of bank finance, where the courts held that simple debt structures lay at the foundation of bank deposit-taking in order to enhance fractional reserve issues, maturity transformations, pooling of default risk, and a vast ensuing expansion of credit. The bank deposit and clearance system, again, does not vary our basic concepts of debt; but the ready shifting of bank ledger entries as a payment system shows that debts became in effect transferable assets long before legislation created a statutory path to debt assignment in 1873, and quite independently of so-called equitable assignments of the benefit of debt that had developed in the preceding century.[34]

2. Enforcement, Asset Partitioning, and Security

One implication of debt being a personal obligation of the debtor is that the contracting of the obligation does not of itself partition, allocate, or bond any assets belonging to the debtor. This is evidenced powerfully by the historical rule that debts being purely personal obligations were cancelled with the debtor's death; the heirs were not bound simply because they took the debtor's assets, because the debt was not imprinted on the assets to create a persistent claim. Historically the law of the church governing personal succession, and the law of wills and estates in the king's courts, each developed methods to apply the precedent debt obligations of deceased persons to bind the executors or administrators handling the deceased estate; for example the law might imply a trust to pay debts binding the executors and heirs as a condition of taking control of the assets from the deceased estate, unless strongly controverting evidence could be adduced.[35] Roman law had similar techniques with the institution of *fideicommissum* novating both assets and liabilities to a representative on death.[36] But these legal moves were necessary to outflank the intrinsically personal nature of the debtor's payment duty that could not survive the person.

[33] Getzler 2026.
[34] Geva 2001, 2011. Walsh 2023 gives a detailed analysis of the fitful introduction of statutory assignment of debts; the point here is the statutory innovation came well after alternative assignment methods had been perfected.
[35] Habakkuk 1994.
[36] Johnston 1988.

The non-specific personal quality of debt has further manifestations, in both Romanic and common-law systems. During life all the debtor's assets are presumptively available to meet all liabilities including voluntary debts. A debtor cannot say—'I owe you a hundred pounds, but you can only collect against my personal bank accounts, not my business assets or my real estate'. Debts may be satisfied by attachment to the general assets in an estate or collection of assets by a number of techniques: a receivership attaching income and selling capital to meet debts may be adopted or imposed where the debtor cannot make a capable repayment plan; and ultimately the creditors can force a bankruptcy or insolvency procedure dissolving the debtor's control of assets entirely and transferring the estate to agents of the creditors for distribution. Earlier insolvency procedures were a more anarchic race to the court door—the first creditor to prove debt and get a judgment for execution could send in bailiffs to seize whatever was available in satisfaction; the laggards got the leftovers, if any. A more coordinated system emerged in modern times, with appointment of trustees in insolvency who were tasked to lock down assets of the debtor in a regulated fund and then proceed to aggregation of assets, rating of liabilities, and distribution to creditors in a fair and orderly manner in order to meet proven debts. This was especially useful where there were rival classes of debtors and a shortfall of assets, with tradeoffs involving timing, order, and methods of liquidation and distribution managed through a court-monitored collective procedure.[37] The Crown maintained super-priority for debts owed to it by subjects, taking first place in the insolvency queue by virtue of the royal prerogative; this fiscal privilege sat alongside entire forfeiture of felon's estates, as well as escheat for land and *bona vacantia* for goods. The court would ensure that the trustees respected prior securities, but otherwise would enforce *pari passu* distribution.

The general availability of assets to meet debts in our modern law betokens a basic commitment to the liberal principle of patrimony—that free persons enjoy autonomy over their rights and must stake their rights to meet their assets. The patrimonial principle is only implicit in the common law system, and was not always observed. A key flashpoint concerned whether land capital could be reached to satisfy debts, to the destruction of the landowner's tenure and estate. An early solution came with the medieval writ of *elegit*, establishing that a part possession akin to a forced lease could be granted to a creditor to extract income from the land, without appropriating the capital and disrupting

[37] Goode 2018.

long-term estate planning. European systems struggled to reach a similar balance between land rights and debt.

Real tenures and estates were remoulded in modern times, with doctrines of conversion and overreaching allowing land to be regarded as a repository of monetary value, easing the extraction of debt from capital. Indeed, owners campaigned for the right to attach debt to their limited estates (life interest, joint tenancies, remainders, and so on) so as to enhance their liquidity potential. Trust beneficial interests were brought within the scope of debt enforcement by the early 1800s in England, with creditors being able to attach equitable interests and take income and capital out of the trust to meet the personal liabilities of trust beneficiaries. However, the trend of recent years, particularly in the United States and the offshore jurisdictions, has been to create asset protection trusts that insulate wealth held in trusts from liability for debt, detracting markedly from the patrimonial principle.[38]

The major arena where contracted debt gives rise to a pre-adjudicative claim to specific assets is where real security is granted over identified assets. Real security is clearly the major conduit by which debt is converted into a form of proprietary claim. The law here is elaborate and precise, imposing requirements that the security be specific, formalized, and publicized for the protection of other trading and creditor parties present and future. Such securitization is usually done at the time of contracting the debt, but in some circumstances security protections can be added on by staking of assets after the debt has been running, typically where the creditor needs further assurance of payment or the debtor needs fresh money. This is common in financial markets, where lending contracts may build in a power to increase collateral posted by the debtor in light of change to market conditions and debtor circumstance (or simply ask for fresh collateral to forestall calling a term to existing debt).

As with payments into court and insolvency controls, the granting of security as an add-on duty does not directly bear on the juridical qualities of simple debt. One can owe a simple debt without any assets to one's name, a common enough phenomenon; and the creditor cannot insist that extant or future property be reserved to pay the debt unless or until a real security or insolvency procedure is in place. The law can imply certain liens and charges into transactions for value in order to secure repayment of debt, for example where a transferee was vested with a specific title prior to payment; or where payment for a specific asset had been tendered prior to completion. Thus, a purchaser of land vested with possession might owe a lien back to the vendor

[38] Hofri & Bennett 2021; Smith 2008, 2017.

prior to payment being tendered, to assist the smooth operation of conveyancing in the property market whilst protecting the vendor.[39] Persons seeking title in the land would be put on notice to look out for the unpaid vendor lien by registrations or the document trail.

Implied and concealed security brings risk fraud on rival creditors. The doctrinal requirement of formalized and specific *ex ante* security, discoverable by other creditors, and creating exceptions to the operation of the *pari passu* credit bargain governed by insolvency laws, was significantly undermined when nineteenth-century equity courts allowed charges to be imposed over future and floating assets under the disposition and control of the debtor, but still apt to secure contracted debt on certain conditions falling in. In the United States such remoulding of secured debt and insolvency principles was resisted until well into the twentieth century, and finally instituted by legislation or code, sweeping away earlier inhibitions.[40]

VI. Conclusion: Personal with Proprietary Characteristics

We can now draw back from the functions, causes, and consequences of debt, and ask again: where does debt sit on the grid of personal and proprietary claims? If debt is a personal obligation to pay over a value, does the law treat that value as an asset with proprietary characteristics?

Our tour through the terrain has shown that contracted debt for an agreed sum had roots in property transfers, particularly of fungibles including coin. There was also an intrinsic element of real enforcement in earlier legal systems with the taking of security into court as intrinsic to the litigation process, together with the ready immobilization of recalcitrant debtors to get at their assets. However, on the analytical plane the debt claim in modern times came to be resolved as a strictly personal obligation between debtor and creditor, particularly so as the action for trespass damages supplanted earlier debt and covenant forms. There were no assets the creditor could claim under simple debt to the exclusion of others.

The law nonetheless added proprietary characteristics back into debt, through attachment via insolvency procedures and ready implication and ascription of real security to buttress recovery of debt sums. The most striking and serious development of a proprietary dimension to debt has been the rise

[39] Cleaver 2024.
[40] Getzler 2006, 2012.

of free debt assignability, beginning with payment offsets brokered by banks, but now spreading so as to make pyramids of assignable debt-based wealth and ready generation of credit a driver of modern finance and commerce. The combination of *ex post* attachment techniques and free assignability does add back a profound property dimension to the debt obligation. The value of legal and historical analysis shows how we reached this point, and may cast light on the path ahead.

References

Abatino, B. and G. Dari-Mattiacci. (2020). 'Agency Problems and Organizational Costs in Slave-Run Business'. *Roman Law & Economics, Volume I: Institutions and Organization.* G. Dari-Mattiacci and D. P. Kehoe. Oxford: Oxford University Press: 273–306.

Baker, J. H. (1971). 'New Light on Slade's Case'. *Cambridge Law Journal* 29: 51–67, 213–236.

Baker, J. H. (2019a). *Baker and Milsom's Sources of English History: Private Law to 1750.* 2nd edn. Oxford, Oxford University Press.

Baker, J. H. (2019b). *Introduction to English Legal History.* 5th edn. Oxford, Oxford University Press.

Birks, P. B. H. (2005). *Unjust Enrichment.* 2nd edn. Oxford, Oxford University Press.

Birks, P. B. H. (2014). *The Roman Law of Obligations.* Oxford, Oxford University Press.

Borges, J. L. (1946). 'On Exactitude in Science'. *Collected Fictions.* A. Hurley. Harmondsworth, Penguin Books: 325.

Buckland, W. W. (1963). *A Textbook of Roman Law.* 3rd edn. P. G. Stein. Cambridge: Cambridge University Press.

Cleaver, M. J. (2024). '*The Equitable Lien: Credit, Security, and Priority in English Law and Economy, 1673–1925*'. DPhil Thesis, University of Oxford.

Daube, D. (1961). 'Derelictio, Occupatio, and Traditio'. *Law Quarterly Review* 77: 382–389.

Desan, C. (2014). *Making Money: Coin, Currency, and the Coming of Capitalism.* Oxford, Oxford University Press.

Fox, D. (1996). 'Bona Fide Purchase and the Currency of Money'. *Cambridge Law Journal* 55: 547–565.

Fox, D. (2008). *Property Rights in Money.* Oxford, Oxford University Press.

Fox, D. and W. Ernst. (2016). *Money in the Western Legal Tradition - Middle Ages to Bretton Woods.* Oxford, Oxford University Press.

Gaius (1946). *Institutes.* F. de Zulueta. Oxford, Clarendon Press.

Georgiou, A. (2025). 'Making contract-breakers pay'. *Law Quarterly Review* 141: 104–130.

Getzler, J. (2006). 'The Role of Security over Future and Circulating Capital: Evidence from the British Economy circa 1850–1920'. *Company Charges: Spectrum and Beyond.* J. Getzler and J. Payne. Oxford, Oxford University Press: 227–251.

Getzler, J. (2012). 'Assignment of Future Property and Preferences'. *Fault Lines in Equity.* J. Glister and P. Ridge. Oxford, Hart: 73–105.

Getzler, J. (2026). 'Equity, Legal Coding, and the Foundations of Banking: *Foley v Hill* (1838–48)'. *Essays on the History of Equity.* D. Foster and C. Mitchell. Oxford, Hart: 403–428.

Geva, B. (2001). *Bank Collections and Payment Transactions.* Oxford, Oxford University Press.

Geva, B. (2011). *The Payment Order of Antiquity and the Middle Ages—A Legal History.* Oxford, Hart.
Glanvill, Ranulf de (1965). *The Treatise on the Laws and Customs of the Realm of England.* G. D. G. Hall. London, Nelson.
Gleeson, S. (2018). *The Legal Concept of Money.* Oxford, Oxford University Press.
Goode, R. M. (2018). *Principles of Corporate Insolvency Law.* 5th edn. K. van Zwieten. London, Sweet & Maxwell.
Graeber, D. (2014). *Debt: The First 5000 Years.* 2nd edn. Brooklyn NY, Melville.
Habakkuk, J. (1994). *Marriage, Debt, and the Estates System: English Landownership, 1650–1950.* Oxford, Oxford University Press.
Hofri, A. and M. Bennett (2021). 'The Use of Trusts to Subvert the Law: An Analysis and Critique'. *Oxford Journal of Legal Studies* 41: 692–718.
Holmes Jr, O. W. (1882). *The Common Law.* London, Macmillan.
Honoré, A. M. (1960). 'Rights of Exclusion and Immunities Against Divesting'. *Tulane Law Review* 34: 453–468.
Honoré, A. M. (1961). 'Ownership'. *Oxford Essays in Jurisprudence.* A. G. Guest. Oxford, Clarendon Press: 107–147.
Hudson, J. (2012). *The Oxford History of the Laws of England, Vol II: 871-1216.* Oxford, Oxford University Press.
Ibbetson, D. J. (1984). 'Sixteenth Century Contract Law: Slade's Case in Context'. *Oxford Journal of Legal Studies* 4: 295–317.
Ibbetson, D. J. (2001). *A Historical Introduction to the Law of Obligations.* Oxford, Oxford University Press.
Johnston, D. (1988). *The Roman Law of Trusts.* Oxford, Clarendon Press.
Justinian (1987) *Institutes.* P. Birks and G. McLeod. London, Duckworth.
Lau, J. (2024). 'Pre-judgment Interest on Liquidated and Unliquidated Sums'. Lloyd's Maritime and Commercial Law Quarterly: 136–161.
Mann, B. H. (2009). *Republic of Debtors: Bankruptcy in the Age of American Independence.* Cambridge, Harvard University Press.
Markham Lester, V. (1995). *Victorian Insolvency: Bankruptcy, Imprisonment for Debt, and Company Winding-up in Nineteenth-Century England.* Oxford, Clarendon Press.
Midrash Rabbah Volume 2 – Exodus, Leviticus. (1977). H. Freedman and M. Simon. London, Soncino.
Milsom, S. F. C. (1985). *Studies in the History of the Common Law.* London, Hambledon Press.
Nietzsche, F. (2013). *On the Genealogy of Morals: A Polemic* (1887). R. C. Holub, et al. Harmondsworth, Penguin Books.
Palmer, R.C. (1993). *English Law in the Age of the Black Death, 1348-1381: A Transformation of Governance and Law.* Chapel Hill, University of North Carolina Press.
Pollock, F. and Maitland, F. W. (1895). *The History of English Law before the Time of Edward I,* 2 vols. Cambridge, Cambridge University Press.
Seabourne, G. (2003). *Royal Regulation of Loans and Sales in Medieval England.* Woodbridge, Boydell Press.
Simpson, A. W. B. (1958). 'The Place of Slade's Case in the History of Contract'. *Law Quarterly Review* 74: 381–396.
Simpson, A. W. B. (1975). *A History of the Common Law of Contract: The Rise of the Action of Assumpsit.* Oxford, Clarendon Press.
Smith, L. D. (2008). 'Trust and Patrimony'. *Revue générale de droit* 38: 379–403.
Smith, L. D. (2017) 'Massively Discretionary Trusts'. *Current Legal Problems* 70: 17–54.

Stoljar, S. J. (1964). *The Law of Quasi-Contract.* Sydney, Law Book Company.

Stoljar, S. J. (1975). *History of Contract at Common Law.* Canberra, ANU Press.

Walsh, X. P. (2023). 'Voluntary Assignments of Legal Choses in Action in England and Australia after the Judicature Act 1873'. *Journal of Equity.* 17: 59–92.

Weber, M. (1985). *The Protestant Ethic and the Spirit of Capitalism* (1904–5). T. Parsons. London, Routledge.

V.

CONTRACT, PROPERTY, AND BEYOND

15

Are Choses in Action Property?

William Swadling

I. Introduction

Orthodoxy has it that our property law divides between real and personal property. But though real property does not further divide, personal property oddly does, between 'choses in possession' and 'choses in action'. On that basis, anything which is a chose in action is *ex hypothesi* a species of property. The argument advanced here is that most 'choses' contained in this category are not 'property' at all, and that the opposition with choses in possession is, nowadays at least, false.

II. Property

'Property' is a notoriously ambiguous word. As a matter of the English language, we use it in many different ways. One is in describing the attributes of physical things, for example, the 'properties' of magnesium. Another is to describe physical things themselves. Laypersons, for example, talk of cars, computers, or plots of land as their 'property'.[1]

In the law, the dominant usage of 'property' is as a qualifier of rights. We see this most clearly in land law, which has the most developed jurisprudence of property rights. The first thing land law teaches us is never to speak of land itself as 'property'; land law would be incomprehensible if we did. We are concerned instead with a particular class of rights, property rights, with respect to the physical thing we call land. Examples of such rights are fee simple estates, leases, easements, and profits à prendre. The hallmark of these rights, what makes them property rights, is that they are rights with respect to physical things strictly binding on third parties. Of course, my right to bodily integrity

[1] *Hocking v Director-General of the National Archives* (2021) 271 CLR 1, [202] (Edelman J).

William Swadling, *Are Choses in Action Property?* In: *The Property-Contract Interface*. Edited by: James Penner, Irina Sakharova, Henry E. Smith, and Zhong Xing Tan, Oxford University Press.
DOI: 10.1093/9780198951995.003.0020

is also strictly binding on third parties. We do not classify it as a property right, however, because it does not exist in relation to a physical thing separate from my person. As will be seen, the common law has no name for such rights, though civilian systems generally call them 'extra-patrimonial'.

Land law also teaches us that not all rights with respect to land are property rights; there are also personal rights, binding only the parties to their creation.[2] There are many examples in the caselaw, including *Hill v Tupper*,[3] where the Basingstoke Canal Company's grant of the 'exclusive right to put pleasure boats on a canal' was held not to be exigible against a third-party innkeeper also renting out boats, and *King v David Allen (Billposting) Ltd*,[4] where a successor in title was held not bound by a contract entered into by the grantor with a company giving them the right to use the side of the building for advertising purposes. Yet another example is the right to the exclusive possession of land in *Prudential Assurance Co Ltd v London Residuary Body*,[5] which failed to qualify as either a fee simple estate (because not indefinite) or a lease (because the term was uncertain). Others are rights which would have qualified as easements had they touched and concerned the land,[6] positive covenants,[7] and rights of pre-emption.[8]

What these cases demonstrate is that there is a *numerus clausus* or closed list of property rights with respect to land. As Lord Brougham famously said in *Keppell v Bailey*, where a negative answer was given to the question whether a covenant entered into by the defendant's predecessor in title with the plaintiff that they and their successors in title would always buy the limestone used in their manufacturing process from a particular source and transport that limestone by a particular railway was binding on the defendant successor in title:

> There are certain known incidents to property and its enjoyment; among others, certain burthens wherewith it may be affected, or rights which may be created and enjoyed over it by parties other than the owner; all which incidents are recognised by the law. In respect of possession, the property may be

[2] The position is slightly muddied by the presence of the economic torts, but these require a high degree of fault and have other dissimilar characteristics: below, text to notes 40–41.

[3] (1863) 2 H & C 121.

[4] [1916] 2 AC 54.

[5] [1992] 2 AC 386. As this case shows, the right was not disqualified from proprietary status because it did not touch and concern the land, but because it was not in the *numerus clausus*. That a right touches and concerns the land is a necessary but not a sufficient condition of proprietary status: cf Chambers (2026).

[6] *Ackroyd v Smith* (1850) 10 CB 164.

[7] *Rhone v Stephens* [1994] 2 AC 310.

[8] *Pritchard v Briggs* [1980] Ch 339. The position was changed by statute in respect of registered titles to land by the Land Registration Act 2002, s 115.

> in one, while the reversion is in another; in respect of interest, the life estate in one, the remainder in tail in a second, and the fee in reversion in a third. So in respect of enjoyment; one may have the possession and the fee-simple, and another may have a rent issuing out of it, or the tithes of its produce, or an easement, as a right of way upon it, or of common over it.... But it must not therefore be supposed that incidents of a novel kind can be devised and attached to property at the fancy or caprice of any owner. It is clearly inconvenient both to the science of the law and to the public weal that such a latitude should be given. There can be no harm in allowing the fullest latitude to men in binding themselves and their representatives, that is, their assets real and personal, to answer in damages for breach of their obligations. This tends to no mischief, and is a reasonable liberty to bestow; but great detriment would arise and much confusion of rights if parties were allowed to invent new modes of holding and enjoying real property, and to impress upon their lands and tenements a peculiar character, which should follow them into all hands, however remote. Every close, every messuage, might thus be held in a several fashion; and it would hardly be possible to know what rights the acquisition of any parcel conferred, or what obligations it imposed.[9]

What this case also demonstrates, as do all those where the right in question failed to qualify as proprietary, is that persons nevertheless have the 'fullest latitude' to create personal rights with respect to land by contract. The reason there is no *numerus clausus* of such rights is simple: since they are not strictly binding on third parties, they do not, as in *Hill v Tupper*, impinge other peoples' freedom; nor, as in *Keppell v Bailey*, do they clog titles. There is no need, therefore, to restrict their number.

Finally, land law teaches us that the assignability has no bearing on the status of a right as proprietary. So, in *King v David Allen (Billposting) Ltd*, the right was no doubt assignable, but this did not make it proprietary. Likewise, the right to occupy not qualifying as a lease in *Prudential Assurance* had been assigned many times over, but that did not mean it crossed the divide between personal and proprietary.

Unfortunately, judges and commentators are sometimes misled by a *dictum* of Lord Wilberforce in *National Provincial Bank v Ainsworth*,[10] where the question was whether 'the deserted wife's equity', the common law right of a wife to be housed by her husband arising by status, was capable of binding third-party

[9] (1834) 2 My & K 517, 535–536.
[10] [1965] AC 1175.

mortgagees. The House of Lords held that it was not a property right and therefore incapable of binding anyone but the husband. However, instead of simply saying that it was not within the *numerus clausus*, Lord Wilberforce held it not to be proprietary because it was not 'definable, identifiable by third parties, [and] capable in its nature of assumption by third parties'.[11]

Although these might well be qualities of property rights, they are also qualities of many personal ones, as the examples of *Hill v Tupper*, *King*, and *Prudential* show. At best, Lord Wilberforce was laying down necessary conditions for the recognition of property rights, not tests of sufficiency; to hold otherwise would be to destroy the *numerus clausus*, a proposition not argued for in that case. Many subsequent cases, however, have taken assignability as the hallmark of a property right.[12] But assignability tells us nothing of whether a right is capable of binding strangers to its creation, which is the concern of the *numerus clausus*.

III. Personal Property

If 'property' describes rights with respect to physical things strictly binding on third parties, then personal property rights must be a species of such rights. This is reflected, to an extent, in the contrast drawn by property lawyers between real and personal property, the latter concerned, at least originally, with property rights in physical things other than land, namely goods or 'chattels'.

What accounts for this bifurcation is not the nature of the rights themselves[13] (if it did, we would not be speaking of two sub-species but of two different species altogether) but the remedies the common law provides to those dispossessed of physical things. If a person with a right to possess land is dispossessed thereof, the common law can grant a specific remedy, an order that they be put back in possession. However, where a person is dispossessed of goods, no order for possession will issue from a common law court.[14] Instead, the court can only order that the plaintiff recover from the defendant the goods themselves or the value of the best right to the goods, the choice being that of the defendant. Because in the case of land the plaintiff gets an order that they

[11] Ibid, at 1247–1248.

[12] Particularly so for cryptocurrency: *AA v Persons Unknown* [2019] EWHC 3556 (Comm); *Tulip Trading Ltd v Bitcoin Association for BSV* [2023] EWCA Civ 83.

[13] Though the list of property rights with respect to goods is different from that with respect to land.

[14] One exception is the action of replevin, a specific common law remedy for unlawful distress. There has also long been an equitable jurisdiction to order up delivery, akin to specific performance of contracts, dependent on a damages remedy being inadequate.

recover the physical thing itself, the *res*, we call it 'real' property, whereas because in cases of goods the plaintiff is guaranteed only a monetary remedy, we call it 'personal' property.[15]

So far, then, personal property is a sub-species of property, lining up with real property to comprise the subject of property as a whole. However, as we will see, this understanding entails a much narrower view of personal property than currently understood.

IV. Choses in Possession

As seen, personal property divides between choses 'in possession' and those which are 'in action'. The meaning of 'chose in possession' has evolved over time. 'What then is a chose in possession?'

'Chose' is simply French for 'thing'. Though 'thing' has many meanings in English (and French), in the context of chose in possession it means 'physical thing'. Originally, to say of someone that they had a chose in possession said nothing more than that there was a physical thing in their possession: according to a sixteenth-century law dictionary, it was 'a thing whereof a man is . . . possessed'.[16] Nor was it confined to any particular type of physical thing, covering both land and goods. If the physical thing was taken by another without their consent, the person no longer had a chose in possession. But it was not then said that they thereby lost their right to possession. The phrase did not originally describe any type of right, merely a state of affairs.

It is occasionally said that choses in possession are physical things *capable* of possession. Thus, the Law Commission of England and Wales say that a chose in possession is 'any object which the law considers amenable to possession'.[17] For them, therefore, fish in the sea would be choses in possession. This is immediately problematic, for it would mean that the word 'chose' in the phrases 'chose in possession' and 'chose in action' meant different things, physical things and non-physical things, with the result that they could not be logically juxtaposed. Nor could it any longer be a subdivision of personal property since such fish are objects of no rights whatever,[18] let alone property rights. Not surprisingly, it is not English law.

[15] This also explains why leases of land are, somewhat awkwardly, called 'chattels real'.
[16] Rastell 1563, entry 'Chose in Action'.
[17] Law Commission (England and Wales) 2023, 3.17.
[18] *Young v Hichens* (1844) 6 QB 606.

V. Choses in Action

The meaning of 'chose in action' has also changed over time. It too originally described a state of affairs, namely that a plaintiff was in a position to obtain a physical thing, to 'reduce' a 'chose' into 'possession' by bringing a court 'action':

> Thing in action is when a man hath cause, or may bring an action for some duty due to him; as an Action of Debt upon an Obligation, annuitie, or rent, Action of Covenant, or ward, Trespasse of goods taken away, beating, or such like, and because they are things whereof a man is not possessed, but for recovery of them is driven to his Action, they are called things in Action.[19]

A chose in action, therefore, was a cause of action to get possession of a physical thing, whereas a chose in possession was a physical thing of which a person was already possessed.

The 'choses' reduceable into possession by 'action' were money and land. If money was sought, and it is important to remember that money was then a physical thing (coinage), the plaintiff was said to have a 'chose in action personal' or 'personal action'.[20] If land was sought, they had a 'chose in action real' or 'real action'.[21] There was thus an equation between the different *forms* of action and the different *choses* in action.

The idea is of a thing being reduced into possession by the taking of court action is still seen today. Thus, in *Curtis v Wilcox*, Wynn-Parry J said:

> It is clear ... that at common law a wife cannot sue her husband for a tort committed before the marriage. If, therefore, the wife had a cause of action which she could pursue after the marriage it must have been because her right of action in tort, which arose before the marriage, was a thing in action forming part of her estate, which she could reduce into possession by action before marriage.[22]

The case concerned the power to sue in tort someone who had caused physical injury to the plaintiff through negligence. It was a chose in action because it was something which, through court action, could be reduced into possession.

[19] Rastell 1563, entry 'Chose in Action'.
[20] For a modern account, see Sutton 1929.
[21] Booth 1811. The real actions were abolished by the Real Property Limitation Act 1833, though they had fallen into disuse long before. Specific recovery of land is, however, still available.
[22] [1948] 2 KB 474, 479.

So far, then, the taxonomy makes perfect sense. Since the word 'chose' in both phrases means physical thing, the two can be logically opposed. The contrast is simply between physical things in a person's possession and those which can be reduced into possession though court action.

Why was this distinction drawn? Its importance lay in assignability. Originally, choses in action could not be assigned, something that changed only in the nineteenth century.[23] But while property rights with respect to land and goods were assignable long before that, this could only be done by feoffment with livery of seisin for land and delivery for goods.[24] Neither was possible where the rightholder was out of possession,[25] who was said to have a 'mere' chose in action.[26]

As seen, a person dispossessed of goods could bring a court action by which it was adjudged that they 'do recover' from the defendant a (substitute) sum of money. There, the chose in action arose because of an interference with the plaintiff's property right. But it was not so confined. As *Curtis v Wilcox* demonstrates, causes of action in tort are choses in action,[27] so the complaint was not necessarily about interferences with property rights. Thus, the ability to bring actions for money for breach of contract were choses in action, as were tort claims for defamation and negligence. We were thus not talking about property at all. As Lindley LJ explained in *Colonial Bank v Whinney*:

> [T]he original idea was that a chose in action was not property of a particular class, but was no property at all. It was not that property was divided into choses in action and choses in possession, but that a chose in action was only a right to sue as distinguished from property.[28]

At some point, however, certain substantive rights came to be included within the phrase. As will be seen, this was probably the work of Blackstone.[29] A good example is *Colonial Bank v Whinney* itself, where the issue was whether company shares were choses in action. Lindley LJ, with whom Cotton LJ agreed, held that they were not, for there was nothing for the shareholder to

[23] Judicature Act 1873, s 25(6).
[24] *Cochrane v Moore* (1890) 25 QBD 57.
[25] There were also concerns regarding maintenance and champerty.
[26] *Edwards v Jones* (1836) 1 My & Cr 226, 236. This is turned on its head in one modern text, where it is said that something cannot be a chose in action unless it is assignable (Liew 2024, [1-07]), the (fundamentally flawed) thinking being that as choses in action are a species of property they will only qualify as such if assignable.
[27] [1948] 2 KB 474, 480.
[28] (1885) 30 Ch D 261, 284.
[29] Text to notes 43–46.

recover by action. The shareholder had the share '... and he cannot get anything more than he has got already. If he is kept out of his dividends he can bring his action for those dividends. They may be choses in action ... but he cannot sue for the share, as he has it already.'[30] Cotton LJ agreed.

Fry LJ dissented. In a judgment later approved (obiter) by the House of Lords, he said:

> [A] share is ... the right to receive certain benefits from a corporation, and to do certain acts as a member of that corporation; and if those benefits be withheld or those acts be obstructed, the only remedy of the owner of the share is by action. Of the share itself ... there can be no occupation or enjoyment; though of the fruits arising from it there may be occupation, enjoyment, and manual possession. Such a share appears to me to be closely akin to a debt, which is one of the most familiar of *choses in action*; no action is required to obtain the right to the money in the case of the debt, or the right to the dividends or other accruing benefits in the case of the share; but an action is the only means of obtaining the money itself or the other benefits in specie, the right to which is called in one case a debt and in the other case a share. In the case alike of the debt and of the share, the owner of it has, to use the language of *Blackstone*, 'a bare right without any occupation or enjoyment'.[31]

For Fry LJ, therefore, 'choses in action' were species of rights, not descriptive, at least not wholly, of causes of action.

However, if we are now speaking of rights, which rights? As seen, when 'chose in action' meant 'cause of action', it covered causes of action in respect of all rights, regardless of whether the underlying right was personal, proprietary, or something else. If we have now switched from causes to rights, or are at least including rights, are we likewise talking about all rights?

It seems not. As Fry LJ's statement demonstrates, the thinking is that we are still dealing with opposed categories, so that choses in possession, which must now be seen as *rights* to the possession of land and goods rather than the fact of their possession, are excluded. As seen, Fry LJ does this by introducing the notion that we are dealing with rights for which the *only* remedy for interference is court action. If self-help is possible, the rights are not choses in action, meaning that plaintiffs dispossessed of either land or goods, who often have self-help 'remedies',[32] no longer, as they once did, have choses in action.

[30] (1885) 30 Ch D 261, 284.
[31] (1885) 30 Ch D 261, 286–287.
[32] Arguably not a remedy at all, merely, in Hohfeldian terms, an immunity from suit.

'Chose in action', therefore, now describes a class of rights not including rights to the possession of physical things, moveable or immoveable, the reason being that these can be 'claimed or enforced' by taking physical possession. Why this should matter, especially when it is remembered that persons dispossessed of land and goods, in addition to their self-help 'remedy', can and usually do go to court to obtain a specific or monetary remedy, is unclear. Indeed, court action will generally be the preferred remedy, with self-help not pursued or possibly unlawful. It is not, for example, possible to enter another's land to retrieve goods, and it is sometimes a crime to retake possession of land.[33] In such cases, we should presumably be reclassifying the underlying rights as choses in action, though that is never done. The distinction is arbitrary at best.

Also seemingly excluded are rights to bodily integrity and the maintenance of a reputation, what civilians (especially in the French legal tradition) call 'extra-patrimonial' rights.[34] The decision to exclude them seems to have been made on the basis that such rights are not assignable and so cannot therefore be a species of property. However, this is difficult to comprehend, for it was not until the nineteenth century that 'patrimonial' rights, for example, the benefit of debts, became assignable in English law.[35] Moreover, company shares, though within the category of choses in action, have never been assignable, only 'transferable' by novation.[36]

Although causes of action do not feature in Fry LJ's definition, they were never expelled, as *Curtis v Wilcox* demonstrates.[37] Presumably also still included are those causes of action arising from the interference with rights to possession of land and goods, even though the underlying right is not.

Thus, the category 'chose in action' nowadays contains an odd mix of almost all 'patrimonial' rights and descriptions of situations where people can sue for money judgments regardless of the nature of the underlying right. However, not included are extra-patrimonial rights and the patrimonial rights to the possession of land and goods.

Moreover, the opposition with choses in possession is now false. Although the word 'thing' now means 'right' in the phrase chose in possession, it means both 'right' and 'cause of action' in chose in action. Further, as will be seen immediately below, the types of right in play are in different categories, those in

[33] Criminal Law Act 1977, s 6; Protection From Eviction Act 1977, s 3.

[34] Birks called them 'superstructural rights': Birks 1997, 11–12.

[35] So-called 'equitable assignment' was not an assignment at all but the creation of a trust in favour of the assignee. Tham 2019.

[36] *Ashby v Blackwell* (1765) Eden 299, 302–303; *Simm v Anglo-American Telegraph Co* (1879) 5 QBD 188, 294; Benjamin 2000, 3.05; Micheler 2002. Bearer shares seem to be an exception.

[37] See text to note 22 above.

choses in possession being proprietary, those in choses in action being a mixture. It is sometimes said that the latter category comprises 'incorporeal' rights and the former 'corporeal' rights, but this does not work: all rights are incorporeal: no one has ever touched a right.

The final point to note is that there is no *numerus clausus* of choses in action. Since choses in action include rights arising by contract, and as seen, there is no limit to the rights people may therby create,[38] there can be no *numerus clausus* of choses in action, something which should make us immediately doubt whether they really can all be property rights.

VI. Choses in Action as Property

Having determined the meaning of the phrase 'chose in action', the question is whether the 'things' under its label are 'property'. It is obviously not true that all 'things' in the category are species of property rights, the most obvious being causes of action, which are not rights at all, let alone property rights.

As to the 'rights' element of choses in action, we need to go through the list to determine whether they are proprietary. Some clearly are not, the most obvious being the benefit of a debt. The right of a creditor to payment from their debtor does not have the same third-party effect as a fee simple estate in land, lease, easement, or profit. If the debtor does not pay, the creditor cannot sue any third party for performance.[39] It is no different with the benefit of contracts. If A contracts with B that B will paint A's house, A cannot sue any third party for performance if B does not do the job. Moreover, this proposition is not contradicted by the presence of the economic torts. So, for example, where a defendant is successfully sued for inducing a breach of contract, they are not compelled to perform, either specifically or through the payment of expectation damages.[40] Indeed, they are not even capable of performing, something only the contractual counter-party can do. Their obligation instead is not to intentionally induce a breach. Moreover, a high degree fault is necessary to trigger these torts,[41] whereas the property wrongs, as seen, are strict.

[38] See the quote from *Keppell v Bailey* (above), text to note 9.

[39] Bizarrely, Smith & Leslie 2018, [1-08]–[1.15]), though acknowledging this fact, nevertheless call it 'bilateral intangible property', opposing it to what they call 'multilateral intangible property', a label they attach to, eg, intellectual property rights. Such a dichotomy is fundamentally flawed: a 'bilateral' property right is, by definition, not a property right at all.

[40] Thus, if TP owes £1,000,000 to P but does not have the means to pay, D inducing him not to pay does not render D liable to be ordered to pay P £1,000,000.

[41] *OBG Ltd v Allan* [2007] UKHL 21, [39].

What is true for debts and the benefit of contracts generally is also true for shares.[42] If a company refuses to pay its shareholder dividends or allow them to vote in a company meeting, the shareholder has a claim against the company alone; no other person can be ordered to perform or is even capable of performing.

By contrast, some rights in this category do have strict third-party effect. These are the intellectual property rights; for example, copyrights and trademarks. However, they are different to rights with respect to physical things in many ways, including in both their modes of acquisition and loss. There is no concept, for example, of copyright arising by taking possession, as there is with land and goods. Nor can copyright be lost by the physical destruction of any subject matter, for there is none. But though not property rights in the same way as are titles to land and goods, intellectual property rights at least come close. Moreover, as would be expected of rights having strict third-party effect, they too have a *numerus clausus*: new species of intellectual property rights cannot be created at the fancy or caprice of the parties, who must instead accept the forms provided by law, for example copyright, patent, and trademark.

VII. 'Propertizing' Choses in Action

Intellectual property rights apart, none of the 'things' in the 'choses in action' box come close to being 'property'. The mystery then is why it is commonly asserted that choses in action are collectively a species of personal property. We might explain this in various ways, none of which, however, work.

1. Property as Collective Noun

The word 'property' is sometimes used to describe the totality of a person's rights, those 'proper to' a person. This seems to underly Blackstone's categorization of choses in action as a species of personal property:

> PROPERTY, in chattels personal, may be either in possession; which is where a man has not only the right to enjoy, but has the actual enjoyment of, the

[42] For a book-length treatment of the question whether shares are a species of property, see Pretto-Sakmann 2005. The author's conclusion is that they are not.

> thing: or else it is in action; where a man has only a bare right, without any occupation or enjoyment.[43]

Elsewhere, Blackstone, who clearly influenced Fry LJ in *Colonial Bank v Whinney*, says of a chose in action that 'the owner may have as absolute a property of such things in action, as of things in possession'.[44]

Blackstone's description of choses in action as 'property' is seemingly dictated by the structure of his *Commentaries*, which are divided into four books: Book I, 'Of The Rights of Persons'; Book II, 'Of The Rights of Things'; Book III, 'Of Private Wrongs'; and Book IV, 'Of Public Wrongs'.[45] By rights of persons, Blackstone did not mean rights belonging to persons but rights such as those of liberty and reputation, 'extra-patrimonial' rights in the civilian tradition. By the oddly named 'rights of things', Blackstone was concerned with 'patrimonial' rights as a whole. But now, since such 'things' were proper to persons, they amounted to 'property'. We see this in his division of rights into two classes:

> First, those which concern, and are annexed to the persons of men, and are then called jura personarum or the rights of persons; . . . secondly, such as a man may acquire over external objects, or things unconnected with his person, which are styled jura rerum or the rights of things.[46]

Thus, choses in action were 'property' because they belonged to persons.

We see similar thinking in the more recent writings of Harris, who said:

> 'Property' comprises (1) ownership and quasi-ownership interests in things (tangible and ideational); (2) other rights over such things which are enforceable against all-comers (non-ownership proprietary interests); (3) money; and (4) cashable rights. That is what property is.[47]

It is important to understand that Blackstone and Harris use 'property' as a collective noun and not adjectivally, to describe a species of right.

[43] Blackstone 1765–1769, ii, 389.

[44] Blackstone 1765–1769, ii, 397–398.

[45] Blackstone is here clearly following the structure of the *Institutes* of both Gaius and Justinian, his fourth book being included to encompass the otherwise omitted criminal law.

[46] Blackstone 1765–1769, ii, 16.

[47] Harris 1996, 139.

But though grammatically unobjectionable, it does not answer our question whether the rights within the category choses in action, though 'proper to a person', are *property* rights. For Blackstone and Harris, all rights, at least patrimonial ones, are 'property'. This sense of the word is therefore unhelpful to our enquiry and, since it is liable to confuse, must be avoided.

2. Choses in Action as Objects of Ownership

Closely allied to the idea that choses in action are 'proper to a person' and therefore 'property' is the notion that choses in action can be the objects of ownership and therefore property. This thinking is equally flawed.

There is much confusion in English law as to the word 'ownership'. It can mean many things, including a type of right and as expressive of a relationship between a person and a right.[48] Land law can again help with our analysis. Although there is no right called ownership in the *numerus clausus*,[49] two or more persons together holding a right are said to 'co-own' it. The right might be a fee simple estate, a lease, or a profit. What can be said of co-owners can also be said of sole 'owners', though we now tend to use the language of 'having' or 'holding', rather than 'owning'. Land law therefore teaches us that persons can have 'ownership' of rights, where ownership is not a right in and of itself, but expressive of the relationship between persons and rights.

It is, however, equally possible to speak of owning personal rights, demonstrating that 'ownership' is neutral as to the type of right in question. As Salmond noted:

> Ownership . . . denotes the relation between a person and any right that is vested in him. That which a man owns . . . is in all cases a right. Ownership . . . extends to all classes of rights, whether proprietary or personal . . . [50]

The possibility of rights being owned, therefore, cannot make them 'property'.

Turning now to goods, there is, as with land, no ownership of the physical thing itself. As noted, though laypeople might speak of owning physical things such as cars, lawyers, at least good lawyers, talk instead of 'having' or 'owning'

[48] We will see below that it is even sometimes used to express a direct relationship between a person and a physical thing.
[49] *Lulham v Crown Estate Commissioners* [2025] EWHC 1572 (Ch), [1].
[50] Salmond 1957, § 89 (300).

rights with respect to cars. Thus, the Sale of Goods Act 1979 defines a contract of sale as one 'by which the seller transfers or agrees to transfer *the property* in the goods to the buyer ... '[51] And if two or more persons hold this 'property', we once again refer to them as co-owners of the 'property': ownership as relation, not right.

It important to understand that we are not saying here that ownership is a right attaching to a right. To take again the example of land law, the fee simple estate or lease is not the 'object' of the right of ownership; it is the land which is the object of the fee simple estate or lease. This is not, however, how some civilian legal systems conceive of ownership, at least according to some commentators. Unlike the common law, they are said to allow for the ownership of physical things with no intermediate right, ownership of the physical thing being a right in and of itself.[52] Then, lining up rights according to the second century Gaian scheme, which speaks of *res corporales* and *res incorporales*, things physical and non-physical,[53] they have ownership (as right) of physical things and ownership (as right) of non-physical things, that is, rights. Thus, writing of Scots law, Reid says:

> Things can be both corporeal and also incorporeal, 'incorporeal things' being another name for rights. From these two propositions a third follows. This is that there can be rights in incorporeal things, which is to say that there can be rights in rights ... Suppose that A owns a car, takes the lease of a plot of land and lends £1000. The car is a corporeal thing. The lease and the debt are incorporeal things, the former being a real right and the latter a personal right. All three are A's property, and accordingly it can be said that A owns the car, the lease, and the debt.[54]

At first sight, this seems to be nothing more than ownership as relation. However, this is not what Reid means, for he goes on to say that ownership of rights:

> ... facilitates a proper analysis of the transfer of rights. Thus if A contracts to assign his debt to a third party, C, ... C has a personal right against A to the transfer of A's personal right against B; and, when the transfer is completed ... C has the real right of ownership to the personal right against B. The end

[51] Sale of Goods Act 1979, s 2 (emphasis added).
[52] For an excellent discussion, see Gretton 2007.
[53] de Zulueta, Gaius, Bk II, 12.
[54] Reid 1996, [16].

> result... is that A has transferred his right of ownership in the thing to C. The analysis would be precisely the same if A had transferred, not an incorporeal thing (the debt) but a corporeal thing (the car).[55]

For Reid, therefore, 'owners' have two 'things', not one: the 'real' right of ownership and the right they own.

The same view has been recently expressed south of the border. According to Goode:

> Property is equated with a thing, an asset, not a relationship, though of course property is significant only insofar as it involves a relationship with a person and what is commonly referred to as a transfer of an asset is in essence a transfer of an interest in an asset exercisable against some or all third persons.[56]

For Goode, therefore, we simultaneously have both 'assets' and 'interests' in those assets, which is no different to Reid's notion of a right of ownership in a right.

This does not, however, work.[57] Take, for example, copyright in a song. The right, the object of the ownership right, is already vested in its owner. Unlike a physical thing, it has no existence separate from its rightholder; unlike physical things, there is no copyright in the air. But the copyright-holder under Reid and Goode's scheme has two rights: the copyright and the ownership of the copyright. The latter, however, has no content. Then, as to assignments, we saw Reid saying that what was transferred was the 'ownership' of the right, and Goode the 'interest' in the asset. Does it follow that the copyright itself is not transferred, that it remains with the transferor? That would be nonsensical. And if not, then the 'ownership' or 'interest' is once again demonstrated to have no content. Once again, Occam's razor needs wielding here.

Even if an accurate description of how some civilian systems operate, it is not how ownership works in English law. As seen, when English land lawyers speak of fee simple estates or leases being the 'object' of ownership, the word does no more than express the link between the right and its holder. There is one right, not two, not 'ownership' *and* the fee simple estate, only ownership *of*

[55] Ibid.
[56] Goode 2023.
[57] Gretton 2007, 836.

the fee simple estate. The fee simple estate is already vested in its holder. There is no need to interpose another right to express this idea.

3. Choses in Action can be the 'Object' of Property Rights

If not the 'object' of ownership, where ownership means a type of right, can we not say that rights such as copyrights, company shares, and debts can be the 'object' of property rights and therefore 'property'? This, for example, is the view of Spence, who defends intellectual property rights as 'property' on the ground that 'the object of the relevant property rights is the legal right itself'.[58] The Law Commission of England and Wales express similar thinking in their recent work on digital assets,[59] section 1 of the Property (Digital Assets etc) Act 2025, the product of their work, providing:

> **Objects of personal property rights**
>
> A thing (including a thing that is digital or electronic in nature) is not prevented from being the object of personal property rights merely because it is neither—
> (a) a thing in possession, nor
> (b) a thing in action.[60]

It will be recalled that the Commission view 'things in possession' as physical things not in possession though capable of being possessed. The wording of the Act demonstrates the thinking that, just as these physical things can be the 'object' of personal property rights, so too can choses in action.

It is, however, impossible for a right to be the 'object' of a property right. We would never say of a fee simple estate in land that it was property because it was the 'object' of property rights; it is a property right in and of itself, made so by its content. Though we can certainly say that land and goods can be the object of property rights, that is, again, because of the need for the intermediation of rights between persons and physical things. As seen, the notion is redundant

[58] Spence 2007, 15–16.
[59] The Commission speak similarly of digital assets 'attracting' property rights: Law Commission (England and Wales) 2023, 142, 2.6, 2.17. 2.51, 2.61, 2.62, 2.70, 3.3, 3.12, 3.67. The notion of cryptocurrency 'attracting' property rights was expressly recognized in *D'Alolia v Persons Unknown* [2024] EWHC 2342 (Ch), though the point was conceded by counsel.
[60] Property (Digital Assets etc) Act 2025.

in the case of rights themselves.[61] In any case, as the discussion above shows, that right could equally be a personal right. Moreover, on Spence's and the Law Commission's thinking, what is there to stop the rights in cases like *Hill v Tupper* and *King v David Allen (Billposting)* being the 'object' of property rights? However, if they were, the *numerus clausus* would be destroyed.

The thinking does not work for the same reason that 'ownership as right' does not work. Just as it is meaningless to speak of a debt being the object of ownership, so too is it meaningless to speak of it as the object of a property right. Once again, what would be the content of this right? The benefit of the debt is already vested in the creditor. What does it add to say that the creditor has a property right to the benefit of the debt? It is impossible to have a right to a right, let alone a property right to a right.

4. Property as Wealth

It is sometimes said that property is wealth. We see this, for example, in a textbook on personal property, where we are told that: 'the law of personal property is the law of property, or in economic terms, the law governing wealth and resources, save that one important category of resources is carved out', that carve-out being interests in land.[62] A similar view is expressed by Goode in the note mentioned above, who said that 'property is anything of realisable commercial value'.[63] If true, choses in action as rights are 'property' because they can be assigned for value and choses in action as causes of action are property because they can sometimes be assigned and in all cases will eventually, assuming a solvent defendant, generate wealth.

The proposition is, however, demonstrably false,[64] betraying a peculiarly non-legal approach to the topic. The benefit of the advertising contract in *King v David Allen (Billposting)* was 'wealth', in that it generated income for the rightholder and could have been sold, but it was not 'property' when that word is used, as it should be, as a qualifier of rights. Likewise, the benefit of the contractual licence to occupy land in *Prudential Assurance v London Residuary Body* was 'wealth', but it was not 'property', save again in this non-technical sense. What seems to be happening here is an equation of the word 'asset' with 'property'.

[61] Discussion above, text to note 57.
[62] Bridge et al 2021, [1-011].
[63] Goode 2023, 4.
[64] See the trenchant reply to Goode by Stevens 2023.

However, many 'things' are valuable and so can be reduced into money. A person's labour, for example, can be bought and sold, but John Locke apart,[65] we would not describe it as 'property'. Likewise, though information can sometimes be turned into money, it is not property *per se*.[66] Simply because a chose in action as right can be turned into money by sale, or a chose in action as cause of action can be turned into money through sale or litigation, does not make either of them 'property'.

5. Assignability

It is sometimes said that because choses in action can be assigned, they are 'property'. This is wrong, for two reasons. First, as seen, assignability is not the test of whether a right is a property right. Although most property rights are assignable, many personal rights are as well.

Second, as also seen, many of the 'things' in the category 'chose in action' either still are[67] or were for many years unassignable. Take the benefit of a debt. Although for centuries considered a chose in action, they were incapable of assignment until the enactment of the Judicature Act 1873.[68] The fact of assignability cannot therefore be the explanation of their 'propertiness'.

6. Choses in Action are 'Things'

As seen, laypersons might describe physical things, plots of land, and bicycles as 'property'. But, as also seen, this is not, or at least should not be, the language of the law. Lawyers need always to divorce physical things from rights. Nevertheless, it is sometimes said that choses in action are 'things' and for that reason alone 'property'.

Harris, for example, says that intellectual property rights are property rights in the same way as property rights are with respect to land and goods because they have as their object 'things' called 'ideational entities'.[69] However, ideational entities, whatever these might be, cannot be equated with physical

[65] Locke 1689, s 27.
[66] *Boardman v Phipps* [1967] 2 AC 46, 89–90 (Viscount Dilhorne), 103 (Lord Cohen), 127–128 (Lord Upjohn).
[67] As seen, company shares to this day cannot be assigned, only novated: text to note 36.
[68] Now the Law of Property Act 1925, s 136.
[69] Harris 1996, ch 4.

things. Take again the case of copyright in a song. The 'ideational entity' cannot be the song itself, which may still be in the composer's head: there is no copyright until it is recorded.[70] Copyright does not protect ideas *per se*,[71] only particular expressions of ideas. Thus, the 'ideational entity' which was the style of face paint used by Adam of the rock group Adam and the Ants was held by the Court of Appeal not to be capable of being the subject matter of copyright as a 'painting'[72] because there was no 'surface' on which anything was painted.[73] Lawton LJ was adamant that copyright was not about the protection of ideas *per se*, only expressions thereof: 'a painting is not an idea: it is an object; and paint without a surface is not a painting. Make-up, as such, however idiosyncratic it may be as an idea, cannot possibly be a painting for the purposes of the Copyright Act 1956.'[74] By contrast, the law of real and personal property attaches to all physical things.[75]

Moreover, even with copyright in a song, interference with that right takes a different form from interference with rights to possession of physical things. If I sing a Beatles' song in my shower, though I may appropriate this 'ideational entity', I do not infringe the copyright of Lennon and McCartney; it is only a breach of copyright if the performance is made in public.[76] By contrast, if in my shower I use without his consent a bar of soap to which Sir Paul has a better title, I commit the tort of conversion. That the 'thing' cannot be the 'ideational entity' is also illustrated by the fact that copyrights generally run out seventy years after the death of the author,[77] even though the 'ideational entity' will still exist. It is the exact opposite with physical things: if a seagull eats my sandwich, both it and my title are destroyed.

Harris's 'entity', therefore, turns out to be nothing more than the right itself; there is no 'thing' independent of the right. Indeed, this is inherent in the word copy*right* itself. Copyrights are different to rights with respect to physical things, which exist in time and space regardless of recognition by the legal system.

[70] Copyright, Designs and Patents Act 1988, s 1(2): 'Copyright does not subsist in a literary, dramatic or musical work unless and until it is recorded, in writing or otherwise.'

[71] 'It is trite law that there is no copyright in ideas': *LB (Plastics) Ltd v Swish Products Ltd* [1979] FSR 145, 160 (Lord Hailsham); see also Lord Salmon at 165.

[72] 'Artistic works' can be the subject matter of copyright, one form of which are paintings: Copyright, Designs and Patents Act 1988, s 1(1)(a) and s 4(2).

[73] *Merchandising Corpn of America v Harpbond* [1983] FSR 32.

[74] Ibid, 46.

[75] Even human beings in darker parts of our history.

[76] Copyright, Designs and Patents Act 1988, s 16(1)(c).

[77] Ibid, s 12(2).

VIII. Why This Matters

Birks once wrote that, 'Flawed classification is a source and symptom of intellectual disorder'.[78] If looking for an example, he could not have chosen a better one than the notion that our law of personal property divides between choses in possession and choses in action.

We have already seen how the false opposition confused the Law Commission in its work on digital assets. It has also led the courts into error. Probably the most egregious example is Lady Hale's speech in *OBG v Allen*,[79] where the question was whether it was possible to 'convert' the benefit of a contract. There is of course a tort of inducing breach of contract, but, as seen,[80] that requires both an inducement and a high degree of fault, neither of which were present on the facts of the case. Lady Hale nevertheless held that the plaintiff could resort to the strict liability tort of conversion, normally reserved for interferences with rights to possession of physical things other than land. She said:

> In a logical world, there would be such a proprietary remedy for the usurpation of all forms of property. The relevant question should be, not 'is there a proprietary remedy?', but 'is what has been usurped property?' The essential feature of property is that it has an existence independent of a particular person: it can be bought and sold, given and received, bequeathed and inherited, pledged or seized to secure debts . . . Once the law recognises something as property, the law should extend a proprietary remedy to protect it.[81]

The flawed taxonomy is leading her ladyship astray. Once it is realized that choses in action are not property rights *per se*, the analogy with property rights with respect to physical things breaks down and the supposed 'illogicality' falls away. Fortunately, the majority in that case, led by Lord Hoffmann, was not misled.

[78] Birks 2004, 20.
[79] [2008] 1 AC 1.
[80] Text to note 41.
[81] *OBG v Allen* [2008] 1 AC 1, [309].

IX. Conclusion

The phrases 'chose in possession' and 'chose in action' originally did nothing more than describe states of affairs; they were not concerned with classes of rights and were logically opposed. Chose in possession described the fact of a physical thing being in a person's possession, while chose in action described the fact of a person having the ability to bring a court action to obtain a physical thing, either land or money. 'Chose' in both phrases meant 'physical thing'.

However, that meaning has changed over time. Nowadays, both categories encompass *rights*, though chose in action continues to include causes of action. They are no longer logically opposed. Causes of action are not rights and do not therefore belong in a supposed taxonomy of rights. Further, a person non-consensually dispossessed of goods has both a chose in possession, their right to possession not evaporating on dispossession, and also a chose in action, the ability to bring an action to recover money as compensation for the infringement of their right, meaning that the categories are not mutually exclusive. Finally, of the rights classified as choses in action, they are arbitrarily defined by the common characteristic of there being no self-help remedy for interference, a criterion having nothing to do with whether a right is proprietary.

Nor can choses in action be made property by the fact that they belong to someone, that they have value, are assignable, or are 'things'. Further, it is analytically impossible to say that they can be the objects of rights of ownership or of rights of property, for that is to assume they behave as physical things do.

What we in fact have in the category chose in action is a miscellany of rights and causes of action, with most of the rights having no proprietary status at all and with causes of action not even being rights. They should not therefore share the same designation or be seen as a subset of personal property. As Lindley LJ pointed out in *Colonial Bank v Whinney*:

> No little confusion has arisen from this extended use of the expression '*chose in action*' . . . Though debts, money in the funds, shares in companies, copyrights and patents are all incorporeal personal property, they are so different in their nature and legal incidents, that care must be taken not to be misled by giving them all a common name which conceals their differences. We all know that our law has not been put into a very scientific shape, and there is often considerable difficulty in determining in what sense a particular expression, such as '*chose in action*', is used.[82]

[82] (1885) 30 Ch D 261, 283–284.

The use of a common name to conceal a plethora of rights and actions has led many to see them as sharing the same characteristics, especially when it is thought that, along with choses in possession, they are part of a wider category of personal property. If choses in possession are 'property', the thinking goes, so too must choses in action.

However, choses in action are not, or at least are not all, 'property' when that label is used as a qualifier of rights. They cannot therefore be juxtaposed with property rights with respect to goods. Though intellectual property rights may rightly claim to be a species of property right, nothing else within the category, either rights or causes of action, can. Only when this is realized will our law be put into 'scientific shape'. In the meantime, judges and law reform bodies will continue to be confused.

References

Benjamin, J. (2000). Interests in Securities: A Proprietary Law Analysis of the International Securities Markets. Oxford, Oxford University Press.

Birks, P. (ed), (1997). The Classification of Obligations. Oxford, Oxford University Press.

Birks, P. (2004). Unjust Enrichment. 2nd edn. Oxford, Oxford University Press.

Blackstone, W. (1765–1769). Commentaries on the Laws of England. 1st edn. Oxford, Oxford University Press.

Booth, G. (1811). The Nature and Practice of the Real Actions: in their Writ and Process: both Original and Judicial. 2nd edn. London, W. Clarke and Sons.

Bridge et al. (2021), Bridge, M., Gullifer, L., Low, K., and McMeel, G., The Law of Personal Property. 3rd edn. London, Sweet and Maxwell.

Chambers, R. (2026) 'Restrictive Covenants'. The Property-Contract Interface. Penner, J., et al. Oxford, Oxford University Press.

de Zulueta, F. (1946). The Institutes of Gaius. Oxford, Oxford University Press.

Goode, R. (2023) 'What is Property?' Law Quarterly Review 139: 1.

Gretton, G. (2007). 'Ownership and its Objects'. Rabels Zeitschrift für ausländisches und internationales Privatrecht (RabelsZ) 71: 802

Harris, J. (1996). Property and Justice. Oxford, Oxford University Press.

Law Commission (England and Wales) (2023). 'Digital Assets: Final Report' (Law Com No 412).

Liew, Y. (2024). Guest & Liew on the Law of Assignment. 5th edn. London, Sweet & Maxwell.

Locke, J. (1689). Two Treatises of Government. 1st edn. London. Awnsham Churchill.

Micheler, E. (2002). 'Legal Title and the Transfer of Shares in a Paperless World—Farewell Quasi-Negotiability'. Journal of Business Law 358.

Pretto-Sakmann, A. (2005). Boundaries of Personal Property: Shares and Sub-shares. Oxford, Hart.

Rastell (1563). Les Termes de la Ley: or Certain Difficult and Obscure Words and Termes of the Common Lawes and Statutes of this Realme now in Use Expounded and Explained. London, printed by the Assignes of John More Esquire.

Reid, K. (1996). The Law of Property in Scotland. Edinburgh/London, Law Society of Scotland/Butterworths.

Salmond, J. (1957). Jurisprudence. 11th edn. London, Sweet & Maxwell.
Smith, M. and N. Leslie (2018). The Law of Assignment. 3rd edn. Oxford, Oxford University Press.
Spence, M. (2007). Intellectual Property. Oxford, Oxford University Press.
Stevens, R. (2023). 'Crypto is Not Property'. Law Quarterly Review 139: 615.
Sutton, R. (1929). Personal Actions at Common Law. London, Butterworth & Co.
Tham, C. (2019). Understanding the Law of Assignment. Cambridge, Cambridge University Press.

16
Having, Doing, Owing

Larissa Katz

I. Introduction

For most of its history, the common law did without the distinction between in rem and in personam rights.[1] Even after its adoption into the Anglo-American legal lexicon as an important if imperfect tool for classifying rights, many common law scholars continued to see it as a Roman Law conceit, ill-suited to traditional categories of contract, debt, tort, property, and equity.[2] It remained a well-used but precarious distinction in common law thinking until the legal realist movement got a hold of it.[3] Building on a Hohfeldian view of rights as bipolar relations, the legal realists pushed aside the idea of property as a right in rem to make room for the idea of property as a collection of bipolar relations (a bundle of rights).[4] Not everyone was sold, of course. Many courts and commentators continued to describe rights as 'in rem' or 'in personam'.[5] By the early 2000s, however, it was increasingly clear that the distinction was headed for obsolescence in the American legal academy.[6] The *Property/Contract Interface* changed that. It effectively rehabilitated the distinction in academic circles. It identified the unique advantage of in rem rights (which it called the exclusion strategy) in terms of the conservation of information costs where there is a large and indefinite audience for the rights. Twenty years later, its legacy endures in a renewed appreciation of the distinction, significance, and

[1] Austin is credited with introducing the distinction into common law thinking. See Austin 1873, 176.
[2] See Williams 1888; Buckland & McNair 1965. On the adoption of the distinction, see Kocourek 1920, 322.
[3] See, eg, Cohen 1954, 373–374. See Kocurek 1920, 322 ('The definition of Austin adopted from the modern civilians has been so often repeated that it seems *prima facie* a doubtful labor at this late day to question it.')
[4] For a discussion of the realist's intervention in American property law and theory, see Smith 2011.
[5] Birks 2000, 21 (describing 'a first division between proprietary rights (rights in rem) and personal rights (rights in personam)').
[6] Balganesh & Katz 2022.

Larissa Katz, *Having, Doing, Owing* In: *The Property-Contract Interface*. Edited by: James Penner, Irina Sakharova, Henry E. Smith, and Zhong Xing Tan, Oxford University Press.
DOI: 10.1093/9780198951995.003.0021

interplay between the two basic types of rights and the strategies—exclusion and governance—associated with each.[7]

In this chapter, I want to isolate three ideas about the nature of in rem and in personam rights and the differences between them, that owe their prominence to the *Property/Contract Interface*.[8] First is the idea that in personam rights (with contracts as the core case) and in rem rights (with property as the core case) form opposite poles of a spectrum of rights.[9] Second, there is the idea that the pressure for standardization intensifies (or eases) as we move closer to (or farther away from) the in rem end of the spectrum because of the information and other costs associated with enforcing rights against a large and indefinite class of others (or against a small and definite class of others).[10] Finally, there is what I will call the non-differentiation thesis, which has a stronger and a weaker form. This is the idea that a pure in rem duty does not entail (in the stronger form of the thesis)[11] or require (in its weaker form) the differentiation of one owner from the next.[12]

In the discussion that follows, I raise some questions relating to these themes and suggest that the general distinction between in rem/in personam rights ought to be understood in terms of two categorically distinct ways we can relate to others in law. This chapter proceeds in three stages. The first advances reasons to shift from contract to debt as the core of an in personam right.[13] Like

[7] A governance strategy supplements an exclusion strategy in a legal order, allowing for refinements to the basic 'keep off' message of an in rem right. Smith 2012, 1693–1694. See also Smith 2002 (identifying exclusion and governance strategies for the delineation of rights).

[8] I note that Merrill and Smith's cost-benefit model of rights contains considerably more nuance and depth than I can hope to capture in this chapter. See, eg, the emergence of an explicitly modular theory of property in later work, such as Smith 2012, 1693 ('Property organizes this world into lumpy packages of legal relations—legal things—by setting boundaries around useful attributes that tend to be strong complements. The law of property in effect encapsulates these lumpy packages, or modules, semitransparently from other modules and the outside world generally.').

[9] On the idea that in rem and in personam rights lie on a spectrum of rights, see Merrill & Smith 2001, 809 ('It should be remembered, however, that we are dealing with a spectrum from in personam to in rem rights, and we will emphasize how familiar problems of incomplete information are increasingly important as one moves toward the in rem pole of the spectrum.')

[10] Ibid, 788 ('In rem rights, in other words, involve indefiniteness and numerosity in two directions. . . . [O]wnership is protected against interference from a large and indefinite class of dutyholders. But each dutyholder also confronts a world containing a large and indefinite class of owned things.'). Ibid, 790 ('*In personam* rights will be governed by flexible legal rules that minimize the costs of tailoring rights and obligations to each particular situation, whereas in rem rights will be governed by bright-line rules that allow large and indefinite numbers of people to identify owned resources at low cost.') The model is not limited to information costs. See, eg, Smith 2021, 17–18 (denying that 'the main purpose of property is to lower information costs' and emphasizing that complexity gives rise to information costs, but 'information costs are but part of the picture'). Finally, see Smith 2012, 1700 ('property itself could and would be otherwise in the absence of transaction costs.')

[11] Penner 1997, 27.

[12] Merrill & Smith 2001, 795.

[13] For what counts as 'classic debt', see *Benjamin D. & Madeline Prentice Gilbert v Commissioner of Internal Revenue*, 248 F 2d 399, 402 (2d Cir 1957) 'The classic debt is an unqualified obligation to pay a sum certain at a reasonably close fixed maturity date along with a fixed percentage in interest payable

a basic contract, debt is a legal relation between singular and definite parties. Unlike contract, debt is necessarily defined in terms of a standardized, inflexible, bright-line rule: pay what you owe, which is always a fixed sum.[14]

The second stage of the discussion raises some doubts about the non-differentiation thesis in its stronger and weaker forms. In rem property rights are better seen as positions of authority that require others to *defer* to the person in charge, the designated agenda-setter for a specific, identifiable thing.[15] By putting owners in charge of deciding who can do what with things, property rights enable the making of plans around, with, or through things. To know what deference requires of her, a non-owner must differentiate owners, as distinct loci of authority. Of course, an across the board keep-off strategy would enable non-owners to avoid liability at a low cost—just like paying 50 per cent of your income in tax, in a system with at most a 50% tax rate, will ensure you do not run afoul of tax authorities. But a rule of abstention whether de jure or de facto does not achieve coordination *through* property as opposed to by other means (eg contract). Deference to an owner's agenda—which requires the differentiation of owners—does.

And, finally, the third stage points in the direction of a different basis for distinguishing in rem/in personam rights, in terms of categorically different ways we can stand in relation to others in a legal order and the kind of wrong essentially associated with each. One kind of right takes the form of authority to decide a question, requiring others to defer to the exercise of that power. And the other kind of right takes the form of a right that stipulates how another should act: 'pay what you owe', 'do as you agreed', and so on. The in rem/in personam distinction also tracks the different ways that we can wrong others (requiring or dispensing with intention).

II. Shifting Focus from Doing to Owing

Merrill and Smith's account takes contractual rights to be the central case of in personam rights. They draw key features of a 'pure' in personam right—for example, their potential flexibility, granularity, customizability—from the nature

regardless of the debtor's income or lack thereof.' *Brown v Budget Rent-a-Car Systems, Inc*, 119 F 3d 922 (11th Cir 1997) ('As long as transaction creates obligation to pay, "debt" is created.')

[14] While contract *may* be standardized for reasons related to its function, simple debt requires it. See Smith 2006, 1176 ('Boilerplate is highly standardized, and when courts interpret boilerplate they treat it as intentionally standardized and not harboring unusual meanings').

[15] *National Provincial Bank Ltd v Ainsworth* [1965] AC 1175 (UK HL) (*Ainsworth*).

of basic contracts. Playing up what we can learn from contractual rights may have the effect of playing down what we can learn from other kinds of pure in personam rights like debt, a right to receive or collect a fixed sum of value from another.

1. Debt as the Central Case?

Here are three reasons to look at the in rem/in personam distinction through the lens of debt. Taken together they suggest that debt is, if not the only pure in personam right, at least a central case that any account of the category ought to reflect.[16]

One reason has to do with history. In the beginning, there was debt and property. A claim of this sort ('you owe me a fixed sum') is foundational in English private law, its place secured long before modern contract law arrived on the scene.[17] English law before the sixteenth century did not recognize a general liability simply for failing to perform an undertaking as agreed outside of a covenant under seal.[18] Instead of a claim-right to another's *doing* something agreed to, English law recognized a claim-right to another's *owing* a fixed sum.[19] Of course, an agreement under which some benefit had been conferred may give rise to a debt (a fixed sum now owed in return). But debt can arise for other reasons too: a court judgment, a statutory obligation to pay dues, a written instrument made under seal (i.o.u.).[20] The dichotomy between having and owing thus preceded the dichotomy between having and doing. Whether

[16] While some debts are contractual, others are not, arising in the context of accounting actions, judgment orders, written instruments. See, eg, Cheshire, Fifoot, & Furmston 1986; Lehman & Phelps 2005, 365 ('a sum of money that is owed or due to be paid because of an express agreement; a specified sum of money that one is obligated to pay, and another is entitled to receive or collect.')

[17] By Tudor times, an action for debt on an obligation was the 'commonest single type of action in the Common Pleas'. Baker 2019, 345.

[18] Covenants under seal were used primarily in relation to land or other long-term relationships rather than in ordinary commercial contexts (eg purchase and sale of goods). Baker, ibid, 339 ('This writ was usually brought to enforce covenants concerning land, such as leases, and was said to have been invented for that purpose, but its wording was not so restricted.') Some scholars have thought that covenants originally were restricted to land although any such subject-matter restrictions were loosened later. See Simpson 1987, 10. Modern contracts emerged later in the sixteenth century, when courts started to recognize liability for non-feasance (failing to do as agreed). See Cheshire, Fifoot, & Furmston 1946, 9–10.

[19] In medieval law, debt might be measured in money or some other defined value or fungible. See Baker 2019, 342 ('The difference between detinue and debt resulted from the necessary distinction between specific chattels, which were owned, and money or fungibles, which were owed.') A creditor could prove debt by producing a document under seal or proving some transaction between the parties sufficient to give rise to debt—the obligation to pay a fixed sum. Ibid, 343 ff.

[20] Halsbury & Hailsham 1931, vol 2, s 11, 262–263; Chesire, Fifoot, & Furmston 1946, 3–4.

you did or did not do something you promised to do was up to you as far as the common law was concerned unless the covenant was made under seal. But whether you owed someone money was a matter that the common law took very seriously, in the form of an action in debt. Given the foundational importance of debt in the development of the common law, one might reasonably expect to see debt reflected in the nature of in personam rights generally.

A second reason for organizing the discussion around debt is that it offers a cleaner contrast with property, all the better to see the basis for the distinction between in personam and in rem rights. Contracts can give rise to an interest in the use of a particular thing or a right to be conveyed a particular thing and even (at least in the case of specifically performable contracts) may convey equitable proprietary rights in that thing. By contrast, it is axiomatic that a claim in debt is and remains a liquidated demand, not a right that implicates the use or conveyance of particular things.[21] Debt, in short, is and remains liquidated in a way that provides a clear contrast with property, which always relates to a specific thing.[22] A debt does not create any interest in property of the debtor: a creditor has no claim to any particular asset of the debtor. That explains why any loss of assets on the part of the debtor has no effect on the persistence of the creditor's right whereas the destruction of a thing to which a property right relates destroys the property right.[23] A debtor's loss of her wherewithal may affect the enforcement, not the existence, of a debt: a debtor cannot be held in civil contempt for a failure to pay as ordered if the debtor lacks the ability to pay. But this has nothing to do with the nature of debt and everything to do with the nature of a court order and its command of obedience. Disobedience must be voluntary to count as contempt. Finally, the categorical distinction between property and debt also explains why a third party can effectively discharge another's debt by paying the sum owing out of the third party's own pocket, with assets that *never* belonged to the debtor.

Finally, there are some doctrinal advantages to thinking about the in rem/in personam distinction in terms of the property/debt distinction. The contrast between property and debt is *the* operative in rem/in personam distinction in many highly visible and salient legal contexts. Take the bankruptcy context. If

[21] See, eg, *Fitzroy v Cave* [1905] 2 KB 364 (CA), per Cozens-Hardy. See below on how debt itself might, through equity's intervention or through statute, become the object of intangible property rights (a right to the debt action). See Williams 1894; Sweet 1895. See also Tham 2019.

[22] See, eg, *Re Goldcorp Exchange Ltd (in Receivership)* [1995] 1 AC 74 (PC), 90 (on the requirement of an identifiable, specific thing). See also *Ainsworth*, 494; Swadling 2013, 177.

[23] Kocourek 1920, 327 (the 'inability of a debtor to pay does not in the slightest way affect the full measure of his legal duty.') See *Videotron Ltee v Industries Microlec Produits Electroniques Inc* [1992] 2 SCR 1065 (SCC) at 1078. See also *Ex Parte Radford* [1918] 18 SR 6 (NSW) at 6, 7 (noting that non-payment of a debt in circumstances in which the debtor is unable to pay is not grounds for contempt).

we want to work out someone's position vis-à-vis the debtor's estate in bankruptcy, we ask whether that person's rights are classified as property or debt, e.g., whether that person is an owner/bailor of some particular thing, with a right to its return (in rem rights), or just a creditor, owed a fixed sum of money (in personam rights).[24] Of course, a person can become a creditor owed a fixed sum *because* of a contract (eg for the amount of the purchase price for something sold to but not paid for by the debtor). But notice that the contracts behind some debts do not figure in the way we organize claims in relation to the debtor's estate in bankruptcy. We ask only if the claim is merely one of debt (or can be reduced to debt) as opposed to property—whether that debt originated in contract or in some other legal event.

The property/debt distinction is just as fundamental in equity as it is in law. For example, it organizes how equity conceives of the beneficiary's position in relation to the trustee following an action for an account. If a trustee embezzles trust funds, equity must determine, through the accounting process, whether the beneficiary is in the end just a creditor owed a fixed sum (debt) or has a proprietary claim to something identifiable as the *res* or its proceeds through tracing. We ask in other words whether the beneficiary *has* something, that is, equitable property in respect of a specific asset or *is owed* something, that is, equitable debt. If the latter, the beneficiary has a right that the trustee pay a fixed sum following an accounting procedure to reconstitute the trust.[25] If the former, the trustee or a third party holds property rights in the original trust *res* or its traceable proceeds for the benefit of the beneficiary.[26]

Finally, debt is often invoked as paradigmatic of rights at the in personam end of the in rem/in personam distinction in a broad swathe of historical and contemporary legal writing.[27] Now of course debt and contract often go hand in hand—as I explain later when describing the parallel ways in which contract

[24] See Kull 1998, 279 ('Unless he can present himself as the owner, legal or equitable, of property that the trustee holds for the bankruptcy estate, even the plaintiff whose restitution claim is good against the debtor will fail to state a claim in restitution as against the general creditors.') Cf Balganesh & Katz 2022 (drawing the in rem–in personal distinction in terms of 'persistent rights.')

[25] See *Libertarian Investments Ltd v Hall* [2013] HKCFA 93 (describing an award in account not as 'granting a remedy for wrong but enforcing performance of an obligation.'). Oosterhoff 2004, 1004 (The nature of the obligation is 'a claim in relation to a fixed amount, that is the amount revealed by the accounting, and in this sense, it is "in the nature of debt" ').

[26] Watson 2016; Smith 2023.

[27] Maitland 1969 (noting two classes of private rights, rights in rem and rights in personam, which map onto the two broad categories of ownership and debt, in the course of complaining that this framework cannot explain the trust.). Even Hohfeld appears to have used debt as the primary example of an in personam right: 'If B owes A a thousand dollars, A has an affirmative right in personam, or paucital right, that B shall do what is necessary to transfer to A the legal ownership of that amount of money.' (Merrill & Smith 2010, 782, citing Hohfeld 1917, 72) Of course, contract is frequently invoked as a classic in personam right, too. See Corbin 1924, 501 and 509 (referring to contracts).

interacts with both in rem and in personam rights (property and debt). But let me ward off any suspicion that debt *reduces* to contract. Notice that: whereas contracts require consideration, debts can arise gratuitously. Whereas contracts are always voluntary, a debt can arise involuntarily (as in cases of mistaken payments, or in accounting actions, where trustees owe a duty in the nature of debt to restore the trust if they turn out not to have received or to have released trust assets contrary to the terms of the trust.). Whereas contracts can be frustrated, debts cannot be: a debt is not destroyed by the debtor's inability to pay.[28] And while contract may be the cause of a debt, debt has other causes, including court judgments, statutes, written instruments under seal (i.o.u), and accounts.[29]

2. Debt and Bright-Line Rules

Across the variety of legal contexts that give rise to debts in law or equity, debt necessarily takes a simple, standardized form: a right to the payment of a fixed sum of money. In its simple prescription—pay what you owe—a debt deploys a strategy for defining rights that Merrill and Smith associate with a core case of in rem rights, property.[30]

While property and debt both have a simple, standardized form associated with lower processing costs, there is nothing more in personam than the creditor–debtor relationship itself. Debt does not generate any proprietary claims in respect of the debtor's present or future assets. That is why a mere (ie unsecured) creditor has no claim to any assets in the debtor's estate-in-bankruptcy but must stand in line with every other creditor to claim a pro rata share in whatever assets are left after in rem rights are satisfied. That is also why it counts just as much as a discharge of a debt if a third party pays the creditor the amount owed with assets that never belonged to the debtor. And that is why debt does not depend for its existence on the debtor having assets at the time the debt is acquired or any time thereafter. A debt as a right to the payment of a

[28] See Kocourek 1920, 326–327. Bankruptcy and insolvency does not destroy so much as transform a debt. See Pistor 2019, 16 ('When insolvency loom, insisting on contract enforcement is no longer an answer; instead, it is time to decide who gets how much and in what order.')

[29] Halsbury & Hailsham 1931, vol 2, s 11, 262–263; Chesire, Fifoot, & Furmston 1946, 3–4.

[30] See, eg, Merrill & Smith 2000 ('The imperative of standardization is strongest when the number of potential dutyholders is greatest. Property rights . . . bind all the world and thus present the greatest need for standardization. Contract rights, which bind only the parties, create no comparable externality and thus can be freely customized.') Merrill and Smith identify intermediate situations, between 'pure' in rem and in personam types of right; eg compound-paucital (rights against numerous defined persons) and quasi-multital (rights against singular but undefined persons). Merrill and Smith 2001, 803.

fixed sum is the opposite of a property right. Finally, debt consists of a bilateral relationship between a creditor and debtor, defined in terms of what the latter owes the former.[31]

Of course, a debt relationship may *itself* serve as an object of a third-party's intangible property right (with the assistance of supplemental rules of legislation or equity that constrain the right of a debtor to discharge the debt by payment to the original creditor, where the latter assigned the debt to someone else with notice to the debtor).[32] The assignability of debt, when coupled with rules disallowing discharge except by payment to the assignee, gives rise to what Merrill and Smith call a quasi-multital situation: a singular definite debtor and an undefined creditor.[33] The law responds, just as Merrill and Smith suggest it should, with protective notice requirements: an assignee's right to payment is enforceable only against a debtor with notice. For my purposes, it is important that the assignment of debt, with the introduction of third-party effects, relates to something that is already, even in the absence of downstream third-party effects, a highly standardized in personam relation between a creditor and a debtor. Debt is not itself quasi-multital and so not itself located at an intermediate point between in personam and in rem poles. Debt is in itself a personal obligation that is distinctly at the in personam end of the spectrum, alongside basic contract rights.

Contract rights, unlike debt, clearly do represent a governance strategy. This feature of contract reveals less about the nature of in personam rights and more about contract itself and its role in qualifying other legal relations, *both* in rem and in personam. Contract serves to refine creditor–debtor relations in a way that parallels its role in relation to property: it has the same governance function in relation to both. Through a supplementary layer of contractual relations on top of the creditor–debtor relation, parties can achieve the granularity that debt alone does not permit. Through contract, they can customize specific terms relating to the schedule for repayment, penalties for missing a payment,[34] interest rates, etc, and even provide for the satisfaction of the debt

[31] See Simpson 1987, 17 (describing an early case requiring the plaintiff to bring an action in covenant not debt to enforce an agreement under seal to pay a third party a fixed sum.)

[32] There is now a huge market in debt but whether debt can serve as the object of a property right is another (and indeed a contested) matter. See Swadling 2013, 175; Pretto-Sakmann 2005, 218; Swadling (forthcoming). For my purposes, whatever the status of an assignee's right to the enforcement of the underlying debt, that right relates to a pre-existing legal relation—the debt itself—which is quintessentially in personam.

[33] Merrill and Smith 2001, 805 ('where the number of parties is small but the identity of one of the affected parties is indefinite, a lack of information about the indefinite party is likely to be a problem'.)

[34] See Downes 1996 (on limits of freedom of contract in this context).

other than through its repayment in full.[35] But notice that contract in all of these cases *adds* a layer of governance to the creditor–debtor relationship rather than subsuming it. If the contract fails for any reason, the debt remains.

3. The Relationship between Function and Strategy

What can we take away from centring the discussion of in personam rights around debt? For one thing, we learn that even pure in personam rights (between definite and singular parties) are not necessarily aligned with any particular strategy for defining rights. Governance and exclusion strategies for defining rights may cut across the in rem/in personam divide. Differences across in personam rights (pliable, customizable rights, like contract or rigid, standardized rights like debt) reflect the different function of each in the legal order. Contract, by enabling us to assume liability for failing to perform our voluntary undertakings, allows the formation of voluntary associations tailored to private purposes. This fits with the idea that contracts add a layer of bespoke governance to other more rigid and standardized legal relations—although I would note that it does so *across* the in personam/in rem divide—in relation to debt and property alike.

Debt's standardized, inflexible form is required by *its* function, independent of the size and indefiniteness of the audience. Debt enables the thinnest form of interpersonal interaction—one abstracted from the purposes or expectations we may have in entering a creditor–debtor relationship in the first place.[36] If a right genuinely is in the nature of debt, then it is a kind of right the content of which does not depend on the intentions or purposes of the parties. This means that the content of a right in the nature of a debt must take the form of something that is fungible: a right to the payment of a fixed sum of money. If it turns out that the specific purposes of the parties in lending/borrowing the sum are intertwined with the content of the rights-duties of the parties, we are no longer dealing just with debt, but something else: a kind of trust.[37]

[35] Traditionally, contracts for the satisfaction of debt for less than its full amount presented problems because of the nature of debt as a liquidated demand. See *Sibree v Tripp* (1846) 153 ER 745, 15 M&W 23; *Foakes v Beer* (1884) 9 App Cas 605 (UK HL). There have been many refinements to this basic rule (eg payment of less by a third party; payment prior to maturity; payment somewhere new, all of which operate as a discharge of the debt by accord and satisfaction.)

[36] Recall that debt does not reduce to contract and so ought not itself to be understood as self-standardization.

[37] Of course purposes of the parties may bear on the initial classification of some relationships as creditor–debtor or something else (bailment, trusts, etc). *Re Lowden*, 1978 CarswellAlta 362, [1978] AJ No 943. Oosterhoff 2019.

In some jurisdictions, this is known as the *Quistclose* trust, which works like this:[38]

> Money advanced by way of loan normally becomes the property of the borrower. He is free to apply the money as he chooses and save to the extent to which he may have taken security for repayment the lender takes the risk of the borrower's insolvency. But it is well established that a loan to a borrower for a specific purpose where the borrower is not free to apply the money for any other purpose gives rise to fiduciary obligation on the part of the borrower which a court of equity will enforce.[39]

Debt serves as the lowest common denominator of all private law relations. It allows more complex relationships (between parties to contracts, between a successful plaintiff and a defendant in a tort action, between a trustee and a beneficiary in cases of breaches of trust leaving no traceable proceeds) to reduce to a simple legal relation defined by a bright-line rule: 'Y, pay a fixed sum of money to X.'[40]

Debt's non-purposive character and its standard form also allow it uniquely to be aggregated and set off against other legal relations of the same kind.[41] Other private law rights cannot be set off against each other in the same way. Two contractual rights cannot be set off against each other because they are not commensurable; for example, my right to a horse against your right to a cart, although of course parties can contractually agree to treat the rights as set off against each other. Nor can your right to bodily security be set off against my right to bodily security for the same reason: for example, your right not to be injured negligently against my right not to be injured negligently. But it is possible to set off a right to collect $100 from you against your right to collect $50 from me, leaving me with a reduced (rather than a whole new) claim that you pay me $50.[42] Rights in the nature of debt can be set off because they are defined just in terms of fixed sum, and not in terms of activities, purposes, or interests that lack a common measure.

[38] *Barclays Bank Ltd v Quistclose Investments Ltd* (1968), [1970] AC 567 (UK HL). For an overview and critical discussion of the idea of a Quistclose trust, see Swadling 2004. For the American approach, see, eg, Linarelli 2009. ('In the United States, the trust would likely be a security interest, and a creditor not pursuing Article 9 secured creditor status would bear significant risk of loss in the event of the debtor's default or bankruptcy.')

[39] *Twinsectra, Ltd v Yardley* [2002] 2 AC 164 (UK HL), [58].

[40] Even specific performable contracts can be reduced to a creditor–debtor relationship if a court orders a monetary equivalent of specific performance. See Berryman 2023.

[41] It is axiomatic that '[i]n its application set-off is limited to money claims.' Halsbury & Hailsham 1938, vol 29, 479, para 676. For a discussion of the distinctive nature of equitable set off, see Stevens 2018.

[42] See note 39 above for discussion.

In this section, I have mostly focused on why it may be useful to start with debt rather than contract in working out what distinguishes in rem and in personam rights. Contract and debt deploy different strategies for defining rights that reflect their different functions.[43] Whereas contracts allow for the creation of highly customizable rights, rights in the nature of debt require adherence to the same standard, simple form. I argued that this may reveal more about the nature and function of each kind of right in the legal order than it does about the audience for in personam rights or the costs associated with defining their content. If we take debt as a core case of an in personam right, the in rem/in personam distinction no longer appears to align as clearly with two distinct strategies for defining rights. Debt, as a pure in personam right, requires definition in terms of a simple bright-line rule: pay what you owe, which is always a fixed sum.

4. The Non-differentiation Thesis Revisited

If we take property and debt as the two poles of the spectrum of rights, the in personam end of the spectrum starts to looks more like the in rem end of the spectrum in terms of the pressure to standardize and resistance to customization. (Debt, like property, is refined through contract.)

On the far in rem end of the spectrum, the situation is less complicated: as Merrill and Smith explain in *Property/Contract Interface*, rights in rem are characteristically defined in ways that allow for certain cost-saving moves by others in processing the content of an in rem right and what it requires of them. One of these cost-saving moves concerns non-differentiation of owners from the standpoint of dutyholders. On the strong version of the non-differentiation thesis, this is because there is simply a single duty owed to the plurality of owners. As James Penner put it: '[w]e are under one duty to the plurality of property holders however their property is distributed amongst themselves.'[44] On a weaker version of the non-differentiation thesis, dutyholders cognize in rem duties as effectively the same duty to keep off what you do not own, which for epistemological and economic reasons avoids the need for

[43] On incentives to self-standardize, see Merrill and Smith 2000, 35, n 135 ('where liquidity is a primary concern, there is an incentive to conform even to nonmandatory standards'); on standardization of contracts for a variety of reasons, see Smith 2006, 1191 ff.

[44] Penner 1997, 27, quoted in Merrill & Smith 2001, 788. See also Penner 2020, 89–90. Austin describes a 'common duty' on the part of all of mankind to forbear from interfering. Austin 1873, 381. See further Stevens, 2018 42 ('We are (or at least were) merely observing that some duties are owed to other individuals, whilst others relate to physical things and give rise to duties owed to the rest of the world.')

costly differentiation of owners and the rules each sets down.[45] The *Property/ Contract Interface* invoke Jeremy Waldron's formulation of the idea that in rem character of property rights reduces the costs of ordinary social interactions:

> [absent the *in rem* quality of property rights,] citizens would have a great deal of difficulty following the rules . . . He would have to acquire a detailed knowledge of the rules for each resource and of his rights, powers, liberties and duties in relation to it. There would be no other way of ensuring in ordinary life that one abided by the rules except to find out what they were and learn them by heart.[46]

It would be impossible or at least very costly for everyone to learn each owner's different rules for every particular thing in the world.

If we think of property rights as defining separate and independent loci of authoritative decisions about things, it may be that a general in rem duty of deference to authority of this kind requires more differentiation of owners than the non-differentiation thesis suggests. Now of course, just as I can sidestep the authority of a state by staying away from its territory altogether, I can avoid the authority of an owner by avoiding any potential interaction with particular—or all—unowed things. But abstention overdoes what rights in rem require of you. Just as someone can avoid committing a crime by avoiding any activity that is even close to the line or can avoid running afoul of the tax authorities by overpaying taxes, so too risk-averse non-owners may for prudential reasons steer clear of other people's things entirely (self-exclude). Note that the same strategy for avoiding liability is not available in respect of liability for breach of contract: the only way to avoid liability is to do exactly what the contract requires and to absorb the costs of figuring out what that is yourself.

A non-owner who ascribes to 'keep off' as their default strategy with respect to things which she does not own is using a prudential strategy to avoid liability. But following a strategy of abstention is not without costs of its own. The costs are exactly what we would expect them to be: the costs of failing to take full advantage of the extent to which the owner has set an agenda that advances our (divergent) plans, rather than requiring a bypass.

[45] See also Smith 2012, 1701 (by defining property rights in terms of things, property law 'walls off" a 'chunk of the world—a thing—under the owner's control, and much of the information about the thing's uses, their interactions, and the user is irrelevant to the outside world. Duty bearers know not to enter Blackacre without permission or not to take cars, without needing to know what the owner is using the thing for, who the owner is, who else might have rights and other interests, and so on.'

[46] Merrill & Smith 2001, 795 citing Waldron 1988, 42–43. See Penner 1997, 29 ('"Things", then, whether physical things or states of affairs such as bodily security, mediate between rights in rem and duties in rem, blocking any content which has to do with the specific individuality of particular persons from entering the right-duty relation.').

III. The In Rem/In Personam Distinction Revisited

One implication of my analysis so far is that the distinction between in rem and in personam rights does not reliably track two strategies for defining rights (exclusion and governance) with intermediate interventions (eg notice and protection strategies) in between these two poles. If it is not the difference between strategies for defining rights, associated with lower or higher costs, that accounts for the in rem/in personam distinction, what does? I could not begin to offer a full answer to this question (if there is one). But it seems to me that in personam rights, like debt and contract, and in rem rights, like property, reflect two fundamentally different ways in which we can stand in relation to others in a legal order.

1. Two Categories of Rights

In personam rights tell other people what to do (pay! perform! Keep off this thing! Come in only on these terms!)[47] whereas in rem rights tell other people who gets to decide a question (my call!). Put another way, in personam rights are rights to another's doing something and in rem rights convey authority to decide a question which command deference—and the exercise of which may produce rights of *either* variety (more in personam rights, like licences or beneficial interests, or more in rem rights, like subordinate rights to possession).[48]

2. Two Categories of Wrongs

This substantive account of the in rem/in personam distinction has an advantage that might appeal to the common lawyer in all of us. It not only organizes the way we think about rights but how we think about what counts as ways we can wrong others.

[47] A duty to perform or pay may be enforced by an order to do that particular act. See, eg, Smith 2019, 50 ('It is common to describe orders in terms that indicate the legal nature of the stipulated act: thus, authors (including myself) frequently refer to orders to "pay damages", "pay a debt", "cease a trespass", or "perform a contract".')

[48] Browder 1960, 1255 (discussing the 'fundamental conception of the divisibility of ownership . . . '); see also Chang & Smith, 2012, 36–37; Worthington 2000, 672–677 (observing that even personal property can be split between owner and bailee, allowing an owner to share an asset while retaining control.) On the *numerus clausus* principle, see Swadling 2013, 175 ('there is in English law, as with all developed legal systems, a numerus clausus (closed number) of property rights.') Merrill & Smith, 2000, 3 ('Generally speaking, the law will enforce as property only those interests that conform to a limited number of standard forms.').

All in personam legal relations concern rights to a particular other's doing something: 'Keep off', 'pay up', 'do as you agreed to do!', 'execute the trust according to its terms'. All of these duties are strict liability for the same reason: if you have a duty to x or not x, you fail to do what you are obligated to do simply by not x-ing. All in rem legal relations concern authority (in the case of ownership, an exclusive position of agenda-setting authority). We can only wrong someone who has authority by denying their jurisdiction or by taking it for ourselves. This kind of wrong requires intention: you cannot exercise someone else's power without intending to do so because exercising a power means *making* a decision, something that requires intention. Thus, all the classic ways to deny or take another's ownership authority (another's in rem property right) require intention: for example, wrongful usurping of ownership (eg adverse possession) requires *animus possidendi* (at least, the intention to exclude the world at large including the paper title-holder); the wrongful interference with possession requires the intention to interfere; denying authority by slandering title, creating doubt as to the owner's right to property (the right to be the agenda-setter for that thing), also requires intention. Trespass does not require intention but then trespass on its own does not usurp or undermine authority.[49] And the cases where trespass is so flagrant as to amount to an injury to the owner's very authority *do* involve intention.[50] Failures to discharge duties in rem (as opposed to the duties particular non-owners owe to particular owners) involve fault-based liability: to flout or usurp another's authority requires intention or reckless disregard.

IV. Conclusion

The *Property/Contract Interface* is a tremendously illuminating and powerful investigation into the cost-based reasons we have to employ different strategies in defining private rights. This chapter has argued that debt complicates the way we formulate that spectrum. While some kinds of pure in personam rights allow for a high degree of customization, for example, basic contracts, others require a high degree of standardization, for example, basic debt relations. The contrast between both flexible and standardized pure in personam rights on

[49] Prosser 1956, 171 ('The theory of trespass was that the plaintiff remained the owner of the chattel, with his possession only interfered with or interrupted, so that when it was tendered back to him, he must accept it.'). See Kocourek 1920, 332 ('What is A's right against B with respect to the duty not to come on the land? By the definition it is a right *in personam*.')

[50] *Jacque v Steenburg Mobile Homes*, 209 Wis 2D 605 (1997) (awarding punitive damages for the flagrant flouting of authority).

the one hand and in rem property rights on the other may, I have argued, lie elsewhere.

References

Austin, J. (1873, 1966 ed). *Lectures on Jurisprudence, or, The Philosophy of Positive Law.* 4th edn. Vol 1. Bristol, Thoemmes Press.

Baker, J. H. (2019). 'Contract: Covenant and Debt'. *Introduction to English Legal History.* Oxford, Oxford University Press.

Balganesh, S. and L. Katz, (2022). 'The In Rem/In Personam Distinction and Conceptual Partitioning for Persistence'. *Wesley Hohfeld A Century Later.* S. Balganesh, T. M. Sichelman, and H. E. Smith. Cambridge, Cambridge University Press: 258–272.

Berryman, J. (2023). 'Equitable Compensation'. *The Law of Equitable Remedies.* Toronto, Irwin Law: 651–680.

Birks, P. (2000). 'Rights, Wrongs, and Remedies'. Oxford Journal of Legal Studies 20: 1–38.

Browder, O. L., Jr (1960). 'Future Interest Reform'. New York University Law Review 35(7): 1255–1278.

Buckland, W. W. and McNair, A. D. (1965). *Roman Law and Common Law: A Comparison in Outline.* 2nd edn. Cambridge, Cambridge University Press.

Chang, Y. and H. E. Smith (2012). 'An Economic Analysis of Civil versus Common Law Property'. Notre Dame Law Review 88: 1–55.

Cheshire, G. C., C. H. S. Fifoot, and M. P. Furmston (1946). *The Law of Contract.* Oxford, Oxford University Press.

Cohen, F. S. (1954). 'Dialogue on Private Property'. Rutgers Law Review 9: 357–388.

Corbin, A. (1924). 'Rights and Duties'. The Yale Law Journal 33: 501–527.

Downes, T. A. (1996). 'Rethinking Penalty Clauses'. *Wrongs and Remedies in the Twenty-First Century.* Peter Birks. Oxford, Oxford University Press: 249–270.

Furmston, M. P., G. C. Cheshire, and C. H. S. Fifoot (1986). *Cheshire, Fifoot and Furmston's Law of Contract.* 11th edn. London, Butterworth.

Halsbury, S. G. and Q. H. Hailsham (1931). 'Bankruptcy and Insolvency'. *Halsbury's Laws of England Being a Complete Statement of the Whole Law.* 2nd edn. London, Butterworths 2: 1–471.

Halsbury, S. G. and Q. H. Hailsham (1938). 'Set-Off and Counterclaim'. *Halsbury's Laws of England Being a Complete Statement of the Whole Law.* 2nd edn. London, Butterworths 29: 477–520.

Hohfeld, W. N. (1917). 'Fundamental Legal Conceptions as Applied in Judicial Reasoning'. Yale Law Journal 26: 710–770.

Katz, L. (2008). 'Exclusion and Exclusivity in Property Law'. University of Toronto Law Journal 58(3): 275–316.

Katz, L. (2020). 'Ownership and Office: The Building Blocks of a Legal Order'. University of Toronto Law Journal 70: 267–286.

Kocourek, A. (1920). 'Rights in Rem'. University of Pennsylvania Law Review 68(4): 322–336.

Kull, A. (1998). 'Restitution in Bankruptcy: Reclamation and Constructive Trust'. American Bankruptcy Law Journal 72: 265–302.

Linarelli, J. (2009). 'Analytical Jurisprudence and the Concept of Commercial Law'. Penn State Law Review 114(1): 119–215.

Lehman, J. and S. Phelps (2005). *West's Encyclopedia of American Law.* 2nd edn. Detroit, Thomson/Gale.

Maitland, F. W. (1969). *Equity: A Course of Lectures.* 2nd edn. London, Cambridge University Press.

Merrill, T. W. and Smith, H. E. (2000). 'Optimal Standardization in the Law of Property: The Numerus Clausus Principle'. Yale Law Journal 110: 1–70.

Merrill, T. W. and H. E. Smith (2001). 'The Property/Contract Interface'. Columbia Law Review 101: 773–852.

Oosterhoff, A. H. (2004, 2019 ed). *Oosterhoff on Trusts.* 9th edn. Toronto, Thomson Reuters Canada.

Penner, J. E. (1997). *The Idea of Property Law.* Oxford, Oxford University Press.

Penner, J. E. (2020). *Property Rights: A Re-Examination.* Oxford, Oxford University Press.

Pistor, K. (2019). 'Minting Debt'. *The Code of Capital: How the Law Creates Wealth and Inequality.* Princeton, Princeton University Press: 77–107.

Pretto-Sakmann, A. (2005). *Boundaries of Personal Property: Shares and Sub-Shares.* Oxford, Hart.

Prosser, W. (1956). 'The Nature of Conversion'. Cornell Law Quarterly 42: 168–184.

Simpson, A. W. B. (1987). *A History of the Common Law of Contract: The Rise of the Action of Assumpsit.* Oxford, Clarendon Press.

Smith, H. E. (2002). 'Exclusion Versus Governance: Two Strategies for Delineating Property Rights'. Journal of Legal Studies 31(2): 453–487.

Smith, H. E. (2006). 'Modularity in Contracts: Boilerplate and Information Flow'. Michigan Law Review 104: 1175–1222.

Smith, H. E. (2011). 'Property is Not Just a Bundle of Rights'. Econ Journal Watch 8(3): 279–288.

Smith, H. E. (2012). 'Property as the Law of Things'. Harvard Law Review 125: 1691–1726.

Smith, H. E. (2021). 'Property Beyond Flatland'. Brigham-Kanner Property Rights Journal 10: 9–56.

Smith, L. (2023). *The Law of Tracing.* Oxford, Clarendon Press.

Smith, S. (2019). *Rights, Wrongs, and Injustices: The Structure of Remedial Law.* Oxford, Oxford University Press.

Stevens, R. (2018). 'Set-Off and the Nature of Equity'. *Defences in Equity.* P. S. Davies, S. Douglas, and J. Goudkamp. United Kingdom, Bloomsbury Publishing Plc: 41–52.

Swadling, W. (ed), (2004). *The Quistclose Trust: Critical Essays.* London, Hart.

Swadling, W. (2013). 'Property: General Principles'. *English Private Law.* A. Burrows, 3rd edn. Oxford, Oxford University Press: 173–306.

Swadling, W. (forthcoming). 'Are Choses in Action Property?'. The Property-Contract Interface. J. Penner et al. Oxford, Oxford University Press.

Sweet, C. (1895). 'Choses in Action'. Law Quarterly Review 10(4): 238–240.

Tham, C. H. (2019). *Understanding the Law of Assignment.* Cambridge, Cambridge University Press.

Watson, J. A. (2016). *The Duty to Account: Development and Principles.* Annandale, NSW, The Federation Press.

Waldron, J. (1988). *The Right to Private Property.* Oxford, Clarendon Press.

Williams, T. C. (1894). 'Is a Right of Action in Tort a Chose in Action'. Law Quarterly Review 10(2): 143–157.

Williams, T. C. (1888). 'The Terms Real and Personal in English Law'. Law Quarterly Review 4: 394–408.

Worthington, S. (2000). *Personal Property Law.* Oxford, Hart.

17

Cash and Credit

Money and the Property-Contract Interface

*James Penner**

Cash, as a medium of transaction in many instances, opens the way for the exercise of many fundamental rights . . . such as the right to 'informational self-determination', freedom of action and freedom of speech . . . The store-of-value function of cash is directly linked to property rights. The easy accessibility to cash, especially for the elderly, the socially vulnerable or minors, allows people to participate in society and, for example, allows children to learn how to handle money. In particular, when socially vulnerable people use cash, they face none of the barriers involved in applying for a credit card or, despite all their efforts, opening a current account.

(Yves Mersch, The Role of Euro Banknotes as Legal Tender (speech given at the 4th Bargeldsymposium of the Deutsche Bundesbank, Frankfurt am Main) (14 February 2018))[1]

* I am grateful to the many who have commented on this chapter as I have presented it in various drafts. I owe especial thanks to Derwent Coshott, Duncan Horne, Jodi Gardner, Federico Lupo-Pasini, Irina Sakharova, and Catharine MacMillan, who led the discussion of my chapter at the Property-Contract Interface Workshop in December 2024

[1] Cited in Lupo-Pasini 2021a, 30.

James Penner, *Cash and Credit* In: *The Property-Contract Interface*. Edited by: James Penner, Irina Sakharova, Henry E. Smith, and Zhong Xing Tan, Oxford University Press. © James Penner 2026.
DOI: 10.1093/9780198951995.003.0022

I. Introduction

The modern legal entity we know as 'money' sits astride the property-contract interface in a way no other legal entity does. It has two forms: a property form, in what we colloquially refer to as 'cash', and a contract form, what I shall explain as 'ledger money', the sort of money one holds in a bank account. The property form came prior to the ledger form, but this too had an intimate relationship with contract. Prior to the introduction of the property form of money, historically coin made from precious metals, the economic problem of the 'double coincidence of wants' in a barter economy was solved by debtor–creditor relationships. The chief 'agency' of the introduction of coin was to mitigate the costs of such relationships. Much later, the free creation of ledger money by commercial banks, moving the world largely to where we are now, paved the way for a number of economic developments, as I shall discuss. We therefore now live largely in a world of the 'contract' form of money. But these forms, true to their property or contract nature, have quite different associated costs and 'sociologies', and I shall argue that these must be carefully taken into account as the world of money progresses.

II. Fiat Money, Barter Money, and the Credit Relationships that Precede Money

I shall characterize the kind of money issued in all modern societies as governmental 'fiat money', which is a combination of negotiable bearer money (cash, ie banknotes and coins) and 'ledger money', the kind of money created by central and commercial banks.[2] But before we get to that characterization, we need to discuss another kind of money which has figured in the economics literature—'barter money'.

Barter money is essentially a 'numeraire' or 'unit of account' *token* theory of money, in which a certain amount of one good, whether a bushel of wheat or an ounce of silver—the 'token'—is used to price all other items.[3] A numeraire token arises by conventional practice to avoid the problem of the 'double coincidence of wants', that is, the unlikelihood that two persons under any given distribution of goods (and this always arises under a division of labour in the production of goods) will each seek exactly the same quantity of goods the

[2] See, eg, Desan 2014, 2020; Keen 2022, ch 2; Pettifor 2017, chs 1 and 2.
[3] See, eg, Desan 2020, 8–10.

other has and wishes to exchange. Instead, the presence of a numeraire token allows more exchanges to take place because, being a universal unit of value by which other prices are determined, it can serve as a kind of money, facilitating exchange, assuming, as Alchian explained, it is easily measurable, reasonably durable, reasonably 'assessible' by non-experts (eg they do not routinely mistake pewter for silver), and reasonably portable.[4]

Yet money, as we find it in the historical record down to the present day, does not arise primarily in response to the infelicities of *barter* but in response to the infelicities of *credit*. Creditor–debtor relationships always precede the introduction of money.[5] Creditor–debtor relationships are the way that societies without money, or without sufficient money, overcome the problem of on-the-spot barter, the double coincidence of wants. To take a very simple example which might realistically occur in a predominantly agricultural economy: a supplier of milk will transfer milk, which they get from their cows daily, to a hay producer on credit, accepting payment from the hay producer in quantities of hay when the hay harvest comes in. Notice, importantly, that extending credit of this kind involves a significant degree of trust between the parties, which will normally mean they are members of the same community in which an individual's reputation for creditworthiness will be uppermost in people's minds. One could not reliably extend credit to strangers. In the absence of credit of this kind, every individual (or more realistically, every family) would need to be a jack of all trades, producing everything needed to sustain themselves; the efficiencies of a division of labour in production would be unavailable.

III. Fiat Commodity Bearer Money: Coin

Coin, which in Western history seems almost universally to be the first true fiat money, always emerges against what might be called a mixed feudal and exchange economy. In such an economy, there are basically two kinds of economic transactions, one of which I shall somewhat misleadingly call 'tribute' transactions, and the other private market transactions.[6] Under the European feudal tribute system, kings largely received benefits from their subjects in kind, principally through forms of what in English law were called 'services', for

[4] Alchian 1977.
[5] Desan 2014, 24, 38–50, 58–62; Graeber 2011, ch 2. Gleeson 2018, 32–33.
[6] I leave aside here the 'gift' economy, which supported the church and which would also cover the rules of inheritance, although this economy was very important as well.

example by the receipt of agricultural goods ('socage') or the provision of soldiers for the king's army ('knight service'). (Lesser nobles in the feudal structure acted as intermediaries, receiving from those below them, and providing to those above.) Alongside was the economy of private market transactions, which as we have seen above was, in the absence of money, an economy burdened by the inefficiencies of barter and debt. The problem of tribute, of course, is that any king might be dissatisfied with what it brought him, and he might wish to take advantage of the non-tribute, or private market, economy to better meet his needs. It seems that what always occurred to kings in these circumstances was to *monetize* tribute. In order to do that, they had to create money.

This was done by a two-edict move in the creation of tokens and their functionality. The king would require his subjects to accept tokens in payment for goods or services, and he accepted that the now monetized tribute obligation could be paid, and indeed must be paid, not by provision of the previous service in kind, but by his subjects paying in the same tokens. In principle, the king could create tokens out of anything, but for reasons discussed below, these tokens were overwhelmingly stamped pieces of precious metal. The advantage of this monetization for the king is sometimes called the 'fiscal' value of money.[7]

Whether owing to the practicality of issuing tokens or by design, the token was always a *bearer* token. That is, in paying the monetized tribute to the king (which is basically akin to what we would today call 'paying taxes'), a person only had to pay sufficient tokens to discharge the obligation, not the very tokens they had previously received in payment from the king. Thus unlike a personal debt/credit account with the king, the king's debtor–creditor relationships were economically decentralized. Tokens, or coin, could pass from one of his subjects to another as a means of payment, ultimately of payment to the king, but intermediately as payment between individuals engaging in private market transactions. As intentionally created tokens of credit as against the king, this money is properly called fiat money.

As the English history of the decline of feudalism shows, the monetization of tribute proceeded apace, a process known as commutation, in which various 'rent services' under the tenurial system were commuted to money payments.[8] Not all feudal transactions were monetized, of course. Serfs largely continued to serve their masters in kind, not as employees paid in money.

[7] Desan 2014, 44–45.
[8] Baker 2002, 228–229, 241.

The chief factual reason why the king was able to undertake this process lay in the fact that the king was the *common creditor* of his subjects under the tribute system. These tokens were constitutively valuable to each of his subjects, since each had obligations to the king (whether mediately or immediately through the feudal ladder of services). Of course only the subjects of the king were obliged to use his coin, so the 'universality' of money, the identity of the common creditor, is always jurisdictional, and that remains true today.[9]

IV. Why Coin? That is, Why a Fiat *Commodity* Bearer Money?

Why, historically, did sovereigns converge, without external coercion, on issuing their credit tokens as pieces of stamped precious metal, that is, using one kind of commodity—precious metal—as the substance of its tokens? Given this convergence, it seems like the commonsense thing to do, but this has given rise to the misguided idea, famously associated with Locke,[10] but also pressed by the barter money theory discussed earlier, that individuals spontaneously fix on units of some good as something that will become universally accepted as payment. The actual reasons are much simpler. Since silver was the traditional metal for English coinage, we can restrict our attention to that precious metal.

Notice first that one of Alchian's claims, discussed earlier, about what makes something a candidate for money—that it be a good that can be assessed by non-experts—implicitly supports the use of silver since a stamped piece of silver can be more or less identified by anyone, and because silver coins can be made in the size of one's choice, it can be issued so that its denomination is of a kind that can be used to represent the values exchanged in the majority of day-to-day transactions. Second, and more importantly, it is not some independent value of precious metals, or some customary or conventional agreement about their value, that made them good material for money. Precious metal is (1) relatively rare, (2) difficult to imitate, (3) very durable, and (4) requires skill to work.[11] In all these respects silver was the best available substance for materializing a debtor–creditor relationship in the form of tangible tokens. The token-holder is the creditor, and the credit it represents can be transferred to a third party, to make gifts of course, but ultimately to discharge existing debts

[9] Henceforward I shall use 'universal' assuming the qualification of its being jurisdictional.
[10] Locke 1970, [46]–[50].
[11] Desan 2014, 52.

or to pay for goods in an immediate sale. Coin was thus the first true universal means of payment, that is, the provision of contractual consideration and the settling of debts by the transfer of a token denominated in a universal unit of account; coin was thus the first *money*.

Although money can be used to pay non-contractual debts (tax debts, judgment debts) and to make payments as gifts, the chief 'agency' or causal impact of the institution of money is the facilitation of exchange because it avoids the infelicities of barter and credit.

V. The Liquidity and Use Values of Silver

How did the common creditor, the king, source the bullion for his coins? Well, obviously there are a number of possible ways: he might expropriate bullion, demand some tribute in the form of bullion, or might, say, work his own silver mines, as properties owned by himself. But in England what occurred was a system of what is called 'free-minting', and this generates two competing sources of the value of silver bullion.

Under free-minting, an individual could bring silver bullion into one of the king's mints (there were generally a number of these spread throughout the country) for minting into coin.[12] This individual would receive less silver in coin than the weight of the bullion they brought in, so in straight 'value of bullion' terms, they would suffer a loss. The mint would mint all the bullion but keep some percentage of the coins for itself, or rather for the king. This right to give back less in coin than was minted was called 'seigniorage'.[13] But coin has a 'liquidity' value that bullion lacks. Payment by coin is by 'tale', by 'tally' or 'count' as we should say today, that is, by number of coins, whereas payment by bullion is by weight.[14] It facilitates payment if the tokens can be counted. And it is inconvenient to have to deal with weights of bullion—payment with bullion is essentially an exchange of one kind of good for another, a form of barter: every change in the value of bullion will thus alter the terms of exchange. Thus, because coin transactions are more efficient than bullion transactions, and significantly, the king could and did demand payment in coin for taxes, there is always a liquidity value of money, and bullion holders would capture some of this by bringing in bullion and taking coin in return. But silver is not useful

[12] Desan 2010, 382.
[13] Desan 2010, 381–382, 383, 391–393.
[14] Ibid, 387. Gleeson 2018, 37–38, ch 3.

only as coin, of course. It has a separate use value: it could be worked for other purposes, typically in the production of luxury goods like jewellery and plate.

Finally, and most obviously, using precious metals to coin money itself creates a market for those precious metals, competing with other non-coinage uses and raising their price. Because these uses compete with the use as coin, the value of bullion at any one time will fluctuate as demand for both coin (the liquidity value) and for its non-coinage uses rise and fall. The fluctuating liquidity and use values established what at any time was the 'minting point' and 'melting point' of bullion.[15] Where the cash or liquidity value of silver coin exceeded its use value, bullion would be minted. Where the cash value of bullion declined to a certain point against its use value, coin would be melted. In a closed economy, where all the players were within the same money jurisdiction, the free minting and free melting could work as a check on inflation. Where there was a general rise in the price of goods, so that coin became less valuable, it would be melted, withdrawing money from circulation. As a consequence, creditor–debtor transactions would increase, bringing with them the costs and inefficiencies of credit, and money would become dearer, and prices would decline. At some point the cash value of money would recover and minting would again be the more profitable way to realize the value of bullion. 'Individuals considering their advantage in matters of exchange melt or mint precious metal in response, tying the total quantity of money and thus prices to the independent and shared supply of metal.'[16] England, of course, was not a closed economy. There was both international trade and, more importantly, other countries' demand for bullion to mint for their own coin. So there was a 'world' price for silver, which fluctuated in part, but significantly, because of other countries' policies regarding coinage. So, for example, when the bullion value of English silver coin was greater on the continent than its cash value in England, English coin would be melted into bullion and shipped abroad.[17]

Other problems attend credit commodity money, which have been well documented:

> Different denomination coins, even of the same precious metal, will have different liquidity values because some denominations will be used for more transactions than others;

[15] Desan 2010, 367, 388–391.
[16] Ibid, 367 footnote omitted.
[17] Ibid, 383, 404–409. Where the world price of the metal rises substantially, this may lead to a currency departing from a precious metal value entirely. For a farcical example, see Friedman 1994, ch 5.

> This problem is exacerbated by 'bi-metallism', i.e where coins of different precious metals are minted, typically silver and gold; not only will the ratio of bullion value of coins fluctuate according to market prices for the metal, these coins will also have different liquidity values given the high- or low- value transactions in which they are used; in particular, maintaining a count value, of, say, one gold noble to 80 silver pennies, that reflects underlying bullion prices is impossible.[18]

Precious metal coin has never been merely a convenient physical unit representing an amount of bullion, to be traded as that weight of bullion. It has a liquidity value. But the ongoing competition between the use value of bullion and the liquidity value of coin cannot but give rise to the sorts of problems just discussed. We can end on the happy thought that modern coins have, practically speaking, only liquidity value. Their use value, their melt value, is trivial.

VI. Common Debtor Money—Banknotes and Bank Money

The next significant step in the history of money was the introduction of banknotes, which in England, both in the case of Bank of England notes and 'goldsmiths' notes', took the form of a promise to pay coin. As a means of payment banknotes passing in currency became subject to the same basic bona fide purchase rules as coins, as decided in *Miller v Race*.[19] These notes are 'common debtor' money, as opposed to the common creditor money of coin. A person or institution, like a bank, makes itself a common debtor when it issues bearer notes which can be cashed by anyone at the issuing bank. When A has an account with bank B, their main contractual right is a Hohfeldian power *to make B pay*, either themselves by withdrawal or at their order to a third party. So long as B is willing to pay third-party holders of documents requiring payment from A's account that B will honour—until recently the typical document was a cheque—B acts as a debtor to anyone coming into the possession of the cheque.

The issue of banknotes takes us to the concept of 'bank money'. Bank money is the 'money' which bank customers hold in 'demand deposits' or 'demand accounts'. As 'demand' indicates, money in these accounts can be withdrawn on demand in the form of cash, or more frequently, it can be 'transferred' to

18 Desan, 2010, Part III, 397, 400–402, 406–407. Gleeson 2018, 39–44, 99–101.
19 (1758) 1 Burr 452 (KB).

third parties by way of a payment system, in the past mostly by cheques, today mostly by way of electronic 'transfer'. 'Transfer' is put in quotation marks to indicate, as we shall see, that it is misguided to think of payments under payment systems as transfers from the payor to the payee. The demand aspect of these accounts means that money in a demand account is essentially equal to cash on hand in terms of its power to pay others, which is why bank money is counted in determining (one measure of) the money supply.

Bank money has three sources. The balance in a demand account can be increased by the deposit of cash, or the receipt of a 'transfer' of bank money from another bank account. In neither case is there an increase in the money supply. But the balance in a demand account can also be increased when the bank issues credit, by lending money to its customer. It may thus increase the customer's 'power of withdrawal/power to pay' by crediting the demand account with the loaned amount, or by extending an overdraft facility. Notice that the customer's power to demand, whether by withdrawal or by ordering payment to a third party, is equally enhanced whether this is by way of crediting the account or by extending an overdraft. This form of bank money is therefore sometimes called 'credit money', because it creates a credit against the bank. But it is not to be confused with the common *creditor* money that indicates money arising from a common creditor such as a king. Rather, this 'credit' money can arise because the bank is situated as a common *debtor*, as explained above. This 'bank money', which is 'made' by banks in this way, constitutes most of the money in the system, on the order of 97 per cent, with cash making up the remainder.[20] For obvious reasons, this power of the banks to lend and increase the money supply is regulated.

Whatever its source, whether by deposit or transfer from another or via the issuance of a loan, all bank money—the money held in bank accounts—is to be treated as 'ledger' money. Ledger money has no physical existence; it is entirely a matter of contract between the bank and its customer; it *is* the modern contractual form of money. Coins and banknotes, that is, cash, remain as the property form of money. Importantly, they are convertible one to the other 'at par'. A bank does not discount the cash it receives when it takes it as a deposit, nor does a cash withdrawal attract any levy.

[20] See McLeay, Radia, & Ryland 2014, 15.

VII. Some Legal Aspects of Money as a Matter of Private Law

As Proctor and Gleeson relate,[21] there is no clear legal definition of 'money' in the law, and its characterization in legal contexts is very sensitive to its economic function.[22] But I want to concentrate on one matter essential to understanding the property-contract interface in this area of law.

First, money as property. A coin has always been a 'negotiable chattel': the right to the money passes upon delivery, and where money passes 'in currency', that is, is used to pay for non-money goods or services, the recipient acquires title to the money so long as they take the money in good faith, for example not being aware that the money was stolen. Banknotes, although originally promissory notes to pay coin, and still in England stated in that form, are now, like coins, negotiable chattels. In respect of this tangible money, in *Moss v Hancock* Darling J said this:

> Money as currency . . . seems to me to have been well defined by Mr. Walker [citing F. A. Walker, 'Money, Trade, and Industry', Encyclopaedia Britannica, sub tit. 'Money' p 4] as that which passes freely from hand to hand throughout the community in final discharge of debts and full payment for commodities, *being accepted equally without reference to the character or credit of the person who offers it* and without the intention of the person who receives it to consume it or apply it to any other use than in turn to tender it to others in discharge of debts or payment for commodities.[23]

The italicized passage is important. In the case of tangible money, the recipient takes no credit risk other than the possibility that the coins or notes are forged, and that possibility concerns the quality of the coins or notes themselves, not the character or credit of the person who offers it, for that person may innocently believe they are genuine.[24] In this respect money is a perfect exemplar of the phenomenon of 'modularity' in property law. As Smith relates:

[21] Proctor 2022, ch 1; Gleeson 2018, 116–117.

[22] This is particularly so with the concept of 'legal tender', which is complex. See, eg. Proctor 2022, 2.24–2.31. Gleeson 2018, 133–135, 136–141. For a recent exploration of the issues, see William Bateman 'Legal Tender And The Micro-Structure of Financial Stability', unpublished manuscript on file with the author. I shall also not explore the intricacies of the related law of 'payment'; see Proctor 2022, ch 7; Gleeson 2018, 103–105, 107–109, 143–146.

[23] [1899] 2 QB 111, 116 (emphasis added).

[24] Proctor 2022, 1.11.

> [An] information-cost theory of money helps explain what we might mean by liquidity services. By coinciding on one standard good (especially one that is itself easy to measure) with standardization, it becomes worthwhile to break a single transaction (say wheat for oil) into two transactions (wheat for money and money for oil). The whole point of money is its negotiability: one need not inquire into its history. Thus a good faith holder can get good title to cash, even from a thief. But in this respect money is an extreme example of what the *numerus clausus* does to property: it modularizes by hiding information and presenting an extremely simple and easy-to-measure face to the world, thereby providing liquidity.[25]

In the case of bank money, the situation is starkly different, for here money is entirely a matter of contract, and here there is always a credit risk. A deposit of cash into one's bank account is just an exchange of one kind of money—property, that is, chattel money—for another—contract, that is, ledger money. The credit risk here is, obviously, the solvency of the bank, and these days we know all too well that banks can fail.[26] And withdrawal and cheque payments are always on terms. To take a simple example, prior to the introduction of cash machines, payment was restricted to the bank's opening hours. I am old enough to remember the long queues on Friday evenings when most people received their paycheques.

Although I can use my agent to pay cash on my behalf, in the case of bank money the bank is always my paying agent when I exercise my power against the bank to make it pay a third party. And nowadays, of course, most money moves electronically by engaging a web of contracts. To take a simple 'transfer' of funds, let us say A has an account with Y Bank, and B has an account with Z Bank. A exercises a power under their banking account contract with Y Bank to order Y Bank to require Z Bank under Y Bank's contract with Z Bank to credit B's account with £1,000. Colloquially, we say that A has 'transferred' £1,000 from A's account with Y Bank to B's account with Z Bank, but this is not a transfer in law. The contractual relationship between Y Bank and Z Bank allows them to participate in a payment system under which they facilitate payments for their respective account holders. As between themselves, Y Bank and Z Bank are merely debtors or creditors inter se, depending upon whether at any one time their accounts vis-à-vis each other show a positive balance for Y

[25] Smith 2011, 160 endnotes omitted. See also Merrill & Smith 2001, 778–779.

[26] Private bank deposits are protected by various levels of insurance in different jurisdictions. See, eg, https://www.fscs.org.uk/what-we-cover/; https://www.sdic.org.sg.

Bank or a positive balance for Z Bank. A similar analysis applies to payments by way of credit card.[27] Where A pays B by credit card, the credit card issuer (CCI) will expend its funds to pay B at the end of an accounting period (minus charges, and so on), and A will be required to reimburse CCI on whatever repayment terms (including charges, interest, and so on) are specified by their contract. As should be clear, none of this involves genuine transfers of anything;[28] rather, in the first case, B's enhanced bank balance arises by a kind of novation, that is, as a new or augmented contractual right against Z Bank to make Z Bank pay; in the CCI case, the payment the retailer receives from CCI to the retailer's bank is, again, a new contractual 'power to make pay' against the retailer's bank.[29]

VIII. Two Main Functions of Banks and the Costs Thereof

Although banks do other things,[30] here I concentrate on two: they provide payment systems and they issue loans. As regards the first, the bank–customer contract is almost a perfect example of what Merrill and Smith call a compound-paucital legal form,[31] in which there is a standard form contract between banks and a multitude of similarly situated counterparties. As they predict, this legal form attracts a clear protection strategy: this contract is one of the most heavily regulated by the state, and beyond the contract itself customers are provided protection with mandatory regimes of deposit insurance, the costs of which are born by banks themselves.[32]

As regards the second, the issuance of loans, this typically involves a much more involved governance regime, containing terms which are tailored to prevailing market conditions and to the assessment of the individual customer, in particular the risk of the latter's insolvency.

I have referred above to the inefficiencies and costs of credit. Regarding payment systems, the most obvious cost is simply that of maintaining records and processing transactions, 'maintaining the ledger', so to speak. As a matter of a bank's business model, some of these payment system costs could be covered with the revenue it earns as interest on its performing loans, but banks also

[27] Proctor 2022, 7.23.
[28] Gleeson 2018, 113.
[29] Proctor 2022, 7.19.
[30] Eg facilitating saving and investment through saving accounts (in particular term accounts).
[31] Merrill & Smith 2001, 786, 790, 797–799, 801, 803–806.
[32] See, eg for the UK, https://www.fscs.org.uk/about-us/funding/; for Singapore, https://www.moneysense.gov.sg/understanding-deposit-insurance/.

cover these costs with various charges and fees. An important point here is that although payment services may be 'free' to the bank customer making, say, a bank transfer within the jurisdiction, paying one's utility bill for example, there are always costs in the system which have to be borne by someone, for example by charges upon retailers receiving credit card or other payments; with electronic wallet payments (such as ones on one's phone) the possibilities expand to providing advertising services informed by data 'scraped' from the users' activities.

An interesting example of the business model of English banks came to light in *The Office of Fair Trading v Abbey National plc.*[33] In order to fund basic current account banking, those customers 'in credit', that is, with positive balances, enjoy 'free banking', that is, they do not pay charges on normal payment transactions. This involves a significant cross-subsidy from those customers who incur charges for unauthorized overdrafts.[34] So, 'banks . . . earned £2.56bn from Relevant Charges in 2006 (against £4.1bn in net interest earned on accounts in credit)'.[35]

Turning to the costs of the lending side of banking, everything turns on the fact that by issuing loans a bank creates money, expanding the money supply. If I make a private loan to you, either handing you £1,000 in cash or by 'transferring' £1,000 from my bank account to yours, that doesn't increase the money supply. By contrast, when a bank creates bank money it does exactly that, for when it grants you an overdraft or raises your account balance, it doesn't transfer anything from itself to anyone; this is new money.[36] Moreover, the creation of this money *is linked to 'creditworthiness' as determined by commercial banks.*

There is nothing nefarious about this: in a sophisticated and well-regulated banking sector banks should be experts in allocating credit to the private sector, both to consumers and to businesses.[37] The fact that interest payments on performing loans are banks' chief source of profit means that they have every incentive to create all the money necessary to facilitate innovative,

[33] [2009] UKSC 6.
[34] Ibid, [1], [54], [80], [87], [88], [105].
[35] Ibid, [36].
[36] Pettifor 2017, 15–20; Keen 2022, 19–25; This is *not* 'fractional reserve banking' as explained by neoclassical economists. See McLeay, Radia, & Ryland 2014; Keen 2011, 307–312; Keen 2020, 20–25; Pettifor 2017, 24–26. Coppola 2019, 34–43. Genuine fractional reserve banking occurs when private banks print their own banknotes, issued to make loans, the value of which banknotes exceeds the value of the bank's reserves of state-issued coin and paper currency, hence 'fractional' reserve banking: the reserves cover only a fraction of the value of the banknotes issued. For a discussion of the operation of fractional reserve banking in the US during the 'free banking' era of the nineteenth century, see Lupo-Pasini 2020, 191–194.
[37] Desan 2020, 20.

productive, commercial enterprise along with sensible consumer finance (most obviously in the housing sector). If properly directed, banks can create all the money we need to invest in productive enterprises which result in economic growth.[38] But banks, in making lending decisions, are just as much as any other 'investor' subject to periodic cycles of conservatism and exuberance in lending.[39] Moreover, lending decisions always respond to the *demand* for credit.

This was most clearly shown by the 'quantitative easing' (QE) following the 2008 financial crisis.[40] Under QE, central banks created money to restore liquidity to the financial sector. They did this principally in two ways: by buying up outstanding government issued debt, which was largely held by financial institutions or other institutional investors such as pension funds, and by buying from banks 'troubled assets' so that they no longer remained on the banks' balance sheets. This indeed flooded the banking system with money, but it did nothing to restore the 'real economy', that is the day-to-day production or consumption for most citizens.[41] It did, helpfully, prevent a crisis for pension funds,[42] so pensioners at least continued to receive their pensions, much of which is used for everyday consumption. But for non-pensioners, nothing significant was done to relieve the mass of consumers of their financial predicaments. Indeed, austerity programmes like the one undertaken in the UK only made things worse for them. And this had clear consequences. What were the now flush-with-money commercial banks to do with it? When the real economy is in recession, there is little demand for real economy investment, as the demand for the products and services that investment would otherwise create is absent if all the prospective consumers of it can ill afford those products and services. So who did receive credit, at historically low interest rates, from the banks in the post-QE era? Largely the wealthy, those we might call the investor class. Money was borrowed to buy assets, art, real property, even wine, driving up their prices.[43] Companies borrowed to buy back their own shares, raising the value of their shares, and thus the value of that asset class.[44]

[38] Pettifor 2017, 5–6, 20–24.
[39] Coppola 2019, 44–46. Gleeson 2018, 19–21.
[40] Coppola 2019, ch 1; Pettifor 2017, 62–76; Keen 2011, 304–312.
[41] This has happened before. See Rajan 2011, in particular his discussion of the US Federal Reserve's response to the DotCom Bust, 105–119.
[42] Coppola 2019, 6.
[43] Ibid, 2, 29–30. Pettifor 2017, 67.
[44] Coppola 2019, 30.

IX. The Dematerialization of Money

By 'dematerialization of money' I mean the withdrawal from the payments systems of coins and banknotes, so that only by using debit or credit cards or other means of electronic payment (eg via 'wallets' on one's phone) can payments be made. Dematerialization could be a government initiative, or it can happen selectively in the private sector. During my recent stays in England, I noticed a growing number of shops and pubs that had 'card only' signs.[45] Complete dematerialization would, of course, amount to the abolition of the property form of money.

Here I just want to provide some reasons why we might consider the costs of dematerialization, in particular complete *de jure* dematerialization by the state no longer producing notes and coins.

First of all—a point which flows directly from the preceding discussion—cash has a certain liquidity value because it alleviates the reliance of private market actors upon credit. It allows one, for instance, to deal with strangers. And of course, one might say, this problem is equally alleviated with credit or debit cards and other means of electronic payment. But these means of payment do not extend to all, and never to all on equal terms. These credit terms can be themselves very costly. We also know that there is a premium on electronic transactions paid for by the retailers themselves. These charges may not be much in percentage terms, but they do constitute a private levy on all goods and services not paid for in cash.[46] And looking towards the future, it is apt to note that:

> [Where there are dominant e-payment providers in the market] [a]t present, the competition of cash keeps e-payment providers' fees low. Yet, experience suggests that in the long term, a monopolistic position will inevitably lead to higher costs and fees for consumers.[47]

I do not deny that there are costs associated with handling cash, the risk of theft being the most obvious, but are they entirely outweighed by the facility

[45] For discussion, see Martin Wolf, 'The Death of Cash: An Ancient Technology on its Way Out', Financial Times (5 June 2017): https://transact.ft.com/death-of-cash/; Eswar Prasad, 'Cash will soon be obsolete. Will America be ready?' Brookings Institute Op-Ed (25 August 2021) https://www.brookings.edu/articles/cash-will-soon-be-obsolete-will-america-be-ready/; Rose Eveleth, 'The Truth about the Death of Cash', BBC News (24 July 2015). https://www.bbc.com/future/article/20150724-the-truth-about-the-death-of-cash; Izabella Kaminska, 'Why the Death of Cash May Have Been Exaggerated' Financial Times, Alphaville (27 May 2016). I thank William Bateman for pointing me to these sources.

[46] Lupo-Pasini 2020, discusses in detail the range of such costs.

[47] Ibid, 230.

of card and other electronic payment means when the costs of those are accounted for?

We must also note, of course, the situation of the unbanked and 'underbanked',[48] who are not served or ill-served by the electronic card and other payment systems, and for whom cash remains an essential means of payment. This problem, while arguably the most important, has been thoroughly dealt with elsewhere so I shall not discuss it here.[49]

It also seems to me that dematerialization would have some significantly detrimental effects, for example with regard to travel. I know that exchanging banknotes from one currency to another is costly and an annoyance, but we also know that bank and credit cards do not always travel well. In these days where banks are always flagging up transactions—and here reliance on one's mobile phone across jurisdictions is also necessary—actual cash is a source of security when the card is declined. Whilst there is one particular downside of cash, that it can be lost or stolen, in some of the literature it seems as if people forget that cards and phones can also be stolen. That might not allow the thief to use a contact credit or debit card for very long if the loser acts quickly to block it, but unlike the loss of cash, it is hugely inconvenient to deal with lost phones and cards. I would much rather lose a few hundred pounds in cash than a wallet containing only my cards—or my phone, which I now need to enter into almost all electronic banking transactions given two-factor identification protocols.

Furthermore, the psychology and sociology of cash is different from that of electronic money, especially electronic money giving rise to debt as in the case of credit cards. As Lupo-Pasini relates:

> There is limited behavioral economics literature on the usage of cash and why people tend to prefer it for certain transactions. Unlike digital payments and standard banking, cash does not require a basic level of financial literacy, which has proven to constitute a major barrier to financial inclusion. Banknotes and coins are widely understood and do not require a prior understanding of how bank accounts work or familiarity with mobile technology.[50]

[48] Crawford, Menand, & Ricks 2021, 125–127.
[49] Lupo-Pasini 2020, 2021a, 2021b; Crawford, Menand, & Ricks 2021, 125–130.
[50] Lupo-Pasini 2020, 202, footnotes omitted.

That 'cash does not require a basic level of financial literacy' applies in particular to children, whose 'learning to handle money' was one of the features stressed by Mersch in the opening quotation.

Moreover,

> In interviews, it is often reported that cash makes budgeting easier as users can more readily contextualize the financial impact of their purchases on their savings; in other words, it gives them a sense of control. On the other hand, even for digitally-savvy individuals, it is sometimes more challenging to track various expenses and understand how they reflect on their account, as most digital payment mechanisms do not show this. The likelihood is that new apps might address this problem in the future. Yet, for persons suffering from compulsive behaviors, the ready availability of digital money might lead to extra spending, even in the presence of apps. In many of the focus groups organized by the UK Parliament and the House of Lords Financial Inclusion Committee, the risk of extra spending and increased debt with digital payments was highlighted as one of the greatest risks. Since the business model of digital payment services is based on very low consumer fees, most of their revenue comes from charging fees on overdrafts and selling consumers' data. The ultimate outcome of this is that those groups that are more prone to overspend, would end up subsidizing the cost of the service for everybody else.[51]

To put the point another way, electronic money, as immaterial money, is 'unseen' in the sense of not being physically there, to be seen and handled—it requires effort to determine just what you have even if that only means checking on one's available credit—very different than just checking what one has in one's physical wallet. One of the first things money advisors tell people to do when they are living beyond their means is to cut up their credit cards. Spending cash has a sobering effect that charging on one's card doesn't. Of course you may respond that the law should not bend to suffer fools, those who cannot stay on top of their finances, yet it is not an entirely irrelevant consideration given the prevalence of cognitive biases and 'nudge' theory.[52]

There are also human rights concerns. By being denied a traditional means of payment, and in turn requiring one to enter into a payment system devised

[51] Ibid, 228–229, footnotes omitted.
[52] See, eg, Bar-Gill 2012, in particular ch 2 on credit card contracts.

entirely by the choices of a certain class of market actors—roughly the financial sector—one is being subjected to a non-democratically created market regime. At the very least in the case of *de jure* dematerialization, the state should be required to make some form of electronic money available to all. I shall consider Central Bank Digital Currencies in the final section.

One of George Orwell's abiding concerns was the freedom and liberty that is only possible with privacy, not being constantly supervised or under surveillance.[53] Credit, including the modern world of electronic credit and money, poses, to my mind, a clear risk that this freedom will be impaired. I have never lived in a jurisdiction in which I would like all of my transactions to be tracked or trackable. Cash is by its nature anonymous, as we have seen. But credit money is not, perhaps not always practicably, but always in principle. Three distinct but related areas concern me, all mentioned in the opening quotation from Mersch. One, 'informational self-determination', which is the idea that not all of one's activities should be monitored, much less recorded. Informational self-determination is clearly related to freedom of speech. It is simply obvious these days that being 'found out' on social media as a contributor to a particular social or political movement can have devastating consequences. I need say no more about that. My second concern is the freedom of minors to do things of which their parents would not approve. If all a minor's transactions are available to their parents in the way that some parents monitor their children's locations via their smartphones, then this is, I think, a serious diminution in freedom for the minor. Finally, let me put in a word for markets in illegal or disfavoured goods or services. States take very different views about what these goods or services are and the ways in which they should be regulated—such as drinking age requirements (21 years old in the United States) or access to abortion pills—or even banned, from cannabis to what might be called the 'obscene', to prostitution, and so on. All of these choices are often discriminatory and irrational. A little rebellion is often a good thing, and I would submit that (and I am not discounting the problems to which black markets give rise) only cash really works in this realm.

X. Central Bank Digital Currencies

A Central Bank Digital Currency (CBDC) essentially creates a debtor–creditor relationship between individuals and a central bank, so, for example, a kind of

[53] See eg, Solnit 2021, 47, 100, 224–225, 249.

bank account which all British citizens might be entitled to have with the Bank of England. This is in contrast with the current situation, where only commercial banks have accounts with the Bank of England. As currently proposed on the Bank of England's website, these accounts would be mediated by commercial companies providing wallets to access this form of electronic money.[54]

As Crawford et al relate, a CBDC could take the form of a crypto token, using the sort of blockchain technology used by Bitcoin.[55] But they also make the following points:[56] whilst people tend to regard these 'tokens' as akin to physical coins, with peer-to-peer transactions being as anonymous as cash transactions, this is confused. Both regular electronic bank account money and crypto 'money' is *ledger* money; nothing physical is involved. What primarily distinguishes crypto from regular electronic ledger money is its anonymity. As they point out:[57] 'Decentralized ledgers can be either permissioned or permissionless; the same goes for centralized ledgers.' The question is a policy one, not a technological one. We could, for example, entirely abandon the now pervasive 'know your customer' rules that apply to banks' opening accounts, and allow people to open bank accounts anonymously or pseudonomously; but for a host of good reasons, that is not the current policy orientation. It would make no sense to carve out an exception to this policy simply because the ledger, as with crypto 'currencies', is decentralized. And whilst it is often said to be a good feature of the dematerialization of cash that it would inhibit large sum transfers for money laundering purposes or otherwise dealing with the proceeds of crime, for a state to endorse a decentralized ledger money with anonymous accounts would be to facilitate such transactions; as we know, facilitating such transactions is one of the main functions of cryptocurrencies today.[58] Any such move by a state would be, to say the least, perverse given its purported desire to squelch such transactions.

Thus the choice between whether a central bank should choose a digital currency in the form of regular electronic ledger money or a crypto token version is a technological one. Given that crypto payments cannot be scaled up to serve as an effective general, much less universal, payment system,[59] and that their value fluctuates so much and so often that they do not provide a reasonably

[54] 'This would be an electronic version of cash issued by the Bank of England and accessed by digital wallets provided by companies.' See https://www.bankofengland.co.uk/explainers/what-is-the-digital-pound.

[55] Crawford, Menand, & Ricks 2021, 117–118, 151–155.

[56] Ibid, 151–155.

[57] Ibid, 152.

[58] Stevens 2023, 627.

[59] Crawford, Menand, & Ricks 2021, 153.

stable value which is essential to the functioning of money, plus their preposterously terrible environmental effects,[60] the choice of the former is, as they say, a 'no-brainer'.

Now that that point has been settled, I shall henceforward just refer to 'Central Bank bank accounts', or 'CB bank accounts'.

The various ways in which CB bank accounts could be used are very much a live issue. Their most obvious beneficial function, as Crawford et al emphasize,[61] is that if such accounts were made available to all citizens or permanent residents within a jurisdiction, the problem of the unbanked and underbanked would be solved. Although central banks have tended to associate the ideas of creating a CBDC with the dematerialization of cash,[62] as if the problem of the unbanked were simply the decline in cash transactions, this is misconceived. The importance of cash, as I have emphasized throughout, is that it facilitates non-debtor–creditor relationships, providing a means of payment which is anonymous, does not depend on creditworthiness or trustworthiness, and which has a very different 'schedule' of costs compared to the other credit–debit forms of payment.

Most of the 'action' in considering the use of CB bank accounts is whether they should be 'basic', in the sense of simply providing for the holding of money up to any limit (thus removing the need for deposit insurance in commercial bank accounts) and the provision of basic payment services, such as providing debit cards, or whether they should be more expansive—in particular whether the CB should engage in the broad panoply of private consumer services, such as credit cards, consumer loans, and overdraft facilities, or providing money deposits in the case of a financial crisis ('people's quantitative easing').[63] It is beyond the scope of this chapter to delve into all the possible options, but I think one point should be made clear. One must distinguish, as I have done earlier, between the function of banking as providing a *payment system*, and the function of *issuing credit*, by making loans or providing overdraft facilities. Crawford et al emphasize that CB bank accounts are primarily designed to provide the former, a universal payment system.[64] Central Banks have no expertise in allocating credit to the private market, so to add this function, in particular so as to dislodge this function from the private banking sector, would involve a myriad of economic and policy considerations, and should not be

[60] Stevens 2023, 627.
[61] Crawford, Menand, & Ricks 2021, 125–130.
[62] See the link cited at note 51.
[63] Coppola 2019.
[64] Crawford, Menand, & Ricks 2021, 123, 159–160.

undertaken lightly. As I mentioned above, there is nothing inherently nefarious in allocating to private banks the function of credit creation through lending, though of course it must be regulated, as indeed it is everywhere, though, as the 2008 financial crisis showed, probably not regulated enough.[65]

But, and this cannot be emphasized enough, none of the foregoing discussion of CBDCs leads to the conclusion that we should dematerialize money. The introduction of a CBDC could ameliorate some of the problems generated by the private banking market, such as the problem of the unbanked, and risk of private bank failure, but it would do nothing to address the concerns about dematerialization explored in section IX.

XI. Conclusion

No legal form rests so thoroughly upon the contract-property interface as money does. In particular, the 'at par' interconvertibility of cash to ledger money and vice versa is a clear demonstration of this. At the same time we have seen that the property form of money, cash, and the debtor–creditor contractual form, ledger money, have very different profiles in terms of costs and the sociology of their use, which must inform policy decisions going forward. Perhaps it is the burden of this chapter to argue that by having both forms, in particular retaining cash, we may approach if not the best then at least a superior economic world than one in which the property form is made to disappear entirely through dematerialization.

References

Alchian, A. A. (1977). 'Why Money?' *Journal of Money, Credit and Banking* 9: 133–140.

Baker, J. H. (2002). *An Introduction to English Legal History*. Oxford, Oxford University Press.

Bar-Gill, O. (2012). Seduction by Contract: Law, Economics and Psychology in Consumer Markets. Oxford, Oxford University Press.

Coppola, F. (2019). *The Case for People's Quantitative Easing*. Cambridge, Polity Press.

Crawford, J., L. Menand, and M. Ricks (2021). 'FedAccounts: Digital Dollars'. *George Washington Law Review* 89: 113–172.

Desan, C. (2010). 'Coin Reconsidered: The Political Alchemy of Commodity Money'. *Theoretical Inquiries in Law* 11: 361–410.

[65] For a compelling argument that the government, via its Central Bank, should not get into the business of private sector lending, in effect turning that function over to state bureaucrats, in spite of her extensive criticisms of the banking sector, see Pettifor 2017, ch 6.

Desan, C. (2014). *Making Money: Coin, Currency, and the Coming of Capitalism.* Oxford, Oxford University Press.

Desan, C. (2016). 'Money as a Legal Institution'. *Money in the Western Legal Tradition: Middle Ages to Bretton Woods.* D. Fox and W. Ernst. Oxford, Oxford University Press: 18–35.

Desan, C. (2020). 'The Key to Value: The Debate over Commensurability in NeoClassical and Credit Approaches to Money'. *Law and Contemporary Problems* 83: 1–22.

Friedman, M. (1994). *Money Mischief: Episodes in Monetary History.* New York, Harcourt Brace & Company.

Gleeson, S. (2018). *The Legal Concept of Money.* Oxford, Oxford University Press.

Graeber, D. (2011). *Debt: The First 5,000 Years.* Brooklyn, Melville House.

Keen, S. (2011). *Debunking Economics: The Naked Emperor Dethroned?* London, Zed Books.

Keen, S. (2022). *The New Economics.* Cambridge, Polity Press.

Locke, J. (1970). *Two Treatises of Government.* Cambridge, Cambridge University Press.

Lupo-Pasini, F. (2020). 'Is it A Wonderful Life? Cashless Societies and Monetary Exclusion'. *Review of Banking & Financial Law* 40: 155–253.

Lupo-Pasini, F. (2021a). 'Financial Inclusion and the "War for Cash"'. *Law and Contemporary Problems* 84(1): 17–33.

Lupo-Pasini, F. (2021b). 'Monetary Transitions and Property Rights: Lessons From India's 2016 Demonetization'. *Banking & Finance Law Review* 36: 209–236.

McLeay, M., A. Radia, and T. Ryland (2014). 'Money Creation in the Modern Economy'. *Bank of England Quarterly Bulletin* Q4: 14–27.

Merrill, T. W. and H. E. Smith (2001). 'The Property/Contract Interface'. *Columbia Law Review* 101: 773–852.

Pettifor, A. (2017). *The Production of Money: How to Break the Power of Bankers.* London, Verso.

Proctor, C. (2022). *Mann and Proctor on the Law of Money.* Oxford, Oxford University Press.

Rajan, R. G. (2011). Fault Lines: How Hidden Fractures Still Threaten the World Economy. Princeton, Princeton University Press.

Smith, H. E. (2011). 'Standardization in Property Law'. Research Handbook on the Economics of Property Law. K. Ayotte and H. E. Smith. Cheltenham, UK, Elgar: 148–173.

Solnit, R. (2021). *Orwell's Roses.* London, Granta.

Stevens, R. (2023). 'Crypto is not property'. *Law Quarterly Review* 139(October): 615–628.

Index

For the benefit of digital users, indexed terms that span two pages (e.g., 52–53) may, on occasion, appear on only one of those pages.

Figures are indicated by an italic *f* following the page number.

S